JEANNETTE RANKIN

JEANNETTE RANKIN

Suffragist,
First Woman Elected to Congress,
and Pacifist

Ted Carlton Harris

ARNO PRESS
A New York Times Company
New York • 1982

10

Publisher's Note: This book has been reproduced
from the best available copy.

Editorial Supervision: Steve Bedney

First publication in book form 1982 by Arno Press Inc.
Copyright © 1972 by Ted Carlton Harris
Reprinted by permission of Ted Carlton Harris
DISSERTATIONS IN AMERICAN BIOGRAPHY
ISBN for complete set: 0-405-14075-4
See last pages of this volume for titles.
Manufactured in the United States of America

Library of Congress Cataloging in Publication Data

Harris, Ted, 1934-
   Jeannette Rankin : suffragist, first woman elected
to Congress, and pacifist.

   (Dissertations in American biography)
   Originally published as the author's thesis
(doctoral--University of Georgia)
   Bibliography: p.
   1. Rankin, Jeannette. 2. United States--Politics and
government--1901-1953. 3. Legislators--United States--
Biography. 4. United States. Congress. House--
Biography. 5. Feminists--United States--Biography.
6. Pacifists--United States--Biography. I. Title.
II. Series.
E748.R223H37 1982   328.73'092'4 [B]   80- 2914
ISBN 0-405-14084-3   AACR2

JEANNETTE RANKIN: SUFFRAGIST, FIRST WOMAN ELECTED

TO CONGRESS, AND PACIFIST

by

TED CARLTON HARRIS

A.B., The University of Georgia, 1955

B.D., Vanderbilt University, 1958

M.A., The University of Georgia, 1969

A Dissertation Submitted to the Graduate Faculty

of the University of Georgia in Partial Fulfillment

of the

Requirements for the Degree

DOCTOR OF PHILOSOPHY

ATHENS, GEORGIA

1972

PREFACE

Jeannette Rankin has always been a woman much ahead of her
time. Like many others born in the simple and rugged West, she has
always been a keen individualist and courageous fighter. This
pioneering spirit is strong and active. At ninety two, she is still
lecturing and lobbying for new social legislation and a more democratic
electoral system.

With the current unrest on our nation's campuses, the demonstrations for equality before the law, the demand for presidential
election reform and the disillusionment over war in general, and
Vietnam in particular, Jeannette Rankin's spirit comes alive to our
age. Over the past few years she has challenged the prevalence of
poverty, the persistence of discrimination, proposed election of the
President by "direct preferential vote" and demanded an end to the
Vietnam war. She has promoted these goals for well over half of a
century with an amazing physical and mental vigor.

I first met Jeannette Rankin in November of 1965 and found her to
be a charming person as well as an interesting historical figure. After
completing my Master's Thesis on her activities in Georgia in the 1920's
and 30's, I decided to attempt a biography for the doctoral dissertation.
With an appreciation for the pacifist view, I dug into the project with
enthusiasm. The purpose of this dissertation, as far as possible, is
to present an accurate account of Jeannette Rankin's life, the forces
that may have influenced it, and the contributions that she has made to

American social and intellectual life.

Research for this topic has been both interesting and rewarding. The basic research tool was Jeannette Rankin herself. Being available in Watkinsville, near my home, I made use of extensive interviews and very frequent consultations. Miss Rankin was most patient and cooperative in this endeavor. These interviews were supplemented by conversations with contemporaries and members of the Rankin family.

Also, I used what manuscripts have been saved of the Jeannette Rankin papers. These are in her personal possession. The research included a trip to Montana, to the Schlesinger Woman's Library at Radcliffe College, to the New York Public Library, to the Swarthmore Peace Collection at Swarthmore College and to the Library of Congress. In addition to the personal interviews, letters and manuscript collections, numberous articles were available in periodicals and newspapers. An informative discovery was a scrapbook on Jeannette Rankin compiled by Joyce Hill, a contemporary and close personal friend of Miss Rankin.

I wish to thank Dr. John Chalmers Vinson for his patient efforts in guiding the research and his valuable suggestions in the writing of this study. Also, Dr. Melvin Herndon and Dr. Earl Ziemke have provided encouragement and inspiration. Certainly appreciation is due to University of Georgia librarians, Christine Burroughs, Susan B. Tate and Leslie B. Kilgore. To Bernice Nichols, Curator of the Swarthmore College Peace Collection, I express gratitude for her helpfulness in locating materials.

Last, but not least, I am grateful to my family for their patience and to my parents for their encouragement.

While many people have contributed to this study, finally, I must accept responsibility for its research and writing.

July 5, 1972   Ted Carlton Harris

▼

TABLE OF CONTENTS

Page

PREFACE   iii

CHAPTER

 I. EARLY LIFE IN MONTANA   1

 II. PREPARATIONS FOR A REFORMER   20

 III. LET THE SUFFRAGETTE OUT   39

 IV. THE MONTANA CAMPAIGN   67

 V. FROM CHEERS TO BOOS   96

 VI. A WOMAN IN CONGRESS   125

 VII. THE SEARCH   163

 VIII. FROM PEACE EDUCATION TO PEACE ACTION   202

 IX. ENOUGH OF JEANNETTE   221

 X. THE ZENITH   243

 XI. A FOOTNOTE IN HISTORY   274

 XII. FROM OBLIVION TO RESURGENCE   309

 XIII. THE DOWAGER OF WOMEN'S LIBERATION   337

 XIV. EPILOGUE   352

APPENDIX   359

BIBLIOGRAPHY   361

CHAPTER I

EARLY LIFE IN MONTANA

Jeannette Rankin, suffragist, first woman elected to the United
States Congress and pacifist, is still on the creative edge of
American life after ninety years. From social worker in 1909 to the
Jeannette Rankin Bridage in 1968, her courage and her ideas have con-
sistently challenged and inspired the political and social life of
American men, women and youth. This early advocate of equal rights for
women, born on a ranch near Missoula, Montana, has shown creative
intenuity, bold individualism and frontier ruggedness as she assailed
the problems of women, legislation and peace. The background for this
unrelenting evotion to high ideals and progressive legislation developed in the primitive pioneer life of Montana at the time of Jeannette
Rankin's birth.

Montana in the last half of the nineteenth century was a land of
opportunity as well as a territory bursting with challenge. In addition
to miners searching for gold, the Homestead Act brought increasing
numbers of ranchers and farmers. The Indians, objecting to these
intruders, fought a losing battle to retain their hunting grounds.
River traffic up the Missouri to Fort Benton helped to open the interior
of the Montana Territory. Providing even faster transportation, the
railroads brought new life to the Eastern Plains and to the Rockies.
Jeannette Rankin's parents, John Rankin and Olive Pickering, came West

1

to profit from these opportunities and to accept the challenge of
frontier life.

John Rankin, remembered as a peppery, Scotch Canadian, was born in
1841 in Apin, Ontario of parents who had emigrated forty years earlier
from Scotland. Being the fourth boy in a family of nine brought special
hardships. After attending only three grades in the local log school,
he dropped out to learn the carpenter's trade. To relieve the family
of further expense, he crossed the border into Shelby, Michigan to
work for his oldest brother in a coke mill. After working there for a
few years, John and his youngest brother, Duncan, decided to seek their
fortunes in the West.[1]

While the rest of the nation struggled to settle the problems of
reconstruction after the Civil War, John Rankin was trying to reach
the Montana Territory. For two and one-half months in the Spring of
1869, he was a "helper" on a Missouri River flatboat. Among his hardships was a diet so limited to watermelons that he never wanted to see
another one. Alongside flatboats, numerous shallow-draft sternwheelers
fought their way between the shifting sandbars, changing channels and
numerous snags of the mighty Missouri. John Rankin's temporary destination was Fort Benton.

---

[1]Dorothy Brown Interview, September 3, 1970, p. 1 of transcript;
Jeannette Rankin Interview, March 31, 1970, p. 1 of transcript; John
Rankin's parents were Hugh and Jenette Stuart Rankin.

Located at the head of river navigation, it became the hub of a web-like network of economic and commercial enterprises.[2]

Unlike many vessels that plied the Missouri, Rankin's boat encountered no Indians, but it ran aground on Cow's Island several miles short of its destination. After gathering up his tools, Rankin set out on foot for Fort Benton. When he arrived, Rankin heard that a fire had destroyed a greater part of Helena, where "Last Chance Gulch" had opened up a new gold strike five years earlier. Since he knew the carpentry trade, he purchased a team of oxen and drove the ninety miles South in search of work. Most of the rebuilding had been finished by the time he arrived. So, with his brother, Duncan, Rankin moved three or four miles up the gulch to Unionville where they constructed a stamp mill to facilitate in the crushing of ore.[3]

Not satisfactorily challenged by these activities, the "Canada boys," as they were often referred to, crossed the Rocky Mountains in the Fall of 1870 into Missoula. Encompassing roughly the land west of the Continental Divide, Missoula County contained about one-sixth of the area in the present state of Montana. Its population in 1870 was 2,554 out of a Territorial census of 20,595; while the United States claimed only 38,858,371 citizens. John Rankin first settled in the Cedar Creek Mining Camp near Superior, Montana to prospect in the mountains for gold. Soon he returned to Missoula and opened construction,

[2]Alton B. Oviatt, "Fort Benton, River Capital," A History of Montana by Merrill G. Burlingame and K. Ross Toole (New York: Lewis Historical Publishing Company, 1957), pp. 137-155; Edna McKinnon Interview, November 16, 1971, p. 1; J. R. Interview, March 31, 1970, p. 1; Elizabeth Huber Interview, September 12, 1971, pp. 3-4.

[3]J. R. Interview, March 31, 1970, p. 1.

sawmilling and other business enterprises.[4]

As was typical of Carnegie, Rockefeller and other barons of the last quarter of the nineteenth century, John Rankin diligently pursued the "free enterprise system" and fulfilled the image of an entrepreneur. Soon his personal properties included land in Missoula, a ranch about six miles out on Grant Creek and one of the first water-powered saw mills in the area. Using his skill as a carpenter while mastering math and geometry through practical experience, Rankin built what was generally considered the first bridge across the Missoula River. The Blockhouse Bridge stretched two hundred and fifty feet across a point five miles from town. In addition to constructing many of the other bridges that spanned the Missoula, the Bitterroot and other western Montana rivers, Rankin designed many residential and business structures. To him also belonged the destinction of having built in 1872 the town's first religious ediface - the Methodist Church.[5]

The saw mill and related milling equipment on Grant Creek became a tremendous source of income for John Rankin. His timber and mill supplied the lumber for the building of Fort Missoula shortly after 1877, and for most of the construction in town. Additional income came from the many houses that he rented to lumber jacks, rail crews and other workers. Within ten years, he had accumulated several thousand dollars in cash and considerable property. Along with these

---

[4]U. S. Bureau of the Census, The Statistics of the Population of the United States (Washington: Government Printing Office, 1872), Volume I, p. 46; Wellington D. Rankin Interview by John Board, March 23, 1964, p. 25.

[5]The Daily Missoulian, June 3, 1951; Joaquin Miller, An Illustrated History of the State of Montana (Chicago: Lewis Publishing Company, 1894), pp. 565-566.

material gains, he had earned the respect of fellow citizens as they
elected him county commissioner in 1878.[6]

With an eligible bachelor loose, Olive Pickering, the future Mrs.
Rankin, entered the picture. The Pickerings were an old line New England
family, dating back to a land grant by the King of England in 1692 to John
Lowe Pickering. The Pickerings settled around Newington and Portsmouth,
New Hampshire. Jeannette Rankin's mother, Olive Pickering, grew up on a
subsistance farm. When asked about her father, Olive said, "Oh, he was
lazy. He would much rather write speeches and articles for the newspaper
than to do any work on the farm."[7] Actually, he had been educated and
trained for a teaching career. Apparently the maternal side of the
family was more practical. Olive Rankin in her earthy New England
sense of humor chuckled over the remark that a traveling preacher
entered in his journal, "Today I traded horses with Deacon Berry and
he cheated me. May the Lord have mercy on his soul."[8] Olive finished
her own education and began teaching school in New Hampshire. She had
no illusions as to her academic accomplishments. She recollected, "I
was young and good looking and dressed well, and the school board
probably knew that I needed a job, so they always gave me one."[9]

On a trip East, William Berry, an uncle and long-time Sheriff

----

[6]Elizabeth Huber Interview, September 12, 1971, p. 3; The Daily
Missoulian, May 4, 1904.

[7]Elizabeth Huber Interview, September 12, 1971, p. 1.

[8]Ibid., p. 1.

[9]Ibid., p. 1; J. R. Interview, March 31, 1970, p. 2; Supposedly
John Pickering and his four brothers came over with the family of Governor
Winthrop and were given land in the New Hampshire grants.

in Missoula County, fascinated Olive Pickering with his tales of the
West. When he indicated they needed a school teacher in Missoula, Olive
begged her parents to let her go. She wanted to leave New Hampshire
because there had been too much inbreeding in the Pickering and Hoyte
families. Additionally, she anticipated the adventure of the West.
Evidently hoping to reduce the risk, her parents agreed on condition
that Mandana, her oldest sister, accompany her. At the time, Mandana
was engaged and did not want to leave. With conniving strategy and a
sense of determination, Olive cried until Mandana gave in. As so, in
a few days, they were off to Montana.[10]

The trip west in 1878 was by transcontinental trail to Corinne,
Utah, and then by stagecoach to Missoula. Giggling all the way,
Olive Pickering, at age twenty, thrilled at the adventure and excitement. The only over night stop on the seven day stage trip was one
night in Butte, Montana, a wide open, wild and rough mining town.
Olive became very upset because Mandana made her stay in the stage
office and would not let her see what was happening outside. But the
next morning she received her thrill on the stage coach ride into
Missoula.[11]

Just outside Butte, the stage had to descend an unusually steep
grade, covered with slick pine needles. The driver tied a huge log
across the back of the stage coach wheels to act as an additional brake.
When asked about what happened, Olive replied, "Oh, we went down the hill.

---

[10]Ibid.

[11]J. R. Interview, March 31, 1970, pp. 2-3; Bingham D. and Betty
Masden, "The Diamond R. Rolls Out," Montana, XXL (Spring, 1971), p. 31.

I laughed and Mannie prayed."[12]

After arriving in Missoula, Olive Pickering boarded with W.O. Dickinson, a trader and merchant. His wife, Emma, had taught school the year before and was a delightful pioneer woman. She and Olive Pickering became life long friends. On the other hand, Olive thought Dickinson was perfectly uncouth because "he wore an Indian scalp on his belt."[13] Olive's New England reserve never permitted her to ask if he took it himself.[14]

While living with the Dickinson's and thoroughly enjoying the refreshing atmosphere of the frontier, Olive Pickering became Missoula's second school teacher. No doubt she was a good one. Nieces remembered her literary sense. "She loved words, the meanings of words and had a great sense of humor about them, especially enjoying puns."[15] Teaching on the frontier was never easy. Indians constantly peeked through the windows. Not wanting the students to see her fright, Olive called for more concentration on the lessons at hand. In the long run, it was not the red skins that proved more upsetting to the class, but the attention of a red-bearded bachelor.

John Rankin, by this time a successful lumber merchant, soon noticed and was immediately attracted to the new teacher in town. Wearing long, curly, brown hair and a red beard, he would occasionally drive

---

[12]Elizabeth Huber Interview, September 12, 1971, p. 2.

[13]Ibid.

[14]One of Jeannette Rankin's other nieces, Virginia Ronhovde, indicated that Dickinson had a strange bald spot on his head, and that Olive learned that he had been scalped and left for dead. Virginia Ronhovde Interview, June 11, 1971, p. 3.

[15]Virginia Ronhovde Interview, June 11, 1971, p. 3.

by the school house in his buggy with its "spanking good team of horses" to catch a glimpse of Olive. The students quickly realized that he was "sparking" their school madam. They greeted these appearances with great joviality and had to be called back to their work by a well-modulated Eastern accent, "Now scholars."[16]

It would have been a short courtship if John Rankin had prevailed. Olive's New England sense of honor to a signed contract made him wait until school ended. The long suffering Mandana returned East for her sister's trousseau and the wedding took place in the Dickinson home in August of 1879.[17] John Rankin took his new bride and her sister to the Grant Creek ranch to live. It was here than Jeannette was born on June 11, 1880, the oldest of seven children. The other members of the family were Philena, who died in childhood; Harriet, later Dean of Women at the University of Montana; Wellington, a Republican politician, District Attorney, and Montana's most famous trial lawyer; Mary, an English instructor at University of Montana; Grace, a homemaker; and Edna, a lawyer and pioneer in the field of planned parenthood.

Grant Creek Mill, since it was better known for its saw milling, was an interesting place in itself. It was not unusual for the Rankin children to play on the logs that were in the mill pond waiting for sawing. In addition to raising horses, swine and cattle, there was always hay to be stacked and grain to be threshed. Irrigation ditches carried water to the more arid areas of the ranch. The farm provided the usual amounts of fruits and berries. Often times, the Indians as

---

[16]Elizabeth Huber Interview, September 12, 1971, p. 3.

[17]J. R. Interview, March 31, 1971, p. 3.

they were traveling through, sold fresh huckleberries to the Rankins.

The ranch house was a wood, framed dwelling with the usual kitchen, living room and bedrooms. For more comfortable sleeping in the summer, the enterprising Rankins used a semi-permanent tent that contained four double beds. Built over the creek stream was the milk house, lined with shelves to hold the tins from which cream was skimmed. There was always plenty of hot cereal and thick cream for breakfast. At times, Olive Rankin made cheese which was sold in Missoula along with quantities of butter and eggs.[18]

As Jeannette neared school age, John Rankin built his town house on Madison Street in Missoula. Meriweather Lewis, of the Lewis and Clark Expedition, camped in 1806 on this site near the conjunction of the Rattlesnake and Missoula Rivers. Even earlier it had been a favorite campsite for the Indians. The family spent the winters in this three story, brick veneer house. It was equipped with the first hot and cold running water in Missoula, a huge zinc bathtub and a wood-burning forced air furnace. Many of the neighboring children thrilled at the opportunity of bathing in Rankin's tub. The bathroom was commodious enough to be a gathering place for all the girls in the family. In front of the "throne" was a register which transferred additional heat from the kitchen stove below. Another of Rankin's ingenious devices was a two hundred pound flour and sugar bin constructed on a pivot in the pantry for Olive's easy use. To give a special Oriental touch to all of this, John Rankin topped his house with a glass enclosed, walk around, Burmese

---

[18]Edna Mckinnon Interview, Nov. 16, 1971, p. 4.

styled cupola. In its time, it was one of the finest houses in Missoula.[19]

Through the years this house served the needs of the growing family.
School friends were always welcome for a visit or a meal. Hot, fresh-
baked bread was available about once a week when the children returned
from school. John and Olive Rankin were well known as delightful hosts.
Quick witted and lively John enjoyed the Scottish jigs and was nimble
enough to jump up in the air and click his heels together three times
before coming down. Friends liked to come to the Rankin place because
Olive always "set a good table," topped with delicious cakes and a
freezer of home-made ice cream.[20]

While the Rankins loved to entertain, they seldom returned social
visits. Olive Rankin always expected people to come to see her. She
was offended if they did not invite her to their parties, but they knew
she would never come. Only on very rare occasions in the summer would
she leave the house to attend the theater. For thirty years, she did
business with her grocer without ever going to his store. It seemed
that her aims were to simply care for the family and to meet their needs.

There were seldom dull moments at the Rankin house. Dinner time
was especially enjoyable. John Rankin always sat at one end of the
dining table. If there were guests they were seated to his left as
he was blind in the right eye and deaf in the right ear as a result of
a cannon accident. Next to the guests would be Jeannette and then

---

[19] Probably not true, but a legend of the Rankin House indicated that
a road agent, typical scourge of early Montana, was hanged from the
unfinished framework by Vigilantes, the unofficial but effective police
of the era. Daily Missoulian, June 3, 1951, p. 6; Edna McKinnon Interview, November 16, 1971, p. 6; Dorothy Brown Interview, September 5,
1970, p. 2.

[20] Elizabeth Huber Interview, September 12, 1971, p. 5.

Wellington. To John Rankin's right sat Harriet, Mary and Olive. At
the end of the table on youth chairs were the younger children, Grace
and Edna. Edna McKinnon recalled that she and Grace were to be seen
and not heard, but that they enjoyed the constant flow of tales, heated
arguments and the interchange of fast talk between guests and family.[21]

Mother Rankin entered very little into the conversation because
she was too concerned about feeding the family. By nature a shy person,
she was very modest with friends. Once when Amos and Rosie Buck, old
friends from the Bitterroot Valley, were eating dinner, the butter was
located in front of their plates. As soon as there was a lull in the
conversation, Olive Rankin said, "Rosie, won't you have some butter?"
She answered, "No, Amos and I don't use butter. Thank you." And the
butter dish stayed there the rest of the meal. Grace and Edna were in
hysterics. Of course, they couldn't eat a meal without butter! Adding
to the amusement was the delight at seeing their mother in a difficult
situation. She was simply too modest to say, "Well, Rosie, if you
don't like it, please pass it."[22]

As the family grew older, these dinners became quite frantic. All
of the children inherited John Rankin's temper and Olive's stubborn
determination. Wellington, the boy of the family, assumed the place of
leadership when his father died, but Hattie and Jeannette also had
ideas of their own. This resulted in tremendous arguments between these
three older children. Occasionally, a glass of water came flying from
the other side of the table to accentuate a point. Many times someone

---

[21]Edna McKinnon Interview, Nov. 16, 1971, p. 3.

[22]Ibid.

left the table in great fury.[23]

John Rankin involved the older children in his work. Hattie, as
his "associate," kept the books and details of the businesses straight.
She aided him by collecting rent from the houses that he owned across
town. While Hattie became her father's right hand man, Jeannette was
the "idea" girl. She proved invaluable in assisting him to understand
new ideas and logically to reason out future projections. Jeannette
could always come up with an answer quickly as to where they should go,
what they should do and how they should do it. Also the older children
spent some time assisting in the operation of the sixty-five room
Rankin Hotel, erected in 1891.[24]

Childhood years for Jeannette were not dull to say the least.
In the summer, the entire family moved to the ranch. There Jeannette
along with the other Rankin children and neighbors attended a summer
school paid for by their father. Prior to school time, the children
took a circuitous route jumping along favorite logs in the mill pond.
Luckily this proved adventureous rather than disasterous. In addition
to romping over the logs, picnicing in the Spring meadow and playing
the usual repertoire of children's games, there was the huge sawdust
pile. It always proved a delight. As Jeannette grew older, basketball,
dancing, and sleigh riding became more popular.[25]

---

[23]Edna McKinnon Interview, November 16, 1971, p. 3.

[24]Rankin Block, a three story brick building, was constructed in
1891 on Front Street and contained sixty-five rooms with electricity, a
call bell system, excellent dining room and a bath on every floor.
Joaquin Miller, An Illustrated History of the State of Montana (Chicago:
The Lewis Publishing Company, 1894), p. 566; Historic and Scenic Missoula
and Ravalli Counties compiled by Wagner and Sevigne, 1899, p. 36 (picture);
Edna McKinnon Interview, November 16, 1971, p. 5.

[25]Edna McKinnon Interview, November 16, 1971, p. 5.

During these years, Jeannette belonged to a social club, the Buds. Rather snobbish, it was typical of those organized by the sons and daughters of the older families in Missoula. There were sixteen members of the Buds and they usually met once a week. Besides enjoying whisk, they planned parties, played games, gossiped and took sleigh rides. Jeannette, however, was never tremendously impressed.[26]

Being inventive and creative, Jeannette was not challenged by these social activities. Simple playing was not enough. One time the neighbors in high dudgeon complained to Olive Rankin about the store in her house. Upon investigation it turned out that Jeannette and one of her friends had hung a diaper out the upstairs window announcing the opening of a dress shop. Actually, the girls only planned to make clothes for dolls. It was typical of Jeannette's ingenuity to establish such a business enterprise.[27]

On one occasion when Jeannette was entertaining a group of her teenage friends, she showed them how to operate the saw mill. Saw milling was an intricate business, but Jeannette brought a log onto the carriage by directing the boys as to what lever to push and which hooks to use. She did not saw the log just to destroy it, but sawed it perfectly to ascertain its maximum useability. To operate a saw mill as a teenager was evidence of the remarkable mechanical talents she has

---

[26]Jeannette belonged to the Buds; Hattie to the Quinza; Wellington to the Phi Del Tau; Mary to the Pelecums; and Grace and Edna to the Brownies, the last club of the pioneer families. Dorothy Brown Interview, September 5, 1970, p. 3; Mrs. Jimmie Rittenour Interview, September 6, 1970, p. 3; Edna McKinnon Interview, November 16, 1971, p. 5.

[27]Elizabeth Huber Interview, September 12, 1971, p. 7. At another time, she inserted an add in the local paper advertising a loaner shop for dogs.

shown throughout her life.[28]

Furthermore, she was versatile enough to switch from a buzzing saw to a sewing needle. Being the oldest of the girls, she became their seamstress and usually made most of their clothes. The sisters may have complained that they didn't have the latest style, but their dresses were always novel and interesting. Jeannette never told the girls what kind of dress that they would have for a party. Indeed, she didn't know. With her flair for creativity, Jeannette usually made their dresses as she went along. It was frustrating, but the sisters knew better than to complain. Later, to improve her workmanship or possibly on demand by the younger children, she took sewing from Margaret Burke, the best seamstress in town.

Edna McKinnon, the youngest of the Rankin girls, remembered that Jeannette once made her a dress for a piano recital. She described it as having "a ruffle right around my stomach. I could have cried, but I knew better." Not saying a thing, but evidently seeing her distress, Jeannette drew from the drawer a piece of Alice blue taffeta ribbon. Crushing it, she stitched it around so that the ruffle did not protrude. In fact, it hid Edna's stomach. In the back was a lovely butterfly taffeta bow. Edna recalled, "Here I was the prettiest child in captivity, but I had suffered agony before it came out perfectly."[29]

From these experiences Jeannette Rankin gradually assumed responsibility for the household operation of the family. In many ways, she almost became a second mother and especially so after John Rankin's death. When decisions

---

[28]Edna McKinnon Interview, November 16, 1971, p. 8.

[29]Ibid.

had to be made, Jeannette made them and generally without consultation.
As an example, when Edna had her tonsils out, she remembered:

> "It wouldn't have occured to Jeannette to tell me.
> She just ordered me to come downstairs and there
> was a thing draped like an operating table. The
> doctor took out my tonsils and adenoids. I had
> nothing to say about it."

Burdened with these daily responsibilities, Jeannette was angry and
annoyed a great deal of the time. Some of the sisters, looking back,
were amused. They felt Jeannette wanted to run the family, but at the
same time insisted she was being imposed upon.[30]

Complementing Jeannette's very practical education in the home and
on the ranch were the elementary school in Missoula, the Preparatory
School and later the University of Montana. John Rankin almost made a
fetish of education. Having such slight opportunity himself, he was
determined that his children receive the best. Knowing that he wanted
his family to receive a college education, he helped to locate the state
university at Missoula in 1896. Subsequently, all the children were
graduates of the University, plus at least an additional year in higher
education. Jeannette studied for a bachelor of science degree with a
major in biology. She wrote her senior thesis on snails under her
favorite biology instructor, Morton J. Elrod. Professor Elrod remembered
her as a "timid girl who worked hard for what she got."[31]

Actually, school was not interesting to Jeannette. She just did not
fit - either thinking too fast or too slowly. With great empathy for

---

[30]Ibid.

[31]_Helena Independent_, November 26, 1916.

today's dropouts, she confessed, "I went on because it was the thing to do."[32] After having entered the preparatory division in 1892, Jeannette, along with seventeen other students, was graduated from the University of Montana in 1902.[33]

The six years following graduation were frustrating and difficult. Yet, in a way, they were most decisive. Jeannette returned with the family to the ranch in the summer of 1902 as a college graduate, but as she remembered, "I was not prepared to do anything."[34] Thus began several years of an agonizing search for identity and for a job.

To find a job was the first hurdle in this struggle. Following in the steps of her mother and because it was about the only thing a woman could do at that time, Jeannette secured a temporary teaching certificate. She taught at Grant Creek, near the Rankin ranch, as the only teacher in a one room school. The next year she taught at Whitehall, a small village near Butte. After three months, she became disillusioned with a teaching career and resigned. On the heels of this experience came a family tragedy.[35]

John Rankin, who married late in life, fathered seven children during the first thirteen years. They soon became a close knit and loyal clan endowed with personal freedom and motivated with the desire to get ahead. Life for John Rankin had been rigorous, but his businesses had been materially rewarding. After a trip into the Bitterroot Mountains

---

[32] J. R. Interview, March 31, 1970, p. 9.

[33] The Daily Missoulian, June 5, 1902.

[34] J. R. Interview, March 31, 1970, p. 9.

[35] J. R. Interview, March 31, 1970, p. 8; Jimmie Rittenour Interview, September 6, 1970, p. 1.

to inspect a pasture, he complained of fever. Within a week, he died at
his home in Missoula, probably a victim of Rocky Mountain Spotted Fever.
With the death of the Rankin patriarch on May 3, 1904, Jeannette under-
went her second difficulty in almost as many years. In addition to
being an emotional shock, his untimely death at sixty-three brought
distinct changes to the family structure.[36]

Because Olive Rankin depended solely on her husband for the management of the family affairs, Wellington had to take over temporary
operation of the various businesses. In addition to this, he operated
the ranch during the summer of 1904. Eventually, the ranch, sawmill and
business properties in Missoula were sold. Wellington, who had an
amazingly keen and decisive mind, negotiated these transactions so that
they would take care of his mother for the rest of her life. While "the
boy", as Olive Rankin called him, took over the financial affairs,
Jeannette assumed complete responsibility for the family. Her mother's
basic contribution was only in running the kitchen. All other decisions
were made by Jeannette and Wellington. Edna McKinnon, the youngest
daughter, recalled that her mother "just couldn't do anything so somebody
always did it for her.... [even to] finding out how much money she had in
the bank. We would find out and tell her."[37] These responsibilities of
caring for the children and seeing that everyone received an education
were quite heavy on Jeannette. Welcome relief came in a trip to Cambridge
in the winter of 1904 and 1905.[38]

---

[36] The Daily Missoulian, May 4, 1904; J. R. Interview, Mar. 31, 1970, p.18.

[37] Edna McKinnon Interview, November 16, 1971, p. 6, 9.

[38] Jimmie Rittenour Interview, September 6, 1970, p. 1; Edna McKinnon
Interview, November 16, 1970, p. 11.

After Wellington returned to Harvard in the Fall of 1904, he became quite ill. Jeannette and a friend, Jimmie Rittenour from Missoula, went East to care for him. They stayed about six months. After Wellington regained his strength, the girls began to date the boys from Harvard. They even considered enrolling in the Massachusetts Institute of Technology if they had located an interesting study. Instead of courses, Jeannette and Jimmie found attractive young men.

One delightful event was a trip down to Washington for the inauguration of Theodore Roosevelt in March of 1905. Senator Joseph Dixon from Montana secured tickets for them to attend the inqugural ball. Jay McCormick of Missoula escorted Jeannette and Wellington accompanied Jimmie. To have a good time in Cambridge and Washington was not enough. Dr. W. P. Mills, brother of Jimmy and a physician from Missoula, was in New York attending a refresher course in medical science. He invited the girls over to New York to spend a few days at the Waldorf-Astoria, and to go sightseeing. But alas, all good things came to an end. Jeannette returned to Missoula with wider experience, but still with no career in mind.[39]

In contrast to such a delightful time in the East, Missoula proved to be boring. To pass the time away, Jeannette thought she might like to make dresses. For several months she served as an apprentice dressmaker in the shop of Margaret Burke. When she grew dissatisfied, Jeannette enrolled in a correspondence course in furniture designing. After a while, this too became uninteresting. As an individual struggling with ideas and seeking personal identity, Jeannette Rankin found no peace.

---

[39]Jimmie Rittenour Interview, September 6, 1970, pp. 1-2.

The accompaning depression resulted in declining health. For such, her usual cure was a trip. Health then became an excuse to visit an uncle in San Francisco. Soon after arriving, Rankin quickly forgot about her own self as she discovered new life and challenge in social work on Telegraph Hill, an Italian settlement in San Francisco. Within four months, a door had opened and the search for identity and a career was over.

CHAPTER II

PREPARATIONS FOR A REFORMER

The insatiable drive that would lead Jeannette Rankin to social involvement was not born in Boston, San Francisco, nor in any particular experience, but was hammered out over the anvil of many years. From childhood, she had dreamed of being a nurse; but because of her apparently weak physical condition, John Rankin encouraged his oldest daughter to do something else. Even though she would eventually enter another field, the characteristic concern for human life and values still remained very active and very real.[1]

In her early teens, Jeannette began to show marked sensitivity and compassion as she cared for the animals on the ranch. Once, when her father, John Rankin, indicated that a favorite horse had town a seven-inch triangular gash on his flank, Jeannette came to the rescue. She secured strong thread and a darning needle from the sewing box. With cool precision, she ordered the horse tied and thrown. With tenderness and compassion, she sewed the gash up as if it were only the normal thing to do. On another occasion, Shep, the Rankins' dog, severed a paw in a gopher trap. Jeannette was not content just to heal the leg; she ingeniously devised for it a false leather paw complete with harness. The dog wore it until his natural death many years later.[2]

---

[1]Edna McKinnon Interview, Nov. 16, 1971, p. 11.

[2]Ibid.

Jeannette transferred this interest and love for animals to individual persons. She cared for five sisters and a brother in addition to the endless duties of ranch life. Rankin grew up wrestling with interpersonal and family problems. Both inside and outside the family, Jeannette expressed concern for the individual and his relationships as a member of society. She wanted to improve mankind by developing basic reform through legislation. Rankin was not content to just provide temporary assistance and relief. As she made application of these ideas to social work, suffrage, politics, and peace, causes and ideas became much more important than individual casework. In the development of these concepts, Jeannette Rankin's early life was a formidable influence.

Within the Rankin family, there was seldom any resentment or prejudice toward minority groups in Montana. This environment at home freed Jeannette in her thinking and in her action with ethnic and racial groups that she saw. Caravans of Indians regularly passed through from Black Foot country. Olive Rankin, keeping her distance, regarded them as physically dirty and was a little fearful of them. As natural with children, the younger Rankins felt no fear. Jeannette and her friends occasionally went to visit Indians who would be camped nearby. At other times, they would go to the reservation to watch the Indian dances and to observe and appreciate their culture. The Rankins apparently were no more conscious of the hideous way in which the Indians were being treated than the majority of people of their time.[3]

There were no Indians attending college with Jeannette. Those privileged to acquire a higher education went east to school. When home

---

[3]Ibid., p. 9.

on vacations, they were usually included in the social parties. Charlie Allard, a handsome, full-blooded Indian boy, was a favorite among the girls of Jeannette's club. Instead of intolerance toward halfbreeds, the Rankins believed it distinctive to have Indian blood. Captain C. P. Higgins, a firstline pioneer Missoula family, married a "quarter breed"; and the Rankins "thought it was nice."[4]

During her early years Jeannette Rankin remembered no Negroes in Missoula.[5] A traveling circus provided Jeannette's first contact with Black men. She recollected a feeling of complete amazement. In fact, the Rankin children made the association of these men with burned stumps in the forest. Since the black stumps had been burned by forest fires, so these black men, too, must have been burned! One day the children came in from play all covered with axle grease. Olive Rankin exclaimed, "What's happened?" The children answered, "We were playing burned men that we had seen in the circus."[6]

Later, there were Black students at the university with Jeannette. Janet and Gustavious Adolphus Stewart were among the smartest in school. Their father was chaplain at Fort Missoula. They had traveled widely and gained valuable experience. While stationed with the Negro regiment at the Fort, Stewart's wife died. Subsequently he courted an old maid sister of Missoula's Methodist minister. Jeannette recalled with delight the

---

[4] J. R. Interview, March 31, 1970, p. 7.

[5] Probably the first Negro to enter the Montana Territory after the founding of the United States was a black slave named "York". During 1804-1806, he accompanied Lewis and Clark on their expedition across the Northwest from St. Louis to the Pacific.

[6] Ibid.

old maid's comment when questioned about marrying a colored person. She reportedly said, "[I'd] rather marry someone with a black face and a white heart than a white man with a black heart." Jeannette loved this story and felt it was typical of the thinking of her friends. Interracial prejudice, in Jeannette's retrospect, was not as intense in Montana as it has sometimes been portrayed.[7] An article written by Jean I. Castles suggested that after the Civil War the Negroes in the West were among the first to experience integration. There was little discrimination on the prairie. At the day's end, all hands were the same color--dust gray. Reflecting Jeannette's feeling, the Negroes were judged more by the work they performed than by the color of their skin.[8]

These humanitarian impulses may have been nurtured, or at least encouraged, by the religious training that the Rankin children received in the Presbyterian Church. It seemed, the children were regular attendants at Sunday School and Morning Worship; but John and Olive Rankin were not. John's religious background came from a long line of Scotch Presbyterians, while Olive Pickering had been baptized by the Baptist Church. Bible stores were very real to Jeannette. Wellington remembered seeing the tears streaming down her cheeks as she read the Old Testament story of Joseph and his brothers.[9] It would be difficult, of course, to ascertain exactly how much influence religious or ethical training had on Jeannette. She maintained no formal ties with religious

---

[7]Ibid., pp. 6 & 7.

[8]Jean I. Castles, "The West: Crucible of the Negro," Montana: the Magazine of Western History, XIX (January, 1969), pp. 83-84.

[9]Wellington D. Rankin Interview with John Board, March 23, 1964, p. 33 of transcript.

organizations. Throughout later years, however, she effectively used
Biblical material to illustrate her talks. Churches, missionary societies,
and ministers were always in focus of attention for her speeches and
organizations.

The West was infamous for its struggle between the Indian and the
White man, but this antagonism was not reflected in the attitudes of the
Rankin family. John Rankin would use force if need be to defend home
and town, but he abhorred mistreating the Indians.[10] From their first
meetings with the White men, the Nez Perce Indians had been friendly.
When Governor Stevens, of Montana Territory, signed an agreement with
them in 1855, the Nez Perce ceded much of their land. Definite areas
were agreed upon for their permanent use. With the discovery of gold
in the Wallowa country of Northeastern Oregon, the Indians were induced
to relinquish even more land. In the summer of 1877, Chief Joseph decided
that the best solution was to attempt to flee to Canada through Montana.[11]

When Montana citizens heard of the Indians' approach, every town
organized companies to repel them. John Rankin joined Kenney's Volunteer
Company, #6, from Missoula, and served from about July 14 to July 30.
These volunteers joined forces with the regular army from Ft. Missoula
under the leadership of Captain C. C. Rawn. About eight miles from the
mouth of Lo Lo Canyon, the soldiers and civilians prepared an entrenchment.

---

[10] J. R. Interview, February 14, 1969, pp. 1-2.

[11] Verne Dusenberry, "Chief Joseph's Flight through Montana: 1877,"
Montana, II (October, 1952), pp. 43-45.

Rawn hoped "to compel the Indians to surrender their arms and annunition, and to dispute their passage by force of arms."[12]

In a meeting with Chiefs Joseph, Looking Glass, and White Bird, who proposed to march peaceably if unmolested, Captain Rawn refused to allow the Indians' passage unless his stipulations were met. When the over 100 or so volunteers from the Bitterroot Valley heard that the Nez Perce had promised to pass peaceably, they decided to provoke no hostility. In groups of one to a dozen, these men left camp. John Rankin was among them. In a fearless and audacious tactical move on July 28, the Indians climbed to a higher ridge and crossed about 800 yards above the rifle pits. They avoided the soldiers' breastwork and entered the canyon about a mile further down. Because he was so out maneuvered by the Indians, Captain Rawn's post at Lo Lo has been popularly known in Montana history as "Fort Fizzle."[13]

Subsequent events brought harsh treatment to the Nez Perce. Pioneers, trading with the Indians as they marched through, became frightened after one Indian secured whiskey and ammunition at Stevensville and Corvallis. Joined by Colonel John Gibbon and his men, the military caught the Indians encamped at Ross' Hole. Waiting until daylight of August 9, they charged the village and massacred the Indians. Chief Joseph escaped but finally surrendered within 30 miles of the Canadian border on October 7, 1877.

[12]A. E. Rothermick, "Early Days at Fort Missoula," Historical Reprints: Sources of Northwest History, Number 23, p. 6; Michael A. Leesen, History of Montana, 1739-1885 (Chicago: Warner, Beers, & Co., 1885), p. 864.

[13]John Barness & Wm. Dickinson, "Minutemen of Montana," Montana, X (Spring, 1960), pp. 2-9.

In his call for peace, he said:

> I am tired of fighting. Our chiefs are all killed.
> It is cold and we have no blankets. The little
> children are freezing to death. My people...have
> run away into the hills and have no blankets and
> no food. Hear me, my chiefs, my heart is sick and
> sad. From where the sun now stands, I will fight
> no more, forever.[14]

The Rankin family discussed these events, and Jeannette remembered her father's objections and "his biting remarks about authorities who would do such a stupid thing."[15] He believed the Nez Perce should have been allowed to pass unharmed through the Bitterroot Valley. On the other hand, John Rankin was not adverse to violence. A powerful man with big hands, he would fight at the drop of a hat. One of those who knew him said, "I've seen him in fights and he could fight! He enjoyed fighting. It didn't disturb him at all."[16] Yet, Rankin was a reasonable man who would provoke no hostility as was shown by his refusal to fight at "Fort Fizzle." The only gun that he ever owned was the one used in the campaign against the Nez Perce. In fact, he never wore a gun nor permitted any to be kept on the ranch.[17]

This antagonism to useless warfare carried over to the military, stationed at Fort Missoula. John Rankin jokingly thought that the Indians were much smarter than the military men and hoped that his family would never get too involved with the soldiers. There was never much said

---

[14]Alvin M. Josephy, Jr., The Nez Perce Indians and the Opening of the Northwest (New Haven: Yale University Press, 1965), p. 630.

[15]J. R. Interview, February 14, 1969, p. 2.

[16]Wellington Rankin Interview with John Board, March 23, 1964, p. 18.

[17]J. R. Interview, February 14, 1969, pp. 1-2; March Elizabeth Huber Interview, September 12, 1971, p. 6.

openly, but the prevalent attitude, and one shared by Rankin, was that
the military was a loafer's job and that anybody with ambition would do
something else. John Rankin appeared "to make fun of them as if they
were dumb people, lazy and didn't work."[18] It definitely was not the
Rankin kind of life. This atmosphere probably had its influence upon
Jeannette, and the atrocities perpetrated against the Indians by the
military may have heightened its effect.[19]

Subconsciously, a part of Jeannette Rankin's abhorrence to war may
have stemmed from observing the tragedy of her father who was blinded
in the right eye and deafened in the right ear by a military weapon.
This cannon was being used in a political celebration in July of 1871.
Instead of shot, it was packed with wadding. John Rankin and William
Raup came around the corner just as it was being fired. Rankin remained
unconscious for about 10 days. His sight and hearing were forever impaired.
How much effect this may have had, if any, remained speculative; but cer-
tainly within the realm of probability.[20]

As Jeannette grew up, she was in school with a boy who had an unusual
experience as a tiny baby. In retrospect, she considered it a unique
privilege to have known him. His mother and father were crossing the
plains as part of a wagon train. As they were encamped one night in a
circle, they heard the Indians approaching. While the men dashed for

---

[18]J. R. Interview, March 31, 1970.

[19]Edna McKinnon Interview, November 16, 1971, p. 9.

[20]Ibid., p. 3; Michael A. Leeson, History of Montana, 1739-1885
(Chicago: Warner, Beers & Co., 1885), p. 865; Joaquin Miller, An
Illustrated History of the State of Montana (Chicago: The Lewis Publish-
ing Co., 1894), p. 565.

their guns, the boy's mother rushed to get him. She took him in her arms
and ran to meet the Indians. As they came near, she fearlessly handed
them her tiny baby as a measure of friendship. They took him, smiled,
laughed, and returned him. She was unable to tell them not to be afraid.
But, when she handed them this tiny baby, they understood and went away.[21]

This relationship had a profound effect upon Rankin in later years.
She enjoyed telling this story in her peace talks to emphasize the fact
that America needed more trust and less fear. Fear, according to her,
led to war. Once in speaking to a high school group, she "brought the
house down" by suggesting, "You can't send your Senator a baby, but you
can write to him and make him know you oughtn't to try to settle disputes
by the war method."[22]

By the time Jeannette reached college, her appreciation for the
value of human life was highly evolved. War to her became an antithesis
to the development of human resources. She remembered the anxiety at
seeing her friends leave for the Spanish-American War in 1898.

Once while in college she was assigned to read publicly Tennyson's
The Charge of the Light Brigade." Jeannette told her professor,
"This is hideous. I can't read it."[23] Thus, her humanitarian ideas
evidently took a pacifist slant while she was young. All of this was to
culminate significantly in courageous votes against American participation
in World War I and World War II.

How much did the frontier influence the development of Jeannette

---

[21] J. R. Interview, February 20, 1969, p. 2.

[22] Ibid.

[23] Jeannette Rankin, "Two Votes against War," Liberation, III (March,
1958), p. 4.

Rankin's personality? Normally, the frontier would bring to mind those characteristics associated with rugged men, individualism, survival of the fittest, violence and warfare with the Indians. Possibly, the frontier experience, prompted by land hunger, had encouraged America's involvement in three wars: the War of 1812, the Mexican War of 1846, and the Civil War. Fortunately, Jeannette received an abundance of the West's ruggedness, love for nature and the out-of-doors, individualism, and courage. But from the violence and Indian wars, she inherited an abhorrence of killing and the settling of disputes with guns.

Alongside these ideas, the West also tended to produce a cooperative spirit among the pioneers. They were far away from governmental services, and thus it became imperative that they work together. Being preoccupied with the conquest of wilderness, westerners developed the concepts of non-intervention and neutrality more readily than other sections of the nation. Jeannette later accepted these premises as the basic foundation of her foreign policy. So her life showed an acceptance of the best of several strains of western culture. All these ideas began to flower after a visit to the East.

While caring for her brother, Wellington, in Cambridge during the winter of 1904-1905, Jeannette Rankin became acutely aware of the contrast of the Eastern slums, poverty, and disease with Montana's open ranchland, abundant opportunities, and invigorating climate. These terrible social and industrial conditions touched the tender heart of the Montana ranch girl. In a way, these experiences became a turning point in her life. She returned to the ranch to resume family responsibilities in 1905 but was destined never to be the same.[24]

After a period of restlessness in Montana, Jeannette Rankin, in 1907, boarded the Northern Pacific for California to seek a change of scenery and to recuperate from inflamatory rheumatism. Instead of resting, she began working in the Telegraph Hill settlement, a social work project in the Italian section of San Francisco. Elizabeth Ash, a social worker, directed the activities of the settlement.

Jeannette worked directly with the children. She cared for them while their mothers attended educational classes and political meetings. She remembered that the boys always ran to the settlement house to be the first to operate the brush-making machine. Jeannette observed, "If you have what interest children, you don't have to make them come. They come because they want to. They come with perspiration running down their faces."[25]

In addition to child care, Jeannette Rankin attended hearings on wage and hour legislation, child labor laws, factory working conditions, and other social legislation being pushed as part of the Progressive Era. In this environment, she gained valuable insight into settlement work and socio-political legislation. The needs of women and children loomed large on her new horizon.[26]

While working with the Telegraph Hill settlement, Jeannette Rankin read avidly. Articles by Jane Addams on social work for young people challenged her thinking. Benjamin Kidd, a British sociologist, made a

---

[24]Peter Clark MacFarland, "Jeannette of Montana," Colliers, LIX (April 21, 1917), p. 7.

[25]J. R. Interview, January 16, 1969, p. 1.

[26]Ibid.; J. R. Interview, April 14, 1970, p. 22.

life-long impression with his book <u>Social Evolutions</u>. Inspired by the
dedication of the social workers at Telegraph Hill and motivated by
social writings of the time, Jeannette's spirit of humanitarianism
grew by leaps and bounds. The needs of the women and children from
Boston to San Francisco stimulated her to action. Realizing that she
needed more than enthusiasm, Rankin enrolled in the New York School of
Philanthropy to acquire a philosophy of social work and to gain practical
experience.[27]

With this in mind, Jeannette entered the New York School in the
fall of 1908. Wellington was at that time completing his last year in
Harvard Law School. The School of Philanthropy, located near New York
City's lower East Side, was the recognized training center for social
workers at that time. Its faculty included Franz Boas, Ben Lindsey,
Louis D. Brandeis, Florence Kelley, and Booker T. Washington. Edward
T. Devine, editor of <u>Survey Magazine</u>, was the guest lecturer for 1908-
1909. His lectures probably were typical of the social thinking of the
time, which challenged classical economics and urged the raising of
standards of living.[28]

Jeannette Rankin grew up in a period of social and economic change.
Many sociologists and economists were challenging the concepts of Social
Darwinism and Classical Economics. Lester F. Ward, <u>Dynamic Sociology</u>
(1881), Henry George, <u>Progress and Poverty</u> (1879), and Edward Bellamy,
<u>Looking Backward</u> (1888), were critics of Herbert Spencer's Social

---

[27]J. R. Interview, January 16, 1969, p. 1.

[28]New York School of Philanthropy <u>Yearbook</u> for 1908-1909; E. T.
Devine, "The New View of Charity," <u>Atlantic Monthly</u>,CII (December, 1908),
p. 739.

Darwinism. They rejected the concept of social progress through survival
of the fittest and substituted the value of the human mind and rational
choice supported by governmental intervention to restrain the strong and
to protect the weak. The Gospel of Wealth idea, emphasizing proof of
special fitness and character through accumulating wealth and distribut-
ing it for charity, no longer carried weight.

Social settlements made a great impact between 1850 and 1915.
Jane Addams' Hull House in Chicago, Lillian Wald's Henry Street Settlement
in New York, and Robert Wood's Andover House in Boston were representative
of the social services performed by this movement. Closely aligned with
this approach was the Social Gospel Movement which advocated moderate
reform in wages, housing, and working conditions. Its leader was
Washington Gladden, a Congregational minister, who defended labor's right
to organize and strike. He denounced the idea that supply and demand
should control wages.[29]

The New York School of Philanthropy operated generally within this
sociological framework. In a letter to her sister, Mary, Jeannette
Rankin spoke of the admiration of the school for Simon N. Patten and
his book, The New Basis of Civilization.[30] Patten, an economic determinist,
wrote that a society's economy influenced, directly or indirectly, all
its ideas and its physical environment. He saw the changing American
economy hopefully leading to a new morality that

> ...does not consist in saving, but in expanding
> consumption; not in draining men of their energy,
> but in storing up a surplus in the weak and young;

---

[29]Washington Gladden, Applied Christianity (Boston: Houghton,
Mifflin & Co., 1886), p. 35.

[30]J. R. to Mary Rankin, February 1909, J. R. Manuscripts.

> not in the process of hardening, but in extending
> the period of recreation and leisure; not in the
> thought of the future, but in utilization and
> expansion of the present.[31]

Other new sociologists and economists concluded that misery and poverty were unnecessary and could be eliminated. Efficiency of society became the panacea. Jeannette Rankin observed, "Everyday we hear about the 'Efficiency Test." They say, 'We don't want good people. We want people good for something.'"[32] This sociological milieu only confirmed Rankin's personal beliefs even more.

While at the School of Philanthropy, Jeannette studied the history of social reform, theory and practice of charity organization, social and racial progress, labor problems, and criminal sociology. In addition to this philosophical instruction in the morning, the program of the school provided for practical experience through actual case work and in special projects. Usually, the afternoons were spent visiting social cases in the slums. With sympathy and tact, Jeannette immediately identified herself with the individual problems and concerns. She was able patiently to secure information needed to help those she was visiting.[33]

One of Rankin's special projects, which lasted two months, was to locate, screen, and secure children to attend the deaf school. First, she familiarized herself with the purposes and program of the school for the deaf by attending classes and studying its curriculum. She secured potential candidates by visiting the public school classes. To her dismay, they reported any kind of affliction and disease as deafness. While

---

[31]Simon N. Patten, The New Basis of Civilization, (New York: Macmillan Company), 1907, pp. 214-215.

[32]J. R. to Mary Rankin, February, 1909, J. R. MSS.

[33]Peter Clark MacFarlane, "Jeannette of Montana," pp. 7-8.

investigating these cases, she saw women and children suffering from every illness imaginable. Jeannette believed that there were no horrible sights on which she had not looked; no woes nor tragedies that she had not glimpsed in the slums of New York. She was touched to the very depths of her heart.[34]

In addition to the case study program, Jeannette Rankin worked two months in the night courts of New York City. She was an understudy of Maude Miner, chief probation officer of the New York City Magistrate's Court.[35] While doing research for a suffrage speech to be given by Maude Miner, Jeannette Rankin was horrified and upset to learn that women in the East had asked for and been denied the vote. From her experience in the West, she simply assumed the right to vote was only a matter of asking. The discovery of the hardships and the struggles that women were undergoing in the East to secure suffrage influenced Rankin's conversations so much that Wellington suggested, "Perhaps that's a better thing to do than social work."[36] Eventually, she took his advice, but that time was still another year away.

In the light of this struggle for suffrage and her study of the concentrated problems of life in a great city, Jeannette began to make an evaluation. Suddenly, she now realized that everywhere she went women

---

[34] J. R. Interview, January 16, 1969, p. 1.

[35] Working with the night court and in the slums of New York City was dangerous for any girl--even Jeannette Rankin. To openly carry a billy club was too obvious an affront to her femininity. She solved this problem by concealing her weapon in a dainty, velvet party bag with draw strings. Edna McKinnon Interview, November 16, 1971, p. 12.

[36] J. R. Interview, March 31, 1970, p. 10.

and children were adversely affected by laws in which they had no direct voice of representation nor power of administration. In her estimation, this was totally unjust and extremely brutal. Having heard the cry of sickness and poverty, Jeannette became convinced it could be answered by political means. From this point on, she was an ardent campaigner for "votes for women."

Her year at the School of Philanthropy had been heartbreaking but abundantly rewarding. In contrast to many of the students, she came to view her training in social work as equipping her to relieve suffering-- not as a means to a job.[37]

Full of enthusiasm and eager to apply her newly acquired knowledge and skill, Jeannette Rankin returned to Missoula after graduation in the summer of 1909. Her first energies, which she remembered as "fun," were devoted to an effort to clean up the city jail. At school, they had been trained to begin their work in any city by looking first at the jail. Knowing the sheriff, Jeannette sought and gained an appointment. She learned that they were placing prostitutes, lawbreaking lumberjacks and all other prisoners into one bullpen because of overcrowded facilities. Inmates also needed more sanitary living conditions, and deserved better food.[38] The situation was ready-made to challenge the ingenuity of the budding young social worker.

Jeannette attempted to talk to the women in the jail, but succeeded in only infuriating them because she talked down to them. "They just smiled at this stupid girl," she remembered. Next, she turned to the

---

[37] J. R., January 16, 1969, p. 1.

[38] Edna McKinnon Interview, November 16, 1971, p. 10.

civil authorities, namely Judge J. W. Webster, a Yale graduate. He was aware that the conditions were ghastly and that something ought to be done by the city officials. When nothing changed, she made a return visit to his chambers. Looking up from the end of the long table where he was reading, he mumbled to himself, "My God, that woman again."[39] The Rankin family laughed at this incident and was amazed at her tenacity and determination to see this project through.

Unable at this point to accomplish her goals, Jeannette took her case to the women in Missoula. She encouraged them to call Judge Webster to discuss the conditions at the city jail and to voice their opinions. One day the county attorney sought to discredit the agitation by telling the Judge, "That is just Jeannette Rankin. It is nothing." Turning to him, the Judge replied, "Then, why are all the good women in town telephoning me?" From this episode, Jeannette valued the lesson learned about the importance of people expressing opinions to elected officials.[40] It was a method she would use over and over again.

Having won moderate success in this endeavor, Jeannette Rankin led a campaign to establish a public bathhouse in Missoula. When the lumberjacks came into town, they had no facilities for bathing and no place to go except the saloon. Attacking at least a part of the problem, she collected quite a sum of money for the construction of baths modeled after those in Europe. Again, she felt this was an excellent idea to help the lumberjacks, tramps, and others to keep clean. After talking to a

---

[39] Ibid.

[40] J. R. Interview, March 31, 1970, p. 12.

lot of people some interest developed but the plan failed to gain
momentum. She dejectedly returned the contributions and left for the
West Coast to seek employment.[41]

With her training in social work, Jeannette soon secured employment as a "home finder" in the Children's Home Society of Spokane,
Washington. These were difficult days for her as she developed an
emotional attachment to the children. It was an agonizing experience.
"There was one instance," she said, "I will always remember. One child
was placed in a home and they decided they didn't want him. He came
back and wept in the office. All these awfully sad things about the
children, I couldn't take it."[42]

From the Spokane Society, Rankin transferred to another one in
Seattle. Here, she lived in the orphanage. In time, she became disillusioned with the program, techniques, and commitment of these professional social workers. She bagan to look for something else to do.
Jeannette remembered, "I didn't fit in at all. I didn't like the way
they were doing it, and I didn't know how to do it."[43] Nevertheless,
in deference to the problems, this work did give her an insight into the
needs of babies, older children, and young adults.[44] It also helped to
confirm her conviction, held since the days of the New York School of
Philanthropy, that reform was needed in many of the institutions dealing
with social problems. Jeannette believed that these conditions were the

---

[41]J. R. Interview, January 16, 1969, p. 1.

[42]J. R. Interview, September 27, 1971, p. 14.

[43]J. R. Interview, January 16, 1969, p. 1.

[44]Bertha Filer, "Our First Woman Congressman," McCall's, XLI
(April, 1917), p. 14.

result of bad laws. As was typical of her later approach, she then determined "to attack the cause in order to do away with the effects."[45]

Disappointed with social work as a career, Jeannette Rankin charted a new course. She enrolled in the University of Washington to study economics, sociology, and public speaking in order to more adequately prepare herself for a career championing social legislation. As her interest in a child welfare career declined, Rankin's involvement in suffrage increased.[46]

---

[45] J. R. Interview, January 16, 1969, p. 1; Lewis Levine, "First Woman Member of Congress Well Versed in Politics," New York Times, November 19, 1916, II, p. 4.

[46] J. R. Interview, January 16, 1969, p. 2.

CHAPTER III

LET THE SUFFRAGETTE OUT

When Jeannette Rankin arrived in Washington State in the fall
of 1909, a women suffrage campaign was well underway. Feminism, as a
movement, had made its debut as a facet of the general reform era of
the 1830's and 1840's. Unfortunately, the struggle over slavery and
the coming Civil War eclipsed the efforts of such feminists as Lucretia
Mott, Elizabeth Cady Stanton, Susan B. Anthony, and Lucy Stone.

During the post-war years, women continued to struggle for equal
rights but reaped few victories. A most significant political gain
came when the Wyoming territorial legislature in 1869 gave women the
right to vote, to control their property, and to serve on juries. The
1890's saw a new flury of feminine activity. Through the years, suffrage
had gained respectability; and, with the passage of time, the animosity
among early leaders had declined. With a new generation of women in a
different atmosphere, the two contesting suffrage associations were able
to merge.

In 1890, Wyoming became the first state to incorporate woman
suffrage into its constitution. Three years later, Colorado gave its
women the right to vote. Utah Territory had granted enfranchisement in
1870, only to see it declared invalid by Congress. After Utah became
a state in 1896, it restored woman suffrage to its statutes. In an
almost uncontested vote, Idaho became the fourth state in 1896 to

grant suffrage to women. But with the winning of Idaho, a long dry spell set in.

Despite the arduous campaigns between 1896 and 1910, suffragists could claim no victories. Anna Howard Shaw, clergyman and physician, succeeded Carrie Chapman Catt in 1904 as president of the National American Woman Suffrage Association when the latter resigned because of family and international women's commitments. Dr. Shaw was an excellent speaker, but an ineffective organizer. She was jealous of suggestions from the grass roots. During her presidency from 1904 to 1915, very little progress was made toward a federal amendment; but the state campaigns continued at a frenzied pace and took on new significance.

The Washington State campaign broke the dry spell. In the spring of 1909, a hostile Washington legislature finally gave the two-thirds majority necessary to get the suffrage amendment on the ballot. It had been 13 years since the last suffrage victory and 11 years since a legislature had let an amendment through. Jeannette Rankin arrived in Washington State in the fall of 1909 to take up work with the Children's Home Societies in Spokane and Seattle. Overcome with anxiety and frustration, she resigned to better prepare herself for a career to change the laws hindering social progress. While a student at the University of Washington in Seattle, she noticed an announcement in the paper offering suffrage posters for distribution. This was part of a "poster brigade" established by the College Equal Suffrage League to assist in putting up the colorful red-and-white placards. The April poster read,

"Roosevelt when Governor of New York in a message to the New York legislature urged woman suffrage."[1]

After replying to the advertisement, Jeannette Rankin received a
bundle of suffrage posters. She covered the entire neighborhood, placeing
them in all the available store windows. A barber shop, certainly a male
citadel, seemed an unlikely place for a suffrage poster, but she felt it
should not be slighted. After an initial rebuff, the barber, on second
thought, decided to take one. Later, from her apartment window, Jeannette
watched the amusing proceedings. Men would be stoically walking along
the sidewalk, and suddenly they would see the poster. Quickly, they would
go in, and she suspected they shared much fun and laughter at the expense
of woman suffrage.[2]

A leading suffragist lived in the neighborhood and was pleased and
surprised to find the streets plastered with suffrage posters. She
inquired at the barber shop as to the name of the individual who put up
them. With this interesting link, Jeannette Rankin entered the suffrage
campaign. Since the spring quarter was about over and she would soon
be leaving for Montana for the summer, Rankin offered her services in
the fall. She indicated she would return without pay if they would only
keep her busy. The Washington suffragists readily agreed.[3]

When Jeannette Rankin arrived in the fall of 1910 in Seattle, she
worked under Emma Smith DeVoe, president of the Washington Equal Suffrage

---

[1]Woman's Journal, XLI (May 7, 1910), p. 75; Adella M. Parker, "The
Woman Voter of the West," The Westerner, XVI (August, 1912), p. 6;
J. R. Interview, March 31, 1970, p. 10; J. R. Interview, January 6,
1969, p. 2.

[2]J. R. Interview, March 30, 1970, pp. 10-11.

[3]J. R. Interview, March 30, 1970, p. 11.

Association. DeVoe's organizational plan was to contact every registered voter. Blanks were supplied to all precinct chairmen. They were to secure the voter's stand on suffrage and convert him if possible. These blanks, with appropriate information, were returned to the state head-quarters so the suffragists could determine where to work.[4] Supplementing posters, booths at area fairs, theatrical productions under the direction of Adella Parker, and house-to-house canvasses were a multitude of speaking engagements.

With no experience except what she had gained in social work, Rankin launched her suffrage work in Ballard, a small lumber mill town. After visiting the known suffragists, she contacted the newspaper editor and the school teachers. Then, Jeannette went everywhere talking woman suffrage. Someone suggested having a public meeting. She secured the city hall and a speaker. In proportion to her efforts, she envisioned 25 to 30 people, but only about 15 showed up. She remembered, "I was just sick."[5] After Ballard, the suffragists moved Jeannette around from town to town. She felt the moves meant she had failed. At the end of the campaign, Mrs. Homer Hill, President of the Washington Equal Franchise Society told her: "Well, when we saw what you had done in Ballard, we thought we were not going to waste her there any longer."[6] Jeannette's enthusiasm was catching, and her effectiveness exceeded all anticipations.

Besides working with Emma Smith DeVoe of the Washington Equal Suffrage

---

[4]"The Suffragist Germ in Washington," Woman's Journal, XLI (March 5, 1910), p. 40.

[5]J. R. Interview, March 30, 1970, p. 11.

[6]J. R. Interview, March 30, 1970, p. 11.

Association and Mrs. Homer Hill of the Washington Equal Franchise Society,
Jeannette Rankin found a new friend in Minnie J. Reynolds, a former
Colorado campaigner and national journalist. Because of her influence,
Jeannette incorporated the peace issue in the suffrage program. Many of
the suffragists already wanted the right to vote in order "to express
the woman's point of view" on other issues. To Rankin it only seemed
natural that a mother's instinct would be for the peaceable preservation
of her race.[7]

While walking along the sidewalk one evening during her three-month
speaking tour of Washington State, Minnie Reynolds saw a brood of baby
chicks in an incubator in a store window. Turning to Jeannette, the
national suffragist said, "The women produce the boys and the men take
them off and kill them in war."[8] Such homely examples as this encouraged
in Jeannette a growing concept of the terribleness of war. From that
experience and others, she began to argue that women should have the
right to vote so as to stop wars and to save their sons. Years later,
Rankin asserted that in countries where women were enfranchised it was
difficult to start war. She hoped after the ballot was granted to
American women they would outlaw war in the same way that public opinion
had outlawed dueling.[9]

From the spring of 1909 to the fall of 1910, the women of Washington

---

[7]Belle Fligelman Winestine to the author, February 23, 1969, in his
personal files; Woman's Journal, XLI (October 15, 1910), p. 171.

[8]J. R. Interview, January 10, 1969, p. 7.

[9]Denver Colorado Post, April 18, 1925, a clipping in the Rankin Folder,
Women's International League for Peace and Freedom Files, Swarthmore College
Peace Collection, hereafter referred to as WIL files, S.C.P.C.

State waged a strenous uphill campaign. The principles under which they
conducted themselves were as follows:

> Keep the issue single. Be for nothing but suffrage,
> against nothing but anti-suffrage. Pin your faith
> to the printed word. It carries conviction. Rely
> upon facts rather than argument. Plead affirmative
> arguments. Put your opponent on the defensive.
> Convert the indifferent--there are thousands of
> them. Let the incorrigible alone; they are only a
> few. Avoid big meetings; they rouse your enemies.
> Avoid antagonizing "big business," but get the
> labor vote--quietly. Be confident of winning.
> Try to have every voter in the state asked by
> some woman to vote for the amendment; this will
> carry it. Always be good-natured.[10]

This campaign in many respects, was the most brilliant ever conducted for suffrage. It broke the deadlock and set a new pace for suffrage
campaigns all over the country. Contrary to previous practice, the
direction of the campaign was in the hands of Washington women. Outside
speakers came at the request of Washingtonians and worked wholly under
their supervision. Also, in contrast to prior campaigns, there were no
"big" meetings or large public debates. Rather than taking the chance
of arousing the opposition, the Washington suffragists went to ready-made
meetings, assembled for other purposes, and secured permission to speak
briefly.[11]

All work and no play would make "Suffragette" a dull girl. To
enliven the campaign, the women gave teas, luncheons, dinners and
receptions. Every assembly had a dash of suffrage talk. There were

---

[10]Adella M. Parker, "The Woman Voter of the West," pp. 37-38;
These directives were not only important for the Washington campaign
but formed a basis for Jeannette's political philosophy in later years.

[11]Adella Parker, "The Woman Voter of the West," p. 37.

parlor meetings, moonlight excursions, card parties, and dances to raise
money to carry on the work. In many towns, they published a suffrage
paper filled not with arguments but with facts and clever cartoons.
These methods made the campaign a pleasure and victory even sweeter.

There were other factors which aided the suffrage cause in Washington
State. The country, as a whole, experienced an upbeat in the democratic
pulse from the progressive program of Theodore Roosevelt. It demanded a
more responsible and responsive democracy. The direct primary law in
Washington helped to put the individual parties on good behavior. The
women were supported by labor and by the Socialists. No doubt, the English
women's violent tactics gave the cause big advertisement. But no other
forces would have won the fight had not the women staged a superhuman
effort. On November 8, 1910, the equal suffrage amendment, winning in
every county, carried by a total of 52,299 to 29,676. It won in fourteen
out of thirty-eight counties by a margin of two to one. This opened the
door for campaigns in Montana, California, and Arizona.[12]

As to an evaluation of Jeannette's place in this campaign, Minnie
Reynolds wrote a note of appreciation to the Woman's Journal. She pointed
out that "Jeannette worked for several months without pay. No service
was too commonplace, difficult or disagreeable. All this was enhanced by
her singularly sweet personality." After Jeannette began speaking late
in the campaign, the noted suffragist said, "I prophesy that she will be

---

[12]Ida H. Harper, History of Woman Suffrage (New York: National
American Woman Suffrage Association, 1922), I, p. 317, hereinafter
referred to as HWS; Woman's Journal, XLI (April 16, 1910), p. 63;
Western Woman Voter, January, 1911, p. 3.

heard of in future campaigns."[13] No prophecy or dream was ever truer!!
Jeannette's next stop was her native state.

Suffrage in Montana was not a new issue. Before 1900, the National
American Woman Suffrage Association, under President Susan B. Anthony,
had promoted suffrage work in the state. Several societies were organized and conventions held. Two early presidents of the Montana organization
were Dr. Maria M. Dean and Clara B. Tower. In 1902, Carrie Chapman Catt,
President of the National American Woman Suffrage Association, Gail
Laughlin and Laura Gregg, field workers, spent the spring and summer
re-activating and organizing suffrage clubs in Helena, Butte, and across
the state. In addition to suffrage groups, they addressed women's clubs,
trade councils, and labor conventions. Laughlin remained in Montana
through the fall swelling the suffrage organization to 30 clubs.
Petitions became a major form of propaganda where organization was
impracticable.[14]

Under the direction of Gail Laughlin, NAWSA field worker, suffrage
legislation was introduced in both houses in 1903. After considerable
debate, the House voted 41 to 23 in favor but not the two-thirds
necessary. The resultion in the Senate, introduced by H. L. Sherlock,
was also defeated.[15] After another serious attempt to secure passage

---

[13]Woman's Journal, XLI (December 17, 1910), p. 242.

[14]Mary G. Peck, Carrie Chapman Catt (New York: W. H. Wilson Co.,
1944), p. 126.

[15]Ida Harper, HWS, VI, pp. 360-361; Among its strong supporters were
Dr. O. M. Lanstrum, J. M. Kennedy, John MacGinnis, Colonel James U. Sanders,
F. Augustus Heinze, Colonel C. B. Nolan, and state senators C. A. Whipple,
W. F. Meyer, and Edward A. Johnson.

in 1905, nothing was done except in a desultory way until 1911. The political equality clubs lingered on as did the presentation of an annual suffrage amendment to the legislature. Encouraged and happy with the "breakthrough" victory in Washington in the fall of 1910, Jeannette Rankin returned to Montana for Christmas. Immediately, she joined the Political Equality Club in Missoula, her home town, and started to work.

Jeannette Rankin gave new life to the club and sparked so much enthusiasm that they elected her vice president. After learning that Dr. J. M. Donahue proposed to introduce a woman suffrage amendment in the Montana legislature, Jeannette called a meeting of the Political Equality Club and interested citizens. There were about 40 men and women present for this public meeting. She indicated a desire and willingness to go to Helena to work for suffrage. They accepted her proposal to represent them.[16]

After arriving in Helena, the newly appointed suffrage lobbyist interviewed Dr. D. J. Donahue. Jeannette Rankin, to her astonishment, learned that he had proposed to introduce the legislation only as a joke. "To men, woman suffrage was the funniest thing in the world," she remembered. In the Washington campaign, children had made funny banners; and the men had told clever jokes. Everyone had laughed and talked about it. Since Dr. Donahue had received the desired repartee, Jeannette replied, "Well, you've gotten the publicity and now you'll have to go through with it. You'll have to introduce the bill."[17] And so he did.

Legislative champions for suffrage were Colonel C. B. Nolan, W. W. Berry, and D. G. O'Shea. In addition, Jeannette secured the support of

[16] J. R. Interview, January 16, 1969, p. 2; Ida Harper, HWS, VI, p. 361.

[17] J. R. Interview, January 26, 1969, p. 2.

several women from Helena. There were strong opponents also. James E.
McNally and Joseph Binnard, legislators, presented such formidable
opposition that Rankin became discouraged and returned to Missoula. In
the meantime, the committee called for a sponsor to speak in the affirmative. Rather than using this as an excuse for pigeonholing the bill,
the committee passed the legislation into the House and called for
Jeannette to address the entire body.[18]

Never had Jeannette Rankin addressed such a large audience in a
formal speech. She made her brother, Wellington, a recent graduate
of Harvard Law School, listen to her preparations and to make suggestions.
When he would remind her, "It's a very important occasion," it nearly
scared Jeannette to death. While she was writing and learning her speech,
the Montana legislature was trying to nominate its senator. Prior to the
session, the people, in a referendum, had selected T. J. Walsh as their
choice. Visitors packed the galleries at the noon hour to watch the
voting. To avoid conflict, the House invited Jeannette to speak at two
o'clock.[19]

As early as one o'clock, there was standing room only. The Senate
refused the invitation of the House to attend officially, but adjourned
and was present. The House floor resembled anything but a legislative
chamber. The members had assessed themselves fifty cents apiece to
buy flowers to decorate the hall and a bouquet for Jeannette. Also, the

---

[18]Ibid.; Peter Clark MacFarlane, "Jeannette of Montana," p. 8, Ida
Harper, HWS, VI, p. 361.

[19]J. R. Interview, January 16, 1969, p. 3.

gaily colored hats of the women blanketed the arched doorways to the room.[20]

Jeannette Rankin arrived at the Capitol in a lovely green velvet dress. A number of old-time suffragists, Dr. Maria Dean, Dr. Mary B. Atwater, Mrs. James U. Sanders, Mary L. Anderson, and May Murphy, proudly escorted her to the reading desk. The reception accorded Rankin pleased the Montana women. After the House resolved itself into a committee of the whole, Representatives C. B. Nolan, H. N. Blake, and D. J. Donahue escorted her to the rostrum. The Helena Independent recorded that Nolan and Chairman Dan O'Hern, in introducing Jeannette Rankin, gave eloquent tributes to her work in varous parts of the country.

To gain rapport with the legislators, Jeannette Rankin's opening sentence began, "I was born in Montana." To this, the men broke into a round of applause so boisterous that she almost forgot her speech. Regaining her composure, Jeannette declared that she wanted suffrage not just for herself but for the six million women who were following the vocations of men and for their children. Naming the countries of the world where women had suffrage or partial suffrage, one-fifteenth of the surface of the world, Rankin said, "Women are voting in those countries that lead in enlightenment, civilization, and education." Then, to the Montana legislators, she poignantly phrased the question, "Which will Montana stand with?" And then even more decisively, she asked, "Which will you stand with?"[21]

By pointing out that the neighboring western states of Wyoming,

---

[20]Ibid.; MacFarland, "Jeannette of Montana," p. 8; Ida Harper, HWS, VI, p. 362.

[21]Helena Independent, February 2, 1911.

Colorado, Utah, and Idaho had granted women enfranchisement, Rankin hoped to encourage a favorable response. She reminded the legislators that the women now were struggling against the same tyranny men had gladly given their lives to crush during the revolutionary period--namely, "taxation without representation."

The most widely used male argument against suffrage was that the "woman's place was in the home." Persuasively, Jeannette countered by asking, "How can they make it a home if they have no control of the influences over the home?" Then she continued by pointing out that in only 13 states did women have equal guardianship of their children. In 23 states the father could will away an unborn child without the mother's consent. Mothers were also concerned with nursing a child through typhoid fever, but it was more important that she have a voice in regulating typhus in the milk supply.[22]

Jeannette Rankin concluded her twenty-minute speech by asking the legislators not to decide the question of equal suffrage but to submit it to voters of Montana. As a prelude to her plea, she read a memorial from the Political Equality Club of Missoula, which supported a constitutional amendment. The tenor of Jeannette's speech did not stoop to begging for support. Neither did it threaten, cajole, or appeal to male chivalry. She simply advanced her argument and asked for sincere consideration.

But many of the men were not intent on giving it serious thought. Representative Joseph Binnard, leader of the opposition, rose to present Jeannette with a bouquet of purple violets. Through the presentation of flowers he attempted to turn the meeting into a facetious affair.

-----

[22]Ibid.

Consequently, the women were just about to burst into tears.[23]

The sentiment changed when Colonel C. B. Nolan, law partner of Thomas J. Walsh and the oldest and most respected member of the legislature, rose to speak. In his brogue, he talked of how hard his Irish mother had worked, how she had taken care of the family and all the things she had done that were hard for women. He summed it up by saying, "A woman like that ought to have the right to vote."[24] With tears in their eyes, the House voted a majority but not the necessary two-thirds.[25]

There were several significant results of this legislative appearance. It gave a new birth of enthusiasm to the suffrage movement in Montana and established a hard core of workers who used effectively, or capitalized on, the propaganda from Washington State. Secondly, the invitation from the House provided Jeannette Rankin an excellent public forum through which to express her suffrage ideas. As a result of newspaper coverage across the state, various women wrote to Jeannette and asked, "Why didn't you tell us? Why didn't you let us know?"[26] In addition to establishing a rallying point, Rankin secured a readymade list of interested suffragists.

---

[23]Ibid.; Burton K. Wheeler, Representative from Silver Bow, remembered that a group of them had previously arranged to have a little fun. He joined Binnard, told funny stories of imagined consequences and evoked lots of laughter. While having dinner that evening with several of the men at the hotel, some of the suffragists entered. He remembered them pointing and saying, "Look at that bunch of crooks!" After having his fun, he voted for suffrage because he said, "If I hadn't I think my wife would have quit me." Burton K. Wheeler, Personal Interview, June 10, 1971, Washington, D.C., p. 2.

[24]J. R. Interview, January 16, 1969, p. 3; Peter Clark MacFarland, "Jeannette of Montana," p. 34.

[25]Woman's Journal, XLII (February 18, 1911), p. 49.

[26]J. R. Interview, January 16, 1909, p. 4; J. R. Interview with Katrina Cheek, November 14, 1969, p. 3.

Essentially, this legislative appearance kicked off the final equal suffrage campaign in Montana. Also, the majority vote of the male legislators indicated a change in their sentiment toward enfranchisement of women. Yet, many of the representatives later told Jeannette they had supported the amendment only because they knew it would not pass.

Jeannette Rankin temporarily accepted a bouquet of violets from the legislators, but she indicated that she would permanently settle for nothing short of equal suffrage. After Minnie J. Reynolds returned to New York from the Washington State campaign, she learned that Harriet B. Laidlaw, chairman of the Manhattan Borough of the Woman Suffrage Party of New York, sought to hire a worker for the area. Reynolds remembered the dedication and enthusiasm of the young women who had accompanied her for three weeks in Seattle. Laidlaw wrote to Montana. Since Jeannette desired to gain a foothold in the organized suffrage movement, she accepted the open door of Laidlaw's personal offer of fifty dollars a month for half a year. In the summer of 1911, she packed her bags and left for New York.[27]

In the years after the turn of the twentieth century, suffrage work in New York, as well as in the nation, was in the doldrums. Its revival must be credited to the enthusiastic work of Harriot Stanton Blatch, daughter of the early feminist Elizabeth Cade Stanton, and Carrie Chapman Catt, immediate past president of the National American Woman Suffrage Association. Having just returned from England where she breathed the Pankhurst spirit for several years, Blatch insisted that the women get involved politically. They must become more militant. Her suffrage group,

---

[27] M. J. Reynolds, "How Miss Jeannette Rankin Started in Politics," The Call, N. D. in Harriet B. Laidlaw Scrapbook at Schlesinger Library, Radcliffe College.

the Women's Political Union, began to lobby and testify before the New
York legislature at Albany. Despite objections from other suffragists,
they initiated the idea of using parades in 1910 and adopted the regular
use of open air meetings.[28]

While Harriot S. Blatch brought militancy and new life to New York
suffrage, Carrie Chapman Catt developed a new scheme of organization.
Admiring the "political machine" of Tammany Hall, she decided to use its
district structure as the organizational pattern for her New York Woman
Suffrage Party. Established in 1909, it became the first suffrage group
to use assembly and election districts. Suffrage had successfully
borrowed the machinery of the city politician.[29]

With this shift to New York, Jeannette Rankin came into a larger
and more sophisticated campaign for woman suffrage. Upon arriving, she
immediately went to work in the assembly districts of the Borough of
Manhattan. Under the direction of the New York Woman Suffrage Party,
she spent much of her time in organizational activity. This meant foot
work on the streets of New York and extemporaneous speaking on the street
corners. Usually, they would try to locate a corner where there was not
a saloon. The normal procedure would be for the suffragists to ask passersby to stand until a crowd gathered. While one would be speaking, others
would be giving out literature and slips of papers on which people could

[28]Harriot S. Blatch, Challenging Years (New York: G. P. Putnam's
Sons, 1940), pp. 91-129.

[29]Harriet B. Laidlaw, "Organizing To Win Votes for Women by the
Political District Plan." in Harriet B. Laidlaw Papers, Schlesinger
Library, Radcliffe College, hereinafter refered to as HBL Papers.

write their names to indicate an interest in suffrage. After these were
collected, Jeannette made a personal visit to secure their help as a
worker or a precinct captain. This took her into practically every slum
and tenement house in Manhattan.

In addition to working under the leadership of Harriet B. Laidlaw,
Jeannette shared responsibilities with Cornelia Swinnerton, Elizabeth
Freeman, and other young women. As they traveled around the city, they
were continually inspired with fresh devotion to the cause of women by
seeing the oppression and degradation to which women were subjected.[30]

Another facet of Jeannette's job included work with employed girls.
Even though they labored long hours at toilsome and oppressive jobs,
many working girls volunteered their evenings for suffrage. Rankin helped to establish girls' clubs in connection with parish houses and church
settlements. She especially enjoyed the many evenings speaking to the
girls at the Junior League House where she lived.[31] Quite frequently,
other groups also invited her to present the suffrage cause.[32]

These months in New York substantially increased Jeannette Rankin's
ability and knowledge. Since she had not done much speaking in Washington
State and Montana, the "street corner oratory" helped her to gain confidence
and to learn the suffrage rhetoric. The work in New York introduced her
to the politics of a metropolitan city. She tenaciously learned, and
never forgot, the precinct scheme of organization. Besides acquiring

---

[30]The Woman Voter, II (January, 1912), p. 25.

[31]The Junior League House, a house on East 86 Street, rented a suite
for seven dollars a week, including meals and transportation through the
East Side to Third Avenue. The Woman's Journal, XLVII (November 18, 1916),

[32]The Woman Voter, II (January, 1912), p. 26.

more experience and new techniques, Jeannette Rankin made many friends
and etched for herself a permanent sketch in the national suffrage
picture. When the call from California came, she was prepared and ready
to do.

Encouraged by the success in Washington State, California suffragists
began a push for victory. In essence, the work had not ceased from the
last defeat in 1896 by the urban centers. As the campaign warmed up,
social settlements, civic leagues, humanitarian groups, labor unions,
socialists, and prohibitionists supported the suffrage cause. Elizabeth
L. Watson, President of the California Equal Suffrage Association, directed the central committee and led the cause to victory. The amendment
passed the California Legislature by a comfortable margin in February.[33]

During the summer of 1911, California called for national help.
Harriet B. Laidlaw offered the services of her newly discovered worker
Jeannette Rankin to the central committee.[34] Along with Jeannette Rankin,
the New York suffragists sent for a period of six weeks Helen Hoy-Greeley,
leader of the Nineteenth Assembly District, and Mrs. A. C. Fisk, chairman
of the Woman Suffrage Party in the Bronx. Jeannette arrived in San Francisco
the last day of August and was quickly handed a full week's schedule.[35]

Rankin's first major talk was on September 5 at Alameda, across the
bay from San Francisco. She was featured with a popular minister Charles

---

[33]Woman's Journal, XLII (February 18, 1911), p. 5; Selina Solomons,
How We Won the Vote in California (San Francisco: The New Woman Publishing Company, 1912), p. 30.

[34]Constance Dean to H. B. Laidlaw, August 5, 1911, in HBL Papers,
Folder 105.

[35]James Laidlaw to Mrs. Frank Deering, August 31, 1911, in HBL Papers,
Folder 105. To save suffrage money, J. R. rode on upper births in the
trains. J. R. to H. B. L., September, 1911, in HBL Papers.

Aked, pastor of the First Congregational Church in San Francisco. Mabel Deering, of the College Equal Suffrage League, wrote, "Miss Rankin's speech at the meeting was a great success.... The audience was greatly taken with Miss Rankin.... She says you never have such enthusiastic applause in New York."[36]

After the rally in Alameda, Jeannette Rankin started north to work in the county districts and rural mining camps of Yolo, Siskiyne, and Butte. This turned out to be rigorous campaigning far away from and in contrast with the picturesque activities of San Francisco. As she entered the towns, Jeannette inquired as to where Hiram Johnson had spoken. Johnson, Governor and later Senator from California, was a growing Progressive political figure in 1911 who advocated progress, efficiency, and reform. With her genius for popular appeal, she wanted to launch her campaign for suffrage from a spot already associated with political sincerity, progress, and success.[37]

While spending time with the "country folk," Jeannette reported to Harriet Laidlaw, "I have not slept in the same bed two nights in succession since I came to California so you know I have been very busy--have spoken fourteen times." In one county seat town, she described suffragist activities as including a band, an auto parade, a meeting in the opera house, and a big crowd. To her, it was a "real political meeting." Jeannette enjoyed that trip so much she described it as "a lovely summer outing."[38]

[36]Mabel Deering to H. B. Laidlaw, N. D. in HBL Papers, Folder 109.

[37]Peter Clark MacFarland, "Jeannette of Montana," p. 37.

[38]Jeannette Rankin to H. B. Laidlaw, September 13, 1911, in HBL papers, Folder 105.

Jeannette traveled by stage coach into the heart of California's historic mining districts. On the way, the stage driver stopped at French Gulch for dinner. Never one to miss an opportunity, Rankin looked around for a group to address. Inside the hotel, she appealed to a man to notify the people on the street that a woman would speak on suffrage from the hotel steps before the stage left. He blushed and demurred. The hotel clerk declined without blushing. Finally, a small boy consented "to tip youse off to de bums." Not many came, but those who did, she reported, listened with wonder and respect.[39]

On the stage to Weaverville was an educator who had organized a women's band. "I tried the men for years," explained the bandmaster, "and they quit on me; but the women have proved faithful."[40] Naturally, the women were delighted to play for Jeannette Rankin. According to reports, her audience included all of the people in the town. When the votes were counted, French Gulch and Weaverville gave suffrage a winning majority.[41]

The women over the entire state of California were hopeful but not confident. Remembering the last defeat led by the urban centers, especially San Francisco, and vested liquor interests, they realized the need to win heavily in the rural areas. The Central Committee sent as many organizers as possible into the rural counties in the hope of enlarging majorities.[42] October 10 began two days of suspension as tabulators counted the votes.

---

[39] Peter Clark MacFarland, "Jeannette of Montana," p. 37.

[40] J. R. Interview, Sept. 25, 1971, p. 2.

[41] Peter Clark MacFarland, "Jeannette of Montana," p. 37.

[42] Mrs. Frank P. Deering to Harriet B. Laidlaw, November 1, 1911, in HBL Papers, Folder 105.

Early returns from San Francisco indicated a decisive defeat for the
women. As results from the rural areas and southern California were
reported, however, the suffragists squeezed out a 3,500 vote victory
out of a total of 247,000 votes cast.[43]

In an article entitled, "Why the Country Folk Did It," Jeannette
Rankin attributed the victory to five factors. First, she recognized
that there was not the same distinction in California as in New York
between professional people and the "people who use their hands." She
illustrated this by pointing out that a cultured man discussing the
single tax issue in the parlor in a San Francisco hotel was the same
man she saw later in work clothes when she addressed a small community
gathering. He was the owner of a local flour mill but worked along with
the men. Apparently, she thought "more educated people work and more
working people are educated in California than in most states."[44]

Adding to this, Jeannette Rankin observed that the men of California
were used to seeing women work. They ran fruit ranches, owned and operated mines, and appeared in all professions and occupations. "In the rural
districts," she wrote, "the women are respected more because they work
and achieve things."[45]

In the third place, Rankin found that some women were the inspiration
of entire communities. They encouraged the discussion of common problems
and lived very democratically. Rankin also contributed an important
educative influence to small town newspapers like the Sacramento Bee.

---

[43]Woman's Journal, XLII (October 14, 1911), p. 45.

[44]Jeannette Rankin, "Why the Country Folk Did It," The Woman Voter,
II (December, 1911), p. 13.

[45]Ibid.

Finally, Jeannette noted the value of Socialists' support. In their meetings she felt that the idea of equal rights for women fell on fruitful
soil.[46]

In summary, Rankin described the prevailing sentiment of the country
districts as very sympathetic. Instead of emphasizing conversion to
suffrage, her goal was to get out the vote. She was very disillusioned
with the wealthy, the liquor interest and the vice lords in the city
who worked against enfranchisement. In what was to become a symbol of
her lifelong career, she declared "We must work with what the great
Lincoln called 'the plain people.'"[47]

After about six weeks of hard work in northern California, Jeannette
Rankin returned to New York City in November to assist Elizabeth Freeman
and Cornelia Swinnerton in open air meetings. She did a systematic canvass
of the Thirteenth Assembly District and opened a clubroom as a center for
district life. Rankin became very adept at using the district organization
plan for suffrage. All of this effort was aimed at securing a woman
suffrage amendment to the New York State Constitution in the legislature
of 1912.

As the year 1912 opened, New York suffragists formed a coalition
of their men's, women's, and collegiate organizations. Included in their
coalition effort were the New York State Woman Suffrage Association, the
Woman Suffrage Party, the Equal Franchise Society, the Political League,
the Collegiate Equal Suffrage League, the Men's League for Equal Suffrage,
and the Women's Political Union. They nominated a Cooperative Committee

---

[46]Ibid., p. 13.

[47]Ibid., p. 13.

and employed Jeannette Rankin to lead the legislative lobby at Albany.
She was assisted by Caroline Lexow and Harriot S. Blatch of the Women's
Political Union and Harriet Mills of the New York Women Suffrage Associa-
tion.[48] Senator Stephen J. Stilwell of the Bronx and Representative
Andrew F. Murray of Manhattan introduced in their respective houses
suffrage legislation for the women.

Besides securing strong legislative sponsors for the amendment,
Jeannette Rankin had to put together an effective organization. Fortunately for the cause of suffrage, this was what she did best. She then assumed
responsibility only for legislative lobbying and delegated the other jobs.
The Central Committee met every Friday to hear Rankin's report, to review
progress, and to make plans for the next week. In addition to lobbying,
the suffragists gathered petitions, wrote letters, attended hearings, and
marched in parades. They knew that they must acquire every means of support
possible.[49]

In all previous attempts, New York legislators had killed constitutional
amendments enfranchising women in the committee before they could reach the
floor for debate. This time Jeannette found the politicians courteous,
well informed, and convinced as individuals of the bill's merit. Yet,
they pointed out two reasons why they would hesitate to vote for it. The
first was "the women of my district don't care anything about it," and
secondly, "some of the women in my district have spoken to be about it, but
not a single man."[50] Thus, voter indifference was one of the large obstacles

_____

[48] Woman's Journal, XLIII (January 13, 1912), p. 14; Harriot S. Blatch
and Alma Lutz, Challenging Years, p. 156.

[49] New York Suffrage Newsletter, XIII (March, 1912), p. 39.

[50] New York Suffrage Newsletter, XII (February, 1912), p. 26.

Jeannette Rankin had to overcome. To counter these objections, she encouraged a writing campaign from the district to inform the representatives of local sentiment.

The suffragists not only wrote to Albany, they came to demonstrate. Harriot S. Blatch, who organized the first parade in 1910, usually led these marchers from the Women's Political Union. While they were in town to march, Jeannette Rankin helped introduce these women to their legislators in order to convince them of backhome interest.[51]

While the suffragists were hard at work, so was the opposition. Mrs. Gilbert James, chairman of the National League for the Civic Education of Women, discovered that the anti-suffragists had mailed letters to generally conservative Wall Street businessmen. They solicited financial aid to stop "this invasion of the home and revolution of social life."[52] The National Association Opposed to Woman Suffrage, organized in New York in 1911 and led by Mrs. Arthur M. Dodge, appeared in strong numbers. E. P. Wheeler, another outspoken New York critic of suffrage, suggested in a speech that motherhood must be protected and conserved by sparing them the burden of the vote. He also said that not every women should have the right to vote and that women could probably exert their influence better through other channels.[53] In addition to these forms of opposition, Jeannette Rankin often took up the gauntlet in debate as typified by one held in Greenwich House in February of 1912 against Professor C. E. Pellew.[54]

[51]New York Call, March 13, 1912, p. 4.

[52]New York Call, March 6, 1912, p. 5.

[53]E. P. Wheeler, February 27, 1912, E. P. Wheeler Manuscripts, New York Public Library.

[54]The Woman Voter, III (March, 1912), p. 2.

To combat anti-suffrage propaganda, the women held a huge parade on the day of the vote in the Assembly, thus drawing attention to suffrage and to a mass meeting planned for Cooper Union the following day. The speakers, Anna H. Shaw and Harriot S. Blatch, lambasted politicians for their inconsistent stand on suffrage, while Congressman William LaFollette appealed for "votes for women." Jeannette Rankin again received the support of Socialist workers. Theresa Malkid, a Socialist writer, wrote in an editorial:

> The female of the human race is standing on the threshold of a new era. Man will no longer carry the progress of evolution on his own shoulders; woman, too, will help share the burdens. Since she is entrusted with responsibilities..., she is fully entitled to all the rights and privileges."[55]

Along with the Socialists, Jeannette secured the support of New York's leading liberal clergyman, John H. Holmes of the Church of the Messiah. Rankin experienced a difficult time converting Franklin D. Roosevelt, a young Senator in the 1912 legislature, to her position on social issues. She told him that some of the women in the western states had the vote and that they were working on others. Roosevelt responded that suffrage was a good idea but that laws to protect women and children would work in one place and not in another. He referred to a fish cannery in New England as an example. The women and children went to the cannery when the boats come in. If another boat came in, they would have to return that night even though they had worked all day. If they were prevented by law from doing so, "the fish might spoil."[56] Jeannette retold this

---

[55]New York Call, January 30, 1912, p. 1.

[56]J. R. Interview, January 16, 1919, p. 4.

story from a woman's point of view, saying, "Perhaps the children might spoil, and that they were just as important as fish."[57]

Another interesting story from this campaign related to getting the bill out of the Assembly Judiciary Committee. Jeannette had urged all the women to telegraph their representatives to insist that the bill be reported out. One woman telegraphed, "Let the suffragette out of the committee."[58] Because it was unusual, it provoked laughter and caught attention. Rankin thought this telegram did more good than the most profound communications.

After considerable political wrangling, the Judiciary Committee reported the amendment out adversely. While the Assembly debated the committee's report, the Senate voted 21 to 19 against woman suffrage. In the House, tactical maneuvering continued. When the vote was taken to agree or disagree with the Judiciary Committee's report, the Assembly disagreed 68 to 63, and for the first time the Suffragists had gotten their bill out of the committee. But an illegal move to reconsider carried 69 to 67, and the bill was dead for the session.[59]

Lacking only a few votes in the Senate, and eight in the Assembly for the necessary seventy-six to pass a bill, the proposed constitutional amendment, giving women the right to vote, almost succeeded. The Woman Voter, official organ of the New York Woman Suffrage Association, concluded:

---

[57]Ibid. Rankin thought this was an awfully funny story. Once when she asked a woman how she liked her story, the woman replied, "I cried."

[58]Ibid., p. 5.

[59]Blatch and Lutz, Challenging Years, pp. 156-187; Harriet M. Mills, who wrote the section on New York Suffrage History in HWS, believed this "resolution to table" was a prearranged deal. Ida Harper, HWS, VI, p. 458.

> Miss Rankin has won for the cause at Albany a respect
> and attention which far exceeds what has been accord-
> ed it in former years. There has been more coop-
> erative spirit. Miss Rankin's work has been most
> gratifying to the women whose emissary she has been.[60]

Although she did not win the majority necessary, Jeannette's work was considered a success. Previously all bills had been stymied in the committee. This effort so effectively changed public opinion that in the following legislature woman suffrage passed both Houses.

In an unusual tribute, three legislators, Stephen Stilwell, Timothy Sullivan, and Andrew Murray, testified to Rankin's steadfast devotion to suffrage and marked ability for legislative lobbying. They wrote, "Her tact, her gentle feminine persuasion, and her ever ready logic have made many converts to woman suffrage."[61] Harriet M. Mills, President of the New York Suffrage Association, called the attention of national suffragists to Jeannette by writing that she showed herself most a capable, wise, tactful, and devoted leader.[62]

When the New Albany program ended, in March, Jeannette Rankin returned to Montana to lay groundwork for another suffrage campaign. Before Jeannette could get started, Harriet B. Laidlaw offered her services to Ohio. Dropping everything, she traveled to assist in the campaign already in progress.[63]

Jeannette arrived in May to work under Harriet T. Upton, Treasurer

---

[60] The Woman Voter, III (April, 1912), p. 35.

[61] Stephen J. Stilwell, Timothy D. Sullivan, and Andrew F. Murray to James Lees Laidlaw, March 12, 1912, in HBL Papers, Folder 109.

[62] Harriet M. Mills, "A Suffrage Revival in New York," Woman's Journal, XLIII (March 16, 1912), p. 85.

[63] The Woman Voter, III (August, 1912), p. 29.

of the National American Woman Suffrage Association. From headquarters
in Warren, Ohio, she traveled to several of the adjoining counties. As
was typical of suffrage campaigns, they tried to tie in with existing
political elections. As President William H. Taft and former President
Theodore Roosevelt struggled for the Republican nomination in 1912, the
Ohio suffragists followed the candidates and spoke to their waiting
crowds. Rankin spoke to both Taft and Roosevelt gatherings in Ravenna
and Kent.[64]

In Ashtabula County, Jeannette hired a carriage and drove through
the countryside visiting the farm homes and fulfilling speaking engagements for a week. In the larger cities of Canton, Cleveland, and Akron,
she conducted street meetings and visited factories. As a general rule,
she campaigned a week or two in each place. In letters to Harriet B.
Laidlaw, Rankin estimated the suffrage sentiment to be good in the areas
where she was working. In fact, she thought it was better than in California. One thing she desired was sufficient literature to give out.
She then urged her friends to send money for spontaneous materials to be
printed in Ohio.[65]

Having been in the field for about eight weeks and much of the time
alone, Jeannette Rankin began to feel the rigors of campaigning. From
the very beginning, the relationship with Harriet T. Upton had been
tenuous. There was never a clear understanding of job expectations and
financial arrangements. Previously Rankin had given her time and energy

---

[64]Harriet T. Upton to Harriet B. Laidlaw, May 19, 1912, HBL Papers.

[65]J. R. to Harriet B. Laidlaw, May 11, 1912, J. R. to HBL, May 16,
1912, J. R. to HBL, June 3, 1912 in HBL Papers.

for suffrage with very little remuneration. In Washington State, she
received no pay, only fifty dollars a month from the Laidlaws while in
New York, and 225 dollars for the three months of lobbying before the
Albany legislature.[66] Unfortunately, Jeannette did not find the same
commitment and devotion to suffrage among the women of Ohio. After she
lost her voice speaking to street meetings and factory gatherings in
Akron, Jeannette became quite despondent. In spite of this, she remained
another week to recuperate and still managed to speak at least once each
day. Overcome with frustration and exhaustion, Rankin hastily left Ohio
for Montana in early July of 1912.[67]

[66]M. J. Reynolds, "How Miss Jeannette Rankin Started in Politics,"
Call, N. D. in Harriet B. Laidlaw Scrapbooks in Schlesinger Library.

[67]J. R. to H. B. L., May 11, 1912, in HBL Papers; Harriet T. Upton
to Harriet B. Laidlaw, July 20, 1912, in HBL Papers; Harriet B. Laidlaw
to Harriet T. Upton, July 24, 1912, in HBL Papers.

CHAPTER IV

THE MONTANA CAMPAIGN

During the twelve months while Jeannette worked in New York,
California, and Ohio, Montana suffrage had progressed slowly. The
suffragists' most important accomplishment was the sponsoring of a
booth at the State Fair in 1911. Ida Auerbach, Freida Fligelman, and
Grace Rankin Kinney erected an attractive booth, giving our suffrage
literature and buttons to passersby. With some experience behind her,
Jeannette Rankin, in the summer of 1912, began to marshall the forces
for a suffrage victory in the next legislative session. She addressed
a gathering of women in the studio of Mary C. Wheeler of Helena and
encouraged them to form a temporary state organization. The logical
choice for chairman was Jeannette Rankin with Ida Auerbach as secretary
and Grace Smith as treasurer. The state organization developed neither
a constitution nor bylaws. In fact, there were no membership lists.
When a decision had to be made, everyone was invited to give advice and
to vote. Normally, they talked things over until a consensus was reached.
Mary O'Neil, who was twenty years older than Jeannette and an excellent
prophetess of political trends, advised and aided Rankin through the
entire campaign.[1]

----

[1]J. R. Interview, January 16, 1969, pp. 6-7; Ida Harper, HWS, VI,
p. 362; For a time, there was a more formally organized suffrage group
in Montana. Its demise came in a "hair pulling" fight among the women
over their constitution.

Starting with this temporary organization, Jeannette Rankin and the women canvassed the state, holding meetings and establishing suffrage clubs. They tried to locate a representative in every one of the fifty counties. To secure the support of the major political parties was a critical step undertaken in the latter part of the summer. Jeannette went from county to county personally contacting every delegate to the Democratic, Republican, Progressive, and Socialist Conventions. She was so successful that the Democrats were forced to put woman suffrage in their party platform. When the women approached the Republicans, they could do nothing less than follow suit. The Progressive and Socialists Parties also recommended the submission to the voters of a suffrage amendment to the state constitution.[2]

With the backing of the major parties, Jeannette Rankin circularized the nominees to secure their individual support for legislation. The main campaign of women took place from the summer until the State Fair opened in September. They wanted to have their work finished so as not to hinder the political work of the party candidates. Everytime a man spoke, a woman would go to him and ask him to mention woman suffrage. All through the audience the women scattered "clacks" who would applaude what the politician said about the proposed suffrage amendment. Each time he increased his appeal for enfranchisement, the applause would be equally greater. In this way, the women actually had the politicians making "their" speeches for them.[3]

---

[2] Alice Moque, "Miss Rankin Has Busy Days," The Woman's Journal, XLVIII (April 14, 1917), p. 85; J. R. Interview, January 16, 1969, p. 5; Ida Harper, HWS, VI, p. 362.

[3] J. R. Interview, January 16, 1969, p. 6; Helena Independent, August 30, September 22 and 25, 1912.

While the political campaign drew to a close, Jeannette Rankin quietly toured the state, stopping in one-half of the counties where she appointed temporary suffrage chairmen. In Butte, the women actively campaigned
against James McNally, an anti-suffragist. Although elected, he was convinced that he had better vote for enfranchisement!! By the time the
legislature met in January of 1913, Jeannette had everything under
control. She had persuaded a respected Democratic senator, Tom Stout
from Fergus County, to introduce a bill submitting to the voters the
constitutional amendment. In the House of Representatives, she secured
a well known Progressive representative, Joseph Pope of Yellowstone County,
to do the same thing. Meantime, the women were conducting a letter writing campaign to their respective senators and representatives. Letters
poured in to Governor S. W. Stewart, urging him to recommend the passage
of the suffrage bill in his message to the legislature. They also wrote
to W. W. McDowell, the Lieutenant Governor, asking for his help as presiding
officer over the Senate.[4]

The first meeting of the State Central Committee in Helena coincided
with the opening of the Thirteenth Legislature. At that time, they elected permanent officers of the Montana Equal Suffrage Association.[5]

[4]J. R. Interview, January 16, 1969, p. 5; Jeannette Rankin, "How
Suffrage Was Won in Montana," Handbook and Proceedings, Forty-sixth
Annual Convention of the National American Woman Suffrage Association,
Nashville, Tennessee, November 12-14, 1914, p. 134; Ida Harper, HWS,
VI, p. 362.

[5]They were chairman, Jeannette Rankin, Missoula; assistant chairman,
Mrs. Louis P. Sanders, Butte; and Mrs. G. M. Gillmore, Glendive; secre-
tary, Mrs. Harvey Coit, Port Timber; treasurer, Mrs. Wilbur L. Smith,
Helena; finance chairman, Mrs. Wallace Perham, Glendive; and press chairman,
Ida Auerbach.

The Committee visited the legislature and joyously heard the Governor read his message recommending passage of woman suffrage. With no discussion this time, the Senate passed the resolution to submit an amendment to the voters by 26 to 2. In the House the vote was 74 to 2.[6] After Governor S. V. Stewart signed the resolution on January 25, the women celebrated its passage in a dozen towns across the state by proclaiming February 1 as Woman's Day.[7]

The suffragists' next hurdle was to convince a majority of Montana's voters, but that opportunity would not come until November of 1914. While Montana was securing a state suffrage amendment, the National American Woman Suffrage Association appointed Alice Paul to head up its Congressional Committee in Washington. Along with her assistant, Lucy Burns, she lobbied for the federal amendment. These two women had received firsthand experience and training under the Pankhursts in England and added a much needed note of "militancy" to American suffrage. To further bolster national work, Jeannette Rankin became Field Secretary for the National American Woman Suffrage Association. After thanking Governor S. V. Stewart for the legislative victory in Montana, Rankin hurried off to North Dakota to take up her first appointment.[8]

---

[6] The four dissenting votes were cast by J. E. Edwards, Senator from Rosebud; I. A. Leighton, Senator from Jefferson; Ronald Higgins, Representative from Missoula; and John W. Blair, Representative from Powell County. Ida Harper, HWS, VI, p. 363; Ellis L. Waldron, An Atlas of Montana Politics since 1864 (Missoula: Montana State University Press, 1958), O. 142.

[7] The Woman's Journal (January 25, 1913), XLIV, p. 25.

[8] Alice Paul Oral Interview, June 10, 1971, at the National Woman's Party, Washington, D.C.; Ida Harper, HWS, VI, p. 378; National American Woman Suffrage Association, Forty-fifth Annual Report, Washington, D.C., November 29-December 5, 1913, p. 135.

In North Dakota, Jeannette Rankin joined Mrs. E. M. Darrow of Fargo, President of the state suffrage organization, who had been lobbying in the legislature. After meeting with the women and studying the situation, Jeannette offered some suggestions. Her principal advice concerned the organization of women. She urged them to secure women workers in every county and in every precinct, if possible. After helping with organizational work, Jeannette made a speaking tour which included the cities of Fargo, Grand Forks and Bismarck. Newspaper accounts reported the attendance as good and described "these ladies as being very peaceable in contrast to the English suffragists." Rankin's pleasing personality and dynamism aroused the enthusiasm of the women of North Dakota.[9]

While Rankin was leading the suffragists to legislative victories in Montana and North Dakota, Alice Paul of the Congressional Committee outlined energetic plans for a suffrage parade on the eve of Woodrow Wilson's inauguration. On March 3, five thousand women paraded down Pennsylvania Avenue. A girl dressed as Sacajawea led the Montana delegation who followed in Indian costumes. Edna Rankin, sister of Jeannette, marched in a white buckskin costume. Unfortunately, the express company delayed delivering their banners, and it was almost impossible to tell whom the marching Indians represented.[10] When Wilson reached Washington and found the streets deserted of well-wishers, he is said to have asked where the people were and was told they were watching the suffrage parade. With a sense for the dramatic, Alice Paul had upstaged

---

[9]Fargo Forum and Daily Republican, February 4,5,6,7,8, and 10, 1913; Woman's Journal, XLIV (February 22, 1913), p. 57.

[10]J. R. to Andrew Beckwith, April 11, 1913, J. R.Manuscripts.

the arrival of the President-elect.[11]

The women gained more than just the attention of suffragists. Even though Alice Paul had a parade permit, Washington police rendered only minimal assistance. The parade turned into a near riot as police protection gave way, and the crowd surged into the street. The marchers, with courage and determination, struggled on. They were spat upon, slapped in the face, tripped up, pelted with burning cigar stubs, and insulted by jeers and obscene language. It took the Fifteenth Cavalry to restore order finally. As a result, this episode aroused public opinion, brought an investigation of the Washington police, and gave "new life" to national suffrage.[12]

In March and April, Jeannette Rankin traveled to Saginaw, Michigan, to organize the city into wards and precincts. She arranged meetings and assisted in state-wide organization. When floods in the East detained Anna H. Shaw, Jeannette Rankin spoke in her place. To complicate voting for suffrage, the election commissioners wanted to put all the constitutional amendments except suffrage on the voting machines. Suffrage was to have a paper ballot. Even though the women overcame this difficulty, the amendment lost by a greater margin than in 1912. Some women blamed the liquor interests, while others believed that Alice Paul's Washington parade took needed money away from the Michigan campaign.[13]

For her fourth legislative campaign since Christmas, Jeannette Rankin

---

[11]Eleanor Flexnor, Century of Struggle (New York: Atheneum, 1971), p. 263; Official Program of the Woman Suffrage Procession, March 3, 1913, Schlesinger Library, Radcliffe College.

[12]U.S., Congress, House of Representatives, 62nd Congress, 3rd session, H. R. Report no. 1594; Baltimore Sun, March 4, 1913.

[13]Saginaw Daily News, March 12, 20, 22, 27, 28, 31, 1913; April 1, 7, 10, 1913.

answered the call of the Equal Franchise League of Jacksonville who wanted Florida to be the first state in the region to enfranchise women. They
looked forward to the visit of the Field Secretary whom they described as
"one of the best schooled and most enthusiastic suffragettes to be found
in America."[14] Before she arrived, Senator John P. Stoker and Representative H. L. Bussey introduced constitutional amendments in the Florida
legislature. To her surprise, Rankin encountered much stronger opposition
than she expected from the men. Yet, it was only typical of the reaction
to suffrage in the South.

Elmo W. Acosta, Representative from Duval County, leveled the charge
that Jeannette Rankin was invading the state as a "paid lobbyist" under
the hire of Yankee women. The agitation of outsiders has frequently
been the mythical ghost in Southern reformism and other efforts to
institute change. Furthermore, he believed that Florida women did not
want the ballot. Other legislators expressed this idea by saying that
they "wanted women of the South to remain in that realm of reverence
which had been made for them by men of the South." They feared that equal
franchisement would result in marital unhappiness, divorce, and disrupted
domestic conditions. In summary, Southern opposition as shown in Florida
felt woman suffrage to be contrary to tradition, history, manners, modesty,
and the best thought of the country.[15]

Even more explosive in the South was the problem of what to do about
giving the vote to the Negro woman. Its political consequences were almost
unthinkable to the Southern white politician. He felt the enfranchisement
of the black woman would open an inconceivable Pandora's box of evils. To

[14]Florida Times-Union, April 18, 1913.

[15]Florida Times-Union, May 4, 1913.

counter this argument, Jeannette wrote for literature to prove that woman

suffrage would not create racial suicide. One legislator expressed mixed

emotions as he read the following letter:

> The colored ladies of Jacksonville are glad that
> you are going to help them get a square deal.
> There is 3,000 colored women...who belongs to our
> clubs and church societies and we is willing to
> pay our pole taxis and vote. Our mens is so
> shiftless they does not vote and we womens want
> a chance. The ladies earns more than the mens
> anyway and we most desirously ask that you give
> us a chance to vote.[16]

One editorial suggested that suffrage had gained momentum until the

spring of 1913. When the militant conduct of suffragists in England and

the march of General Rosalie James and her hikers became widely publi-

cized, Florida suffrage cooled. Many women became apathetic and uninterest-

ed.[17] All these problems, combined with opposition from the liquor interests,

helped to defeat suffrage in the 1913 session of Florida's legislature.

When the defeat became inevitable, Jeannette Rankin teased the Florida

women by saying that the chivalric gentlemen who talked so much about

chivalry did the cause more good than she. "It is a winning fight and is

bound to prevail," Jeannette prophesied.[18]

The following month of June, Rankin returned to Montana to lead the

second meeting of the State Central Suffrage Committee in Livingston

---

[16]Cora V. Brown, Secretary of Mount Sinai League to State Legislature
as reported in Florida Times-Union, May 4, 1913.

[17]Florida Times-Union, April 28, 1913.

[18]Florida Times-Union, May 3, 1913; An interesting advertisement by
the Shredded Wheat Company contained the following copy: "Two million
women will have the right to vote at the next presidential election.
Twenty million women have already voted for emancipation of American
womanhood by serving shredded wheat for breakfast." Florida Times-Union,
May 3, 1913.

after the convention of the State Federation of Women's Clubs. All parts
of the state reported great progress in interest and in organization.
Additional officers elected were Mrs. John Willis of Glasgow, recording
secretary, and Mary Agnes Cantwell of Hunter's Hot Springs as chairman
of literature. The State Committee appointed a chairman for every county
and designated workers for each precinct.[19]

While strengthening the state organization, Jeannette Rankin gathered
petitions for the July 31 demonstration in Washington, D.C. The tremendous publicity gained from the pre-inaugural parade in March gave
Alice Paul's Congressional Committee fresh momentum. Pilgrimages, bearing petitions collected at the grass-roots level, were organized to
descend on Washington on July 31. Jeannette Rankin left Butte by car on
July 7 with Montana's petitions for the federal amendment.[20] During the
600-mile trip, she held eleven meetings in Montana, nineteen in North
Dakota, and addressed audiences in St. Paul, Minnesota, Chicago, Illinois
and Indianapolis, Indiana. Along the way, Rankin collected more signatures
and increased interest in the national amendment.[21] When she arrived at
Hyattsville, Maryland, the Montana suffragist was tired and hoarse, but
happy.

From Hyattsville, the pilgrims advanced on the Capitol with a 72-car
procession led by Alice Paul, Lucy Burns, Ruth Hayes, and NAWSA members.
Jeannette, wearing a broad hat tied with a green ribbon, proudly held

---

[19]Ida Harper, HWS, VI, p. 363; NAWSA, Handbook and Proceedings,
46th Convention, p. 134.

[20]Nashville Democrat, July 30, 1913, in H. B. Laidlaw Scrapbook,
1912-1917.

[21]Congressional Union for Woman Suffrage, Report for 1914 (Washington:
Congressional Union, 1914), p. 12.

the Montana banner. Two by two, suffragists from across the country called their senators and representatives to the Marble Room to receive their petitions. Mary Land from Whitehall assisted Jeannette in presenting Montana's signatures to Senator Henry L. Myers. Following the meeting with congressmen, the suffragists celebrated with a dinner at the Brighton Hotel.[22]

For the next two weeks, Jeannette Rankin remained in Washington. During the day, she lobbied the Senate under the direction of the Congressional Committee. They gave her the Southern senators to visit. Jeannette found them warm and understanding toward her persuasive arguments but not convinced. She sought out their position on peace, as well as suffrage, and thought she discovered underneath "a wonderful peace sentiment." When she went to John Sharp Williams, Senator from Mississippi, to ask for suffrage, he summed up the Southern position. He said, "That's all right for your women in the North, but we can't have it in the South on account of the colored women." Knowing that the "grandfather clause," among other restrictions, kept the Negro man from voting, Rankin replied, "Can't you use the same thing against the women that you use against the men?" At that, he jumped up and stormed out, "You can't hit your baby's nurse over the head with a club."[23]

Another interesting experience took place when Rankin and Emily Perry, member of the committee, visited Congressman Hoke Smith from Georgia.

---

[22]Rankin, along with Harriet B. Laidlaw, Mrs. John Turney of Tennessee, Mary W. Dennett, Helen Todd, Rheta Childs Dorr, and Champlain Riley, made speeches that evening. Woman's Journal, LXIV (August 9, 1913), p. 251; Winifred Mallon, "An Impression of Jeannette Rankin," Suffragist, V (March 31, 1917), p. 7; NAWSA, Forty-fifth Annual Report, p. 135; The Daily Missoulian, November 14, 1916.

[23]J. R. Interview, February 14, 1969, p. 4; Mallou, "An Impression," p. 7.

When the lobbists entered his office, he addressed them, "As you are
suffragists you won't mind standing." Throughout the interview Smith
sat lounging comfortably in his chair. While he took out a cigar and
lighted it, the young women said what they had to say standing. The
Woman's Party index card noted that Hoke Smith smoked contemptuously on.[24]

While doing legislative work in the daytime, Jeannette Rankin spoke
every night for two weeks in the streets of Washington. The novelty of
a woman addressing a crowd in an open air meeting attracted many curious
onlookers. With charm, charisma, and the plea of suffrage, she absorbed
their complete attention.[25] One observer, using the tennis vernacular,
described her as one of the first suffragists to put "the lob" in lobbying.[26]

Jeannette Rankin returned to Montana in August, 1913, to get the
suffrage campaign moving earnestly. The third meeting of the Montana
Equal Suffrage Central Committee assembled in Butte on September 22 and
23. Rankin participated in the campaign as both state leader and Field
Secretary for the National American Woman Suffrage Association. She
encouraged the chairman of each county to establish a "county" central
committee. Jeannette advised that local precinct work should be dictated
by the methods best suited for each locality. Obviously, she was using
the "district" organizing plan to its maximum potential.[27]

---

[24]Inez Irwin, The Story of the Woman's Party (New York: Harcourt,
Brace and Co., 1921), pp. 317-318.

[25]Mallou, "An Impression," p. 7.

[26]The Daily Missoulian, November 14, 1916.

[27]Montana Progressive, August 28, 1913; The Woman's Journal, XLIV
(August 23, 1913), p. 272.

After oiling the Montana suffrage machinery and spreading propaganda from a booth in the State Fair, Rankin returned East. Along with Mrs. Thomas Stout, Mrs. A. P. Anderson, and Mrs. J. M. Evans, all of Montana, she attended the Washington Convention of the National American Woman Suffrage Association and made her report as Field Secretary. During the year, Jeannette had tried to bring the National association closer to the states and to acquaint the states in a more intimate way with national suffrage. In addition to state legislative work in Montana, North Dakota, Michigan, and Florida, she visited state officers in Alabama, Tennessee, Missouri, Nebraska, and South Dakota to discuss problems and make recomendations. When the convention ended, Jeannette helped to lead a "Suffrage School" to train workers. She talked on "Field Campaigning," while Mrs. Sherman Booth gave many suggestions on the "Art of Lobbying." Others were to speak on automobile campaigns, street meetings, and how to reach the rural voter.[28]

Even though the National American Woman Suffrage Association voted to retain Jeannette Rankin as Field Secretary for another year, she decided to resign to take active leadership of the Montana campaign for equal suffrage. Jeannette returned to Montana in January of 1914 to begin the sustained push for victory. With the State Central Committee, she mapped out the year's work. They started the campaign by holding precinct meetings weekly to get reports so as to determine weak spots in the organization.[29]

---

[28] Washington Star, November 29, 1913; Woman's Journal, XLIV (December 20, 1913), p. 403; Ida Harper, HWS, V, p. 368.

[29] Woman's Journal, XLV (January 17, 1914), p. 18.

One of the largest difficulties that the women had to overcome was the opposition of women anti-suffragists and liquor interests. Early in the 1914 campaign, Clara E. Markeson, representative of the National Anti-Suffrage Association, went to Butte to confer with the liquor interests. When Jeannette discovered the meeting, she exposed it in an article entitled, "Gumshoe Methods Not Popular in Montana." Rankin suggested that Markeson's purpose was to ally with the liquor interests as they were doing in other campaign states. The New York Evening Post reported that the anti-suffragist had traveled to Butte to outline a proposed program and to secure the approval and cooperation of the National Forum, the organ of the liquor interests.[30] Whatever the reason, the Montana suffragists gained a round in their fight for victory.

Actually, the suffragists were in a difficult situation. They wanted to offend no one. Yet, they needed all the votes possible. Jeannette Rankin did not want to conduct woman suffrage on a prohibition platform. She had a single goal: enfranchisement of women. To soften the anti-liquor stance, the suffragists made it clear that they were "neither for nor against social reform."[31]

In addition to the wet-dry fight, the women faced 118,000 voters (less than one voter to a square mile) scattered over the third largest state in the union. Much of the canvassing had to be conducted in rural districts across the mountains and through the snow. Also formidable opposition came from the Anaconda Company who feared that giving women the vote would bring a demand for reform in Montana politics. Casting

---

[30] New York Evening Post, February 25, 1914.

[31] Helena Independent, February 26, 1914; Belle Fligelman Winestein Interview, Helena, Montana, September 2, 1970, p. 5.

a pallor over economic forces, the labor war between miners and owners made campaigning difficult for the suffragists. In spite of these contending elements, Ruth McCormick, chairman of the National Campaign Committee, wrote, "I spent twenty days in Montana. I think I found more general interest than in any other state."[32]

Congressman Tom Stout, who had introduced the suffrage resolution, believed that suffrage would win because labor and the working men were behind it. Also, he pointed out:

> They have such a splendid leader. Jeannette
> Rankin is one of the most successful campaigners
> that I ever knew. I have seen her go into a
> Democratic Convention...and secure an endorse-
> ment. Then she went to the Republican Conven-
> tion where the opposition was stronger and
> won there. She achieved all this by the charm of
> her manner and the force of her arguments.[33]

To win, the suffragists knew they had to do more than just contend; they had to educate. The first step in that plan was the opening of state headquarters at Butte in February. In a circular letter to all the voters of Montana, Jeannette Rankin, as President of the Montana Equal Suffrage State Central Committee, announced the official beginning of the campaign. The aim of this letter was educational. Rankin pointed out that nine western states and Alaska could vote, that Montana adjoined two suffrage states, and that four million women in the United States could vote for the President. She asked, "Why not the women in Montana?"[34] To gain workers, Jeannette encouraged all who believed in equal suffrage to send a postal card to headquarters. In an effort to cross as many

---

[32]NAWSA, Handbook and Proceedings, 46th Convention, p. 122.

[33]Woman's Journal, XLV (March 7, 1914), p. 80.

[34]Circular Letter to Voters of Montana, February 7, 1914, in H. B. Laidlaw Scrapbook, New York Historical Society.

barriers as possible, the letter stated, "Women in our organization are from all walks of life, every political party and every religion and faith. We unite on one point: We all want to vote."[35]

To kick off the nine month campaign, Jeannette Rankin invited James and Harriet Laidlaw, both strong suffragists from New York, to tour the state. Their first stop was in Billings and then on to Helena, Butte, and Missoula. In Helena, Wellington Rankin, brother of Jeannette and President of the Helena Men's League for Woman Suffrage, called a mass meeting in the city auditorium. Colonel C. B. Nolan, a well known lawyer, presided over the meeting and gave suffrage a boose of respectability. In addition to Rankin and Laidlaw, Mary O'Neil, President of the Butte Club of over three hundred members, and Margaret Rossa, first woman to be elected to a school board in Montana, spoke to large crowds.[36]

As the suffragist express rolled into Missoula, the women plastered the town with attention-getting posters. One read:

> "STOP: LOOK: LISTEN. Provided you are a live one. If dead already, stay where you are and be run over by the Suffragette Express that will overtake the fast male at the Missoula Theatre."[37]

Another one advertised:

> "Miss Jeannette Rankin of the greatest city on Earth will act as an engineer and introduce Mr. James L. Laidlaw of New York, second greatest city, and Mrs. James L. Laidlaw, who will discourse eloquently on the latest agricultural stunt of making two votes grow where one grew before. N.B.--Have your life insured and bring your firearms for there are going to be many bombs exploded and many balloons punctured.

---

[35] Ibid.

[36] New York Evening Post, February 25, 1914.

[37] Poster in the H. B. Laidlaw Scrapbook, 1912-1917.

Come one. Come all. Come seven. Come eleven."[38]
Missoula provided the Laidlaws with their largest mass meeting on the
tour. Ex-governor Joseph Dixon entertained James Laidlaw at lunch,
while Mrs. Tyler B. Thompson, President of the State Federation of Women's
Clubs, honored Harriet Laidlaw with a reception in her home. The women
had lots of fun but also put in long hours of hard work.

They tried to make the campaign a personal one by house-to-house
canvassing. Jeannette Rankin was a dynamo on the campaign trail. One
writer described her as just one of the crowd until she started speaking.
"Let her get started," he wrote, "and she is as ardent as Sylvia Pankhurst.
You would put her down as a determined 'men-you-just-have-to-do-it' and
'we-won't-take-no-for-an-answer' suffragist."[39] Jeannette was not the brick
bat, hunger striking, firebrand type of suffragette common in England; nor
would she be in sympathy with such methods. Rankin believed, "We do not
need militancy over hers. We are getting the vote without resorting to
violence."[40] Yet, Jeannette believed that American suffrage had benefit-
ed from the publicity given English militancy.

As a sample of her many tours, one campaign trip found Jeannette
traveling 1300 miles over seven large counties, making twenty-six speeches
in twenty-five days and electing twenty precinct leaders. She held meetings in court houses, schools, theatres, opera houses, YMCA's, dance floors,
and union halls. She tried to secure speaking opportunities before as
many ready-made meetings as possible. Organizationally, Rankin hoped to

---

[38]Ibid.

[39]Clipping in the H. B. Laidlaw Scrapbook, 1912-1917, with no source
of date.

[40]Ibid.

locate leaders in every voting precinct and get them to form a county
central committee. Representatives from these county committees formed
the State Central Committee, which directed the overall campaign. As she
toured these counties, Rankin found enthusiasm growing and was overjoyed
when she discovered one county publishing "a suffrage weekly." One of
Rankin's county chairmen was a woman with eight children. She was
Catholic, and her husband was a saloon keeper. Rankin described her "as
one of the best workers I have ever seen. If there is anything she has
not read, I do not know what it is."[41]

The basic concept in Jeannette Rankin's argument for suffrage was
that it would free women for a greater degree of responsible action in
society. "Even in primitive women," she said, "the most compelling force
is the instinct to preserve and improve the race." As woman became better
educated and more culturally refined, the responsibility to her race increased. To act responsibly, she must be morally free to make choices
as implied by her training and conscience. Women can do this only if
they are economically free. "But," Rankin said, "no class has ever been
economically free until it was politically free." With the attainment
of the ballot, she believed woman could initiate her progress toward
political, economic, and moral reform.[42]

In more specific terms, Rankin encouraged the men to give them the
vote because it showed evidence of a more enlightened civilization. As
was common with other suffrage speakers, she suggested that the franchise

[41]J. R. to Mary W. Dennett as quoted in Woman's Journal, XLV (May
16, 1914), p. 157.

[42]Montana Progressive, June 4, 1914; Helena Independent, September
20, 1914.

would help both the woman in the factory and the woman in the home.
Through the use of the ballot, women could advocate laws to protect themselves in the factory and to regulate the forces that affect life in the
home, such as health and sanitation.[43]

Jeannette Rankin recalled that she was in the middle of Montana
campaigning for suffrage when fighting broke out in Europe in August of
1914. Upon learning the news, she was furious that her education had
been so poor "that she didn't realize this thing was coming."[44] The
mining region around Butte, Montana, had many immigrants from Eastern
Europe; thus, the newspaper posted regular bulletins concerning the war.
To a crowd gathered there once, Jeannette, in a moment of excitement,
said, "If they are going to have war, they ought to take the old men and
leave the young men to propagate the race."[45] The papers condescendingly
replied that was not a nice thing for an unmarried woman to say. Rankin
worried about the war, talked it over with the women, and became very
discouraged. She remembered:

> I felt the end of the world was coming if we were
> stupid enough to go to war. I said, "Well, if we
> don't win suffrage, I'll just let God take care
> of it himself. I'll just not do any more." I
> wasn't going to go on with everything against
> us.[46]

Years later, in explaining the psychology of her famous vote against World
War I, Miss Rankin said of the suffrage campaign:

---

[43]Helena Independent, February 2, 1911; Daily Missoulian, May 3,
1914; Ronald George Coleman, "A Historical Survey of the Rhetorical
Proofs Used by Women Speakers of the Suffrage Organizations: 1868-1919,"
an unpublished Ph.D. dissertation at Case Western Reserve University, 1968.

[44]J. R. Interview, February 14, 1969, p.2.

[45]J. R. Interview, February 14, 1969, p. 8.

[46]J. R. Interview, February 14, 1969, p. 2.

> In talking to women, urging suffrage, we said
> over and over again that war was stupid and
> futile and couldn't be used successfully in
> adjusting human relationships. It was women's
> work which was destroyed by war. Their work
> was raising human beings, and war destroyed
> humans to protect profits and property.[47]

Suddenly, a new argument now entered the Montana suffrage rhetoric.

Women wanted the vote to keep their husbands and sons out of war. Follow-

ing this line of reasoning, the Woman's Journal asked a number of people

if war would be less frequent if women could vote. One woman replied:

> I think war, as war, still has a fascination for
> men. Huge armaments, far from preventing, provoke
> war. I think that women would be less apt than
> men to vote public monies into drednoughts and
> standing armies, or to keep in office public
> servants who are known to be belligerent.[48]

Other women felt this war would not have happened if women could have

voted and established public opinion against it.[49] Lillian Wald, of the

Henry Street Settlement, believed women would strip war of its glamour

and "see in it a demon of destruction and hideous wrong--murder enthroned."[50]

In general, women did not like to see their offspring killed or maimed,

left in bitterness and poverty, nor quarrelsome with others. Mrs. F. W.

Pethick-Lawrence, an English suffragist, summed it up when she wrote,

"Women the world over have one passion and one vocation...the creation and

preservation of human life."[51]

---

[47]Washington Daily News, April 6, 1937.

[48]Woman's Journal, XLV (November 14, 1914), p. 300.

[49]The Suffragist, II (August 15, 1914), p. 2.

[50]Boston Traveler and Evening Herald, August 13, 1914.

[51]F. W. Pethick-Lawrence, "Motherhood and War," Harper's Weekly,
LIX (December 5, 1914), p. 542.

During the entire campaign, there was a steady stream of out-of-state suffragists criss-crossing Montana. They represented the best of women speakers and brought with them the full repertoire of suffrage arguments. During April, Jane Thompson, Rankin's successor as Field Secretary of NAWSA, came to the state to speak and to help with organization. Together, they secured endorsement from the Republican and Democratic Central Committees for the suffrage amendment. Grace B. Cotterill, from Seattle, spoke to many labor unions in May and June. She argued that "as an American mother, I feel that I deserve as much voice in the government under which I and my children must live as does my Chinese laundryman who has been in this country only a few years, or an Italian laborer, who has just taken out his naturalization papers."[52]

Following Cotterill was Margaret Hinchey, an Irish laundry worker from New York, whose direct appeal to the labor unions Jeannette appreciated. Rankin noted, "Hinchey is a member of the Woman's Trade Union League and the union men here all seem to have heard of her work."[53] Edna Rankin, Jeannette's sister, took her on a speaking tour to Coeur d'Alene, St. Regis, and Taft, reputedly the toughest town in the Northwest. During the train trip to Taft, cinders from the locomotive covered Hinchey's white dress. While Edna had gone to get it washed and to get some handbills printed, Hinchey created quite an incident when a man broke into her hotel room. In the meantime, Edna was having difficulties of her own. The manager of the general store volunteered to locate the

---

[52] Helena Independent, May 27, 1914; J. R. Interview, April 20, 1970, p. 19.

[53] Mary O'Neil to Leonora O'Reilly, June 20, 1914, Folder #54 in the Leonora O'Reilly Collection, Schlesinger Woman's Library, Radcliffe College; Belle Fligelman Winestein Interview, September 2, 1970, p. 4.

printer if she would watch his store. A drunk came in and chased her up
and down the aisles and round and round. Fortunately, Edna recalled,
"The store owner came back in time to save my virtue."[54]

Margaret Hinchey, always attracted by cemeteries and expressing
curiosity about epitaphs on the tombstones, usually spent an hour wherever
they found burial plots. One afternoon, as Edna and Margaret were canvassing house to house, they could get no one to come to the doors.
Upon returning to Main Street, Edna noticed a string of red lights
festooned in scallops and circles indicating the "red light district."
They had a huge laugh and went right on knocking on doors.

At one white cottage, Edna had difficulty getting the picket fence
gate open. Finally, she succeeded and knocked on the door. All the
time she heard a dog yapping in the background. She inquiried, "May I
come in and talk to you about voting for woman suffrage?" The woman
looked at Edna and said, "You hussy, You ought to be home. This is
nothing for a young girl to be doing. Women should never have the vote.
Come here, Fido. Get her!!" She barely made it back to the gate in time.[55]

On Saturday evening, Edna Rankin and the tall, big, buxom Irish woman
obtained two strong soap boxes and proceeded to call a street meeting.
As her guide, Rankin introduced the New York Irish laundress to the "tight"
miners and railroad workers. With rough and ready tempo, as only an
emotional Irishman can acquire, Hinchey addressed the audience. She
threatened what laundresses would do to men's shirts if they did not vote

---

[54] Edna McKinnon Interview, November 17, 1971, p. 2.

[55] Edna McKinnon Interview, November 17, 1971, p. 3.

for woman suffrage. She predicted that, if women were given the ballot,
they would seek a mother's pension, a minimum wage, improved industrial
conditions, and prison reform. She clinched her speech by saying,
"Isn't your sister, and your wife and your daughter a person? And if
they are, haven't they the right to be distinguished from the lower
animals and non-entities by the possession of the ballot?"[56] When the
speech was over, a strong arm grabbed Edna and began leading them to the
hotel. It was the "furnace boy" who had stayed with the Rankins while
at the University the previous year. He commented, "You shouldn't be
here. This is no place for women."[57] With that, he locked them in their
room, and thus ended an amazing tour.

As interesting as the Irish laundress were the colorful "General"
Rosalie Jones and "Doc" Ida Craft, suffragists from New York. They were
the star speakers in a campaign in southeastern Montana. Kathryn D.
Blake, a school principal in New York, also gave a month of her vacation
time to campaign. She was inspired by the prospectors back in the mountains
who were saying, "What would our state have been without the woman? You
bet you can count on us."[58] As she finished speaking one evening, an
elderly man grasped her hand and said, "I have been waiting thirty years
for the chance to vote for this measure."[59] In these rural districts,

----

[56]Helena Independent, July 19, 1914.

[57]Edna McKinnon Interview, November 17, 1971, p. 3.

[58]Ida Harper, HWS, VI, p. 365.

[59]Woman's Journal, XLV (August 8, 1914), p. 231.

a dance usually followed the suffrage rally.[60]

In addition to the effective coverage by the speakers, the State
Central Committee sent out reams of propaganda. Early in the campaign,
the women mailed letters to women's clubs, granges, labor unions, and
farm organizations requesting their support. Mary O'Neil, press secretary,
wrote a weekly letter to all the newspapers in the state and mailed monthly letters to the county chairmen, giving them instructions and keeping
them informed. A few weeks before election, the Committee mailed 20,000
letters, bearing no return address, to voters in the country districts.
These contained special leaflets for the farmers.[61]

The climax to the suffrage campaign came with a gald week in
September. It began with a booth at the Montana State Fair where the
women passed out leaflets, buttons, and banners. Mary O'Neil, Mrs. L. O.
Edmunds, Mrs. M. E. McKay, and Belle Fligelman, all newspaper women,
edited The Suffragist Daily, which was sold throughout the week. A parade
on Friday evening, September 25, was the most spectacular event of the
two-year struggle for enfranchisement. Six hundred Montana suffragists,
costumed in white dresses with yellow jackets, marched down Main Street
in Helena. Anna H. Shaw, escorted by Jeannette Rankin and Maria M. Dean,
led a mile-long procession of horseback riders, two bands, two women
buglers, floats, men's organizations, twenty automobiles, and Helen Sanders
of Butte, dressed as Sacajawea, to the city auditorium. Rankin, chairman

---

[60]Jeannette Rankin, Belle Fligelman, Grace Hellmick, Maggie S.
Hatheway, Mary O'Neil, Dr. Maria M. Dean, Lucile D. Topping, and many
other volunteers conducted rallies in the mining camps and country
settlements. Ida Harper, HWS, VI, p. 364.

[61]Ida Harper, HWS, VI, p. 363; NAWSA, Handbook and Proceedings, 46th
Convention, pp. 134-135.

for the evening, introduced the first speaker, Judge E. K. Cheadle.

He asserted:

> There is only one reason why women should have the
> right of franchise, and that is because justice
> demands it. If equal suffrage does nothing but
> convince the people that government is not found-
> ed upon physical force, upon cannon and gatling
> guns, but upon opinions, upon love and faith,
> it will be worth any cost to get it.[62]

Anna H. Shaw, President of NAWSA, followed Judge Cheadle and gave

the principal address. She chastized the men for talking about true

democracy, which they would not put into practice. Dr. Shaw, with tongue

in cheek, questioned the inconsistency of putting the patriotic training

and education of youth into the hands of political nonentities. To give

women the same privileges as granted to immigrants was her greatest de-

sire. In fact, she seemed quite nativistic in her attitude toward

foreigners. Finally, Dr. Shaw reiterated what Jeannette had been saying

throughout the campaign, that women should have the vote to determine

whether their men went to war.[63]

With this note, the suffragists concluded most of their state

campaigning, except for the work of local women. They planned to leave

the month of October to the politicians, who endorsed suffrage openly,

but privately may have opposed it. Jeannette believed this endorsement

was due to their campaign against James McNally in 1912. On November

2, the day before the election, Montanians celebrated Suffrage Day.

Women distributed leaflets and gave hat bands inscribed, "I want my

---

[62]Helena Daily Independent, September 26, 1914; Belle F. Winestein
Interview, September 2, 1970, p. 4.

[63]Helena Independent, September 26, 1914.

mother to vote," to the school children, even to those of the anti suffragists.[64]

The following day, Montana men, after one final struggle, gave their
women the right to vote. In many counties the ballots were sealed up
without a count on the constitutional amendments, and this caused the
women to fear fraud. Rankin telegraphed Mrs. Medill McCormick, Chairman
of NAWSA's Congressional committee, who suggested sending a delegation
of women to Anaconda and Boulder. After days of anxiety and tension,
the amendment carried 41,301 to 37,588.[65]

Because of the slow count, Jeannette Rankin arrived late at the
National American Woman Suffrage Convention in Nashville, Tennessee.
Nevertheless, it was a victorious celebration with Nevada also being added
to the suffrage states. Rankin addressed the Convention and thanked them
for the moral and financial support which attributed to a successful
campaign.[66]

When Jeannette Rankin returned home, she called for a meeting of
Montana suffragists in Helena on January 6, 1915. At that time, most of
the suffrage groups merged into Good Government Clubs whose purpose was

---

[64]NAWSA, Handbook and Proceedings, 46th Convention, p. 135.

[65]Anna H. Shaw Diary, 1914 in Dillon Collection; Woman's Journal,
XLV (November 14, 1914), p. 297; HWS, V, p. 402.

[66]Nashville Tennessean, November 15, 1914; Woman's Journal, XLV
(November 21, 1914), p. 309; While at the Convention, Jeannette spoke
to Saturday night street crowds, despite a steady drizzle of rain. Along
with Jane Thompson, NAWSA Field Secretary, and Ethel P. Howes, Executive
Secretary of National College Association, Rankin spoke to the students
at Vanderbilt and organized an Equal Suffrage League with forty-six
members. Nashville Tennessean, February 25, 1914; Elizabeth Taylor,
The Woman Suffrage Movement in Tennessee (New York: Bookman Associates,
1957), p. 37.

to obtain political action on reform measures. One of their first
accomplishments was to repeal the law through which a man could will
away his unborn child. Then, the women secured an equal guardianship law,
a mother's pension, and a new vocational home for girls who had previously
been placed with the boys at Miles City. Under urging from the women,
the legislature established an eight-hour day for women and split up the
Child and Animal Protection Bureau so the children could have more attention. Probably the most significant contribution of the suffrage movement in Montana was to elevate women to equal voting citizenship.[67]

While Jeannette was organizing the Montana women for political action,
the NAWSA Congressional Committee began pushing the Shafroth-Palmer Amendment adopted at the Nashville Convention. It was the work of Mrs. Medill
McCormick, the new chairman of the Congressional Committee, and a group
of advising senators. The amendment required any state to hold a referendum on woman suffrage when eight percent of the voters at the last
election signed an initiative petition. Its supporters claimed that
this amendment would make it easier to overcome the barriers of many
state constitutions and solve the problem of state's rights. There was
much opposition within the National and obviously in the Congressional
Union, led by Alice Paul. In effect, this amendment committed NAWSA to the
old state-by-state approach.[68]

In early 1915, Jeannette Rankin joined the Congressional Committee
consisting of Antionette Funk, Laura Puffer Morgan, and Mrs. Medill

---

[67] Belle F. Winestein, September 2, 1970, p. 3.

[68] NAWSA, Handbook and Proceedings, 46th Convention, December 14-19,
1915, "Report of National Congressional Committee"; Ida Harper, HWS, V,
pp. 451-452; Eleanor Flexner, Century of Struggle, p. 268.

McCormick. They were assisted by Mrs. Winston Churchill, a member of the
National Campaign Committee. Antionette Funk and Jeannette Rankin worked especially hard to inform the House and Senate members of the Shafroth-
Palmer approach. They made no effort to bring the measure forward for a
vote but considered its presentation worthwhile. This group of lobbyists
were reported able to hold their own against any constitutional lawyer.[69]

Many suffragists were not only concerned with enfranchisement but
with peace. Katherine D. Blake, a New York school teacher and active
suffragist, organized "The Twentieth Century Children's Crusade." They
gathered a petition containing over 350,000 signatures of school children
from nearly every state in the union. Six Washington school girls brought
the petition to Secretary of State William J. Bryan. Jeannette Rankin and
Ethel M. Smith represented the Congressional Committee in the presentation
ceremonies. These petitions, addressed to the rulers of the warring
European nations, were to be forwarded by the State Department.[70]

When the congressional session ended, Jeannette Rankin made a speaking tour to New Hampshire. She addressed the Registered Nurses' Association in Concord, the Equal Suffrage League in Manchester, and visited
Dover, Portsmouth, and Somerworth. She assisted several members of the
Concord High School with preparations for a suffrage debate. Jeannette
enjoyed returning to New Hampshire with her mother as she was a direct
descendant of two of the state's oldest families, the Pickerings and
the Lockes.[71] From New Hampshire, Rankin went to western Pennsylvania

[69] Woman's Journal, XVI (January 23, 1915), p. 32.

[70] Woman's Journal, XVI (March 6, 1915), p. 72; Concord Evening Monitor, February 23, 1915.

[71] Concord Evening Monitor, March 8, 1915; Ida Harper, HWS, VI, p. 405.

and then to Missoula to chair the convention of the Montana Good Government Association.[72]

Tired by the six years of arduous and intensive work in the campaigns from the Pacific to the Atlantic and from lobbying before the sessions of Congress, Jeannette Rankin needed a complete rest. Even more pressing was an operation she had postponed. After surgery in Seattle, she caught a boat to New Zealand to rest. A secondary reason for going was to study the effects of woman suffrage on social conditions since that nation was considered one of the most advanced in progressive legislation.[73]

After discovering New Zealand to be a very restful country, Rankin decided to stay longer than she had planned. To obtain an entrance into the homes of the women to discuss suffrage and to help meet her expenses, Jeannette Rankin advertised her services as an American dressmaker. Jeannette, refusing to accept the standard wages of five shillings, asked for twelve and obtained all the work she could do. While in New Zealand, she boarded in a cooperative home called "Girls' Friendly." She encouraged these young women to seek increased wages and suggested various methods of organization.

In addition to learning about how women were using their vote and getting involved in helping to increase wages for seamstresses, Rankin studied the unions, observed arbitration and conciliation laws, and discussed progressive legislation in general. The experience was a good one, and Jeannette returned to Montana in the spring of 1916 restored and

---

[72]Woman's Journal, XVI (June 19, 1915), p. 196.

[73]Edna McKinnon Interview, November 16, 1971, p. 10; J. R. Interview, January 16, 1969, p. 8.

anxious to begin another campaign.[74]

_____

[74]New York Tribune, February 27, 1917; J. R. Interview, January 16, 1969, pp. 7-8.

CHAPTER V

FROM CHEERS TO BOOS

When Jeannette Rankin returned to Montana in the spring of 1916, she faced several occupational choices. Would she remain as a worker for national suffrage, seek a career as a lobbyist for social legislation, or seize the excellent opportunity in Montana for a woman to run for Congressional office? Hopeful that they would win the struggle for suffrage in 1914, the women had discussed what their next step would be. They wanted to send a woman to Congress. The logical choice was Jeannette Rankin because she was known all over the state. An additional advantage for the women was that Montana elected two Congressmen-at-large. The suffragists estimated that many would vote for a man and a woman, and perhaps the woman could come in second. When Tom Stout decided not to seek re-election, Rankin's possibility for nomination increased.

Early in the spring, Jeannette called a meeting of women from all across the state. After discussing all these possibilities, the women suggested that it would be more reasonable for her to run for the state legislature and then later run for Congress. Wellington, her brother and an acute political observer, attended the informal gathering in Missoula and bolstered Jeannette's bid for a seat in Congress. He encouraged his sister and the women by saying, "You run and I'll elect you." She followed his advice and, subsequently, he became her campaign manager and prime supporter.[1]

---

[1] J. R. Interview, January 27, 1969, p. 1.

The organization for her campaign came from the Good Government Clubs, organized in 1915 to replace the suffrage structure. Their leadership was almost a duplicate of the suffrage associations and was quite favorable to Jeannette Rankin's candidacy. On July 8, over two hundred women attended the meeting of the Good Government League of Missoula County. They heard Mrs. Tyler Thompson, President, nominate Jeannette Rankin "as the candidate of all the women of Montana, and of a majority of the men."[2] Her nomination was seconded by Mrs. W. H. H. Dickinson, the first school teacher in Missoula and a personal friend of the Rankin family. This created a storm of applause and eager approval. Because she had led the fight for suffrage only two years previous, the women felt a deep sense of loyalty, and their organizations across the state immediately gave approval and geared for the campaign.[3]

Feeling that Congress would provide an excellent avenue to advance the cause of woman suffrage and other social issues, Jeannette Rankin was grateful for the opportunity. On July 11, 1916, she formally announced her candidacy for the Republican nomination and adopted a platform advocating:

> Equal national suffrage; Protection of the children of the nation; Revision of the tariff; Preparedness that will make for peace; Prohibition; and Revision of the rules of the House of Representatives so that it may be known where the Representatives stand on the floor and in the committees.[4]

---

[2] The Daily Missoulian, July 9, 1916.

[3] Ibid.

[4] Helena Independent, July 14, 1916; Statement of Candidates for Nomination, Republican Party, Primary Election, August 29, 1916, Secretary of State, p. 12, J. R. MSS.

Jeannette Rankin, as the first woman to become a candidate for Congress, indicated, "The primal motive for my seeking a seat in the national Congress is to further the suffrage work and to aid in every possible way the movement for a nation-wide suffrage."[5] By serving responsibly in Congress, she hoped to convince members of Congress, as well as the men and women of the country, that women could vote wisely and that they could discharge the duties of office well.[6] Within this concept of woman's interest, Jeannette also expressed the idea of going to Washington to represent the interests of the nation's greatest asset, its children.[7] To illustrate her feelings, Rankin pointed out that the previous Congress appropriated $300,000 for a study of fodder for hogs, while setting aside only $30,000 to study the needs of children. She said, "If the hogs of the nation are ten times more important than the children, it is high time that women should make their influence felt."[8] With this platform, the support of the Good Government Clubs and the newly organized Jeannette Rankin Clubs, and a well organized campaign machine, she went to the people.

In a campaign to "Let the People Know," Jeannette Rankin crossed the state speaking on the street corners, in schools, kitchens, mines, union halls, dance halls, and everywhere people gathered. Her candidacy caught the attention of the nation as telegrams and letters prophesied that she would make a remarkable contribution to Congress. General Rosalie

---

[5]Helena Independent, July 11, 1916.

[6]Woman's Journal, XVII (July 29, 1916), p. 4.

[7]Montana Record-Herald, July 12, 1916.

[8]The Portsmouth Times, November 24, 1916.

Jones, a marching New York suffragist, wrote:

> We are watching your political fight with great
> interest and your New York friends believe that a
> better Congressman could not be found and a vic-
> tory for you will mean a victory for suffrage
> throughout the country.[9]

Other endorsements spoke of her work with the New York Legislature as
efficient and as having gained the confidence of the legislators.[10]

As the campaign moved into its final stages, the women redoubled
their efforts. Mrs. Harvey Coit, President of the Montana Good Government Club, sent women into all parts of the state to campaign. The women
realized that they would not be voting for the first time in the approaching election if it had not been for Rankin's effective work. Brass bands,
good crowds and remarkable enthusiasm convinced many male candidates of
the efficacy of endorsing her campaign.[11] A telephone campaign, conducted
by the women on the day before election helped to insure her victory.[12]
When the ballots were tabulated on August 29, 1916, Rankin led the field
of eight candidates for the Republican nomination with 22,549 votes.
George W. Farr, the second Republican nominee, received 15,469 ballots.
In the general election, they would face Democrats John M. Evans and
Harry B. Mitchell.[13]

---

[9] Montana Progressive, August 10, 1916.

[10] Helena Independent, August 9, 1916.

[11] The Daily Missoulian, August 9, 1916; August 23, 1916.

[12] Helena Independent, August 27, 1916.

[13] Ellis Waldron, An Atlas of Montana Politics since 1864 (Missoula:
Montana State University Press, 1958), p. 153.

Having convinced the Republicans of her vote getting ability,
Jeannette had September and October to win over a majority of the total
electorate. She concentrated on enlarging her share of the woman's vote
and winning more of the agricultural vote. While speaking to the wheat
and sheep raising sections of Montana, Rankin discussed the "downgrading"
of wheat, a rural credits law, and promised to support a protective
tariff against European goods. In essence, she endorsed the Farmers'
Equity platform of a state inspection law to supervise grading of grain,
construction of state-owned terminal warehouses, and a state farm-loan
system with lower interest rates.[14]

Because the state Republican leaders still did not like the idea of
a woman's being elected to Congress, they gave her a campaign itinerary
in the thinly populated areas that would have insured defeat. After
threatening to work out her own itinerary and to reveal to the voters
what the Republicans had attempted, the State Committee gave her choice
places and dates. She traveled with J. B. Annin, Republican nominee for
Lieutenant Governor and a good solid citizen. Most of the political
observers believed that John M. Evans, incumbent Democrat, would win
easily; so the contest boiled down to selecting the second representative
since Montana elected two Congressmen at large. For obvious reasons,
Rankin pushed her own candidacy more than the party ticket and thereby
incurred the wrath of the other Republican nominee.[15]

In addition to a good itinerary, Belle Fligelman, a former reporter
for the Helena Independent, provided an excellent publicity campaign.

---

[14] Montana Progressive, October 12, 1916; Theodore Salues, "The Montana
Society of Equity," Pacific Historical Review, XIV (December, 1945), pp.393-
408; The Daily Missoulian, November 2, 1916.

[15] J. R. Interview, Jan. 27, 1969, p. 2.

Another important source of strength came from the Rankin family.
Wellington Rankin, a Helena attorney, chairman of the Montana Executive
Committee of the "Bullmoose" Party in 1912 and its nominee for U. S.
House of Representatives in 1914, conducted a strategic telephone cam-
paign with state and local political leaders. Jeannette's sisters, Grace
R. Kinney, Mary R. Bragg, and Edna Rankin, also campaigned vigorously
for her.[16]

In the last two weeks of the general election campaign, the tide for
Jeannette Rankin swelled to a crest. Everywhere she spoke to packed
auditoriums, and many were turned away. Loud and prolonged demonstrations
left no doubt as to the attitude of her audiences. Her meetings in Great
Falls, Butte, and Bozeman were among the largest political gatherings ever
held in those cities. Rankin's arguments in favor of legislation that
would promote Montana's reclamation projects and agriculture won favor
with the farmers. Endorsement of her candidacy by Theodore Roosevelt
during this tour added to her popularity.[17]

An overflow crowd gathered at the theater in Missoula to hear Rankin's
last speech on November 6. Harry Parsons was chairman of the meeting and
spoke first. Only applause, foot stomping, and cries of "Rankin, Rankin"
stopped him an hour and three quarters later. The crowd was furious
because they came to hear the first woman that was going to sit in the
U.S. Congress. She reiterated her interest in special legislation for
women and children, equal suffrage, a federal children's bureau, prohibition and reform of the House rules. She left the audience in laughter

[16]The Daily Missoulian, October 23, 1916.

[17]Helena Independent, November 6, 1916; The Daily Missoulian, November
2, 1916.

by surmising, "I need only every other vote and then one to make a majority."[18]

With the election on the following day, Jeannette Rankin did not have long to wait. Awakening about one o'clock in the morning after election, she called The Missoulian and asked about Wilson and Hughes. They told her Hughes had won. Not revealing herself, she asked about Jeannette Rankin. The reporter replied, "Oh, she has lost."[19] While she went back to bed, thinking she had lost, Wellington Rankin and Belle Fligelman were watching returns in Helena. Another suffragist was standing beside Belle when the newspaper interrupted with a "Philly" baseball score. This woman said, "Imagine calling us Phillies." As a ranch woman, she knew a filly was a young horse, but not that they were also the National League baseball team in Philadelphia. Belle remembered thinking it was no use explaining to her because the madder she got, the better suffragist she was going to be.[20] Wellington called Jeannette on the morning after the election and, contrary to the reported news, told her she had won. Before the returns were complete, he had discovered certain trends which he felt would give his sister the election. As he had predicted, Evans polled 84,499 votes and Jeannette 76, 932 to win Montana's two Congressional seats. Immediately, many explanations began to be offered for her election.[21]

The Helena Independent attributed her success to having the "best

---

[18]J. R. Interview, January 27, 1969, p. 2; The Daily Missoulian, November 7, 1916.

[19]J. R. Interview, January 27, 1969, p. 2.

[20]Belle Fligelman Winestein Interview, September 2, 1970, p. 6.

[21]Ellis Waldron, An Atlas of Montana Politics since 1864, p. 155.

organization of any of the candidates."[22] Others indicated that she was swept into office on a wave of sentiment for woman suffrage.[23] Because of her recent campaign for suffrage, there was no one who had a more extensive acquaintance with the voters than she, and her ability to communicate with the rural populace, as well as the city dwellers made her almost a sure winner. It was not difficult for her to win in the Republican primary since there were seven men to split the male vote, and, being a popular idol of Montana women, it was obvious that she would receive their votes. Miss Rankin secured an additional advantage when most of the male contestants in the primary endorsed her candidacy in an attempt to secure the women's votes.[24] In accessing her own victory though, Jeannette Rankin said, "Both the men and the women did it. The men of Montana have always given the women what they wanted."[25] In an attempt to obtain a larger vote, she had run almost a non-partisan campaign. As a master stroke of political strategy in most places she had said, "Vote for your local man and vote for me."[26] It was evident that party affiliation was of minor importance to her. Certainly, her election was a combination of many things, but the two most important seemed to have been the women's vote and Jeannette Rankin's own talents as an excellent organizer, a keen thinker and a powerful speaker.

Election to the United States House of Representatives brought Jeannette Rankin to the threshold of a new life. The fulfillment of a desire to work

---

[22]*Helena Independent*, November 12, 1916, p. 10.

[23]*New York Times*, November 9, 1916, p. 2.

[24]*Daily Missoulian*, August 10, 1916, p. 2.

[25]*New York Times*, November 19, 1916, II, 4.

[26]Jeannette Rankin, personal interview, January 27, 1969, p. 1 of transcript.

creatively for progressive legislation had been accomplished. Experiences of thirty-six years prepared her to meet the challenge admirably and to satisfy her strong inner commitment to relieve suffering. But first, she had to meet the challenge of war which loomed on the European horizon.

During the suffrage campaign, Jeannette Rankin spoke out against the European conflict and urged giving women the ballot so that they could vote to keep their sons out of war. By the time she ran for Congress in 1916, the possibility of the United States' getting involved in the First World War was greater. Even though President Woodrow Wilson urged the nation "to be impartial in thought," some Americans sympathized with the Central Powers, while most supported the Allies. "To be impartial in action" was even more difficult because the United States was the belligerents' great source of food, munitions, and credit. Yet, to many the chance that America would go to war was remote.

In formulating her platform, Rankin listed a peace plank along with those advocating social reform, tariff revision, and responsible democracy. She advocated "a preparedness that will make for permanent peace."[27] To avoid any possible entrance of the United States into the European War, Jeannette promoted a system of "coastal defense only" with no preparations that would lead to participation in a war in a foreign country.[28] There was very little discussion of the war question by the Rankin campaigners except in general terms. She recalled, "I didn't think it would come up so soon.... I knew how I'd feel, but we talked in general about the war."[29]

---

[27]Montana Progressive, July 20, 1916; Helena Independent, July 14, 1916.

[28]J. R. Interview, February 14, 1969, p. 4.

[29]Jeannette Rankin, personal interview, January 27, 1969, p. 3 of transcript.

Belle Fligelman, Jeannette Rankin's press secretary, remembered that in
the frequent letters to workers they stressed a "preparedness for permanent peace" and "I'm sure left no doubt that we were opposed to the
war."[30]

The Good Government Clubs across Montana occasionally heard leading citizens speak out against war and especially American involvment
in the European War. W. W. McDowell, a leading political figure in the
state, was representative of these views when he said to the delegates of
the Montana Good Government League assembled in the Placer Hotel:

> "Do you not think that the one great thing every
> good citizen desires above everything else is
> that we keep out of the conflict? And if you
> feel that way about it, do you not think your
> organization should go on record as favoring
> a cessation of hostilities in Europe, and to
> also let it be known that you are opposed to
> the United States becoming involved in the war?"[31]

Concerning this power of woman's opposition, Jeannette Rankin believed
that no war could continue for any considerable length of time without
the support of the women.[32]

The most important slogan of the campaign of 1916 was one coined by
President Woodrow Wilson's supporters -- "He kept us out of war." As the
slogan appealed to the general desire in Montana for peace, President
Wilson gathered overwhelming support, but Jeannette Rankin thought he was
deceiving the people. She said, "It was too good a slogan. It didn't
commit him to anything, and yet it gave the impression that he was going

---

[30]Belle Fligelman Winestine, Helena, Montana, Letter, February 23,
1969, to the author.

[31]Helena Independent, June 14, 1916, p. 1.

[32]New York Times, November 19, 1916, II, 4.

to keep us out of war."[33] In time, Miss Rankin believed that Wilson was going to take the country to war, but Wellington, her brother and campaign manager, would not let her say publicly, "This man who was for peace was a scoundrel," because it would damage her election hopes.[34] With all the male prejudice against a woman already in politics, this was one thing she did not need, so she remained silent in her belief that Wilson would lead the nation to war. As she looked back later, the only thing she misjudged was the time, "I didn't think they were going so soon."[35]

After the election of the first woman to Congress, reporters and photographers swarmed into Missoula. Things became so hectic that cameramen were banned from the Rankin residence. In addition to satisfying the demands of the news media, there were other decisions to settle. Under Wellington's counsel, Jeannette Rankin accepted a speaking tour and a year's contract as special correspondent to the Chicago Herald.[36]

After winning the Republican primary and the general election, Jeannette said in her first public statement, "I am deeply conscious of the responsibility resting upon me. I earnestly hope that I may be of some service, however slight, to the men and women of Montana... and of the nation."[37] In a certain sense she also felt it was her special duty

---

[33]Jeannette Rankin, personal interview, February 14, 1969, p. 6. of transcript.

[34]Jeannette Rankin, personal interview, February 14, 1969, p. 3. of transcript.

[35]Jeannette Rankin, personal interview, February 14, 1969, p. 6 of transcript.

[36]W. D. Rankin Interview by John Board, March 23, 1964, p. 12; Jeannette Rankin eventually made twenty speeches, at five hundred dollars apiece, before Wilson called the Special Session of Congress in April of 1917.

[37]Daily Missoulian, November 18, 1916, p. 10.

to express "the point of view of women" and to help them realize that Congress was a body which dealt with their problems.[38] With these goals in mind, she began to make her way to Washington, D.C.

There were various opinions voiced and written about the "Lady from Montana" as she began to be called. Many looked for a "Montana suffragist -- right out of the cattle country" packing a 44 six-shooter and trimming her skirts with chaps fur.[39] A Montana rancher in replying to an interview said, "Jeannette will make 'em sit up and take notice. She comes from fighting stock and carries a kick in her arguments."[40] Her brother, Wellington, chose other words to describe his sister: "Her life is devoted to the cause of mankind and government, first, last and always."[41] Dr. Louis Levine, from the University of Montana, wrote that the Congressmen will find in their midst "a strong and well-balanced personality, scientifically trained, accustomed to strict reasoning, well versed in the art of politics, inspired by social ideas, tempered by wide experience."[42] With the circulation of these descriptions, it was no wonder that the press hung to every word that she uttered.

Jeannette Rankin arrived in New York in late February to begin her speaking tour. Under pressure of news reporters, she granted an interview in the home of the James Laidlaws'. Playing a safe role, she feigned knowledge about the politics of the House. To an inquiry about universal

---

[38]New York Times, November 19, 1916, II, 4.

[39]Bert Lennon, "The Lady From Montana," Chicago Sunday Herald, December 10, 1919, V, 3.

[40]Ibid.

[41]Ibid.

[42]Louis Levine, "First Woman Member of Congress Well Versed in Politics," New York Times, November 19, 1916, II, 4.

military training, the new Congressman answered that the West had not been
disturbed about the question. She was also non-committal on whether she
would work as an Independent or as a Republican. Miss Rankin would not
state whether she was a pacifist but was certain women would generally
support their country. As to tariff legislation, she said, "I will study
it to see if it means the protection of the workers, and if it does, I
will support it."[43] Taking a more positive note, Jeannette Rankin favored the federal suffrage amendment, extension of child welfare work, state
and national prohibition, a farm loan law, and greater publicity in
Congressional committees.[44]

Jeannette Rankin's maiden speech after election was to an audience
of 3,000 in Carnegie Hall in New York City on a snowy March 2, 1917. After
a congratulatory letter from former President Theodore Roosevelt, Carrie
Chapman Catt introduced the Honorable Jeannette Rankin, who wore a white
chiffon dress and looked as if she were a debutante on the way to the
coming-out party of women into the class of real people. Entitled
"Democracy and Good Government," this speech praised the values of the
unusual state of Montana. She referred to its mineral deposits, thirty-
three billion board feet of sawable timber, widespread use of electricity,
natural gas, and agricultural production (enough wheat to make eighteen
loaves of bread for every man, woman, and child in the United States).
Jeannette was very appreciative of the egalitarian position taken by
Montana men toward their women. It had resulted in her election.[45]

---

[43]New York Sun, February 25, 1917.

[44]New York Tribune, February 25, 1917.

[45]New York Tribune, March 3, 1917.

As to Montana's problems, Jeannette recognized that the natural
resources and their public utilities were concentrated in the hands of
a few. With the change of time, labor problems became increasingly
severe. For her, the solution to these problems lay in a democratiza-
tion of government, industry, and social life. "'Let the People Know'
through education and they can be trusted to choose the right for themselves," said Miss Rankin. Not only must the people have "the vote,"
but they must have the political machinery to make it effective. At
this point, she suggested an absentee voter law, a corrupt practices
act, and a direct popular vote for president, rather than through the
electoral college. She felt, "Direct election of presidents would increase the possibility of each vote having the same value. True democracy
demands that each man have a vote and one man one vote."[46] It was not
until 1962 that the Supreme Court incorporated this principle into state
and Congressional elections.

Extending the "one man—one vote" principle, Jeannette Rankin advocated the use of a direct nominating primary. It had the advantages of
placing more importance on the candidate rather than the party and educating the electorate to be more selective in its choice of candidates. Within
this system, the candidates tended to reflect more adequately the ideas
of the people. To maintain control over their elected officers and legislation, Rankin endorsed the recall, the referendum, and the initiative.
Besides making the legislatures more sensitive to the demands of the
people, these measures placed more responsibility for government on "the
people."

---

[46]Ibid.

Using John Stuart Mill's definition of democracy as "the government
of the whole people by the whole people represented," Rankin advocated a
system of proportional representation. In this way, the ideas of all the
people, both majority and minority, were to be represented according to
a percentage of the total vote. Proportional representation was adopted
in Japan, Switzerland, Belgium, Denmark, and Finland. After World War I,
it was used temporarily in France, Germany, and Poland.

Up to this time, Jeannette Rankin had been careful to grant only
limited interviews and had been guarded in her statements. In Carnegie
Hall there was nothing timid, halfhearted, or guarded about the manner
in which she approached a democracy suitable for government, industry,
and society.[47]

While in New York, Jeannette Rankin, accompanied by her brother,
Wellington, stayed with the James Laidlaws',friends from suffrage days
of 1911 and 1912 when she worked for the New York Woman Suffrage Party.
Knowing that a war vote was a possibility, various pressure groups began
to urge Miss Rankin to vote affirmatively. Mrs. Laidlaw, preferring
that Jeannette vote for war, arranged a visit at Oyster Bay with former
President Theodore Roosevelt. Hoping that he could influence her thinking, Roosevelt told her of his experience with the Germans, their background, their excellent training, and how they were to be feared. The
theme of the dinner conversation concluded with the possibility that
America might have to enter the war. But Miss Rankin remembered that he
never asked her explicitly to vote for war.[48] This was only the beginning

[47]Manuscript of Carnegie Speech in J. R. MSS; New York Tribune,
March 3, 1917.

[48]J. R. Interview, January 26, 1969, p. 7; Great Falls Tribune, March
16, 1937, p. 5.

of immense pressure that climaxed in her vote on April 6, 1919.

After a whirlwind speaking tour in the East, South, and Midwest, Jeannette Rankin arrived in Washington on April 1, 1917, to answer President Woodrow Wilson's call for an emergency session of Congress. On the following day, Miss Rankin attended a breakfast in her honor sponsored by the suffragists at the Shoreham Hotel.[49] She heard congratulatory remarks from the leaders of hostile feminine factions: Carrie Chapman Catt of the National American Women Suffrage Association and Alice Paul of the National Woman's Party, the newly founded militant suffragist organization. Not only were they rivals as to the method of gaining suffrage, but they held opposing views toward the approaching war. Alice Paul was a great advocate of the pacifist position while Catt was pro-war. After Maude Park Wood, chairman of the Congressional Committee of NAWSA, and Anne Martin, chairman of the Legislative Section of the National Woman's Party, gave brief speeches, Jeannette Rankin rose to speak. With trembling voice, she said, "There will be many times when I will make mistakes. I need your encouragement and support. I know I will get it. I promise...." There her voice broke, and she sat down.[50]

Jeannette Rankin struggled with these tensions as she tried to enjoy the beginnings of a momentous occasion. From breakfast she went to NAWSA headquarters and made an appearance on the balcony. Then, Carrie Chapman Catt, Harriet B. Laidlaw, and Jane Thompson accompanied her to the Capitol.

_____

[49]Included among the sponsors were Katharine Anthony, Elizabeth Irwin, Cornelia Swinnerton, Helen Todd, Elizabeth Watson, Mary Beard, Lou Rogers, Katherine Luckie [Lecky], and Jane Thompson.

[50]"The Capitol Welcomes Jeannette Rankin," The Suffragist, V (April 7, 1917), p. 7; Daily Missoulian, April 7, 1917; Daily Missoulian, June 5, 1916.

At eleven fifty-five o'clock John M. Evans, the other Representative
from Montana, escorted Congressman Rankin (Jeannette Rankin preferred
to be called "Congressman" rather than Congresswoman" and likewise
"woman" rather than "lady") into the House chamber as members rose and
the gallery applauded. The first session of the Sixty-fifth Congress
began with the calling of the roll. When the clerk called Jeannette
Rankin's name, both sides burst out in applause. She stood and bowed
first to the Republican side and then to the Democratic side.[51] In the
gallery, Olive P. Rankin and Wellington listened with pride and joy,
while on the floor it was a happy moment for the Congressman from Montana;
but it could not last. She would soon have to struggle with a declaration
of war against Germany.

Events that precipitated this special session began while Jeannette
Rankin was campaigning for suffrage in the summer of 1914. Archduke
Ferdinand, heir to the throne of Austria-Hungary, was assassinated at
Sarajevo on June 28, 1914. This led to a general conflict among the
nations of Europe. Americans personally wanted to stay out of the war,
but they could not avoid expressing sympathies either to the Central
Powers or to the Allies.

Refusing to abridge the rights of American citizens to travel on
belligerent ships, President Wilson faced the loss of 128 Americans in
the sinking of the Lusitania on May 7, 1915. Diplomatic protests accomplished nothing. After the loss of American lives on the Arabic, August 19,
1915, and the Sussex, March 24, 1916, Wilson issued almost an ultimatium.

---

[51] New York Times, April 3, 1917; Terrell D. Webb, Washington Wife,
Journal of Ellen Maury Slayden from 1897-1919, (New York: Harper and
Row, Publishers, 1962), as quoted in Washington Post, March 28, 1963,
B14.

In the face of probable American intervention, Germany retreated for
several months. Early in 1917 the need to cut off England's supplies
in order to break her war effort seemed to justify the gamble that America
would not enter open warfare, or in any event become effective quickly,
caused German military leaders to resume unrestricted submarine warfare
on January 31, 1917. This forced the arming of American merchantmen.
Public opinion was enflamed by publication of the Zimmerman note, pro-
posing a German-Mexican alliance. Germany made good her threat of unrestricted submarine warfare by sinking the unarmed Algonquin on March
12. In view of his position toward submarine warfare and American travel,
President Wilson seemed to have had no real choice than to call for a
declaration of war.[52]

On the evening of April 2, 1917, President Wilson appeared before a
joint session of the House and Senate to ask for a declaration of war.
He stated that neutrality was no longer feasible or desirable; the peace
of the world and the freedom of its people were at stake. The United
States had no selfish interests to serve but was prepared to battle for
those things that were even more precious than peace, for democracy, for
the rights and liberties of small nations and for "a universal dominion
of right by such a concert of free peoples as shall bring peace and
safety to all nations and make the world itself at last free."[53]

---

[52]Foster Rhea Dulles, American's Rise to World Powers, 1898-1954
(New York: Harper and Row, Publishers, 1954), pp. 87-105; Arthur S.
Link, Wilson: Campaigns for Progressiveism and Peace, 1915-1917
(Princeton: Princeton University Press, 1965), pp. 391-430.

[53]U.S., Congress, House of Representatives, 65th Congress, 1st
Session, April 2, 1917, Congressional Record, LV, Part I, pp. 118-120.

The Senate was the first to pass a resolution favoring war by a vote of eighty-two to six with eight abstentions.[54] Attention then shifted to the House of Representatives and the initial vote of the first United States Congresswoman.

With debate beginning in the House, the time for Jeannette Rankin's decision was imminent. She recalled, "Everyone [except the pacifist suffragists] was trying to educate me to vote for war."[55] Advocates of the war resolution wanted to enlist her aid because of the effect a woman's utterance would have on the pacifist group in the House and throughout the country.[56] The suffragists, including her personal friend, Mrs. James L. Laidlaw of New York, wanted her to support the war measure because her negative vote might damage the position of the suffrage movement. On the other hand, there were other suffragists like Alice Paul of the Congressional Union who were presurring Miss Rankin to vote against war.[57]

A great comfort in the midst of these demands was Wellington Rankin, her brother and closest advisor. He had come East with her to be present for the opening session of Congress. He did not want war, but he viewed his sister's new political position as a significant one and urged her to do nothing that would harm it. Personally, he preferred that she vote "a man's vote" on the war issue, because "otherwise she would discredit herself and justify the charge that women were all alike and

---

[54]Ibid., p. 261.

[55]Jeannette Rankin, personal interview, January 26, 1969, p. 2 of transcript.

[56]Daily Missoulian, April 7, 1917, p. 8.

[57]J. R., personal interview, January 26, 1969, pp. 3-4.

opposed to war for sex reasons."[58] When Wellington mentioned the possibility that she might never be elected again, Jeannette would get furious. It was not a question of her personal gain, but of the futility of war and the destruction of lives.[59] Realizing that the final decision must be hers, Wellington always advised: "Now vote your convictions...now vote your conscience."[60]

In addition to the arguments of her friends and of Wellington, Miss Rankin spent many hours listening to the debate in the Senate and then in the House.[61] She was much impressed with the reasoning of Representative Claude Kitchin from North Carolina, Majority Leader of the House, as he argued with tears running down his face:

> "In view of the many assumptions of loyalty
> and patriotism on the part of some of those
> who favor the Resolution, and insinuations of
> cowardice and disloyalty on the part of those
> who oppose it....let me at once remind the
> House that it takes neither moral nor physical
> courage to declare a war for others to fight."[62]

With this encouragement, she was prepared to vote.

The House of Representatives debated throughout the evening and into the early morning hours of April 6 before the first roll call took place.[63]

---

[58] Helena Independent, April 26, 1917, p. 1.

[59] W. D. Rankin Interview, March 24, 1964, p. 15.

[60] J. R., personal interview, January 26, 1969, pp. 2 and 5 of transcript.

[61] Helena Independent, April 26, 1917, p. 1.

[62] J. R., personal interview, January 26, 1969, p. 3 of transcript; Jeannette Rankin: "Twenty Years After," The Christian Herald, April, 1937, p. 10; U.S., Congress, House, 65th Congress, 1st Session, April 5, 1917, Congressional Record, LV, 332.

[63] New York Times, April 7, 1917, p. 4.

Miss Rankin did not respond to the first roll call but instead brushed
back her hair, looked up at the ceiling, rubbed her eyes and clasped
and unclasped her hands as one under great mental anguish. She believed
that she was voting for a commercial war and that the idealistic hopes
entertained by so many would not be realized. "To make the world safe
for Democracy" was a task beyond the power of war to accomplish. She was
gripped by a fear of offending votes desperately needed to secure the
passage of the suffrage amendment and by a desire to express a woman's
horror of war and her principles against it. She also knew the latter
was neither the popular nor expedient to do.[64] Knowing that a second
roll call took place for all who did not answer the first, she promised
her friends to wait until the last moment, and, if she could vote for it,
she would.[65] When Representative Joe Cannon of Illinois entered the floor,
he learned what had happened. He went to her desk and was understood
to have said:

> Little woman, you cannot afford not to vote.
> You represent the womanhood of the country in
> the American Congress. I shall not advise you
> how to vote, but you should vote one way or the
> other -- as your conscience dictates.[66]

As the roll call came around the second time, all the eyes in the
chamber and in the galleries were upon her. When the clerk called her
name, again she did not answer. Because they had been calling everyone
who was against the declaration of war a traitor, Miss Rankin remembered,
"I just unconsciously got up and said, 'I want to stand by my country, but

---

[64] New York Times, April 7, 1917, p. 4; Jeannette Rankin, "I Would
Vote No Again," Christian Science Monitor Weekly Magazine, April 1,
1936, p. 2.

[65] J. R., personal interview, January 26, 1969, p. 3 of the transcript.

[66] New York Times, April 7, 1917.

I cannot vote for war'."[67] Barely audible above the sudden clamor was her last sentence, "I vote no."[68] In the first part of an unprecedented remark during roll call, Rankin established her patriotism; and, when she concluded, "I cannot vote for war," she proved her womanhood. The roll call droned on with the House voting to declare war on Germany, 373 to 50, with 9 members not voting.[69]

Most of the newspapers carried various interpretations of a dramatic, weeping scene as Miss Rankin voted. She denied this, remembering that "I wept for a week. When the time came to vote, it was just too awful to even weep."[70] To Jeannette, these "weeping" stories, as a form of ridicule, were the only effective weapon the militarists could use.[71] Many times people asked Representative Fiorello La Guardia of New York, a progressive who had voted for the war resolution, to ascertain whether Miss Rankin had wept or not. He replied, "I do not know, for I could not see because of the tears in my own eyes."[72]

To Jeannette Rankin's "negative vote," there was an enormous response. Suffrage leaders pardoned her and, at the same time, admired her for standing

---

[67]J. R., personal interview, January 26, 1969, p. 4; New York Times, April 7, 1917, p. 4; The Daily Missoulian, April 7, 1917, p. 8; Columbia University, Oral History Memoir of Frances Witherspoon and Tracy D. Mygatt, pp. 13-15 of transcript; This broke a hundred and forty years precedent of having no speeches made during roll call in the House of Representatives.

[68]New York Times, April 7, 1917, p. 4.

[69]U.S., Congress, House of Representatives, 65th Congress, 1st Session, April 5, 1917, Congressional Record, LV, Part I, 412-413.

[70]J. R., personal interview, January 26, 1969, p. 3.

[71]Statement of J. R. contained in a speech by Karl Stefan over WOL, Washington, July 25, 1935, in J. R. MSS.

[72]Fiorello H. LaGuardia, The Making of an Insurgent: An Autobiography (New York: J. B. Lippincott Company, 1948), p. 141.

by her conviction. Harriet Laidlaw indicated, "While I should have liked for her to have voted differently, she did her duty as she saw it after one of the most terrible mental struggles any woman ever had."[73] Harriot S. Blatch, a New York suffragist, regretted that she voted no, but also admired her courage.[74] Carrie Chapman Catt excused Rankin and said that she had predicted two weeks ago that no matter which way she voted, she would be criticized. If she voted for war, she would offend the pacifists, and, if she voted against it, she would offend the militarists. Mrs. Catt was asked, "Do you think Miss Rankin neglected an opportunity to make a million or more votes for suffrage by voting as she did?" She answered, "I do not believe Miss Rankin was guided by any such consideration." Then, in a conscious effort to disassociate her vote from the suffrage movement, Catt said, "You must remember that Miss Rankin was not voting for the suffragists of the nation--she represents Montana."[75] Privately, Catt wrote to Mary G. Peck that "our Congress Lady is a sure enough joker. Whatever she has done or will do is wrong to somebody, and every time she answers a roll call she looses us a million votes."[76] A week later, the Congressional Committee of NAWSA, showing their contempt for her vote, cancelled plans for a reception for Miss Rankin.[77]

Suffragists in Omaha generally expressed themselves in sympathy with Rankin's vote. Mrs. Draper Smith, State President of Nebraska Suffrage

[73] New York Times, April 7, 1917, p. 4.

[74] New York Tribune, April 7, 1917.

[75] New York Times, April 7, 1917, p. 4.

[76] Carrie C. Catt to Mary Gray Peck, April 8, 1917, in C. C. Catt Papers, Schlesinger Library, Radcliffe College.

[77] Minutes of Congressional Committee of NAWSA (April 11, 1917), Maude W. Park, Women's Rights Collection, Schlesinger Library, Radcliffe College.

Association, said, "If women in all nations had a voice, I feel that we would never have a war." Others said it was unthinkable for a woman to vote for war and that Miss Rankin expressed the viewpoint of most of the women of the country.[78]

In the South, Atlanta suffragists had varied opinions. Emma T. Martin, a prominent suffragist and head of the Wilson campaign in Atlanta, declared that she was sure the women of the South did not think like Jeannette Rankin. On the other hand, Mary L. McClendon, pioneer suffragist in Georgia and President of Georgia Woman's Suffrage Association, believed that the United States should not go to war with Germany. "I am for peace and arbitration unless our country is actually invaded," she said. McClendon chided Jeannette by adding that woman's *forte* was talking and that she should have made a speech telling why she was against the war.[79]

Wellington Rankin, who walked his sister home after the vote, knew she had "crucified" herself.[80] He recalled saying to her afterwards, "You know you're not going to be reelected. You know there will be a lot of feeling."[81] Miss Rankin did not let him continue but said, "I'm not interested in that. All I'm interested in is what they will say fifty years from now."[82] In a letter to Wellington on the following

---

[78]*Omaha, Nebraska News*, April 7, 1917.

[79]*Atlanta Journal*, April 6, 1917.

[80]J. R. Interview, January 26, 1969, p. 5.

[81]Wellington D. Rankin, Helena, Montana, personal interview with John Board, March 23, 1964, as quoted in John Board, "The Lady from Montana: Jeannette Rankin," Unpublished Master's Thesis, University of Wyoming, 1964, p. 133.

[82]Ibid.

Tuesday, Jeannette said, "I am sorry I had to disappoint you. I still feel that this was the only way I could go."[83] Wellington believed that he had never seen a person more defiant of public opinion. In his sister he saw an independence which would defy all consequences, and he felt, "She would consider it more dishonest not to vote your conviction than it would be to rob a bank.... She just won't pretend."[84] From this initial vote, Wellington concluded that perhaps her "conscience" would be her greatest political weakness.[85]

Clark Howell, editor of the Atlanta Constitution, wrote that if woman's first vote was bathed in tears, it was upon an issue near the maternal heart of woman: the issue of war or peace. He believed that the fact she wept did not prove her weak, but womanly, and predicted that her "tears will some day move all the women of the world to be consulted before the "War Lords" tear their sons from their bosoms."[86]

Many other newspapers, and individuals, were critical of Miss Rankin, and her vote as the first and only Congresswoman of that date. An editorial in the New York Times, entitled "Patriotism with a 'but'", declared, "This beginning...as a national legislator is most unfortunate for her. She starts wrong, for she has justified distrust of her judgment and of her opinions."[87] Henry A. Wise Wood, in an address delivered at Cooper Union,

---

[83]J. R. to Wellington Rankin, April 10, 1917, J.R. MSS.

[84]Wellington D. Rankin, Helena, Montana, personal interview with John Board, March 23, 1964, as quoted in John Board, "The Lady from Montana: Jeannette Rankin." p. 133.

[85]Christine Evans, "Woman Against War," Scribner's Commentator, XI (November, 1941), p. 27.

[86]Atlanta Constitution, April 7, 1917, p. 8.

[87]New York Times, April 7, 1917, p. 12.

saw in her vote an eloquent confession of woman's inability to support
the strains of war council in the moment of national crisis.[88] The
Reverend Dr. Robert Watson, Scotch Presbyterian Church, New York, assailed
Miss Rankin by saying, "If our first woman Congresswoman is not willing
and able to stand by her country in this terrible and trying hour, let
her resign at once."[89]

Back in Montana, the papers carried her vote story with little comment.
In Helena, her vote occasioned no surprise as her views on war were well
known.[90] Antagonism to her ideas did not gather until the early summer
months when patriotism had risen to fervent heights in Montana. The Helena
Independent, in an article, entitled "Montana's Congresswoman Now Very
Popular," wrote, "Her mind is honest and open and she has evident courage
to back her convictions."[91] Mrs. J. E. Erickson of Montana made a toast
to Jeannette, saying:

> Thereupon in that gray tense dawn, there arose
> in the cold Congressional Halls a strange sound.
> It was a new born sound. It was like the sob
> of a mother's heart! By virtue of this heroic
> stand of Jeannette Rankin, I herein voice our
> appreciation, our deepest gratitude and our
> loyalty to her.[92]

In reply to a Montana constituent who wondered if she was a failure,
Jeannette Rankin explained:

> I am glad to have an expression of your opin-
> ion because I am glad to know what the people

---

[88]New York Times, May 3, 1917, p. 14.

[89]New York Times, April 16, 1917, p. 4.

[90]New York Evening Journal, April 9, 1917.

[91]Helena Independent, April 26, 1917, p. 1.

[92]Mrs. J. E. Erickson, "Toast to Jeannette Rankin," 1917, J. R.
Collection, Montana Historical Society Library.

think. In the campaign last fall, I judged
the sentiment in Montana was overwhelmingly
against war. Of course, the situation had
changed when the vote was taken and yet the
letters and telegrams that came to me were
sixteen to one against the war resolution.
I tried to let Montana people know that whenever a question arose on which I had received
no definite instructions I would vote in
accordance with my highest ideals.[93]

Indeed, Jeannette Rankin had voted her highest ideals in the early

hours on Good Friday, April 6, 1917. In retrospect, she felt it signifi-

cant that the first woman's vote in Congress was cast against war. It

was not a decisive ballot which would alter the final results, but it

was a personal vote which expressed "woman's point of view" and Rankin's

personal philosophy. Her vote provided women with a precedent for question-

ing the rightness of war. Her conviction against the war method for settl-

ing disputes, evidenced by her vote, cemented a relationship with the peace

movement and shaped her activities that were to span the next twenty years.

Before those events could take place, Congressman Rankin had to face the

immediate tasks of executing the war with Germany.

Generally, after her negative vote on the German war resolution,

Miss Rankin reluctantly supported administration policies. While con-

scription was being debated in the Congress, several civic groups from

Bozeman, Butte, and Hamilton telegraphed to advise her "to stand firm

by the President in his plans, if need be, alone."[94] Although she had

favored the volunteer method of raising an army, Rankin finally voted for

_____

[93]"Our Busy Congresswoman," Literary Digest, LV (August 11, 1917),
p. 43; J. R., personal interview, January 27, 1969, p. 5 of transcript.

[94]O. H. P. Shelley to J. R., April 24, 1917, J. R. MSS; Wellington
Rankin to J. R., April 22, 1917, in J. R. MSS; Helena Independent,
April 27, 1917, p. 5.

the army bill with its selective draft. The Daily Missoulian indicated

that sentiment in that city was overwhelmingly in favor of the draft.[95]

When the Declaration of War against Austria-Hungary came up for

debate in the House, many of the members expected another anti-war out-

burst. She listened attentively and toward the end of the debate rose

to speak. Miss Rankin said:

> I still believe war is a stupid and futile way
> of attempting to settle international difficul-
> ties. I believe war can be avoided and will be
> avoided when the people, the men and women in
> America, as well as in Germany, have the con-
> trolling voice in their government. Today
> special privileged commercial interests are
> controlling the world.[96]

Jeannette Rankin rationalized that the present vote was not a "declaration

of war" because, when America declared war on Germany, it virtually de-

clared war on her allies. She then said, "This is a vote on a mere

technicality in the prosecution of a war already declared. I shall vote

for this as I voted for money and for men."[97] In an editorial, the New

York Times chided her by writing, "It is better to be right part of the

time than wrong all the time."[98]

By voting against the German declaration, Jeannette Rankin fulfilled

her commitment to her pacifist ideals. Having once stated her conviction

on the main issue, she then moved to another position. Rankin expressed

---

[95]New York Times, May 1, 1917; Helena Independent, April 29, 1917,
p. 1. Daily Missoulian, April 26, 1917, p. 1.

[96]U.S., Congress, House of Representatives, 65th Congress, 2nd
Session, December 7, 1917, Congressional Record, LVI, Part I, p. 98.

[97]Ibid.

[98]New York Times, December 10, 1917, p. 14.

124

her unique combination of idealism and practicality by voting for the
Austria-Hungary resolution. That vote, to her, was a practical extension
of a war previously declared. As with many pacifists, Rankin passively
cooperated, as far as conscious would allow, in the war effort.

CHAPTER VI

A WOMAN IN CONGRESS

Even though the Sixty-Fifth was a War Congress and Jeannette Rankin's vote against war stood out as a significant contribution for women, she was involved with other legislative measures. Women and children continued to be her special interests.

Her maiden speech in the House of Representatives came on May 28, 1917, as she introduced an amendment to the Lever Bill. Her amendment suggested that women be employed, as far as practicable, in the gathering of information on the production, supply, distribution, and obligation of food as authorized under the proposed legislation. Jeannette Rankin hoped that woman's involvement in the census program would stimulate in her a keener interest in the government and in national food economy. She believed, "[Women] must turn from individual domestic problems to this new international problems of feeding the people of the world." In less than five minutes, she recorded her first legislative victory. Also, Rankin attached the same type of amendment to the Fourteenth and subsequent Decennial Censuses.[1]

Although she could not defeat the declaration of war against Germany,

---

[1] Jeannette Rankin, "Genuine Recognition of Woman's Wrath in our National Crisis," Atlanta Constitution, July 29, 1917, Magazine Section, p. 2. U.S., Congress, House of Representatives, 65th Congress, 1st Session, May 28, 1917, Congressional Record, LV, Part 3, p. 2998; New York Times, May 29, 1917. U.S., Congress, House of Representatives, 65th Congress, 2nd Session, June 25, 1918, Congressional Record, LVI, Part 8, p. 8276.

Miss Rankin tried to reduce the ill effects of war on women. In published articles, speeches and through legislation, she pointed out the changes
that war would bring. "Women," she said, "must not only prepare themselves...for thrifty administration in their kitchen, but also for professional and paid work."[2] While women economized, Jeannette pushed for
assurances that the grain they saved would not be made into alcoholic
drinks and that their thrift would also be protected from food speculators.

To keep the soldiers in the field required an equal number of women
working on the home front. This woman in industry was of special concern
to Representative Rankin. For her efficiency and health, she urged that
this worker be paid adequate wages, provided sanitary working conditions,
and limited to reasonable hours. Failure at any of these points would
bring bad results for the woman, the nation, and the conduct of the war.
She prophesied "Small use will it be to save democracy for the race if
we cannot at the same time save the race for democracy."[3] For this
reason, Rankin opposed the Brown Bill in the New York Legislature which
proposed to abrogate labor laws for the protection of women and children
and to suspend compulsory education. Fortunately, New York Governor
Charles S. Whitman vetoed this bill which had been carried along on the
waves of patriotism.[4] While some were urging economy in public education,
Jeannette recommended that schools operated on a twelve-month basis to
insure trained minds to cope with the problems of reconstruction after

---

[2]Jeannette Rankin, "What We Women Should Do," _Ladies Home Journal_,
XXXIV (August, 1917), p. 17.

[3]Jeannette Rankin, "At the Front with the Women," _General Federation
Magazine_, XVII (August, 1918), pp. 13-14.

[4]_The New York American_, February 18, 1918.

the war and to counteract domestic uncertainties.[5]

Many of these problems were exemplified by conditions existing in the Bureau of Printing and Engraving. In addition to the normal load, the administration called on the Bureau to print the first Liberty Loan Bonds. Employees, many of whom were women, worked twelve to fifteen hours a day, six days a week, and had all leave cancelled. Many women fell at their machines from exhaustion. News of these conditions leaked out to the press and pulpits. Several of the women approached Congressman Rankin. Through the courtesy of Representative Charles D. Carter of Oklahoma, Jeannette secured a visitor's pass and toured incognito the Bureau with Elizabeth Watson, a private investigator from New York.[6]

Previous efforts by the National Consumers League, National American Woman Suffrage Association and National Women's Trade Union League had failed to gain the attention of the Secretary of the Treasury, William G. McAdoo. With a stack of affidavits acquired by special investigator Watson, Congressman Rankin and Belle Fligelman, her secretary, went to McAdoo's office on June 30. She threatened congressional investigation if the Bureau was not on an eight-hour day by July 5. McAdoo's assistant pulled his chair up and wiggled his finger in Rankin's face. Condescendingly, he said, "You can't do that. In government things can't be done that fast." She replied, "Well, I just thought I'd let you know what's going to be done." In the evening paper, McAdoo announced an eight-hour

---

[5] Jeannette Rankin, "What We Women Should Do," p. 17.

[6] Belle F. Winestein Interview, September 2, 1970, p. 12; New York Telegram, July 13, 1917; New York Times, July 2, 1917.

shift beginning July 5 and the appointment of an investigating committee.[7]

The Committee began its study on July 9 and was swamped by over two hundred girls who came to testify. After only six hours of interviewing, the Committee reported to McAdoo and recommended, among other changes, the permanent adoption of the eight-hour shift. To make up for loss of pay from longer hours, Jeannette introduced a bill to equalize wages paid to men and women employees in the government who perform similar labor.[8] She also attempted to add an amendment to a Sundry Civil Bill to raise pay to $2.24 per hour for the Bureau.[9] Before the conclusion of the agitation, the workers received eight-hour schedules, a half-day on Saturday, annual leave restored, better working conditions, and a new Bureau Director. For this help, the Women's Union of the Bureau of Engraving gratefully presented Jeannette with a banner of appreciation.[10]

In the summer of 1917, Congressman Rankin introduced legislation to provide a pension fund for the dependents of American soldiers called to fight against Germany. She believed that the nation should recognize the value of the service performed by women in wartime. She said:

> When the breadwinner goes to the front to protect
> our country, the women who are left behind will

---

[7]"Political Power in the Hands of a Woman," Survey, XXXVII (July 21, 1917), p. 357; Belle F. Winestein Interview, September 2, 1970, p. 12.

[8]U.S., Congress, House of Representatives, 65th Congress, 2nd Session, January 4, 1918, Congressional Record, LVI, Part 1, p. 617.

[9]U.S. House of Representatives, 65th Congress, Second Session, June 12, 1918, Congressional Record, LVI, Part 8, p. 7701.

[10]"Bureau of Engraving and Printing Meeting an Enormous Demand," The Plate Printer, XVI (July 7, 1918), pp. 1-2; this banner is in the Jeannette Rankin MSS; The Woman Citizen, I (July 21, 1917), p. 136.

> bear the burden of providing for the family....
> We cannot allow the ravages of poverty to disinte-
> grate our social structure.[11]

One of the most important pieces of legislation introduced by Jeannette Rankin in the 65th Congress was a bill to encourage instruction in the hygiene of maternity and infancy. She had previously studied and evaluated the English Bill for maternity aid and wanted to apply it to the needs of mothers and infants across America. Vast distances between mother and the nearest doctor in the West underscored the need for maternity clinics in every county, combined with a rural nursing as widespread as the postal service.[12] Julia Lathrop, head of the Children's Bureau, established by Congress in 1912, discovered in a study of birth registrations an unusually high rate of infancy mortality. In her annual report for 1917, she suggested a plan for public protection of maternity and infancy. Encouraged by the Children's Bureau, Congressman Rankin incorporated these ideas into her bill.[13]

Its purpose was to supply educational materials to needed areas; to provide instruction in pre-natal, post-natal, and infancy care; to regulate midwifery; and to improve generally the health of mothers and infants. The Rankin-Robinson Bill, using the familiar principle of joint federal and state action, would appropriate money to be distributed among the states and administered in cooperation with the Children's Bureau in the

---

[11]U.S., Congress, House of Representatives, 65th Congress, 1st Session, July 10, 1917, Congressional Record, LV, Part V, p. 4931; New York Times, July 11, 1917; Jeannette Rankin, "U.S. Aid for Families of Soldiers," Chicago Sunday Herald, August 5, 1917, II, p. 5.

[12]Jeannette Rankin, "What We Women Should Do," p. 17.

[13]Josephine Goldmark, Impatient Crusader: Florence Kelley (Urbana: University of Illinois Press, 1953), pp. 93-106.

Department of Labor.[14] After a speech before the Council of Organizations by Rankin and hearings before the House Labor Committee, the bill failed to pass. Jeannette Rankin returned in 1920-21 as lobbyist for the National Consumers' League and helped to secure its adoption.[15]

Other legislation for women introduced by Representative Rankin included an independent citizenship bill. The purpose of this measure was to help American women retain their United States citizenship when they married foreigners. Also it aimed to regain citizenship for those women now married to foreigners living in the United States.[16]

While all this special legislation was important, Jeannette Rankin's main goal was "Votes for Women." In her campaign for Representative from Montana, she had promised to work for a federal amendment for suffrage. Suffrage was not the ultimate goal in Jeannette's philosophy, but only the means through which she believed that women could express "their point of view." Enfranchisement was to become the vehicle of communication for women and children. While on a speaking tour previous to the opening of Congress, she urged the adoption of the Susan B. Anthony amendment. Upon arriving in Washington, as had been noted, Rankin was feted by the leadership of the two rival suffrage groups: the National American Woman's Suffrage Association and the Congressional Union. Actually, she felt ill at ease with both groups.

---

[14]U.S., Congress, House of Representatives, 65th Congress, Second Session, July 11, 1918, Congressional Record, LVI, Part 9, pp. 8559-8560; "Federal Mothers' Aid," Survey, XLI (February 1, 1919), p. 640.

[15]U.S., Congress, House of Representatives, Committee on Labor, Hygiene of Maternity and Infancy, Hearings, on H. R. 12634, 65th Congress, Third Session, 1919, pp. 5-7.

[16]Helena Independent, January 22, 1918; Woman Citizen, II (December 22, 1917), p. 78.

Relations with Carrie Chapman Catt became very tenuous after Jeannette Rankin announced her candidacy in 1916. Catt, as President of NAWSA, wrote Rankin a very condescending letter asking about sponsors, the nature of her political ambitions, and what her candidacy would do to suffrage. Rankin remembered the suffrage leader expressed much apprehension as she wrote, "I feel as though I am living on a volcano."[17] Probably more than anything else, Catt, an international suffrage figure, was horrified by the possibility of a young "unlettered" Westerner becoming the first woman to serve in Congress. This letter only made matters worse since Jeannette, for her part, was already unhappy over the replacing of Dr. Anna H. Shaw by Carrie C. Catt as president of the national organization.[18]

On the other hand, Alice Paul, leader of the Congressional Union, was a pacifist and a good friend. Yet, her militant methods and tactics were not characteristic of Jeannette Rankin's philosophy. In the struggle over the Shafroth-Palmer amendment between the Congressional Union and NAWSA in 1914 and 1915, Jeannette worked for and supported this amendment to change the method of getting suffrage before the voters in individual states. While Jeannette assisted Mrs. Medill McCormick of NAWSA, the Congressional Union remained faithful to the Susan B. Anthony federal amendment. Drawing tactics from the English political system, Alice Paul and her supporters charged the Democratic Party with failure to get a suffrage amendment through Congress. They substantiated this charge by working against the Democratic candidates in the 1916 election. Jeannette Rankin could not accept this philosophy. On the other hand,

---

[17] J. R. Interview, January 26, 1969, p. 12.

[18] J. R. Interview, January 26, 1969, p. 14.

NAWSA remained nonpartisan and by 1916 again extolled the virtues of a federal amendment.[19] Thus, generally speaking, Jeannette remained friends with Alice Paul and the Congressional Union, but retained her relationship in NAWSA until they ostracized her after voting against war.

Feeling that she could ill afford to decline, Carrie C. Catt had accepted the invitation to introduce Congressman-elect Rankin at Carnegie Hall in early March. She did not know Miss Rankin very well and sought an interview. Later, in a memorandum to NAWSA board members, Catt described her as "well poised and apparently very level-headed and sensible. I found that the Congressional Union people worked against her and not for her, so that she is under no obligation to them."[20] She also reminded the board that the Congressional Union would probably claim Jeannette Rankin but that the Congressman-elect would not embarrass NAWSA by seeming to belong to their rivals. Catt secured Jeannette's promise to introduce a federal suffrage amendment and believed that with her help the measure would pass the House during the winter of 1917-1918.[21]

On the opening day of the Special Session of Congress in April, 1917, Jeannette Rankin and five other Representatives, along with five Senators, introduced resolutions providing for federal suffrage.[22] When the Democratic

---

[19]Helena Independent, September 9, 1916. J. R. Interview, February 14, 1969, p. 5.

[20]C. C. Catt to NAWSA Board Members, March 23, 1917, Maude W. Park Files, Women's Rights Collection, Schlesinger Library.

[21]Harriet B. Laidlaw to Maude W. Park, March 19, 1917, Maude W. Park Files, Women's Rights Collection, Schlesinger Library.

[22]U.S., Congress, House of Representatives, 65th Congress, First Session, April 2, 1917, Congressional Record, LV, Part 1, p. 128.

and Republican leaders decided to consider only legislation related to
war measures in the special session, suffrage moved to secondary consideration. Fortunately, there was enough work to keep the women busy
in committee hearings and in congressional lobbying. If they could not
hope for passage, at least they could attempt to win committee approval.

On April 20, 1917, the Senate Committee on Woman Suffrage held its
first hearing to consider the resolution of Andrieus A. Jones, Senator
from New Mexico and chairman of the committee. His constitutional amendment provided that the right of citizens shall not be denied or abridged
on account of sex. The hearing room, decorated with the flags of the 22
nations that had given women partial suffrage, was a picturesque setting.
Spectators and suffragists crowded the room and overflowed into the hall.
Jeannette Rankin, dressed in a blue serge suit with a thin white shirt-
waist, spoke with warmth and intelligence about the need for a federal
amendment. Experience as field secretary of NAWSA provided her with
firsthand knowledge of state hinderances to suffrage. She reported that
probably the women in New Mexico could never be enfranchised except by a
federal amendment. To amend their state constitution, the law required
a three-fourth's majority in each house, three-fourths of all votes cast
in the election, and at least a two-third's majority in each county. Other
difficulties encountered in securing suffrage by the state method were the
problems involved in calling a constitutional convention, securing two
consecutive legislatures to pass constitutional changes, the frequency
with which defeated amendments could be resubmitted, and fraudulent count-
ing of the votes. Rankin indicated that voting irregularities had cost
women the vote in several states and that recourse to a federal amendment

was the best solution.[23]

Carrie Chapman Catt, who organized the pro-suffrage witnesses, obtained, in addition to Representative Rankin, a galaxy of Senatorial stars, including Hiram Johnson of California, Reed Smoot of Utah, and Thomas J. Walsh of Montana. The goal of most of the speakers was to answer the objections raised against woman suffrage. Senator Walsh testified to the constitutionality of a federal suffrage amendment. After a week's recess, the hearing resumed with representatives from the National Woman's Party, led by Anne Martin, Vice Chairman. Jeannette Rankin, along with Mary Beard and Dudley Field Malone, collector of the Port of New York, spoke in favor of suffrage as a war measure.[24] Rankin, concerned that labor standards might deteriorate during the war, urged the enfranchisement of women as an incentive to uphold and raise their industrial standards. She advised:

> The standards which we seek to protect and develop
> will rise in proportion to the amount of democracy
> we have in our institutions; in proportion to the
> amount of individual responsibility that is felt
> by the workers themselves.[25]

For Jeannette Rankin, the ballot would symbolize the establishment of this responsibility in women and would give to them a greater awareness of their involvement in social and political life.

Mrs. Arthur M. Dodge, President of the National Association Opposed to Woman Suffrage, apologized for having to take up Congressional time to

---

[23]U.S., Congress, Senate, Committee on Woman Suffrage, Woman Suffrage, Hearings, S. J. Resolution #2, 65th Congress, First Session, 1917, pp. 20-21.

[24]Inez Haynes Irwin, The Story of the Woman's Party (New York: Harcourt, Brace, & Co., 1921), p. 300.

[25]Ibid., p. 57.

argue the suffrage question. Her associates urged that the federal
amendment be laid aside until the war was over. Despite this opinion,
on September 15 the committee issued a favorable report on the suffrage
resolution to the Senate.

While suffrage sailed through the Senate committee, it ran into
difficult sledding in the House of Representatives, where the resolutions
were assigned to the Judiciary Committee. Besides having blocked suff-
rage in the past, the committee was now snowed under with war legislation.
To circumvent this possible obstruction, the Congressional Committee of
NAWSA decided to push for creation of a separate woman suffrage committee.
Representative John Raker introduced the enabling resolution after
Jeannette Rankin and other suffrage advocates had secured the approval of
Speaker Champ Clark. An internal committee, consisting of Representative
Rankin, and five others from Western states secured signatures of House
members to a petition supporting the Raker resolution. Upon seeing the
petition, the Rules Committee called for a hearing on May 18, 1917.

Jeannette Rankin addressed the House Rules hearing and urged the
creation of a woman suffrage committee. She believed it would have ample
time to investigate and evaluate the need for suffrage by a federal amendment. President Wilson on May 14 told E.W. Pou, chairman of the Rules
Committee, that he felt the establishment of a woman suffrage committee
would be "a very wise act of public policy, and...an act of fairness to
the best women who are engaged in the cause of woman suffrage."[26] On
June 6, the Rules Committee, by a close vote of six to five, adopted the

---

[26]Ray Stannard Baker, Woodrow Wilson: Life and Letters (New York:
Harper and Brothers, 1939), VII, p. 68.

resolution establishing a Committee on Woman Suffrage.[27]

After the conclusion of pending war legislation, the House debated the question. Representative Rankin again stressed the fact that the Judiciary Committee was too overburdened with other work to give sufficient consideration to woman suffrage. The resolution passed on September 24 by a vote of 180 to 107, with three answering present and 142 not voting.[28] Since it was so late in the term, the new committee did not organize until the second session began in December.

From the time of the introduction of suffrage resolutions in April of 1917 to the opening of the second session in December, several interesting things happened to give publicity to suffrage and to increase the possibility of its passage. The Congressional Union began to picket the White House with silent sentinels carrying banners which asked, "Mr. President, What Will You Do For Woman Suffrage?" and "How Long Must Women Wait for Liberty?" Unsure of how to handle the novelty, the police left them alone. That was, until the pacifists began to include the war in their slogans. When officials from the Russian Kerensky government came to visit Wilson, the signs read:

> President Wilson and Envoy Root are deceiving
> Russia. They say, "We are a democracy. Help
> us win a world war so that Democracies may sur-
> vive." We the women of America tell you that
> America is not a democracy. Twenty million
> women are denied the vote. President Wilson is

---

[27]U.S., Congress, House of Representatives, Committee on Rules, Creating a Committee on Woman Suffrage in the House of Representatives, Hearings, House Resolution 12, 65th Congress, First Session, May 18, 1917, pp. 5-6.

[28]U.S., Congress, House of Representatives, 65th Congress, First Session, September 24, 1917, Congressional Record, LV, pp. 7372-7373.

the chief opponent of their national enfranchisement.[29]

Violence greeted the appearance of these banners, and the police began
to make arrests.

At first, those arrested were dismissed without sentence. After
continued picketing and violence, the courts began imposing jail terms
from six weeks to six months. The demonstrators encompassed the whole
spectrum of feminine society, including professionals, working women,
wives of administration officials, and wealthy socialites of the area.
They served their jail sentences in the infamous Occuquan Workhouse
in nearby Virginia. In addition to brutal treatment, prison living
conditions were atrocious. To protest, the women went on a hunger strike
and became martyrs when they were forcibly fed.

Jeannette Rankin sympathized with the picketers and privately encouraged them. Not agreeing with all their tactics, she said to them,
"Go ahead, but you won't get it that way. But anything that is done for
suffrage helps."[30] Representative Rankin believed that sentiment for
suffrage was growing in Washington but not necessarily because of the
pickets. In a speech in New York, she surmized:

> The public in Washington does not confuse the
> pickets with the whole suffrage organization
> and they do not blame the mass of women...for
> the mistaken policies of the few.[31]

---

[29] Helena Independent, June 27, 1917.

[30] J. R. Interview, February 14, 1969, p. 6.

[31] New York Evening Sun, October 10, 1917; The Woman Citizen,
I (November 3, 1917), p. 436.

On one occasion Jeannette visited the Occuquan Prison with her secretary,
Belle Fligelman, and Senator McLain from Connecticut. They found the
suffragists, dressed in homely grey flannel gowns with braided hair, in
stark contrast to the prostitutes, who were gaudy with heavy cosmetics
and dressed in the latest styles. As publicity and public sentiment
mounted, President Wilson pardoned the women just before Congress re-
convened in December.

While the pickets and their subsequent treatment attracted publicity,
the women gained the vote in 1917 in North Dakota, Ohio, Indiana, Rhode
Island, Nebraska, Michigan, and Arkansas. The crucial referendum on which
all eyes were focused came in the fall in New York. Because of her vote
against the war, the central committee of the New York Woman Suffrage
Party rejected a resolution inviting Jeannette Rankin to make addresses
in the state. Although not wanted by some members of the state organization, local groups of women invited her to speak. She spoke in Brooklyn
in late September and visited state headquarters in early October to help
paste the signatures of one million women in New York who wanted the vote
onto boards for a suffrage parade.[32] Fearing it was too dangerous to
alienate potential women voters, Tammany Hall did not oppose the suffrage
amendment. It carried by a margin of more than 100,000 votes.[33] In
addition to securing the ballot in these states, it also meant that their
representatives in Congress would now support suffrage legislation. These
were strategic victories for women.

Another factor that may have influenced pro-suffrage sentiment was

---

[32]New York Times, August 31, 1917; Buffalo News, September 24, 1917;
New York Tribune, October 7, 1917.

[33]New York Times, November 7, 1917.

the sacrificial way in which women assumed responsibility in a nation at war. As Germany announced resumption of unrestricted submarine warfare on January 31, many women's groups came to the aid of Wilson. The National Council of Women, representing twenty-seven women's organizations (of which NAWSA was a part), encouraged women to enroll in factories and industries.[34] The Atlanta Business Peoples' Suffrage Association adopted a resolution which read: "In the event of an emergency [we will] work in the mills, factories, offices and on the farms and, if need be, enlist for the war."[35] Anna H. Shaw, honorary president of NAWSA, was chosen by the Council on National Defense to head a committee of eight women to organize women's defense work.[36] By March of 1919, The Woman Citizen reported that everyone in NAWSA from the honorary president to the last director had some job in the war effort.[37]

Yet, there were those who disagreed. When Carrie Chapman Catt pledged the support of NAWSA in case of war, many pacifist suffragists were outraged. For this reason, the Women's Peace Party dropped her from its membership.[38] At the same time, a group of New York pacifists, led by Elizabeth Freeman of the Emergency Peace Federation, rebuked Mrs. Norman de R. Whitehouse for offering New York Governor Charles S. Whitman the services of 500,000 suffragists in case of war.[39]

[34]Washington Star, April 4, 1917.

[35]Atlanta Constitution, April 6, 1917.

[36]Helena Independent, May 5, 1917

[37]"A Report to Make the Bones Fat," The Woman Citizen, III (March 29, 1919), pp. 926-927.

[38]New York Sun, April 1, 1917.

[39]New York Times, February 9, 1917.

Why were women so anxious to support Wilson's program? Jeannette
Rankin and others believed the answer lay in what had happened in the
fall of 1916. Rankin was campaigning in Montana and could not attend
the NAWSA convention in Atlantic City. Her friends returned from the
meeting and reported that Carrie Chapman Catt had sold out to Wilson
and in case of war would support the administration in return for his
aid in securing a federal amendment for woman suffrage.[40] Catt had
earlier visited Wilson in August and later told reporters that she had
gone over plans for the suffrage campaign and that "the President is
weakening in his opposition to the federal amendment."[41] It was interesting that Wilson, who advocated the "state" method, was invited to
address the convention rather than Charles E. Hughes, who supported
federal enfranchisement.

President Woodrow Wilson addressed the national convention of NAWSA
in mid September, 1916. He told the 4,000 cheering women, who had been
trying to gain his favor: "I have come here to fight with you," and
predicted a triumph for the cause of woman suffrage. The President did
not mention how this was to be accomplished, nor did he mention his previously expressed belief that suffrage should come through state legislatures.[42] In view of wanting to do nothing to hurt suffrage nor to
damage relations with Wilson, the convention adopted a nonpartisan
resolution pertaining to the national candidates.[43] When the

---

[40]J. R. Interview, January 26, 1969, p. 6.

[41]Helena Independent, August 2, 1917.

[42]Helena Independent, September 9, 1916, p. 1; The Woman's Journal,
XLVII (February 5, 1916), p. 47.

[43]Helena Independent, September 9, 1916, p. 7.

Congressional Union later picketed the White House saying Wilson was the chief opponent of national enfranchisement, NAWSA denied the truth of these statements and said, "He has done more [for suffrage] than all the other Presidents put together."[44]

With the convening of Congress in December, the House established the Woman Suffrage Committee. Ten members, including Jeannette Rankin, were pro-suffrage; and three were opposed. There was some movement to make Rankin chairman, but Representative Joseph Walsh from Massachusetts, an ardent anti-suffragist, led the fight against her in the Republican caucus. Actually, Jeannette did not want to be chairman because "I thought we might lose a vote." The caucus then endorsed her only as the leading Republican member.[45] Judge John E. Raker, Democrat of California and pro-suffragist, received the appointment.

In the meantime, the Judiciary Committee reported "without recommendation" a suffrage resolution. It was unacceptable to the women because the Committee limited to seven years the time in which state legislatures could ratify it. A Minority Report from the Judiciary Committee contained the views of Jeannette Rankin. She advocated passage because "suffrage for women was fundamentally just." Since woman, as an individual, had attained her legal and industrial status, it was now indeed logical to recognize her as a political entity. Jeannette pointed out that woman suffrage was inevitable because twelve states, including New York, had already passed it. She called for the federal amendment to alleviate the

[44]Helena Independent, June 27, 1917, p. 4.

[45]New York Times, December 13, 1917; Ethel M. Smith to Maude W. Park, October 3, 1917, Maude Wood Park Files, Women's Rights Collection, Schlesinger Library; J. R. Interview, January 30, 1969, p. 5.

situation where part of the states were ruled by the "voice of all the
people; and the rest ruled by an autocracy of sex." To her, the time
had come for women's groups to turn from educational propaganda to political action and to induce the few in power to grant the demands of the
many. Jeannette, hoping to gain support from the "war hawks," reminded
the House that passage of a federal amendment would divert to war service
all the time, energy, and money normally spent in state campaigning.
Finally, Rankin opposed the Majority Report which fixed a limit to the
length of time for ratification.[46]

While Congressmen were discussing federal suffrage in the Capitol,
so were the women who gathered in Poli's Theater for the 1917 annual convention of NAWSA. Suffragists, elated over the vote in New York, were
now hopeful that total victory was in sight. Jeannette Rankin, already
looking beyond enfranchisement to full civil rights, spoke to the delegates about the unfairness of imposing upon women the citizenship of
their alien husbands and indicated that she had recently introduced in
Congress a bill to adjust that discrimination.[47] In writing for the New
York American about the convention's threat to enter political campaigns
unless suffrage passed, Rankin told about a Negro woman in Washington
who said, "When a woman sets out to do a thing, she is the most conquering
thing there is." Jeannette insinuated that was fair warning to the anti-
suffrage Congressmen.[48] The women backed their threats by pledging, if

---

[46]U.S., Congress, House of Representatives, 65th Congress, Second
Session, The Judiciary Committee, Minority Report on H. J. 3, Woman
Suffrage by Federal Amendment.

[47]NAWSA, Handbook and Proceedings of the 49th Annual Convention,
Washington, D.C., December 12-15, 1917, p. 521.

[48]New York American, December 16, 1917.

needed, more than $100,000 for the campaign. While in Washington, Carrie Chapman Catt urged the delegates to visit their Congressmen and to secure their votes for suffrage.

With the fury of women turned loose, the Committee on Woman Suffrage announced hearings for January 3-7, 1918. The National Woman's Party, NAWSA, and National Association Opposed to Woman Suffrage presented their arguments.[49] When the Committee favorably reported the woman suffrage resolution, Washington saw a new flurry of activity. Democratic cabinet members McAdoo, Daniels, and Baker quickly endorsed the resolution; but President Wilson remained silent. Suffragists knew all along that he would not mention it in his message to the new Congress. But, they understood from an administration "mouthpiece" that he would work for the suffrage resolution. On January 9, the opponents of suffrage claimed a safe margin despite intimations from the suffragists that a trump card was yet to be played. When Democratic leaders went to the White House on the eve of the vote to seek Wilson's advice, they reported that he counseled "us to vote for the amendment as an act of right and justice to the women of the country and the world." Was that trump card Wilson's support? If so, Rankin and her friends may have been right in thinking that an agreement had been worked out with the President.[50]

While the Democrats were scurrying around, Theodore Roosevelt urged support from the National Republican Committee. Chairman William R. Willcox then went to Washington to line up congressional support. Along

---

[49]U.S., Congress, House of Representatives, Committee on Woman Suffrage, Extending the Right of Suffrage to Women, Hearings, on H. J. Resolution 200, 65th Congress, Second Session, 1918.

[50]Ida Harper, HWS, VI, p. 636; Helena Independent, January 6 and 10, 1917; J. R. Interview, January 26, 1969, p. 6.

with the action of political parties, hundreds of women descended on the
offices of their Representatives. Senators urged their colleagues to give
women the ballot; congressional secretaries compared notes as to how certain representatives would vote; and pages anxiously awaited the outcome.
One elderly gentleman stopped Representative Rankin in the hall and said,
"It's coming," as if it were a plague. On the day before the vote,
Jeannette Rankin surmised, "Everyone is ready for the question. The
woman's hour has struck."[51]

Shortly after noon on January 10, Joe Walsh of Massachusetts requested that Chairman Raker permit the woman from Montana to speak first.
Walsh had been Jeannette Rankin's greatest adversary in the House until
she won him over by speaking very highly in his district of his honesty
in procedural affairs on the floor.[52] With a flair of progressive
philosophy in her speech, Representative Rankin decried America's waste
of natural and human resources in time of war. "Something was still
lacking," she said, "in the national effort." She suggested the difficulties lay in the fact that men traditionally thought in terms of commercial
profit and found it hard to adjust to thinking in terms of human needs. To
the House of Representatives, Jeannette queried, "Is it not possible that
the women of the country have something of value to give the nation at this
time?"

Rankin continued by enumerating the ways in which women, even before
they got the vote, tried to serve the national welfare. They learned to
read and write, listened to each other's problems, became a stabilizing
influence in the home, and stood back of their pioneering men. While

---

[51]New York American, January 10, 1918.

[52]J. R. Interview, January 26, 1969, p. 10; January 30, 1969, p. 5.

doing all that they were allowed to do, the women desired the political
machinery which would enable them to do even more. She felt that their
participation was especially important in the war effort.

Realizing that suffrage needed Southern support, Jeannette addressed that problem. She asked, "Are you gentlemen...going to retaliate
after fifty years for the injustice you believe was done you so long ago?"
She hoped that they had learned through the struggle for adjustment how
to be broad and open-minded in dealing with another franchise problem.
Jeannette reminded the Southerners how their women had stood by them in
every trial and now wanted only the vote to help them more effectively.
To allay fears of the number of Negro women who might vote, she pointed out,
"There are more white women of voting age in the South today than there
are Negro men and women together." Having chided the Southerners, she
insisted that the real concerns of the time ought to be national rather
than regional.

Representative Rankin pointed out that this nationalizing process
was already at work. President Wilson had taken over the railroads and
was presently concerned with food and fuel supplies. She emphasized,
"Americans must think as a nation and not as separate states." This gave
her the opportunity to say that the country did not declare war nor
mobilize troops state by state but through Congress. "That same action,"
she encouraged, "should be used for women who are struggling for democracy."

The final theme in Jeannette Rankin's speech centered around the
idea of democracy. Capitalizing on President Wilson's distinction between
the German people and the German government, she questioned, "May [others]
not see a distinction between the Government of the United States and
the women of the United States...when we deny the first steps in democracy

to our women?" With a ringing crescendo, she challenged her fellow
Representatives, "How can we explain the meaning of democracy if the
same Congress that voted a war to make the world safe for democracy re-
fuses to give this small measure of democracy to the women of our country?"[53]

Before debate on the suffrage resolution opened, Jeannette Rankin
went to Joe Walsh, a very effective and persuasive speaker, and asked him
not to make a speech against suffrage. Knowing his staunch feeling, Rankin
would not ask him to vote for it, but just not to use his influence in the
negative. She was successful. He did not make a speech.[54] The debate
continued until five o'clock when amendments were offered. After they
were defeated, the voting began. The suffrage resolution won by a frac-
tion less than one vote (274-136) over the necessary two-thirds.

This accomplishment was the result of devotion and loyalty on the
part of several men. Thetus Sims of Tennessee (D), Robert Crosser of
Ohio (D), Henry Barnhart of Indiana (D), and Republican House Leader
James Mann of Illinois came from sick beds, while Frederick Hicks of
New York (R) returned to cast his affirmative vote while his wife lay
a corpse. Jeannette Rankin described their arrival:

> [When they came in] the House stood up and
> applauded and applauded. Tears ran down
> everybody's face and mine. I didn't wipe
> them because I didn't think they could
> see them from the gallery. We carried
> by one vote. [55]

In the recapulation, Representative Walsh, who had voted against suffrage,

---

[53]J. R. Speech in J. R. MSS; U.S., Congress, House of Representatives,
65th Congress, Second Session, January 10, 1918, Congressional Record,
LVI, p. 771.

[54]J. R. Interview, January 26, 1969, p. 10.

[55]J. R. Interview, January 26, 1969, p. 11.

watched the count and said to wavering candidates, "If you change your vote, I will change mine."[56] Jeannette credited his action with saving the vote for suffrage. When the clerk announced the final tabulation of 274 to 136, women's voices spontaneously sang out the verses of "Old Hundred"; and the familiar hymn echoed throughout the capitol. As a momento, Doorkeeper J. J. Sinnot later presented Rankin with the flag that flew over the House during the debate.[57]

After the House victory, Jeannette Rankin claimed credit for Republican leadership. She released the following statement:

> It has been to Republican legislatures and Republican leadership that women (apart from their own undaunted efforts) chiefly owe their enfranchisement in the suffrage states. Mr. Hughes more than a year ago, and Mr. Roosevelt even before, declared for the federal amendment. We look to Republican Senators to go on with the work. We are grateful to Mr. Mann's vote as we have been for his presence and his support.[58]

Representative Rankin was estatic about the removal of the political obstacle which had blocked the path of women for seventy years. She was so happy that she proclaimed January 10 as "Independence Day for the Women of America."[59] Yet, in reality, that day was nearly two and one-half years away.

When the Senate of the 65th Congress failed to pass the measure, it meant another year's delay. With the convening of the 66th Congress in special session, suffrage was revived. It overwhelmingly passed the house

---

[56]Ibid.

[57]Woman Citizen, II (February 9, 1918), p. 212.

[58]Handwritten release in J. R. MSS.

[59]New York American, January 11, 1918.

in May and the Senate in June of 1919. Tennessee became the thirty-sixth
state to ratify the amendment, and Secretary of State, Bainbridge Colby
declared it a part of the federal constitution on August 26, 1920.

While Representative Rankin struggled with Congressional duties in
the summer of 1917, labor difficulties broke out in Montana. Always
sensitive to the needs of human beings, she wanted to help. During her
campaigns for suffrage and for Congress, Jeannette Rankin established
herself as a friend of the common people. She could speak their language,
listen to their problems, and, most important, offer some hope. Her
speeches were not empty phrases, but expressed real concern for the
well-being of men, women, and children at work. She urged the adoption
of the eight-hour day to decrease danger from diseases contracted through
weakened resistance, to lessen industrial accidents caused by fatigue,
and to provide leisure time for creative enjoyment and educational opportunities.[60]

Not only did she advocate an eight-hour day but also sufficient pay
so that the laborer would not have to work overtime to make a decent living.
She believed the American working man was "entitled to eat his dinner at
home and to enjoy his family." Jeannette Rankin felt the Constitution
guaranteed him enjoyment of life, liberty, and the pursuit of happiness;
and only adequate wages could accomplish these goals.[61]

With the coming of the war, Jeannette Rankin became a one-member
team to see that labor and industrial standards did not deteriorate.
She wrote:

> The misguided patriots who urge the breaking

---

[60] Chicago Sunday Herald, March 25, 1917.

[61] Chicago Sunday Herald, August 12, 1917.

> down of all our standards at this time apparently
> understand the laws of psychology as little as
> they understand the laws of human conservation.[62]

Thus, when women and men began to write to her about the labor problems
between miners and owners in Butte, Rankin conscientiously hoped to
alleviate the unwarranted conditions. The dominate labor union among the
men had been the Western Federation of Miners until about 1914. Gradually after the turn of the century, it was infiltrated by representatives
of the Industrial Workers of the World, a radical socialist group believing in sabotage and the general strike, and detectives of the Anaconda
Copper Company, the largest of the mining operators. These individuals
split the WFM into radical and conservative factions. The conservative
group, dominated if not controlled by the company, gained power and
cooperated with the mine owners. As early as 1912, the Anaconda Company
began using a rustling card for employment. Theoretically, it was an
innocuous device, but radical miners knew the rustling card certified
approval of management and prevented them from securing a job.[63]

In June of 1917 an explosion, killing 164 men, rocked the Spectator
mine. Seething with indignation over safety conditions, Butte miners,
led by Tom Campbell and Joe Shannon, organized the Metal Mine Workers'
Union and promptly walked off their jobs. They demanded better working
conditions, a six dollar minimum daily wage and abolition of the rustling
card.[64] On June 20, the MMWU asked Jeannette Rankin to influence Secretary of Labor, W. B. Wilson to initiate a federal investigation.[65] The

---

[62]Chicago Sunday Herald, July 22, 1917.

[63]Melvyn Dubofsky, We Shall Be All: A History of the Industrial
Workers of the World (Chicago: Quadrangle Books, 1969), pp. 301-303.

[64]Ibid., p. 367.

[65]Helena Independent, June 21, 1917.

investigator, who went to the area, reported a need for "conciliation" rather than "investigation."[66] As tension grew tighter, the MMWU requested that Representative Rankin come to Butte herself. Getting only the "runaround" from Bernard Baruch, Chairman of the War Industries Board, W. B. Wilson, Secretary of Labor, and President Wilson, she decided to intervene directly.[67]

John D. Ryan, President of Anaconda, did not respond to Representative Rankin's telegram suggesting that they discuss the issues. In the meantime, the MMWU wired that the situation in Butte had become extremely dangerous. Before she could introduce appropriate legislation, Frank Little, a member of the IWW who came to Butte to agitate, was hanged by six masked men on August 1, 1917. Believing that these difficulties were hindering the production of copper for war materials and that the miners were being treated unfairly, Jeannette Rankin introduced a resolution into Congress. It gave the President power "to take over and operate the metalliferous mines for the common defense of the nation."[68]

In her speech, she exposed the grievances of the miners, including unsafe mining conditions and the rustling system and laid the responsibility at the feet of John D. Ryan. Not only was she concerned about labor standards, but she released news that the companies had discontinued sale of copper to the government pending a hoped-for raise in price by the Committee on War Purchases.[69] This resolution and subsequent speech placed Jeannette

---

[66]Telegram from W. B. Wilson to J. R., July 30, 1918, in J. R. MSS.

[67]J. R. Interview, June 25, 1969, p. 4.

[68]U.S., Congress, House of Representatives, 65th Congress, First Session, August 7, 1917, Congressional Record, LV, Part 6, p. 5896.

[69]Ibid., pp. 5896-5897; newspaper clipping of Rankin speaking before the House, J. R. files at Swarthmore College Peace Collection.

Rankin in the uncomfortable position of mediating between the Anaconda
Copper Company, whom she feared as a political foe, and the IWW, whose
methods of sabotage and violence she abhorred.

Later in August, Congressman Rankin made a trip to Montana to attempt
mediation. Because of her speech on the House floor, Anaconda officials
in Butte found her unacceptable as a mediator and refused to confer.[70]
When she arrived in Butte, five thousand miners, townspeople, and women
met her train. The police, expecting violence, separated Jeannette from
Wellington who had boarded the train in Eastern Montana, forced her into
a waiting car and took her to a hotel. The local paper indicated she was
escorted, but Jeannette thought she was "kidnapped" to keep her away from
the people.[71] This thwarted a proposed parade and demonstration. Unable
to effect a reconciliation, Rankin addressed the miners on August 18 at
Columbia Gardens just outside the city.

For an hour, Jeannette Rankin stood before a crowd of fifteen thousand,
who jammed the baseball park to the outfield fence, and told the results
of her investigations. She denounced the murder of Frank Little, con-
demned the rustling card, pleaded with the IWW not to injure the nation's
wheat crop, and predicted that, if the strike interferred with the supply
of copper for manufacture of munitions, the government would take control
of the mines. The thousands of miners yelled their approval and frequently interrupted her with applause. Jeannette Rankin was their heroine.[72]

---

[70]Telegram from Cornelius Kelley to J. R., August 11, 1917, in J. R.
MSS.

[71]Belle Fligelman Winestein Interview, September 9, 1970, p. 2;
Charles Merz, "The Issue in Butte," The New Republic (September 22, 1917),
pp. 215-217.

[72]"Jeannette Rankin, Friend of Miners, Flay Owners," newspaper clipping with no name in J. R. MSS.

Speaking from a platform containing Tom Campbell, MMWU representative, James Larkin, IWW Chief, and Judge J. J. Lynch of the district bench, Representative Rankin made no effort to hide her opinions. She was outspoken and direct. Pulling no punches, she continued;

> I have no patience with that spirit which seeks to destroy property to satisfy personal grievances, or in the thought that direct action can right existing wrongs.... It is misguided patriotism which believes that direct action has a place in civilized society.[73]

She had no regard for Frank Little's alleged utterances but, on the other hand, greater contempt for the action which permitted his murder. Characteristic of Rankin, she said that it made no difference who Frank Little was. To her, it was not a question of whom they hanged; it was a matter of lawlessness.[74]

As to her stand on the relationship of capital and labor, she continued:

> It is unpatriotic for labor to strike without just cause, especially in time of war. But it is equally unpatriotic for capital to take advantage of men whose patriotism causes them to continue to work under conditions which mean the daily unnecessary risk of their lives.[75]

In this specific Montana struggle, Representative Rankin believed the demands of labor were just, the rustling card reprehensible, and their wages too low.[76] She concluded her speech by telling the miners, "I pledge

---

[73]Interview with Ida Craft, who quoted from clippings about the Butte question, in the Brooklyn Eagle, September 9, 1917.

[74]U.S., Congress, House of Representatives, 65th Congress, First Session, August 7, 1917, Congressional Record, LV, Part 6, p. 5896; Helena Independent, August 19, 1917.

[75]Chicago Sunday Herald, September 23, 1917; Brooklyn Eagle, September 9, 1917.

[76]Chicago Sunday Herald, September 23, 1917.

you my word that I shall always do my utmost to bring about better conditions"; and then she urged them to "strive to bring about a peaceful
solution to existing troubles" because the country is at war.[77]

Despite continued efforts on Jeannette's part to get a federal
investigation, nothing was ever accomplished. The miners finally returned to work in December with their rustling cards. While the miners continued to face the hazards of working conditions, Jeannette Rankin reaped
the whirlwind of attacks as an IWW sympathizer. Unlike most Congressmen
in Washington, she worked for all her constituents, not just to be re-
elected. She was a friend of the working man, independent in action, and
sympathetic but not emotional.

This association with the IWW became only one of several difficulties
to plague Rankin's re-election in 1918. Realizing the tremendous advantage
that the election of two "Congressmen at large" gave to a woman candidate,
the Montana legislature in 1918 divided the state into an Eastern and a
Western district. As applied to her situation, Jeannette Rankin felt she
had been "gerrymandered" into a strongly Democratic district as a deliberate move to defeat her.[78]

In February of 1918, W. W. McDowell, Lieutenant Governor, surveyed
the political situation for Thomas J. Walsh, the incumbent Democratic
Senator. With the new districts, he believed Jeannette Rankin could not
defeat Democratic Representative Evans in the Western district even if she
obtained the Republican nomination. Because of this, McDowell indicated
that, since she had reached such national prominence, he expected her to
announce for the Senate. With words of assurance, he confidently told

_____

[77]Brooklyn Eagle, September 9, 1917.

[78]Louis Levine, "Politics in Montana," The Nation, CVII (November
2, 1918), p. 507.

Senator Walsh that he had nothing to fear.[79] Rankin supporters also came to similar conclusions and were disheartened. Through political spies, the Democrats learned that Wellington himself was worried as to his sister's political future.[80]

In addition to the political liabilities incurred by her vote against war, and support of the miners in the labor dispute at Butte, Jeannette Rankin aroused further opposition by introducing into Congress a resolution for Irish freedom. It proposed:

> ...That this government [The United States] recog-
> nize the right of Ireland to political independence
> and that we count Ireland among those countries
> for whose freedom and democracy we are fighting.[81]

Although many of her Irish constituents petitioned her for this resolution, Jeannette's stated motives were "to preserve democracy in all cases of peoples held in subjection."[82] She regretted that the government had not taken a stand. Irish Montanians were pleased with their Representative's action, but others saw it as an instrument of the Sinn Feiners, a strongly anti-British Irish nationalist group led by Eamonn de Valera. Many Americans considered the Sinn Feiners, who were doing everything they could to hinder the English war effort, to be pro-German and anti-American.[83]

The Helena Independent, in attacking Jeannette's resolution, quoted the German newspaper, Koelnische Zeitung, which had commended the efforts

---

[79]Letter of W. W. McDowell to T. J. Walsh, February 27, 1918, Box 177, T. J. Walsh MSS, Library of Congress.

[80]Letter of Will Campbell to T. J. Walsh, June 30, 1918, Box 177, T. J. Walsh MSS.

[81]Copy of H. J. Resolution #204, 65th Congress, Second Session, January 4, 1918, in J. R. MSS.

[82]J. R. to George Dougherty, July 24, 1917, in J. R. MSS.

[83]Helena Independent, January 6, 1918; New York Times, January 6, 1918.

of German-Americans, Irishmen, and Socialists who were obstructing
America's war preparations. The German editorial named Senator Robert
La Follette of Wisconsin as the leader of this movement in the Congress.
The editorial of the Helena Independent thus concluded that Jeannette
Rankin was "rapidly earning the title of the 'female La Follette'."[84]

Consistent with her pacifist stance, Jeannette was reluctant to speak
in behalf of the Liberty Bonds. By the time she did make a swing around
Montana in early spring of 1918, she encountered bitter opposition.
Montana's Liberty Loan Committee avoided her, and the Republican Party
definitely showed no enthusiasm in her representing them across the state.[85]
In many places, she had difficulty securing a meeting hall. Yet, she
"urged her hearers to buy Liberty Bonds and to do all in their power to
help the country in its prosecution of the war."[86] Having been criticized
severely for not backing the bonds, when Rankin did come to speak for them,
the newspapers attacked her visit as hypocritical. They insisted that she
was needed more in Washington to support the wheat legislation. At the
mercy of the Anaconda Company and Democratic newspapers, she could not
seem to win for losing.[87]

The decision to offer for re-election was a long and painful struggle.
Montana newspapers began to insist on her defeat as early as February of
1918; and, indeed, it seemed her chances for victory were minimal. In a
letter to Wellington, she wrote, "I do not want my family and friends to
make the necessary sacrifices unless they feel that there is a chance for

[84]Helena Independent, January 17, 1918.

[85]Helena Independent, April 27, 1918.

[86]Helena Independent, April 18, 1918.

[87]Helena Independent, April 29, 1918.

success."[88] With absolutely no opportunity to win in the House contest,
Jeannette Rankin announced officially for the Senate on July 16, 1918.

Wellington helped to formulate her platform which included the
promise:

> If I am nominated and elected I will...support
> the President in the vigorous prosecution of
> the war to a victorious conclusion and...will
> vote for every measure he may recommend to more
> efficiently prosecute the war.[89]

The peace movement generally shared her position and campaign slogan,
"Win the War First." The remainder of her political statement seemed to
implement this promise. She advocated legislation to prevent profiteering and thus protect the consumer, to secure adequate compensation for
farmers' products, to give the administration power to fix food prices, to
secure national equal suffrage, to prohibit the consumption of grain for
manufacture of liquor, and to establish national prohibition.[90]

With this announcement, Jeannette Rankin began an arduous six-week
campaign for the Republican nomination for the Senate. She received
support from labor, especially the Butte miners, and the farmers, who
were led by A. C. Townley's Non-Partisan League. In the spring of 1918,
the Non-Partisan League sent Charles E. Taylor to launch the Producers
News in Plentywood and to wage Montana's first League campaign.[91] North

---

[88]Helena Independent, February 1, 1918; J. R. to Wellington Rankin,
N. D., but postmarked March 3, 1918, in J. R. MSS.

[89]1918 Election Campaign Pamphlet in J. R. MSS; Telegram of
Wellington Rankin to J. R., July 5, 1918, which proposed ideas similar
to those eventually adopted.

[90]Ibid.; Helena Independent, July 17, 1918.

[91]Charles Vindex, "Radical Rule in Montana," Montana, XVIII (January,
1968), p. 50.

Dakota farmers organized the League in 1916 to promote progressive legislation for state banks; state-owned terminal elevators, flour mills, and packing plants; a rural credits system operated at cost; and state hail insurance on crops.[92] Because of these socialistic trends, the League became quite suspect in Montana.

The Non-Partisan League was not new to Jeannette Rankin, as she had addressed a convention at St. Paul, Minnesota, in September of 1917.[93] She found their basic goals to be valid and welcomed their support. During the campaign, Jeannette, along with Senator Lynn Frazier of North Dakota, spoke to many "Non-Partisan League Picnics"; and the newspapers thus labeled her as a friend and co-worker with the so-called "unpatriotic and disloyal" Townley.[94] Her response was, "The man we can point to as unpatriotic is the man who comes out of the war with a bigger bank account than when he entered it."[95]

In conjunction with the labor and farm blocs, Jeannette Rankin hoped to attract the women's vote. Her platform contained planks of interest to women on prohibition, suffrage, and consumer protection. While in Washington, she regularly sent materials on baby care to mothers and, during the campaign, emphasized that her record in Congress had shown a concern for women and children. To strengthen her position with working women, Rankin distributed a letter of appreciation from the women in the

---

[92]H. C. Peterson and Gilbert Fite, Opponents of War (Madison: University of Wisconsin Press, 1957), p. 64.

[93]MS of speech delivered at Non-Partisan convention in St. Paul, Minnesota, September 20, 1917, in J. R. MSS.

[94]Helena Independent, January 4, 1918; July 14, 1918; July 24, 1918.

[95]Helena Independent, July 15, 1918. This was a theme which she later developed in the 1930's.

Bureau of Printing and Engraving.[96]

Some women, divided in their feelings, were favorable to Jeannette's social work and suffrage, but not her politics. One women said, "It is hard to know her personally and not feel a very real affection for her, but since she has entered politics, we feel that she has been the narrowest of politicians and as a congressman a colossal failure."[97]

While Congressman Rankin attempted to gather the support of labor, farmers, and the women, Montana newspapers attacked her constantly. Immediately after her vote against war, there was little discussion. As patriotism began to boil, many Montanians, forgetting that once they had been against intervention, criticized her decision. With her attack on the Anaconda Company, the level of newspaper opposition mounted steadily as the company controlled many of the presses. Rankin's proposal for government ownership of newspapers did not win her any bouquets from publishers. Her idea was for each town to have a free paper owned by the people.[98] The most vehement in their opposition to Jeannette Rankin were the Helena Independent, the Anaconda Standard, and the Butte Miner. On the other hand, only the Havre Daily Promoter, owned by Wellington Rankin, and the Butte Daily Bulletin, published by radical labor, supported her.[99]

Aided by charismatic personality, dynamic energy, and courage that knew no fear, Rankin almost won the Republican Senatorial nomination.

---

[96]Helena Independent, July 5, 1918; Mimeo letter to Montana Mothers in J. R. MSS, June 1, 1917; Annabel M. Rooney to Thomas J. Walsh, August 7, 1918, in T. J. Walsh MSS.

[97]Letter of Annabel M. Rooney to Thomas J. Walsh, August 7, 1918, in T. J. Walsh MSS.

[98]Helena Independent, August 8, 1918.

[99]Louis Levine, "Politics in Montana," The Nation, CVII (November 2, 1918), p. 507.

Campaigning against all odds, she lost to Dr. Oscar M. Lanstrum by a slim vote margin of 17,091 (37.7%) to 18,805 (41.5%).[100]

Immediately after the narrow and bitter defeat, rumors began to spread that Jeannette Rankin would run as an independent on the National Party ticket. One of the stories circulating around Helena political circles indicated that O. M. Harvey, member of the Republican State Central Committee, on the day after the election held a conference with Wellington Rankin. He urged the attorney to persuade his sister, Jeannette, to run on an independent ticket. According to Democratic supporters, Rankin's candidacy would take away from Walsh the votes of the miners, Non-Partisan League farmers, and other radicals that he would get if Jeannette were not in the race.[101] Colonel C. B. Nolan in a letter to his former law partner, Senator Walsh, wrote that "her running would be disastrous to you.... Every influence possible should be brought to bear upon Wellington not to have her run."[102]

Democratic political henchmen tried to get Walsh to offer Jeannette a position with the government, preferably overseas, as a bribe to get out of the race. In writing to Senator Walsh, A. E. Spriggs, who, as a Democrat would have normally been degrading Rankin, insisted:

> To our mind she is entitled to something excep-
> tionally good along this line as she has endeavor-
> ed to serve the country loyally and comprehensive-
> ly during the past year.[103]

---

[100]Ellis Waldron, An Atlas of Montana Politics, p. 167.

[101]Helena Independent, August 31, 1918; Letter of Josephine Spriggs to T. J. Walsh, August 30, 1918, in T. J. Walsh MSS.

[102]Letter of C. B. Nolan to T. J. Walsh, August 30, 1918, in T. J. Walsh MSS.

[103]Letter of A. E. Spriggs, September 2, 1918, to T. J. Walsh, in T. J. Walsh MSS.

Even though he was anxious to defeat Lanstrum, Wellington would not participate in anything to his sister's disadvantage.[104] With the rumor of
bribes on both sides, Wellington suggested to Jeannette that she would
have to run to prove she did not take any.[105]

In the middle of September, O. H. P. ("One Horse Power") Shelly, head
of the Montana branch of the National Party announced Rankin's candidacy.
John Spargo had formed the National Party as a new organization of pro-war
socialists, prohibitionists, progressives, and farmers of the Northwest.[106]
Democrats still believed they had been beaten by the Republicans "who had
outbid us at every turn," and that Jeannette got "quite a sum of money
for running, presumably to pay her expenses."[107] Congressman Rankin campaigned only half-heartedly because she realized it was hopeless.

With Jeannette Rankin in the race, the Democrats ran an uneasy
campaign. Walsh's supporters finally induced him to ask for Burton K.
Wheeler's resignation. Wheeler, as District Attorney, was a liberal and
had been accused of being soft on radicals. This resignation now enabled
the conservatives to support Walsh's re-election vigorously. R. R. Purcell,
Mayor of Helena, urged Walsh "to arrange with John D. Ryan to have the
company quietly get in line because you have a hard fight on your hand with
Jeannette Rankin in the field."[108]

---

[104]Letter of C. B. Nolan to T. J. Walsh, September 2, 1918, in T. J.
Walsh MSS.

[105]J. R. Interview, January 27, 1969, p. 4.

[106]Helena Independent, September 20, 1918; New York Sun, September
20, 1918.

[107]Letter of C. B. Nolan to T. J. Walsh, September 14, 1918, in T. J.
Walsh MSS; Wellington Napton to T. J. Walsh, September 29, 1918, T. J.
Walsh MSS.

[108]Letter of R. R. Purcell to T. J. Walsh, October 2, 1918, in T. J.
Walsh MSS.

Since Frances Willard, National President of Women's Christian
Temperance Union, wrote a personal letter in behalf of Jeannette, Walsh
countered with an endorsement by Carrie Chapman Catt, President of NAWSA.
Catt expressed appreciation for his "continued and invaluable aid to
federal suffrage."[109] Exclusive of paid advertisements, the newspapers
generally avoided mention of Rankin's candidacy and regarded Lanstrum
and Walsh as the major contenders. An exception was an editorial in the
Butte Daily Bulletin. In comparing Jeannette Rankin and the other candidates, it noted:

> Walsh bowed to the wishes of Anaconda and appointed
> a company politician as District Attorney. With a
> steadfast courage...she has spoken for the lowly
> and the oppressed with no possibility of reward....
> She is stronger than the servile Lanstrum...and
> brave enough to risk her political fortunes for
> what she believes is right.[110]

Campaigning against great odds and an influenze epidemic, Jeannette ran
third behind Walsh and Lanstrum respectively.[111]

Jeannette Rankin's term in Congress reflected her "progressive"
spirit and "pacific" nature. True to the goals set for herself in
Congress, she had promoted suffrage legislation and other reform measures
benefiting women and children. It was unfortunate for her political
hopes that her negative war vote received so much criticism; but, in
writing about it twenty years later, she still said, "I would do it over
again."[112] This "vote against war" endeared her to the peace movement

---

[109]Letter of T. J. Walsh to Mrs. Tyler B. Thompson, October 14, 1918,
in T. J. Walsh MSS; Helena Independent, October 24, 1918.

[110]Butte Daily Bulletin, October 24, 1918.

[111]Ellis Waldron, An Atlas of Montana Politics, p. 168.

[112]Washington Daily News, April 6, 1937.

and opened new doors of service to her country. It was to these opportunities that she disciplined the next twenty years of her life.

CHAPTER VII

THE SEARCH

The years following the armistice of 1918 received various titles;
but "The Search for Peace," used by Robert H. Ferrell, seemed most descriptive of the era in which Jeannette Rankin began her professional
peace career.[1] World War I almost succeeded in destroying the peace
movement; yet, its conclusion and subsequent treaty revived interest and
enthusiasm within peace circles. In the United States peace societies
dated back to a New York group organized in 1815.[2] A little later, the
American Peace Society, founded by William Ladd in 1828, became the first
"national" peace organization.[3] Even prior to the outbreak of war in
Europe, peace groups were still being organized in the United States.

In 1910 Andrew Carnegie and Edward Ginn established the Carnegie
Endowment for International Peace and the World Peace Foundation to
intensify public education against war. Later assisting in this task
were the Woodrow Wilson Foundation, formed to perpetuate Wilsonian ideals,
and the American Foundation, established to administer the Bok Peace Plan
Award.[4]

---

[1]Robert H. Ferrell, Peace in Our Times: The Origin of the Kellogg-
Briand Pact (New Haven: Yale University Press, 1957), p. 13.

[2]Arthur C. Beales, The History of Peace, (New York: The Dial Press,
1931), pp. 45-46.

[3]Jerome Davis, Contemporary Social Movements (New York: Appleton-
Century Company, 1930), p. 774.

[4]Robert Divine, Second Chance: The Triumph of Internationalism in
America During World War II (New York: Atheneum, 1967), pp. 18 and 21.

163

As a result ot a suggestion that a "league of nations" be established
as an international body for arbitration by Hamilton Holt, editor of the
Independent, and Irvin Fisher, professor at Yale University, the League
to Enforce Peace was organized in Philadelphia in June, 1915.[5] The
League launched a massive campaign to win support for ratification of
Wilson's League of Nations, but became embroiled in the "reservation controversy" in the Senate. This fight dated the decline of the League,
but there was a resurrection under a new group, The League of Nations Non-
Partisan Association, in 1923.[6]

The National Council for Limitation of Armament, established in 1921
to direct activities related to the Washington Conference on the Limitation
of Armament, did not consider itself a peace society, but a loose coordi-
nator of peace activities of seventeen groups across the country. Its
federation included, among others, farm, labor and women's organizations.
At the head of the Council was Frederick J. Libby, a pacifist Congregational
minister turned Quaker. After the Washington Conference, the Council continued to work for disarmament and against militarism. To reflect better
the new goals, Libby changed the name to The National Council for
Prevention of War.[7]

Probably the greatest ideological gift to the peace movement was
Salmon O. Levinson, head of a firm of corporation lawyers in Chicago, who
turned his efforts to international affairs when the war in Europe began

---

[5]Hamilton Holt, "The Way to Disarm: A Practical Proposal,"
Independent, LXXIX (September 28, 1914), pp. 427-429.

[6]Ruhl J. Bartlett, The League to Enforce Peace, (Chapel Hill:
The University of North Carolina Press, 1944), pp. 167-204.

[7]Merle Curti, Peace or War, the American Struggle, 1836-1936 (Boston:
J. S. Canner and Company, 1959), pp. 272-273.

to affect the stock market and his ventures. In 1918, he first proposed to "outlaw" war. He believed war was presently legal and that it could never be abolished until it was made a crime under international law. In addition to "delegalizing war," Levinson desired to codify international law and to create a world court to supervise this law in international rela- tions.[8]

Out of a dinner party in his home on December 9, 1921, Levinson creat- ed the American Committee for the Outlawry of War as a sounding board for his idea. Working with enormous energy, he gathered many prominent people to his cause -- John Dewey, the philosopher; the Reverend John Haynes Holmes, pacifist minister of New York's Community Church; Dr. Charles Clayton Morrison, a minister of the Christian Church (Disciples of Christ) and editor of The Christian Century; and Colonel Raymond Robbins, wartime head of the American Red Cross activities in Russia. A wavering, hesitant convert to "outlawry" was Senator William E. Borah, Chairman of the Senate Committee on Foreign Relations. Through a resolution, he placed outlawry before Congress on February 14, 1923.[9]

Stirred by the sufferings of the nations at war, Jane Addams and Carrie Chapman Catt in 1915 called a convention of women. Out of this grew the first national organization for women designed solely to promote peace -- the Women's Peace Party. In 1919, this group chose to become the American Section of the Women's International League for Peace and

---

[8]S. O. Levinson, "The Legal Status of War," The New Republic, XIV (March 9, 1918), pp. 171-173.

[9]Robert H. Ferrell, Peace in Their Time, p. 36; U.S., Congress, Senate, Borah Resolution No. 441, 67th Congress, 4th Session, February 14, 1923, Congressional Record, LXIV, Part 4, 3605.

freedom.[10]

In addition to the American Section of the W. I. L., there were
basically three other women's peace organizations -- the Woman's Peace
Union, the Women's Peace Society, and the National Committee on the
Cause and Cure of War. The first two occupied the extreme left of the
peace movement, wanting "peace at any price" and standing against all
participation in war on the ground that human life should be held sacred
and inviolable under all circumstances.[11] The National Committee on Cause
and Cure of War, led by the energetic Miss Catt, was a federation of
women's organizations which sponsored several annual conferences on the
"cause and cure" or war. These conferences usually concluded that war was
a futile means of settling disputes, that war should be renounced as an
instrument of national policy and that machinery should be created to
settle international arguments.[12]

Probably, Jeannette Rankin's first definitive association with
peace organizations came with the formation of the Woman's Peace Party
by Jane Addams and Carrie C. Catt in 1915. She participated in the
organizational conference at Washington's New Willard Hotel on January
10-11. Its purpose was "to enlist all American women in arousing the
nations to respect the sacredness of human life and to abolish war."[13]

In its "Program for Constructive Peace," the women urged an immediate

---

[10]Florence Brewer Boeckel, Between War and Peace; Handbook for Peace
Workers (New York: Macmillan Company, 1928), p. 111.

[11]Ibid., p. 114.

[12]Ibid., p. 116.

[13]Marie Louise Degen, The History of the Woman's Peace Party (Baltimore:
Johns Hopkins University Press, 1939), p. 38; J. R. Interview, June 25,
1969, pp. 6-7.

convention of neutral nations to secure the cessation of hostilities and to insure terms of settlement that would prevent this war from being a prelude to another. They advocated a League of Neutral Nations, whose members would settle their disputes by arbitration; an international police force; limitation of armaments; education of youth in the ideals of peace; further humanizing of governments by extension of franchise to women; and removal of the economic causes of war.[14] This group ante-dated the League To Enforce Peace by about six months and represented a very popular cause. In fact, "I didn't Raise My Boy to Be A Soldier" was one of the popular tunes of 1915.

Despite the cooperation of women's organizations around the world, assurances from heads of state, and the spectacular voyage of Henry Ford's "Peace Ship," the women made no headway in settling the war. When Carrie C. Catt, President of NAWSA, as earlier noted, renounced pacifism and offered the service of the suffragists in case of war to President Wilson, Jeannette Rankin chose to remain ideologically with Jane Addams and the pacifists. In reprisal against her actions, Catt was not re-elected as honorary vice president of the New York City Branch of the Women's Peace Party.[15]

After finishing her term as Representative from Montana, Jeannette Rankin accompanied Jane Addams in April of 1919 to Zurich, Switzerland, as one of twenty-five U.S. delegates to the Second International Congress of Women for Permanent Peace (soon to become the Women's International League for Peace and Freedom). Rankin was one of the five members of the permanent national committee, along with Lucia Ames Mead, Florence Kelley,

---

[14]Ibid., pp. 41-42.

[15]Ibid., p. 88.

Alice Thacher Post, and Lillian Wald.[16] In discussing the approaching

congress, Jeannette said:

> I intend to place the problem of stopping the
> spread of Bolshevism before the Congress....
> The League of Nations will also come up...and
> the necessity of having laws safeguarding the
> original citizenship of women who marry men
> of another country....[17]

At its world meeting in 1915 the Congress planned to assemble in the

city where the peace talks would take place. After arriving in Paris,

Jane Addams, the President, discovered that the French would not grant

visas to the delegates of the Central Powers. Zurich became the next

choice. Before leaving Paris, the American delegation visited various

officials of the peace conference and made a five-day tour of the devas-

tated war regions which only strengthened their repugnance of warfare.

Mary Church Terrell, black educator and first president of National

Association of Colored Women, was often a companion and roommate of

Jeannette Rankin during this trip to Zurich.[18]

While the Peace Conference in Paris was deciding the fate of Europe,

one hundred and fifty women from nineteen countries met in an old cathedral

in Zurich to discuss common international problems from a feminine point

of view. Emmeline Pethick-Lawrence, an English suffragist and pacifist,

described one particularly moving scene. As a French delegate spoke of

horrible episodes of destruction and appealed to "les forces de demain,"

---

[16]Among the twenty other delegates were Jane Addams, Emily Greene
Balch, Madeline Z. Doty, Dr. Alice Hamilton, and Mary Church Terrell.

[17]New York Times, April 10, 1919.

[18]Jane Addams, Peace and Bread in Time of War (New York: The Macmillan
Company, 1922), pp. 152-156; J. R. Interview, Apr. 3, 1970, p. 4; Mary
Church Terrell, A Colored Woman In A White World (Washington: Ransdell,
Inc., 1940), p. 331.

a German delegate sprang to her feet holding out both hands to the speaker.
Pethick-Lawrence wrote:

> As these two women--German and French--stood on
> the platform in fervent handclasp, the audience
> rose, and I for one found difficulty in re-
> straining tears. ...All who were present dedi-
> cated themselves...to the promotion of world
> peace.[19]

Jeannette Rankin, much younger than most of the women in the Congress,
served as a member of the Feminist Committee. Its report welcomed the
admittance of women to all positions in the League and the extension of
suffrage to Ireland and Denmark. They urged that a Woman's Charter be
included in the Peace Treaty to help establish political, social and
economic equality of women with men. The committee also insisted that
women be allowed to vote in any plebiscite taken under the Treaty.[20]

Along with these actions, the Congress became one of the first public
groups to pass a resolution of protest against the terms imposed on the
defeated nations in the Treaty of Versailles. Interestingly enough,
the English delegates were the most vigorous in their denunciations. By
guaranteeing the fruits of secret treaties, sanctioning secret diplomacy,
denying the principles of self-determination, and recognizing the principle of the spoils of war, the women felt the Treaty could only lead
to future wars.[21]

After participating in discussion with these European women and
observing the tactics of the Conference statesmen, Jeannette Rankin

---

[19]Emmeline Pethick-Lawrence, My Part in a Changing World (London:
Victor Gollanez, 1938), p. 326.

[20]Report of the International Congress, Zurich, May 12-17, 1919
(Geneva: Congress of International Committee for Permanent Peace, N.D.),
pp. 242-243, 439.

[21]Degen, The History of Women's Peace Party, pp. 229-231.

observed, "It was a vicious treaty" and prophesied "[It] was not going
to solve anything."[22] In writing to Henry White, the sole Republican
member of the United States Delegation, Rankin had asserted, "There will
be war as long as we have secret international relations, and governments...protect special economic privileges." Instead she urged the
commission to recognize that the earth and its treasures belong to all
the people and that human relations msut be considered from a world viewpoint.[23]

The Chicago Evening News, in a critical review of the Congress,
objected to the women's taking positions not truly representative of
the world's womanhood. It declared that, whereas most women had realized
the issues of justice involved in the war, "women like Miss Addams and
Miss Rankin had failed in this respect."[24] On the other hand, the Nation
regarded the resolutions of the women as an honest reminder of the vast
gap between the international justice promised by the Fourteen Points and
the character of the actual settlement.[25]

In January of 1920, the Women's International League sent Jeannette
Rankin to Washington as its representative to encourage the State Department to seek early release of all prisoners of war, especially those in
poor health, and to remove blockades to the free circulation of relief
for the suffering. During the war, many Americans had become victims

[22]J. R. Interview, June 25, 1969, p. 4.

[23]J. R. to Henry White, November 30, 1918, Box 23, in Henry White
MSS, in Library of Congress.

[24]Chicago Evening News, May 19, 1919.

[25]"The International Congress of Women," Nation, CVIII (1919), p. 819.

of the emotional hysteria created by the Committee on Public Information.
Conscientious objectors and other opposed to war were imprisoned and
often treated roughly. Jeannette urged the immediate release of these
political offenders.

With the rise of communism in Europe, Americans transferred this
"fear of the Hun" to "fear of the Reds." Bombing, general strikes and
raids on aliens and radicals characterized the immediate years after
Versailles. Rankin protested against the spirit and methods of these
"raids" and the sudden deportation of those designated as "Reds."[26]

A special joint committee of the New York Legislature, headed by
Clayton R. Lusk, reflected this popular intolerant mood by investigating
so-called revolutionary and subversive movements. It reported that Dr.
David Starr Jordan, once President of Stanford University and Treasurer
of the People's Council of America, conducted in 1917 "Courses of Instruction" for Congressmen who were unsympathetic with the war effort.
The list of Congressmen included Jeannette Rankin. In a letter of June
12, 1917, to Louis Lochner, Executive Secretary of People's Council,
Jordan emphasized that the Council must "keep in touch with Miss Rankin."[27]

In its investigation also of the American Civil Liberties Union, the
Committee noted that Jeannette Rankin was one of two vice-chairmen. It
was interesting to note other names on the ACLU National Committee: Jane
Addams, Felix Frankfurter, John Haynes Holmes, Helen Keller, A. J. Muste,

---

[26]American Section, Women's International League for Peace and
Freedom, Executive Board Minutes, January 7, 1920, in WIL Files at
Swarthmore College Peace Collection.

[27]Report of the Joint New York Legislative Committee Investigating
Seditious Activity, Revolutionary Radicalism: Its History, Purpose and
Tactics (Albany: J. B. Lyon Company, 1920), Vol. I, p. 1054.

Norman Thomas, and Oswald Garrison Villard.[28]

Florence Kelley, general secretary of the National Consumers' League and daughter of "Pig Iron" Kelley of Pennsylvania, had been among the delegates to the Zurich Congress. Previously, she had worked with Jane Addams at Hull House and had served as the first women factory inspector for the State of Illinois. For thirty years the League had worked for a minimum wage, an eight-hour day, child labor laws, and related legislation for the protection of women and children. During the four-month trip to Europe, Kelley observed Jeannette Rankin's "straight forward" thinking and later offered her a position as Field Secretary in November of 1920. Jeannette gladly accepted.[29]

Rankin's first task in her new position was to lobby in Washington for the Sheppard-Towner Bill, which provided instruction in the hygiene of maternity and infancy. She had introduced similar legislation in the last session of Congress and was anxious to see its passage. The Consumers' League supported this measure, which had previously been endorsed by Julia Lathrop, Director of the Children's Bureau, and twelve women's organizations. The National Association Opposed to Woman Suffrage, certain red-baiting groups like the Woman Patriots and Sentinels of the Republic, and some sections of the medical profession fought passage of this federal-state maternity and infancy care program. Typical of the "Red Scare"

---

[28] Ibid., Vol. II, p. 1989.

[29] J. R. Interview, April 14, 1970, p. 18; "National Consumers' League," The Survey, XL (December 4, 1920), p. 372.

period, many called the bill "Russian," "socialistic," and "bolshe-
vistic."[30]

On December 21, 1920, Jeannette Rankin, Julia Lathrop, and Florence
Kelley appeared before the House Interstate and Foreign Commerce Committee
in behalf of the Sheppard-Towner Bill. Rankin related personal experiences
of the hardships of women in isolated Western areas and the background for
her own bill. After coming to Congress, she had asked Julia Lathrop,
head of the Children's Bureau, to make a study of Montana. The statistics
revealed that mortality rates were higher than the national average. After
conferences with women from across the United States, the bill was drawn
to meet their needs and to use existing facilities. Jeannette assurred
the committee that the women supported this bill because they needed it to
"help them save the mother and babies."[31] After more hearings, the succeeding session of Congress passed the Sheppard-Towner Bill, and President
Harding signed it into law on November 23, 1921.[32]

From Congressional lobbying in Washington, Jeannette Rankin traveled
to the Mississippi Valley to work for minimum wage and hour legislation.
The Consumers' League desired to increase public opposition to the 1895
Ritchie Case, in which the Illinois Supreme Court had ruled unconstitutional
an eight-hour day law. In the meantime, in Muller v. Oregon, Louis Brandeis,

---

[30]Josephine Goldmark, Impatient Crusader: Florence Kelley (Urbana:
University of Illinois Press, 1953), pp. 107-108; Report of Jeannette
Rankin, Field Secretary, November of 1920-August of 1921, in National
Consumers' League Files, Box 43, Library of Congress.

[31]U.S., Congress, House of Representatives, Committee on Interstate
and Foreign Commerce, Public Protection of Maternity and Infancy. Hearings before the Committee on Interstate and Foreign Commerce, 66th Congress,
3rd Session, pursuent to H. R. 10925 (Washington, Government Printing
Office, 1920), p. 87.

[32]Florence Kelley, "My Philadelphia Story," Survey, LVII (October
1, 1926), p. 50; Goldmark, Impatient Crusader, p. 106.

a liberal Boston attorney and later U.S. Supreme Court Justice, argued
from an economic and sociological brief to secure a favorable decision
for a ten-hour day law in Oregon from the state Supreme Court.[33] Encouraged by this and the subsequent 1914 Stettler v. O'Hara case in
which the U.S. Supreme Court sustained the Oregon decision, the women
renewed their efforts for more state wage and hour legislation.

Rankin's work was both educational and legislative. She waged a
relentless speaking campaign before chambers of commerce, Rotary Clubs,
trade unions, various women's organizations, churches, high schools, and
universities in the six states of Nebraska, Iowa, Missouri, Illinois,
Ohio, and Kentucky. Jeannette assisted organizations in introducing
legislation, planning hearings, and lobbying their state senators and
representatives. By constant publicity and pressure, she made wage and
hour legislation a "live issue."

For many one-day events, the women bought Pullman tickets. They
would ride to Springfield during the night, lobby the legislature or
attend a hearing, and return home the next night. For longer hearings,
they secured four-bed "drummers" rooms in the hotel. In addition to the
hard work, these women gained compensations from living together and
sharing experiences.[34]

When a chairman in the Illinois House adjourned his committee without listening to Jeannette's witnesses, she suggested that they should
elect a woman in his place. In a speech at Downers Grove, Illinois, Rankin
repeated the suggestion; and, after a long campaign, Lottie O'Neal was
elected to the state legislature. To welcome her to Springfield, the

---

[33]Josephine Goldmark, Crusader, p. 142.

[34]J. R. Interview, March 9, 1971, pp. 2-3; April 4, 1970, pp. 19-20.

women planned a dinner and invited their representatives. Julia Lathrop
was a charming and witty master of ceremonies. Before the evening was
over, Rankin remembered with a sense of delight having the legislators
sing "O Promise Me To Pass the Eight-Hour Bill" and "To Be Nice to
Lottie" to the lyrics of "O Promise Me."[35]

To coordinate regional activities, Jeannette Rankin organized a
Mississippi Valley Conference whose purpose was to consider standards
for industrial legislation that might apply to the total area. Under
sponsorship of the Illinois Committee of the National Consumers' League,
reoresentatives from eleven states met January 5-6, 1923, at Chicago's
City Club. They discussed industrial legislation and the courts, administration and enforcement, the work of women's bureaus, the minimum wage
and the eight-hour day. In addition to directing the conference, Jeannette
Rankin spoke on the state campaigns for minimum wage.[36]

Florence Kelley, commenting on the success of the conference to the
National Consumers' League Board of Directors, recommended that it be
held annually until unified legislation was enacted in the Mississippi
Valley states.[37] Thus, during 1923, Jeannette Rankin continued her educational campaign. While the Illinois legislature met in Springfield,
she lobbied the men for an eight-hour day and a forty-eight-hour week.
For only the second time, the eight-hour day law passed the House; but,
by the end of the session, all legislation for women and girls had been
defeated. Julia Lathrop jocosely observed, "Illinois, at least, passed

---

[35]J. R. Interview, Mar. 9, 1971, p. 2.

[36]Program of Mississippi Valley Conference on Industrial Legislation,
January 5-6, 1923, Box 43, N.C.L. MSS.

[37]Report on Mississippi Valley Conference on NCL Board of Directors,
January 24, 1923, Box 2, NCL MSS.

a law adopting a state flower." Unfortunately, that was women's total legislative harvest for 1923.[38]

Having been so successful with the first conference on labor and welfare, Jeannette Rankin planned another for February 27-28, 1924, at Hull House in Chicago. The Second Mississippi Valley Conference on Industrial Legislation included a business luncheon and a Jubilee dinner, honoring Florence Kelley's twenty-five years of service to the National Consumers' League. Other items discussed on the agenda were employment agencies, employment insurance, the Woman's Bureau, Children's Amendment, and the legislative program for 1925. Since the Legislature of 1923 had given only token response to industrial legislation, Rankin encouraged the conferees to determine the position of candidates before the election primaries. Then, they were to vote for those nominees who favored industrial legislation.[39] The closing act of the conference sent a telegram to Representative I. M. Foster, sponsor of a Federal Child Labor Amendment, urging an immediate favorable report in the Senate and House.[40]

Jeannette Rankin continued to work in the Mississippi Valley until June of 1924. Over the past nine years, she had seen thirty-nine states either enact new legislation or strengthen their existing laws for the protection of women. But, with the decision of the U.S. Supreme Court in Adkins v. Children's Hospital, realistic prospects for wage and hour

---

[38] Report of Florence Kelley to Board of Directors, October 25, 1923, Box 2, NCL MSS.

[39] Announcement of the Program of the Second Mississippi Valley Conference in Box 43, NCL MSS.

[40] J. R. to Florence Kelley, November 24, 1923, in Box 43, NCL MSS; Report of Florence Kelley to Board of Directors, March 27, 1924, Box 2, NCL MSS.

legislation died. The Court pointed out that prescribed minimum wages
for women deprived them of their freedom of contract. Since this decision
set a precedent affecting state laws as well, minimum wage legislation
lapsed into the doldrums and was not resuscitated until the New Deal.
Jeannette was already tired of writing endless reports and of making numerous
speeches to promote legislation. When her brother, Wellington Rankin,
enetered the Republican Senatorial Primary in the Spring of 1924, she obtained a leave of absence from the National Consumers' League to campaign
for him.[41]

Before leaving for Montana, Jeannette Rankin addressed the Fourth
Congress of the Women's International League for Peace and Freedom, which
met in Washington from May 1-7, 1924. Even though her salaried job for
the past four years had been the National Consumers' League, Rankin remained active in the Women's International League as vice-chairman, field
organizer, and a member of the Executive Board. By this time, Rankin
was an ardent supporter of S. O. Levinson's "outlawry of war" plan. In
a session entitled, "Political Aspects of a New International Order,"
she said:

> The human spirit...must be won by a positive
> vision of a world at peace, a world in which
> life and not death is honored, humanity and
> not wealth is valued, love and not hate is
> practiced. ...A nation must see that war
> is a crime before there can be a spiritual
> awakening...to find another way out.[42]

Once war was declared a crime, she urged, as did Levinson, codification

---

[41] Report of Florence Kelley to Board of Directors, November 13, 1924,
Box 4, NCL MSS.

[42] Report of the Fourth Congress of Women's International League for
Peace and Freedom (Washington: Women's International League for Peace
and Freedom, 1924), p. 51.

of international law on that basis and the establishment of an international court to hear and decide controversies. Rankin trusted the enforcement of its judgments "to an enlightened public opinion." She pointed out to the assembled women that the electorate must learn that every vote cast is a vote for or against war. "Equally", she related, "every legislative body considers measures that make for war or peace."[43]

After a heart-breaking, narrow defeat of her brother, Jeannette Rankin did not return to the National Consumers' League, but began to look for a home instead. In the transition period from promoting social legislation with the National Consumers' League to a fifteen-year professional peace career with the Women's International League, the Woman's Peace Union, and the National Council for the Prevention of War, Rankin came to Georgia, bought a farm, and made it her "second" home.[44] With her arrival in Georgia, Jeannette entered one of the most interesting phases of her career. In Georgia, she was to become "A Rebel with a Cause."[45]

Jeannette Rankin desired another residence other than the Montana ranch and her present New York apartment for vacations and "a place that would be mine" to store memorabilia, files and other things. The ten-day round trip to Montana used too much precious time, so she searched for a location closer to New York and Washington. Her friends had second homes in Connecticut and around New York, but since she usually took vacations in the winter, Miss Rankin preferred a warmer climate. To consider the

---

[43]Ibid., p. 52.

[44]With the financial aid of Wellington Rankin, she now owns a 1,250-acre ranch in Montana and an apartment in Carmel, California. She maintains her legal residence in Montana.

[45]Gregory Favre, "Jeannette Rankin: A Rebel with a Cause," Atlanta Journal and Constitution Magazine, June 21, 1959, p. 8.

South, then became logical.[46]

In addition to its climate, the mystique of the South beckoned to Miss Rankin's interest. During the 1913-14 attempts at federal suffrage legislation, she had lobbied Southern Congressmen and found their nature to be warm and understanding. She gathered from these Congressmen that there was a wonderful peace sentiment in the South and she wanted to learn more about it. Even though she was working for suffrage, she remembered,

> I brought in peace in everything, because I
> know I judged men as to whether they were for
> peace or not -- as much as whether they were
> for woman suffrage.[47]

In addition to the attraction of the peace sentiment, Jeannette Rankin wished to learn more about the South, its customs and its people. Especially was she interested in civil rights of the Negro, as her early association had only been with Negro porters. She considered the South a "foreign land" to which she must go, and in later years, she expressed satisfaction by saying, "I've been glad I came because I feel that I know the South as most people don't. It was a great education and a great pleasure.[48]

With a yearning to live on a small farm in the South, Jeannette Rankin wrote to Baptist ministers, because of their number, across the Southern states and asked them to recommend reliable realtors. The response was immediate. Most realtors wanted to sell her a plantation, or, at least several hundred acres, but Epting Real Estate of Athens, Georgia, replied that they had small or large acreages for sale. Friends, who had been to

---

[46]J. R. Interview, May 24, 1969, p. 1.

[47]J. R. Interview, February 14, 1969, p. 4.

[48]J. R. Interview, May 24, 1969, pp. 1-2.

Athens, encouraged her by describing it as a lovely town. Thus, during
Christmas, 1924, she came to Athens and bought a sixty-four acre farm
on the Monroe Road, ten miles west of the city.[49]

Because the farm contained only a small "cotton house," Jeannette
Rankin envisioned a new residence set among the Georgia pines and honey-
suckle. With the aid of a keen visual projection and local carpenters,
she constructed a large, one-room wood frame house with a screened porch
along one side. The porch contained Jeannette's bed, dining table and
chairs, a chintz-covered couch and rockers. She usually slept out there
until the water froze in her glass on the night stand. Eventually, Rankin
added two bedrooms and an upstairs office.

A unique, compact circular stairway led to the upstairs. On her first
trip up the small stairway, Olive Rankin's corset hung on one of the steps.
Dorothy Brown, Jeannette's niece who was living with her, remembered
that Olive, a large grandmother, was "laughing and full of good advice
all the time we were pulling, tugging and hauling her down."[50] Dorothy
McKinnon Brown and her mother, Edna Rankin McKinnon, were in Georgia
during the time of the construction of the house. Through the 1930's,
Dorothy stayed with Jeannette when she was at home in Georgia and attended
several grades in the local school.

The living room, gaily decorated with drapes and paintings, was very
comfortable with a large fireplace and swinging kettle. Typical of Rankin
ingeniousness was a radiator device to provide additional heat. Along

---

[49]J. R. Interview, January 30, 1969, pp. 6-7; Ibid., May 24, 1969,
p. 2 of transcript; Georgia, Clarke County Deed Book, XLI, 517, dates
the deed from S. L. Autry on January 26, 1925.

[50]Dorothy McKinnon Brown Interview, September 5, 1970, pp. 9-10.

one side of the room, Jeannette installed a car radiator with pipes running to the fireplace. As the water heated in the pipes, it circulated
warmth through the radiator to that area. A bay window, on the opposite
end, completed the physical arrangement of the original house.[51]

Compatible with many Southern homes, Jeannette did not have a kitchen,
but a "cook house." Cooking was done on an old four-legged stove in the
refurbished log "cotton house," which was moved nearby and connected to
the proch by a gangplank. Painted tar paper covered the walls and roll-
roofing the floor. To keep from walking outside to dump water, especially
in inclimate weather, Jeannette countersunk a large gasoline funnel in the
cabinet top. She attached a hose to drain the water into the yard. The
cook room had a little closet affair which contained a shaped zinc tub
and an imaginative "apple box" commode. There was a trap door on the
outside where one would remove the johnny and empty it down the lane.[52]

There was no electricity and no running water in the house. The
well, located near the entrance to the cook house, operated with a water
bucket, rope, and windlass. Jeannette lodged overnight male guests and
other visitors in a guest house about one-quarter of a mile away. They
secured water from a lovely spring down the hill which always attracted
many snakes. If the rustic surroundings had not alarmed these "city
fellers," the snakes probably did![53]

On the sixty-four acres, Jeannette planted several hundred pecan
and peach trees. Wild fruits flourished in their chosen soil. Neighbors

---

[51]Ibid., p. 9; Rosa Nell Spriggs Interview, June 11, 1970, p. 1.

[52]Katherine Anthony, "A Basket of Summer Fruit," Woman's Home
Companion, XL (August, 1926), p. 12; Dorothy M. Brown Interview, September 5, 1970), p. 8.

[53]Dorothy M. Brown, Interview, September 5, 1970, pp. 11-12.

rented much of the tillable acreage for the planting of velvet beans and
corn. Jeannette would always invite her friends to "come out to the
farm." A visitor from Athens once remarked, "Well, Jeannette, this is
the most unique farm I've ever seen. I've been all over and have not
seen an animal."[54] After thinking it over, Jeannette gave Rosa Nell
Spriggs, her friend and personal secretary, twenty-five dollars to pur-
chase a Jersey cow. They housed the cow in an abandoned chicken house.
A neighbor boy taught Rosa Nell and Dorothy to milk. After Grandmother
Rankin churned the milk in an old fashioned crock, Jeannette moulded it
for home use and to give to friends when she went into Athens.[55]

After getting her new house well under construction, Jeannette Rankin
accepted a position with the American Section, Women's International League
for Peace and Freedom. As field secretary, she traveled widely, making
speeches and organizing district work. Her speeches in various cities
and to local branches of the Women's International League expressed all
the fire, vigor, and candor that had characterized her earlier campaigns
for suffrage and Congress. To an audience in Cleveland, Ohio, Rankin
said, "The work of educating the world to peace is the women's job, because men have a natural fear of being classed as cowards if they oppose
war." To her, women were a strong force in moulding public opinion, and
no woman with honor could ask her son to go to war unless she had done
everything in her power to bring about peace. That "everything" included
working for the outlawry of war, for the establishment of a world court,
and for the rule of law, not force. Rankin observed that, in the past,
women had nothing to say about giving their men to war, but that they

---

[54]Rosa Nell Spriggs, Interview, June 11, 1971, p. 8.

[55]Ibid.

would from now on.[56]

Queried as to the possibility of a woman president, Jeannette Rankin
replied, "Why, certainly. It is inevitable, and more important, every
desirable. That time is not very distant--probably fifty years, possibly sooner."[57] "Will the men want a woman president?" she was asked.
With a chuckle in her voice and a sparkle in her eye, she answered,
"They'll be delighted. A man inherently likes to be governed by a woman.
Matrimony proves that."[58]

In addressing a luncheon in Cleveland, Jeannette described war as
a "mad-dog that should be locked up." The task for womanhood was to
create public opinion for world peace. She warned women about the caustic
nature of arguments being raised against peace propaganda. "My family,"
she said, "always have been alarmed at the inclination I have to select
unpopular causes, but at the present time I see no more urgent cause for
women to back than...outlawing war."[59] Many women were derogatorily
being called "pacifist," while peace organizations were described as
solialistic, communistic, or linked with the IWW movement. Jeannette declared, "The only thing for them [the women] to do is to stand by their
guns until they have won the cause just as they did the suffrage amendment."[60]

Rankin encouraged the women to form councils devoted solely to the

---

[56]Cleveland Plain Dealer, March 26, 1926; The Herald, Duluth, Minnesota,
March, N.D., 1925, in WIL Files at Swarthmore College Peace Collection.

[57]Boston Advertiser, March 9, 1925. Shirley Chisolm, a black Congressman from New York, is running for President in the Democratic Presidential Primaries, Spring of 1972.

[58]Ibid.

[59]Cleveland News, March 27, 1925.

[60]Ibid.

promotion of peace. When asked why it was necessary to have special peace organizations, she answered, "Because the others...have such full programs that peace could only get a small part of the attention it should have."[61] Her ideal was to have a women's peace organization associated with the WIL in every community.

In April of 1925, the Women's International League Board of Directors named Jeannette Rankin chairman of a fund to manage work west of the Mississippi River. Speaking in Great Falls, Montana, she pointed out the significance of this work. "Western states hold a preponderance of influence in the Senate."[62] To the Executive Committee of the WIL Board on October 13, 1925, Rankin reported that influencing the Senate was the key to stimulating international relations. With the West's holding the balance of power, she felt it imperative to arouse political action in these states.[63]

In the Western organization, Jeannette Rankin proposed two units. Each was to contain two field workers and a secretary, located in a central headquarters. She budgeted $1,000, including her own salary of $250 plus $100 travel expenses, for the first group and $700 for the second. Rankin envisioned these workers contacting local women, organizing WIL chapters, training volunteers, outlining programs, and conducting district and state meetings. The Executive Committee voted to proceed with the plan, provided that $6,000 could be raised for at least six months of operation of

[61]Cleveland Plain Dealer, March 26, 1925.

[62]Great Falls Tribune, April 22, 1925.

[63]Minutes of the Executive Committee of WIL, US, October 13, 1925, in WIL Files, Swarthmore College Peace Collection.

one unit.[64] Realizing that raising money along with organizational work
would be too strenuous, Jeannette Rankin declined to undertake the proposal.[65] Instead, she returned to Georgia to her house and to oversee
operations on her newly acquired farm.

In the summer of 1925, Jeannette Rankin, reverting to her interest
in social work, organized clubs for the girls and boys in the Bogart
community. The girls "Sunshine" club met on Saturday afternoon, and she
taught them how to sew, cook, and to enjoy folk games. Because the girls
had no bathing suits, Jeannette drove to the nearest cotton mill and secured a bolt of Canton flannel. Unrolling it on the floor, she cut seven
garments. The girls regarded these short-skirted suits, which looked like
winter underwear, coldly, to say the least. Jeannette rescued the situation by dying them a bright rose in a neighbor's iron wash pot.[66]

While the girls were organizing a club and learning parliamentary
law, the boys' group, which met on Saturday night, had no president and
was much less structured. Sometimes the boys would ride over on a mule
and bring a watermelon for refreshments. She read stories of Gandhi
to the smaller boys and the older ones put together crystal radio sets.
Some boys enjoyed playing the Jew's harp and the French harp, while others
clapped their hands and lifted their feet in a ragtime dance. Rules of
membership were never strict, and nonmembers were as welcome as regulars.[67]

[64]Ibid.

[65]Ibid., November 11, 1925.

[66]Sunshine Club Record Book in the possession of Jeannette Rankin;
Katherine Anthony, "Living on the Front Porch," Woman's Home Companion,
XL (September, 1926), pp. 32, 34.

[67]Ibid.; Blanche Butler Interview, Watkinsville, Georgia, (a former
club member and life-long friend), February 13, 1969; Atlanta Journal,
November 24, 1963).

Having gotten this project underway, Jeannette Rankin became anxious to also promote peace.

Her attention turned to the nearby town of Athens. Interests in social movements, reform ideas, and internationalism dominated its cultural life in the late 1920's. In addition to the flavor provided by University of Georgia programs and professors, Lucy Stanton, Georgia's famous miniature portriat painter, demonstrated an unusual interest in social reform. The first Athens woman suffrage meeting met in her studio as she early felt the need for women to be interested in the political life of the nation because of its influence on their own and their children's welfare.[68] Occasional international figures and visiting scholars brought new ideas to Athens' social and intellectual life.

It was quite natural for Lucy Stanton, with her interest in woman suffrage, E. Merton Coulter, professor of history and faculty advisor to the International Relations Club at the University of Georgia, Roberta Hodgson, professor in the History Department at Georgia Teachers College, and Jeannette Rankin to become friends and to organize a group to study the foreign policy of the United States. A group of 35 interested persons met for the first time in the one room studio of Lucy Stanton, 552 Cobb Street, on February 9, 1928.[69] Inez Burnet, prominent Athenian and wife of the Director of the University of Georgia Library, became president; E. Merton Coulter, vice-president; and Jeannette Rankin, secretary.[70]

This study group, made up of prominent men and women related basically

---

[68] Athens Banner-Herald, March 19, 1931, p. 3:6.

[69] Ibid.

[70] Athens Banner-Herald, Feb. 10, 1928, p. 1.

to Athens and the University of Georgia Community, met irregularly, usually convening only when Jeannette Rankin was in town. She kept close reins
on the group by having the "power to call meetings" entrusted both to the
president and to the secretary. The original purpose of the society was
"to study the foreign policy of the United States for the purpose of
encouraging the settlement of international disputes by arbitration,"
and to propose programs for other organizations and groups.[71] But, by
October, 1929, Miss Rankin was already referring to the society as a
"propaganda" organization.[72]

This first meeting adopted a resolution on "War and Human Nature,"
which was later printed and circulated by the group. It pointed out that
the proponents of the war method of setting international disputes maintain that war cannot be abolished. At the present stage of social development it was "human nature" to settle disputes by fighting. The resolution
argued that the advocates of war were confusing war and the causes of war,
because war was a "human institution." It said,

> The dispute may have its roots in the present,
> but the method of settling the dispute is one
> of those passing institutions that are the ex-
> pressions of man's state of enlightenment.
> Therefore war can be abolished without changing
> human nature.[73]

---

[71] Athens Banner-Herald, February 10, 1928, p. 1; "Working Politically
for Peace in Georgia," January 5, 1932, Georgia Peace Society Folder,
Swarthmore College Peace Collection, hereinafter cited as Georgia Peace
Society Folder, S.C.P.C.

[72] Jeannette Rankin, to Emilie Behre, Louisiana League for Peace and
Freedom, October 4, 1929, Rankin File Drawers, National Council for Prevention of War, Swarthmore College Peace Collection.

[73] Athens Banner-Herald, February 10, 1928, p. 1:4; "War and Human
Nature," Georgia Peace Society Files, S.C.P.C.; The wording of this
resolution was very similar to words, phrases, and ideas of Jeannette
Rankin. It may be surmised that she wrote, or at least heavily influenced,
the composition of the resolution. Mrs. J. F. Greve was the mother of
Mrs. M. P. Jarnagin.

Since duelling had been outlawed as an honorable recourse in settling disputes, so could the war method. War should be made a legal crime and nations would then resort to courts of law to settle their disputes. The resolution concluded by saying, "War is an outworn institution, as untrustworthy as the duel, in the present enlightened stage of 'human nature'."[74]

The Athens Foreign Policy Club, as designated by the Banner-Herald, in its second meeting "adopted" the name of "The Georgia Peace Society," thereby providing continuity to an earlier peace group organized under the same name.[75] John Morris, professor of German at the University of Georgia, had been a member of the older society and suggested accepting its name. This group had been started by Henry C. White, University of Georgia professor of Chemistry and later President of the State College of Agriculture and Mechanical Arts.[76]

Shortly after coming to the University in 1872, Henry C. White and some of his colleagues organized the Georgia Peace Society with the immediate aim of lessening the tension and healing the wounds left by the Civil War. It affiliated with the American Peace Society and sponsored arbitration addresses and conferences. Dr. White was a great believer in universal peace and for several years attended the annual arbitration conferences at Lake Mohonk (New York), inaugurated in 1895 by Albert Smiley, a Quaker philanthropist. In 1908, H. C. White addressed the Mohonk Conference on the topic, "How Can the Average American College

---

[74]Ibid.

[75]Athens Banner-Herald, March 11, 1928, p. 8.

[76]J. R. Interview, May 24, 1969, p. 2.

Best Promote the International Arbitration Movement."[77]

Under the presidency of Dr. White, the Georgia Peace Society co-sponsored with the Atlanta Chamber of Commerce a "peace jubilee" on May 28, 1911. This mass meeting, addressed by Congressman Theodore Burton of Ohio, was part of a vast nationwide campaign to endorse the arbitration negotiations conducted by President Howard Taft with England and France. It attracted 3,000 Georgians who expressed their moral support for President Taft's humanitarian arbitration ideals.[78]

In addition to adopting a name, the new Georgia Peace Society discussed the proposed Kellogg-Briand Pact. Early in the 1920's, Jeannette Rankin began to favor Salmon Levinson's "outlawry of war" proposal. At the Fourth Congress of the Women's International League, 1924, she asserted, "...not until war is made a disreputable crime can the power of physiological forces be used effectively against war."[79]

James T. Shotwell, a professor at Columbia University, shared Levinson's concept for the "outlawry of war" with the significant additions of sanctions to enforce any agreement. Aristide Briand, French Foreign Minister who had been indoctrinated by Shotwell, according to the professor, proposed a

---

[77]Athens Banner-Herald, December 1, 1927, p. 1; Report of the 14th Annual Meeting of the Lake Mohonk Conference on International Arbitration, 1908 (New York: Lake Mohonk Conference on International Arbitration, 1908), p. 181.; Report of the 16th Annual Meeting, 1910, p. 205.; Report of the 17th Annual Meeting, 1911, p. 2.; Report of the 18th Annual Lake Mohonk Conference on International Arbitration, 1912, pp. 173-175.; In the H. C. White Collection in the University of Georgia Libraries was a signed pledge card to the World Peace Army, April 16, 1914, and a banquet folder from the Pennsylvania Arbitration and Peace Conference, May 19, 1908.; Athens Banner-Herald, October 6, 1935, p. 10.

[78]Atlanta Constitution, May 29, 1911, p. 1.; Curti, Peace or War, pp. 221-224.

[79]Report of the Fourth Congress of Women's International League, p. 51.

mutual agreement to outlaw war between France and the United States. The
State Department saw the hazards of such a bilateral agreement and suggested expanding the proposal into a multilateral pact.[80] By this time, the
American peace movement had aroused public sentiment into a chorus of
approval. Riding the crest of this public interest, Jeannette Rankin
urged support from the Goergia Peace Society.

As the practice was to become for most of their meetings, this
support came in the form of a resolution. In addition to asking the
President by what authority he was carrying on the war in Nicaragua
and expressing appreciation for refusing materially to increase the Navy,
the Peace Society revealed gratification,

> Over the advance made in treaty making indicated
> by our recent treaty with France [The Kellogg-
> Briand Pact]. We believe the desire to renounce
> war as an institution for settling international
> disputes is deeply rooted in the hearts of the
> American people, and a treaty which will make
> war a crime against the law of nations will have
> public sentiment for its support.[81]

The Georgia Peace Society in 1928 made intensive efforts to persuade the presidential possibilities and Georgia's delegates to the Democratic and Republican conventions to exert every possible influence on
the selection of a platform and nominees that favored,

> the negotiation of treaties with every nation,
> or of a world treaty, condemning recourse to
> war for the settlement of international dis-
> putes and solemnly renouncing war as a solution
> to international disagreements.[82]

---

[80] Ferrell, Peace In Their Time, pp. 67-69; L. Ethan Ellis, Republican
Foreign Policy, 1921-1933 (New Brunswick: Rutgers University Press, 1968),
pp. 214-228.

[81] Athens Banner-Herald, March 11, 1928, p. 8.

[82] Athens Banner-Herald, April 10, 1928, p. 14.

As a means of bringing pre-convention pressure to bear, questionnaires were mailed to all prospective presidential candidates to ascertain their views on the outlawry of war by treaties.[83]

Carrie Chapman Catt brought together nine women's organizations in the National Committee on the Cause and Cure of War to explore the problems of peace and war. National Conferences were held in December of 1925 and 1926, and in January of 1928. The third conference agreed to support the renunciation of war as an instrument of national policy; the use of existing, and the creation of needed international machinery to care for the common concerns of nations; and the peaceful settlement of international disputes. To strengthen its activity on the local level, the National Committee designed forty-eight state interpretive conferences.

Inez Burnet, president of the Georgia Peace Society, and Jeannette Rankin joined with leaders of the Georgia League of Women Voters in planning the first Georgia Conference on the Cause and Cure of War for May 31, 1928 in Athens. The purpose of the conference was to discuss methods for effectively organizing the sentiment for peace in Georgia into a constructive program -- emphasizing the importance of the adoption of multilateral treaties as the next step toward universal peace. The Georgia Society and nine cooperating organizations sponsored the one-day conference.[84]

The Georgia Conference, the first of the forty-eight planned, opened

---

[83]Athens Banner-Herald, May 20, 1928, p. 1.

[84]Athens Banner-Herald, May 24, 1928, p. 4. Co-sponsors were the Association of University Women, Council of Women for Home Missions, Y. M. C. A., Georgia Members of Women's Trade Union League, Women's Christian Temperance Union, Georgia League of Women Voters, Georgia Council of Jewis Women, Georgia Federation of Women's Clubs and Federation of Women's Boards of Foreign Missions of North America. Most of these were the Georgia affiliates of the National Committee for the Cause and Cure of War.

on May 31, at the Y. M. C. A. with delegates attending from ten sponsoring organizations plus representatives from the Association of Georgia Colleges, Georgia Safety Council, United Spanish War Veterans, Georgia Federation of Labor, Georgia Library Association, University Georgia International Relations Club, Georgia Committee on Inter-Racial Cooperation, Wesleyan Alumnae Association, State Committee on Law Enforcement and the Unior Red Cross.[85]

"What has the world done thus far to prevent war?" was the theme for the Luncheon-symposium presided over by Inez Burnet. Within this framework, J. H. T. McPherson, History Professor at the University of Georgia, discussed the Hague Tribunal; John Morris, German professor at the University of Georgia, the League of Nations; Mrs. J. D. Miller, president of Georgia Parent-Teacher Association, the World Court; and Roberta Hodgson, History professor at Georgia State Teachers College, the Locarno Pacts. With the exception of Mrs. Miller, the Georgia Peace Society provided the leadership for this luncheon-symposium.[86]

Subjects for the round table discussion in the afternoon included: "A multilateral treaty renouncing war as proposed by Secretary Kellogg -- what is it," "What must the modern peace treaty contain in order to be effective in actually preventing war," "What are the chief provisions of the Root treaties," "What were Briand's objections to the multilateral treaty and how are they likely to be adjusted," "What are the chief provisions of the Bryan treaties," and "Is the covenant of the League of Nations a peace treaty?" Participants in these discussions were Raymond

---

[85] *Athens Banner-Herald*, May 31, 1928, p. 1.

[86] *Ibid.*

Robins, a former Red Cross worker, close associate of Levinson in the
outlawry movement and a national peace advocate; E. Merton Coulter;
Jeannette Rankin; Eleanor Raoul, a member of the Atlanta League of Women
Voters and Mrs. J. N. McEachern, president of the Atlanta League.[87]

The concluding session met at the University Chapel under the chair-
manship of the Reverend W. P. King, pastor of the First Methodist Church,
Athens, and a member of the Georgia Peace Society. Colonel Raymond Robins
was the speaker. He championed the "outlawry of war" and anticipated the
development of other means of settling international disputes. Members
of the audience were asked to pledge themselves to support this movement
"to liberate mankind from the war evil because as long as war is legalized
the nations will use that method of settling their disputes."[88] The only
way to stop war, he concluded, was to outlaw it altogether.

Three important peace resolutions came from the conference. The
first, a duplicate of the resolution adopted the National Conference on
the Cause and Cure of War in January, 1928, endorsed the multilateral
treaties in behalf of the outlawry of war and urged the ratification of
the Kellogg-Briand Pact by the United States Senate. The second, directed
toward the Republican and Democratic platform of 1924, expressed the
appreciation of the Georgia Conference for the adoption of a position favoring arbitration of international difficulties. It also urged the reiteration
and strengthening with unequivocal party support the renunciation of war as
a national policy and the settlement of disputes by means other than warfare. The third resolution called to the attention of the men and women

[87]Athens Banner-Herald, June 1, 1928, p. 1.

[88]Athens Banner-Herald, June 1, 1928, p. 12.

of Georgia the vital question of outlawing war declaring, "It was their personal responsibility to make known their sentiments to the President, Congressmen and legislators."[89] The real purpose of these resolutions, and of the conference as a whole, was to arouse public support for efforts to outlaw war and establish amity among the nations of the world.

The state press reacted enthusiastically to the Georgia Conference. The Atlanta Constitution was glad for Georgia to have had the first conference of this kind and commented, "It did a valiant and patriotic service to the nation and civilization in the adoption of the three resolutions."[90] Editorially, the Macon Telegraph wrote that out of the tragedy of the World War several ideas emerged: War seldom, if ever, settled anything; war in its nature was a matter of psychology; and war between nations was no more intelligent than war between citizens. These convictions, W. L. Anderson, the editor, commented, led to the establishment of the Georgia Peace Society. He then complimented the Conference for its practical plan and definite action. Believing that the chief value of the conference was that it aroused interest in the outlawry of war, the editor concluded:

> If world peace is to become a reality, it will become so because the great masses of men and women have been taught to feel a vital rather than a languid interest in the question and to believe in at least the possibility of outlawing war. This is the task in education which the Georgia Committee on the Cause and Cure of War has set for itself.[91]

---

[89] Athens Banner-Herald, May 31, 1928, p. 1.

[90] Atlanta Constitution, June 2, 1928, p. 8.

[91] Macon Telegraph, June 2, 1928, p. 4.

Because of the ratification of the Kellogg-Briand Pact by the Senate in January of 1929, the Second Georgia Conference on Cause and Cure of War, meeting in Atlanta in May of 1929, did not create the interest nor receive the public acclaim as did the first. Jeannette Rankin pointed up the hope of the Conference for world peace with an address, "Civilization Outgrows War." Other participants on the program were John Allen, professor of Journalism at Mercer College who spoke on "Press, Public Opinion and Peace," and Phillip Weltner, educator and later chancellor of the University System in Georgia, who discussed "The [Elihu] Root Formula and American Adherence to the World Court." James G. McDonald, Chairman of the Foreign Policy Assiciation of New York, described the Pan-American situation in the evening session.[92]

The goal of the peace movement of the 1920's, including the Georgia Peace Society, had been to "educate" the public concerning the outlawry of war. But the Women's Peace Union, organized in 1921, went one step further. They sought to implement outlawry in the United States through a constitutional amendment. Section One of the amendment, drafted in 1923 by Elinor Byrns, legal advisor for the Union, proposed:

> War for any purpose shall be illegal, and neither
> the United States nor any state, territory,
> association or person subject to its jurisdic-
> tion shall prepare for, declare, engage in, or
> carry on war or other armed conflice, expedi-
> tion, invasion, or undertaking within or with-
> out the United States, nor shall any funds be
> raised, appropriated, or expended for such
> purpose.[93]

---

[92] Atlanta Constitution, May 24, 1929, p. 24; May 28, 1929, p. 3.

[93] U.S., Congress, Senate, S. J. Resolution 45, 71st Congress, First Session, May 24, 1929, Congressional Record, LXXI, 1930 (for copy of entire resolution, see page 2748).

To take charge of this political work in Washington and to represent them across the nation, the Women's Peace Union wanted to employ Jeannette Rankin for six months in 1929. Anxious to do lobbying and willing to do extensive traveling, she replied, "I have been in the 'country' long enough to be quite thrilled with the idea of getting into the fight again."[94]

In May of 1929, Jeannette Rankin went to Washington to supervise lobbying for the constitutional amendment. The Working Committee of WPU suggested that she try to find one member in each congressional district to serve on their Congressional Committee. Jeannette wanted to make this woman primarily responsible for contacts with her representative. She also hoped to locate two women in each state to work with their senators. One of Rankin's responsibilities was to write and send a position statement to these women as often as possible. Knowing Jeannette's individualism, the WPU resolved that:

> We make it clear to Miss Rankin that we want
> only such a degree of success and rapidity of
> success as is possible without any compromise
> with either the letter or the spirit of our
> Amendment.[95]

After a week's work in the Congress, Jeannette Rankin suddenly realized the meaning of their caution. She wrote, "Mrs. [C. L.] Babcock was quite right in thinking there would be more opposition than I anticipated.

---

[94]Elinor Byrns to J. R., April 1, 1929, Rankin Folder, WPU Files, Swarthmore College Peace Collection; Working Committee Minutes of WPU, March 13 and April 25, 1929, in C. L. Babcock Papers, Folder 77, in Schlesinger Library at Radcliffe; J. R. to Elinor Byrns, April 6, 1929, Rankin Folder, WPU Files, Swarthmore College Peace Collection.

[95]Working Committee Minutes, WPU, May 16, 1929, S.C.P.C.

It is very great indeed."[96] In calling on the senators from Montana, she discovered that T. J. Walsh listened attentively but would not support the amendment. Burton Wheeler, who was a good friend, thought "the Peace Pact meant very little to the Senate...and there was no hope at all for the amendment."[97] In fact, Jeannette received so little encouragement that she reported the senators and congressman to be very friendly and cordial but brutally frank.[98]

While Congress was in recess, Jeannette Rankin came to Georgia in July of 1929 to address the annual meeting of the Department of Classroom Teachers of the National Education Association. Her lecture, "Teachers and World Peace," emphasized the importance of their supporting the Kellogg-Briand Pact and stimulating thinking that would contribute toward the growth of a world at peace. She expressed horror at the double standard in America between what was wrong for an individual (duelling) might be legal for a nation (war). The renunciation of war as an instrument of national policy helped greatly to alleviate this dichotomy. Since the Paris Pact allowed wars of self-defense, the WPU thought the next logical step in the United States was to amend the Constitution to divest Congress of its "war declaring power." Rankin said, "For the treaty to be taken seriously we must demand that governments proceed earnestly with the task of building the structure and temper for peace."[99]

Comparing the Kellogg-Briand Pact in significance to the Declaration

[96] J. R. to Mrs. Mary B. Orr, May 25, 1929, WPU Files at Swarthmore College Peace Collection.

[97] Ibid.

[98] Ibid.

[99] National Education Association, Proceedings and Addresses, 1929, p. 342.

of Independence, Jeannette hoped the teachers would secure a copy for each classroom and memorize its wording. In answer to those who were calling it a scrap of paper, she reminded the teachers that all treaties were scraps of paper unless they were supported by the masses of people. Believing that classroom teachers were moulders of a crystallized public opinion, she charged them, saying, "The responsibility is upon you...to make world peace."[100]

Attempting to initiate action while in Georgia, Jeannette Rankin went to the state legislature and secured the cooperation of two Representatives from Fulton County, George T. Brown and Luther Still. They were to ask the Georgia House to memorialize the Congress to make was legally impossible by Constitutional amendment as proposed by Senate Joint Resolution No. 45, introduced by Senator Lynn Frazier of North Dakota. Representative George T. Brown, an Atlanta physician, had been closely associated with the peace movement as vice-president of the American Peace Society, vice-president and American Secretary of the International Society for the Prevention of War (Paris), and a member of the Hague Peace Conference.[101] Luther Still was an active member of a typographical trade union and served on a number of boards of arbitration between capital and labor.[102] Since the labor movement was sympathetic to the peace advocates in Georgia, he was happy to co-sponsor Georgia House Resolution No. 34 to "memorialize the Congress of the United States

---

[100]Ibid., pp. 342-343.

[101]Georgia, Secretary of State, Official Register, 1929 (Atlanta: Stein Printing Company, 1929) pp. 92-93.

[102]Ibid.

that the Congress make war legally impossible by constitutional amendment...."[103]

Privileges of the floor were granted Jeannette Rankin to address
the House concerning the Frazier Resolution as proposed by the Women's
Peace Union. Miss Rankin later wrote, "They seemed interested and I
asked Senator Russell (Richard B. Russell, Speaker of the Georgia House)
if they were going to pass it." "If I think they are," he told me, "I'm
going down there and stop it."[104]

And stop it he did! Along with John W. Weekes of DeKalb County,
Richard Russell introduced a substitute resolution condemning unqualifiedly
the measure introduced in the United States Senate by Senator Frazier and
"memorializing Congress to resist every effort to abridge or qualify the
right of America to defend herself in time of national stress."[105] After
extended debate, the substitute resolution was adopted.

In writing to a friend in Connecticut about the Georgia experience,
Miss Rankin called the defeat a "great victory." She said that it usually
took many attempts to get new measures introduced and vote upon. The
very fact that the resolution was introduced, debated and voted upon she
interpreted as encouraging. Since the Connecticut legislature was also
in session, Miss Rankin urged the Meriden Peace Seekers Club to push for

---

[103]State of Georgia, Journal of the House of Representatives, 1929
(Atlanta: Stein Printing Company, 1929), pp. 235-236.

[104]Gregory Favre, "Rebel With a Cause," Atlanta Journal and Constitution Magazine, June 21, 1959, p. 24; State of Georgia, Journal
of the House of Representatives, 1929, p. 235.

[105]State of Georgia, Journal of the House of Representatives, 1929,
p. 235; J. R. to Caroline Babcock, July 3, 1929, WPU Files, S.C.P.C.

a similar resolution.[106]

Of all the peace endeavors supported by Jeannette Rankin, the constitutional amendment to make war legally impossible was probably the
most utopian. Having secured its introduction, the Women's Peace Union
directed Rankin to arrange for a hearing before the Judiciary Committee
of the House. Between July and October, her principal work consisted of
compiling material and writing speeches for the anticipated hearing, which
never materialized. As to the question of defense, the Working Committee
of the Women's Peace Union requested Jeannette to deal with it only inci-
dentally, as their position negated participation in any war, defensive
or otherwise.[107] By the fifth month of her contract, she had interviewed
twenty-two senators and fifty representatives, secured introduction of
the Women's Peace Union's resolution, written four speeches, developed
a plan for a congressional hearing, increased the number of members on
their Congressional Committee, and spent several days on lecture tours.

As the sixth month expired, Jeannette had become disillusioned with
the Women's Peace Union's methods for pushing the amendment. She advised them that to be effective politically they must arous sentiment on
the state and district level and must supply these people in the districts
with elementary answers to the common arguments for war and defense.
Then, the local people must be taught how to express effectively their
sentiment. The Women's Peace Union disagreed with this emphasis on

---

[106]Jeannette Rankin to Mary L. Butterfield, August 14, 1929, Rankin
File Folder, W.P. U. Files, S. C. P. C.

[107]Working Committee Minutes, June 13, 1939, C. L. Babcock, papers at
Schlesinger Library Radcliffe College.

local, grassroots involvement and did not extend her contract.[108]

Before her six-month contract expired, Jeannette Rankin began to
search for another position; but, in the fall of 1929, jobs were not
plentiful. Frederick J. Libby, Executive Director of the National Council
for Prevention of War, did invite her to attend and address their annual
business meeting in late October. Abiding by the guidelines of the Women's
Peace Union, Rankin restricted her remarks to an explanation of their proposed Constitutional amendment.[109] In addition to addressing the directors,
she was able to meet and converse with the NCPW personnel. After the meeting, Libby suggested that Jeannette join the NCPW staff on November 15.
He was able to offer her only expenses until February of 1930. Idealistic-
ally, Libby foresaw the possibility of Rankin opening an office in Atlanta.

Under these inauspicious beginnings, Jeannette entered her work for
the next ten years.[110]

---

[108]Working Committee Minutes, October 7, 1929, C. L. Babcock Papers
at Schlesinger Library, Radcliffe College. Also J. R. did not wish to
raise runds; and, from indications, the WPU may have wanted her to take
on this additional portfolio.

[109]Annual Board Meeting Minutes, October, 1929, listed J. R. attending as member of WPU in National Council for Prevention of War (hereinafter called NCPW) Files at Swarthmore College Peace Collection; Statement of J. R., October 26, 1929, NCPW Files, SCPC.

[110]Frederick Libby to J. R., November 5, 1929, Rankin Folder, NCPW
Files, located in Swarthmore College Peace Collection unless otherwise
noted; Executive Board Minutes, December 18, 1929, NCPW Files, SCPC.

CHAPTER VIII

FROM PEACE EDUCATION TO PEACE ACTION

Because the United States Senate adopted the Kellogg-Briand Pact earlier in the year, Jeannette eagerly anticipated beginning her work in the fall of 1929 with the National Council for Prevention of War. With the government's have renounced war as an instrument of national policy, she envisioned a new day for peace. Paralleling her association with the National Council was a developing popular belief that America should not intervene in the political affairs of foreign countries. For a long time, Rankin had advocated this approach to foreign policy. These directives enabled Jeannette Rankin to continue her struggle for the dissolution of the war system of settling disputes by emphasizing a reduction in military spending, by encouraging disarmament, and by establishing a relationship of amnity with all nations.

One of her first assignments was to return to Georgia to attend the third and final state Conference on the Cause and Cure of War. Its program centered on the themes of Naval Construction, World Court, and Public Opinion. Rankin reported on the work of the National Committee on Cause and Cure of War and led a forum on how women could influence public opinion. She concluded that the best way was "to keep up a continuous barrage of letters to the President, Senators, and Congressmen." Traveling with Rankin was Lucia Ames Mead, from Boston and a vice-President of the National Council for the Prevention of War, who spoke on "How to get the

202

Cooperation of the Press," and on "The World Court."[1]

The Georgia delegates adopted, on behalf of the London Naval Conference, a resolution urging complete and immediate abolition of battleships and substantial reduction of other classes of naval ships. Jeannette Rankin always enjoyed coming to work in the South because she felt it was easier to talk peace where big industry, such as shipbuilding, had no selfish motives in promoting war. At the passage of their resolution, she commented:

> The attitude of the South is toward peace, for
> another war would not necessarily mean more
> production, higher prices, and more grain.
> It is easier to talk to a people who are
> interested in humanity more than in cold
> dollars.[2]

A second resolution placed the Georgia Conference on record as supporting in every way possible such action as will lead to the entrance of the United States into the World Court because it "would give greater effectiveness and afford evidence of the sincere purpose of our government to uphold its commitments made through the Paris Pact."[3]

Jeannette Rankin's itinerary for this trip to Georgia showed her stamina and enthusiasm for peace work. She attended a tea at Lucy Stanton's studio in Athens, arranged the meeting and spoke to the Jefferson (Georgia) Women's Club, in Jefferson some 17 miles away, and planned a supper meeting for the Georgia Peace Society at Inez Burnet's back in Athens. Lucia Ames Mead, who was traveling with Miss Rankin, spoke to the Peace Society.

---

[1] *Athens Banner-Herald*, February 13, 1930, p. 1.

[2] *Macon Evening News*, February 11, 1930, p. 1.

[3] *Athens Banner-Herald*, February 12, 1930, p. 1; February 13, 1930, p. 7.

While on the way to Macon the next day, Miss Rankin visited the newspaper offices in each town, beginning with Athens, until she arrived in
Macon. In addition to attending the conference on Cause and Cure of War,
she addressed a group of 500 students at Mercer College and spoke before
the Macon Kiwanis Club. She declined an invitation to Wesleyan College
because of a conflict. On the day following the conference, she was
guest of the Agnes Scott College International Relations Club (Atlanta).
The next two days found her speaking to the students at Capital View
School (Atlanta) and to the Hartwell (Georgia) Women's Club. Rankin
concluded her report of these activities by writing, "Tired but happy."[4]
Throughout the year, she duplicated this itinerary many times in speaking trips across the United States.[5]

One of the techniques of the National Council for Prevention of
War was to send its staff into Congressional districts to try to influence public opinion and to bring pressure upon the representatives.
Carl Vinson, Representative of the Tenth District in Georgia, was a
ranking member of the House Naval Affairs Committee. In September of 1930,
Jeannette Rankin made a tour of his district to build peace sentiment,
visiting newspaper editors and interviewing as many people as possible.
In two days, she made thirty-one calls and drove 250 miles. Included was
a luncheon visit with Representative Vinson himself in Milledgeville. She
explained what she was doing, and Vinson replied, "What you are doing is

---

[4]J. R. to the Staff of National Council for Prevention of War,
February 13, 1930, Rankin File Drawer, NCPW Files, SCPC.

[5]Nashville Tennessean, January 6, 1930; New York Herald, February 24,
1931; Cardine Woodruff to F. Libby, October 18, 1930, NCPW.

getting a lot of these people so they will write to you next winter when the Navy bills come up."[6] To the Georgia Peace Society, she reported finding sentiment in Georgia growing in favor or the League of Nations, the World Court, disarmament conferences, and the Kellogg-Briand Pact.[7]

Disappointed at the failure of the Geneva Disarmament Conference in 1927, peace workers looked forward to the London Navel Conference in 1930. After prolonged and acrimonious arguments, the United States, Britain, Japan, France and Italy signed the London Naval Pact of 1930, although France and Italy subscribed only to relatively unimportant clauses. The outcome was a partial victory for disarmament as an upper limit was fixed in all categories of vessels, but peace advocates could only hope for another conference.[8]

This hope became reality when the League of Nations announced that the disarmament conference planned since 1925 would be called for February of 1932. During 1931, Jeannnette Rankin began to make plans to support the Geneva Conference. In speaking about disarmament to the District Missionary Societies of the North Georgia Methodist Conference in the Spring of 1931, Rankin stressed recognition of the principle that all nations, including Germany and the other powers already disarmed by the Treaties of Power, were entitled to equality of treatment. She advocated a ten percent a year reduction in total expenditure for armaments for

---

[6]J. R. to Mary Ida Winder, September 6, 1930, Rankin File Drawer, NCPW Files, SCPC; 1930 Annual Business Meeting, Report of J. R., NCPW Files.

[7]Athens Banner-Herald, October 5, 1930, p. 1:5.

[8]Thomas A. Bailey, A Diplomatic History of the American People (New York: F. S. Crofts and Company, 1964), pp. 651-652; Robert H. Ferrell, American Diplomacy in the Great Depression: Hoover-Stinson Foreign Policy, 1929-1933 (New Haven: Yale University Press, 1957), pp. 194-214.

five years; direct limitation and reduction of the weapons of land warfare; and the prohibition of preparation and use of poisonous gas and
bacteriological methods of warfare. She also urged the members of the
societies to ask the President to appoint a recognized peace advocate to
the American delegation at Geneva.[9] Actually, her Georgia Peace Society
went on record as endorsing either Newton D. Baker or Judge Florence E.
Allen, both of Ohio, for appointment to the United States Delegation to
the February Geneva Conference.[10]

This interest in disarmament resulted in the formulating of plans
in June of 1931, for a Georgia Committee on the Disarmament Conference.
Jeannette Rankin was appointed to direct the Committee's activities.
Its purpose was to keep every community in Georgia informed about disarmament, to arouse public opinion to express its interest in the President's appointing an "advocate of peace" to the United States delegation
(in which all National peace groups were interested) and to organize sentiment in the state to exert an effective influence upon the Geneva Conference.[11]

An introductory letter was sent to 1,700 men and women whose names
were supplied by Georgia League of Women Voters, University of Georgia
Alumnae Association and the Southern Methodist Missionary Conference. In
three weeks, Jeannette Rankin had secured three hundred members from
ninety-one towns, and by the end of the year membership had grown to over

---

[9] Athens Banner-Herald, June 8, 1931, p. 2:4; In one week Jeannette
Rankin spoke at Dallas, Marietta, McDonough, and Monroe.

[10] Athens Banner-Herald, December 20, 1931, p. 1.

[11] Athens Banner-Herald, June 25, 1931, p. 2:1; Hartwell Sun, December
4, 1931 (no page given); Jeannette Rankin, Form Letter, July 10, 1931,
Georgia Peace Society Folder, S.C.P.C.

five hundred.[12] The members of the Georgia Committee were to read material
pertaining to the Geneva Conference, to select six people to whom they
would distribute disarmament material and to write letters to the President,
the Secretary of State, the two Georgia Senators, District United States
Congressmen and to each of the delegates representing the United States
in Geneva. An attached post card was to be filled out when these letters
were completed. Miss Rankin used this technique to confirm their having
done what she suggested, or to report other activities and accomplishments.

From the suggested duties, letter writing seemed to be the principle
part of the campaign. Jeannette Rankin provided the Committee members
with ten sample questions, each in a different form, asking President
Hoover if he did not think it would be well to have one who believed in
disarmament on the United States delegation. Letters to the State Department requested material on the Disarmament Conference. The Senators were
asked about United States' entrance into the World Court. For the questions
to the Congressmen, the Committee sent eight statements on military training in schools and members were asked to form one of them into a question
for his Congressman. The technique was to get original letters, asking a
variety of questions, rather than just stating an opinion.[13]

While establishing this sentiment in Georgia for the Geneva Conference,
Jeannette Rankin took a nine-week trip to Europe basically under the auspices
of the NCPW to study the Assembly of the League of Nations. Prior to
the convening of the Assembly, she participated in a two-week study course

---

[12]"Working Politically for Peace in Georgia," January 5, 1932, Georgia
Peace Society Folder, S.C.P.C.

[13]Ibid.

in Geneva sponsored by the Women's International League for Peace and
Freedom.[14]

While never particularly impressed with the League, Jeannette Rankin
considered it useful as a "channel for communication between the nations."
She saw it as a continuing conference, ready to function as the nations
desired. To her, its greatest value came as an instrument to promote
world understanding. Rankin advocated disarming to such an extent that
nations could not participate in a war on a moment's notice. With this
delay, public opinion could be registered; and the League would have time
to function.[15]

Conflict between Japan and China came into the open with an explosion
on the Japanese-controlled South Manchurian Railroad near Mukden on
September 18, 1931. Jeannette Rankin was observing the Assembly as the
Japanese rushed troops into Manchuria. China, unprepared to fight,
appealed to the League of Nations and to the United States. Writing a
month later, Jeannette observed:

> The crisis in the Orient has demonstrated beyond
> doubt the great necessity of reducing armaments.
> With the League of Nations ready to register the
> public opinion of the world and with China un-
> prepared for instant war, sufficient delay was
> secured--we hope--to prevent this dispute from
> developing into a world war.[16]

In addition to calling attention to the Kellogg-Briand Pact, the
Nine Power Pact, the League set up the Lytton Commission to report on the

---

[14]Laura P. Morgan to J.R., April 16, 1931, J. R. Correspondence File
for 1931, NCPW Files, S.C.P.C.

[15]J. R., "As a Woman Views Europe Politically and Economically,"
NCPW Files, S.C.P.C.

[16]Ibid.

crisis. Unfortunately, contrary to Rankin's hope, the Japanese armies were ready to fight and by January of 1932 had crushed all Chinese resistance in Manchuria. Had the armaments of all nations been reduced, according to Rankin, there would have been a chance to prevented war.[17]

While the Japanese overran Manchuria, the Democratic Party caucus named Representative Carl Vinson from Georgia as Chairman of the House Naval Affairs Committee. He had previously served as a member of the Committee for sixteen years.[18] His first decision as the new Chairman was to introduce a $616,000,000 naval building program. Jeannette Rankin challenged the bill for detailed proof of the necessity for increased naval expenditures. She also claimed that the Vinson Bill was a violation of the London Naval Treaty, would jeopardize the success of the disarmament conference opening the next February, and that it was unwise to spend such large sums of money when the United States treasury was virtually empty.[19]

In protest to the Vinson Navy Bill, Georgians sent in 159 post cards from 62 towns in a referendum poll conducted by Jeannette Rankin. These cards were presented to Representative Vinson on January 1, 1932.[20] The work of the Peace Society and the Committee on Disarmament resulted in the Georgia papers debating the advisability of such a large appropriation.

---

[17]Ibid.

[18]Macon Telegraph, December 15, 1931, p. 1; Mr. Vinson was born in Baldwin County, 1883. He served as its solicitor for three years, served four years in Georgia General Assembly, and was elected to the United States House of Representatives in 1914.

[19]Athens Banner-Herald, December 20, 1931, p. 1:2.

[20]Jeannette Rankin to Members of Georgia Committee on Disarmament, January 26, 1932, Georgia Peace Society Folder, S.C.P.C.

The <u>Macon Telegraph</u>, from Vinson's home district, took up the argument
by commenting editorially, "It is absurd for a nation with a tremendous
deficit to go spending money on 'shooting irons' when it will have to buy
bread for a great many of its family."[21] As a result, Jeannette believed
Representative Vinson let the navy supporters express themselves, but did
not ask for a vote. Later when Senator Hale passed the billion-dollar
building program in the Senate, Representative Vinson did not report it
from his committee. The bill was shelved on January 25, 1932.[22] It was
finally adopted by Congress in 1934.

After lobbying against naval expenditures, Jeannette Rankin turned
her attention to the political conventions of 1932. Along with Florence
Boeckel, Education Secretary of NCPW, and Emily Wold, Women's Committee
for World Disarmament, she organized a "To Chicago" plan. The idea was to
have women and college students converge in Chicago in June to register
antiwar sentiment upon the Republican and Democratic parties. In speaking to a WIL meeting urging greater political activism, Rankin said,
"There is tremendous peace sentiment in the United States which has not
been given expression because it is not yet politically conscious."[23]
In a press release, she wrote, "We propose to make it clear to the political leaders, assembled at their conventions, that the people want peace.

---

[21]As quoted in <u>News Bulletin</u> of National Council for Prevention of
War, February, 1932, p. 5.

[22]"Working Politically for Peace in Georgia," January 5, 1932,
Georgia Peace Society Folder, S.C.P.C.

[23]"Women To Put Massed Power Back of Peace," <u>Christian Science Monitor</u>,
April 15, 1932.

Nothing else is of such immediate and pressing importance."[24] They

planned to make public demonstrations, to contact delegates, and to urge

peace planks in the party platforms.[25]

With "peace" banners flying, Jeannette Rankin and Emily Wold led the

caravan of a half-dozen cars as it left Washington, D.C., on June 2. They

anticipated speaking stops along the way and hoped to join similar groups

starting from various parts of the country. Prior to each convention,

the women organized a peace parade with automobiles representing many

states and colleges. Following the parades were hearings before the

Platform Committee. Jeannette, representing the "unorganized women of

the country," shared in the thirty minutes allotted to peace organizations

by the Republicans, while others spoke before the Democratic Committee.[26]

The Republicans in their platform advocated proportional reduction of

armaments and decried increased military expenditures, while the Democrats

endorsed a navy and army adequate for national defense, accompanied by a

reference to economy in expenditures. Both parties supported membership

in the World Court and an international agreement for reduction of arma-

ments.[27]

During 1932 and 1933, Jeannette Rankin traveled widely for the NCPW,

speaking in behalf of disarmament and the Geneva Convention, the Kellogg-

---

[24]Press release, "Statement of Jeannette Rankin," NCPW Files, SCPC.

[25]NCPW News Bulletin, XI (April, 1932), p. 3; Harry Terrell, Mid-West
NCPW Secretary, to author, February 4, 1972; J. R. to Janet Kinney,
University of Idaho, May 5, 1932; Jane Addams to J. R., April 13, 1932,
in J. R. Correspondence File, 1932, NCPW.

[26]NCPW News Bulletin, XI (June, 1932), p. 6; New York Times, June 3,
1932; NCPW News Bulletin, XI (July, 1932), p. 1.

[27]NCPW News Bulletin, XI (July, 1932), p. 4.

Briand Pact, and the moral power of public opinion as an agent to enforce peace. During November and December of 1933, she made one hundred and twenty-five speeches to approximately 27,000 people.[28] Speaking to a Flagstaff, Arizona, Rotary Club, Rankin pointed out the inconsistency between cutting compensation for war veterans because of the depression while increasing the appropriations for armed services and national defense. Contrary to the press releases, she believed the hugh expenditures for defense were only to make profit for shipbuilders and munitions makers at the expense of the people.[29]

Through the 1920's, many Americans increasingly became disillusioned with their recent venture into international affairs, namely World War I. It had not been the "War To End War," much less "A War for Democracy." Wilsonian idealism had not become the panacea for international ills that many had hoped it would. Also, historians, like Sidney B. Fay, punctured America's self-righteous balloon by presenting evidence that the Central Powers had not been entirely responsible nor the Allied countries wholly guiltless in the recent war.[30] In 1921 a League of Nations Commission investigated the European armaments industry and charged it with false reports, fostering an armaments race, bribing government officials, and instigating war scares.[31]

---

[28]J. R. to Mrs. C. A. Broadus, March 5, 1934, J. R. 1934 Corresponddence Files, NCPW Files, S.C.P.C.

[29]Flagstaff Coconino Sun, November 10, 1933.

[30]Sidney B. Fay, "New Light on the Origins of the World War," American Historical Review, XXV (July, 1920), pp. 616-639; C. Harley Grattan, Why We Fought (New York: Vanguard Press, reprint, 1969); Sidney B. Fay, The Origins of World War I (New York: Macmillan Company, 1931).

[31]The First Sub-Committee of the Temporary Mixed Commission of the League of Nations, Report A 81, C. 321 (Geneva, September 15, 1921).

Significant followup in the United States on this theme did not materialize until ten years later.

When Congress created in 1931 the War Policies Commission, a joint congressional-cabinet arrangement, to hear and discuss plans to equalize the burdens of war and to prevent war profiteering, Pandora's box opened. English journalist Norman Angell and Labor Party leader Ramsay McDonald whetted American interest with their publications, The Secret International (1932) and Patriotism (1933). These books exposed the international cartels in armaments. Having become convinced that the munition makers were reaping huge profits while supplying both sides, Dorothy Detzer, national secretary for Women's International League, enlisted the help of Senator George Norris. After careful scrutiny of potential senators to push an investigation of the munitions question, they selected Gerald Nye, former newspaperman and Republican of North Dakota.[32] In the Spring of 1934, the Senate created a Munitions Investigating Committee and appointed Nye as its chairman.

The NCPW and Jeannette Rankin supported the Nye Committee by developing material, lobbying in Congress, and lecturing in its behalf on tours.[33] Speaking on "Why We Need an Investigation of the Munitions Industry," Jeannette Rankin recalled that European armament firms had been active in forming war scares, attempting to bribe government officials, and spreading

---

[32] Dorothy Detzer, Appointment on the Hill (New York: Henry Holt and Co. 1948), pp. 155-156.

[33] Norman Angell and Ramsay McDonald, The Secret International: Armament Firms at Work (London: Union of Democratic Control, 1932); Patriotism, Ltd: An Exposure of the War Machine (London: Union of Democratic Control, 1933; See also Fenner Brockway, The Bloody Traffic (London: Victor Gollanez, Ltd., 1933); John E. Wiltz, In Search of Peace: The Senate Munitions Inquiry, 1934-36 (Baton Rouge, Saint Louis Press, 1963.

false reports about the naval program of various countries in order to stimulate armament expenditure. She also indicated that armament manufacturers had tried to influence public opinion by controlling newspapers and had raised the price of war material by organizing international trusts.[34]

"We are walking in the direction of war and we can get a war anytime the minitions makers and profit makers demand it," Jeannette Rankin prophesied for the B & PW Club in Jackson, Michigan. She revealed how there was always a relation between war scares and legislation, between approrpriations for the army and propaganda fostered by the makers of munitions. When Congressman Vinson of Georgia introduced his "Billion Dollar Naval Building Program" in 1933, she remembered Senator George Norris saying, "Well, we are going through our annual scare with Japan. It means money out of our pockets into the pockets of the profiteers."[35] Jeannette Rankin continued, "If we do not crystalize public opinion we are going directly to war because the munition makers...must use up their stockpiles." She warned her hearers not to be trapped by slogans and silly pretenses into the need of going to war as a means of self defense.[36]

Rankin always urged her audiences or correspondents to write the senators on the munitions investigation committee and inquire about profits made in the last war and that are still being made today. "Be not satisfied," she demanded, "with a reprint...about profiteers in Europe, but insist upon having information regarding our own American patriots who are

---

[34]Jeannette Rankin, Radio Address over Athens WIFI as reported in Athens Banner-Herald, May 31, 1934.

[35]Athens Daily Times, December 20, 1934.

[36]Jackson (Michigan) Citizen Patriot, May 10, 1934.

willing to give the life of your son for their profit."[37]

The Nye Committee charged that armament firms in the United States bribed government officials, disregarded national policies, sold weapons to both sides in time of war, stimulated arms races between nations, lobbied for military appropriations, and thrived on excess profit. Their findings provided some documentation for the charges that American intervention in World War I stemmed from economic causes. Charles Beard demonstrated in his The Devil Theory of War that American prosperity depended on Allied success in the War, and thus intervention was determined by national economic interests. However, Beard showed that the prosperity reached all areas of the economy and was not limited to a few munitions makers.[38] While the investigation continued, Englebrecht and Hanigher released their book, Merchants of Death, which chastised the war industries for their blindness to the social consequences of munitions propaganda. All of this publicity, butressed by the Nye reports, aroused public interest and created an environment in which the peace organizations thrived.[39]

To Jeannette Rankin, the profits by armament makers plus allied banking, industrial, and commercial firms produced a vested interest in continuing the system of war. Contrary to the usual position of the NCPW, she encouraged anti-profit legislation. Rankin reasoned that, by removing profits from war endeavors, one might eliminate war. Certainly, the findings

---

[37]Athens Daily Times, December 20, 1934; see also Great Falls Tribune, June 20, 1934.

[38]Walter Millis' book, The Road to War (Boston: Houghton Mifflin Co., 1935), also contained an economic emphasis linking America to the European Allies; Charles Beard, The Devil Theory of War (New York: The Vanguard Press, 1936).

[39]H. C. Englebrecht and F. C. Hanigher, Merchants of Death: A Study of the International Armament Industry (New York: Dodd, Mead & Co., 1934).

of Senate munitions investigations strengthened this argument.

Before the House Committee on Military Affairs in January of 1935,
Jeannette Rankin reluctantly attacked the McSwain Bill, which was to take
profits out of war by establishing ceilings on various industrial activities. She described this as leading "the people" into a false sense of
security. She agreed with John McSwain's objective but disagreed with
his method of approach. He described World War I as a "rich man's war";
to which Miss Rankin added "fought by the poor man." Characterizing
herself as representing the masses of unorganized women and men, Jeannette
said: "It is perfectly possible to take the profit out of war, but...not
by any of the schemes that the rich men suggest; and you haven't had any
proposals...from the poor man." She suggested that, once war had been
declared, Congress should create a medium of exchange, good only during
the duration of the war. When war ceased, the money would become illegal,
thus insuring that no profits would be made. Rankin proposed:

> You should pay $30 a day [probably she meant
> month], or whatever the soldiers' wage is, to
> everyone, and let everyone have a tin cup and
> bread card and subsist on the same food that
> the soldier does, beginning with the President. [40]

For members of Congress who had voted for war, she advised paying them
the $30 a month and giving them the honor of carrying the flag in battle.

Believing that "the people" do not want war, Jeannette Rankin labeled
all statutory anti-profit legislation as an attempt to blind them into
thinking war can be carried on without profit. She pointed out that as
a result of wartime hysteria, many things were accomplished by Executive

---

[40]U.S., Congress, House of Representatives, Committee on Military
Affairs, Hearing on Taking the Profit out of War, on H.R. 3 and H.R.
5293, 74th Congress, 1st Session, pp. 307-308.

Order without statutory foundation. Rankin further asserted that con-
scription had to be instituted in WW I because the poor man was unwilling
to fight the rich man's war. Pursuing her line of thought, a committee
member asked, "So you think we made a mistake in going to war with Germany?"
She replied, "I made no mistake. I voted against it."[41]

The conversation then shifted to the topic, "Who won the war?" One
member ventured, "We all lost." Another asked, "Who won the San Francisco
earthquake?" With quickness of wit, Rankin observed, "You can no more win
a war than you can win an earthquake." Aware that the committee now saw
the futility of war, Jeannette put forth her own idea for a constitutional
amendment to place war declaring power in the hands of the people as the
only real solution. Cognizant that the people might vote to declare war,
she added to it her "profit removing" currency idea.[42]

While hammering away at the munitions makers, Jeannette Rankin continued organizational work in Representative Carl Vinson's Sixth Congressional
District in the Fall of 1934. Jeannette knew it would be difficult to
secure volunteer workers for propaganda work on a national level. She
sought peace supporters in Putnam, Jasper, Laurens, Bleckley and Twiggs
Counties, covering the counties precinct by precinct. Under her plans,
each precinct was to have an active organization headed by a member of
the Georgia Peace Society. In addition to personal contacts, Miss Rankin
spoke to a meeting on the Court House steps in Eatonton, to a high school
in Dublin, to the Women's Club, high school and a Methodist prayer meeting

---

[41]Ibid., p. 312.

[42]Ibid.

in Cochran, and to an evening group in Monticello.[43] By December, she had

been in ten of the sixteen counties of the Sixth District and had secured

292 new members to the Georgia Peace Society. They represented seventy-

three different precincts and included prominent political leaders in

each county. The opposition to Representative Vinson was greater than she

had expected, but she unwisely concluded that with a good candidate, Vinson

might be defeated in the election of 1936.[44]

While she was in the state, the Georgia Peace Society honored her ten

years of service in Georgia. Rabbi Abraham Shusterman of the Athens Syna-

gogue paid tribute for the Society by saying that she had given it a three-

fold philosophy:

> She had indued us with the conviction that the
> individual effort is meaningful and efficacious....
> She has brought us the enthusiasm to make ours
> a truly moral nation....Finally, Miss Rankin has
> brought us a new vision of the meaning of democ-
> racy.[45]

At this meeting the Reverend John Tate, the new president, initiated a

state campaign for members and enlarged the board of directors to make

it state-wide in personnel including all past Society presidents. Also

included were Roberta Hodgson and W. P. King, who by this time, had moved

to Nashville, Tennessee. Six hundred letters were then mailed to pros-

pective members in the state, and the Georgia Peace Society was about

---

[43]Jeannette Rankin to Frederick Libby, October 1, 1934, Rankin File
Drawer, N. C. P. W., Files, S. C. P. C.

[44]Jeannette Rankin to Frederick Libby, December 7, 1934, Rankin File
Drawer, N. C. P. W. Files, S. C. P. C.; Nonpareil (Council Bluffs, In.)
Dec. 30, 1934.

[45]Athens Banner-Herald, September 28, 1934, p. 1.

to embark on its most active period.[46]

In the Fall, county agricultural fairs provided an excellent opportunity to advertise the work of the Georgia Peace Society and to educate the public for peace. "All they that taketh the sword shall perish by taxes," and "You can no more win a war than you can win an earthquake" were pungent slogans displayed in the Athens District Fair in 1934. Photos showing the horrors of war were displayed along with a large map of Europe. Those who managed the booth distributed literature on the Senate munitions investigation, petitions for entrance into the League of Nations and membership cards for the Georgia Peace Society.[47] To stir up enthusiasm and to help with attendance, the Peace Society sponsored a "Children's Day." Students from Athens and surrounding towns presented posters and short talks on peace at the booth. The Georgia Peace Society planned to make visitors to the booth peace conscious and to convince them that they could help preserve peace. Jeannette Rankin believed preservation of peace to be more of an individual responsibility than a government enterprise. Thus, the people must be educated to believe in the settlement of disputes by arbitration. She said, "When they have been taught the sensible and civilized manner of settling disputes, they will vote against warfare and we shall have world peace."[48]

Such was Jeannette Rankin's devotion that she accomplished the work in Georgia in the Fall of 1934 without the aid of a secretary or the use

---

[46]Athens Banner-Herald, September 28, 1934, p. 1; Jeannette Rankin to Frederick Libby, October 1, 1934; Rankin File Drawer, N. C. P. W. Files, S. C. P. C.

[47]Membership was of two kinds: active -- those who contributed; A. A. Members -- those who signed a membership card and declared their moral support.

[48]Athens Daily Times, November 4, 1934, p. 5.

of a telephone. She contributed the traveling expenses and the mailing
of letters out of her own purse. Constantly, she was torn between
requests for speaking engagements and the organizational work in the
rural districts. Her love for "peace work" and suffering humanity provided the strength necessary to sustain the long hours and arduous miles
of travel.

CHAPTER IX

ENOUGH OF JEANNETTE

During the mid-1930's Jeannette Rankin had two experiences which were probably representative of much of the hardship, insinuation and slander that pacifists faced during the inter-war period. In the Fall of 1934, the Blue Ridge mountain town of Gainesville, Georgia awakened suddenly to find itself the center of a boiling controversy between the "fire-eating" American Legion and its music oriented, liberal arts institution, Brenau College. The widely publicized controversy arose when the Atlanta Post No. 1 of the American Legion objected to the appointment of Jeannette Rankin to a Brenau "Chair of Peace." This opposition came as a surprise because Miss Rankin had spoken at Brenau on other occasions without stirring objections.[1]

In the first of a series of lectures on disarmament, Jeannette Rankin spoke to the political economy and journalism classes and was guest at a luncheon on October 25, 1934.[2] In introducing her to the class, H. J. Pearce, Jr., vice president of the College and professor of history, expressed a pleasantry about hoping to establish a "Chair of Peace" at

---

[1]Jeannette Rankin to Dr. Iola K. Eastburn, February 8, 1930, Rankin File Drawer, N. C. P. W. Files, S. C. P. C. - indicated Jeannette Rankin took Lucia A. Mead to Brenau to speak; Dr. Iola K. Eastburn to Jeannette Rankin, April 2, 1931, N. C. P. W. Files, S. C. P. C. - arranging a date for Jeannette Rankin to speak to Student Chapel.

[2]Athens Banner-Herald, October 26, 1934, p. 1.; Gainesville News, October 31, 1934.

Brenau and, if so, he would nominate Miss Rankin as "Professor of Peace."
The news media in reporting her address translated the wish of the future
into the fact of the past. The reporter stated that Brenau College had
established a "Chair of Peace" and had elected Jeannette Rankin.[3]

After her second lecture, Armistice Day, November 11, 1934, on
"There is more thrill in building up ideas than in destroying lives,"
the Atlanta Post No. 1 charged that the establishment of a "Chair of Peace"
with Jeannette Rankin as professor was "un-American." Kenneth Murrell,
commander of the post, said "the chair of peace, designed to promote the
principle ideas of a peaceful society, is detrimental to the welfare of
American youth."[4] There was great unrest throughout the world. To create
any "ism" other than Americanism among the youth of the country, was unpatriotic, a hinderance to progress, and an obstacle to military preparedness. The post adopted a resolution condemning Brenau for encouraging
pacifism among its students. Included in the resolution passed by the
Atlanta Post No. 1 of the American Legion were two poignant paragraphs:

> WHEREAS, Janet [sic] Rankin has long been ob-
> noxious to those persons who believe that this
> country should be prepared to maintain its
> position as a world power and to protect its
> lives and property and who believe that its
> land, sea and air forces should not be render-
> ed impotent, and
>
> WHEREAS, it occurs to this Post that the
> unusual department thus created by Brenau
> College could serve only the propaganda
> purposes of those pacifists closely akin
> to communists and that no good could come
> by reason of the opportunity afforded this

---

[3]"The Chair of Peace," The Brenau Bulletin, XXVII (February, 1935),
p. 1.

[4]Atlanta Constitution, November 16, 1934, p. 6.

pacifist to preach un-American doctrines to the young womanhood of the South...."[5]

DeLacy Allen, State Commander from Albany, Georgia added the endorsement

of the state organization, saying:

It is the aim of the department to try to prevent any such communistic ideas being taught in the state and we will utilize every effort possible to combat the policies being encouraged at Brenau College."[6]

Those efforts were promoted by circularizing every Legion Post, D. A. V.

Chapter, V. F. W. Post and news agency in the state, condemning the "Chair

of Peace" and Miss Rankin.

Haywood Pearce, Jr., in the absence of his father, H. J. Pearce,

Sr., who was President of Brenau, replied to the American Legion attack.

He indicated that there would be a Chair of Peace established to teach

the students what economics, politics, international law, diplomacy and

international history might indicate about the causes, antecedents and

costs of war. He had difficulty seeing the organization of such a body

of knowledge and its presentation as "un-American." Dr. Pearce was in

Paris in the Spring of 1919 when the Legion was organized by Theodore

Roosevelt and was a charter member of the Paul E. Bolding Post of the

American Legion. He refused to accept Commander Murrell's contention

that "the establishment of a Chair of Peace was detrimental to welfare

of American youth."[7]

---

[5]Resolution by Atlanta Post No. 1 of American Legion, Rankin File Drawer, N. C. P. W. Files, S. C. P. C.

[6]Atlanta Constitution, November 15, 1934, p. 2.

[7]Atlanta Journal, November 15, 1934; Atlanta Constitution, November 16, 1934, p. 6.

In a newspaper account of Haywood Pearce, Jr.'s reply, two things came to light. The "pleasantry" had changed to fact. Indeed, a "Chair of Peace" was to be established to integrate as much knowledge as possible about war and peace into the students' studies. Secondly, Pearce cited his service record in World War I and his own membership in the American Legion to discredit any charge of un-Americanism on the part of Brenau leadership. This argument was effective. At this point, the Legion Post shifted its attack from the College to Miss Rankin personally. The Legion Post objected "to the radical views of war held by Miss Rankin," and said, "Atlanta Post No. 1 does not want the school of thought propagated by Miss Rankin to take root in the South or anywhere else."[8]

Haywood Pearce, Jr., pointed out the real issue by inviting Kenneth Murrell to speak to the Brenau students or to share a forum with Miss Rankin. Pearce wrote that the Post really disapproved of all discussions of pacifism and wished to shut off discussion of the "advisability" of a big army, big navy or military training in the college. "Let us not obscure the issue by epithets," he concluded.[9]

When H. J. Pearce, Sr., Brenau President, returned to the campus, he vigorously defended the College's invitation to Jeannette Rankin to deliver a series of three lectures. He saw the Legion's position as interference with the academic freedom, vital to college inquiry. No hint of un-Americanism in her lectures was discernable to him, but he pointed out Brenau did not necessarily endorse all its lecturers' opinions. In reference to the

---

[8]Atlanta Constitution, November 17, 1934, p. 10; Lucile Adams to Kenneth Clark, President of Brenau, February 25, 1969, which contained an excerpt from letter of Haywood Pearce, Jr., to his sister, Lucile Adams.

[9]Atlanta Journal, November 23, 1934.

"Chair of Peace", he wrote that Miss Rankin's lectures might well lead to such a position, but that it had not been established. He was quick to add "the only obstacle is the deplorable lack of funds."[10]

For her part, Jeannette Rankin prepared a statement for President Pearce saying that she was of Seventeenth Century American Stock, had never subscribed to the doctrines of communism, and was presently an independent in politics. She was willing to be called a "pacifist," if you defined it as committing oneself to settlement of disputes by peaceful means - like our forty eight states settle disputes by appealing to the Supreme Court." She pointed to the adoption of most of the progressive and humanitarian legislation which she had championed. Finally, she wrote, "The sum of my radicalism seems to be my opposition to war, to competetitive armaments and predatory interest."[11]

Support for the "Chair of Peace" idea came from newspaper editorials, college professors, peace advocates, the Georgia Peace Society, current magazines, leading citizens and former Brenau students. T. W. Tippett, pastor of Prince Avenue Baptist Church in Athens, and a good friend, said, "Personally, I appreciate the work of Miss Rankin in the interest of peace. She deserves the confidence and support of the people. I resent the unfair charges against her."[12]

The New Republic wrote: "If the American Legionnaires thought they could turn Miss Rankin from her purpose, they were most naive. Having braved the ill wind of a whole nation, it is most likely she will be

---

[10]Gainesville Eagle, November 22, 1934, p. 1:3.

[11]Jeannette Rankin to H. J. Pearce, November 22, 1934, Rankin File Drawer, N. C. P. W. Files, S. C. P. C.

[12]Athens Banner-Herald, October 18, 1934, p. 1:1.

disturbed by empty flag waving and a few harsh words."[13] An editorial in the Brenau student publication defended the project by asking why should not students learn that peace was the only way to gain world security and democracy, and why should not they be taught the horrors, costs and methods of war? Then the student editor predicted, "A Chair of Peace at Brenau may be the greatest step toward progress that has ever been made."[14]

The Journal of Labor rejoiced, some what prematurely, that Brenau had set up a chair of peace and added Jeannette Rankin to its faculty. It felt that someone should speak of peace in the midst of Georgia's military campuses, naval accoutrements, high school and college military training, and propaganda parades. Editorially, labor took the position that the attacks on Jeannette Rankin were symptomatic of the military leadership and the military mind in which the seeds of war thrive and grow.[15]

Unpreturbed by the response to the establishment of a "Chair of Peace," the "100 percent" American Legionnaires continued their barrage. The James K. Fleming, Jr. Post (Athens) passed a resolution objecting to Miss Rankin's work in various radical groups while using popular organizations as a front.[16] Endorsement of the Legion's views came from other Posts around the state and from state and national leaders.[17]

---

[13]The New Republic, Vol. LXXXI (December 26, 1934), p. 177.

[14]Brenau Alchemist as quoted in Athens Banner-Herald, December 17, 1934, p. 8:5; Alchemist not available in Brenau Library.

[15]Journal of Labor, December 7, 1934, p. 2.

[16]Athens Banner-Herald, December 23, 1934, p. 1:7.

[17]Gainesville Eagle, November 22, 1934, p. 1.

Because of the severity of these charges, Jeannette Rankin considered a libel suit against Kenneth Murrell and Atlanta Legion Post No. 1.
Charges of "communism" and "seditious utterances," which would damage a
person's reputation, presented possibilities for winning a court trial.
Miss Rankin said that, if she alone were concerned, she would ignore the
charges. Anyone who urged reduction of armaments with it consequent decrease of profits must be prepared for bitter and unfair attack by the
tools of these interests. Such charges had been made quietly ever since
she came to live in Georgia. Rankin was glad finally to have a real opportunity to answer them openly. A court case would provide persons who had
no time to inquire into the truth of these charges, an opportunity to see
the real facts. Despite all of these arguments in favor of court action,
the libel suit was never filed. Evidently, she decided she could not win.
Community sympathy was the only real libel, and those charges of communism
were only by association.[18]

The Legion turned down invitations to hear Miss Rankin's last lecture
at Brenau and sent a committee composed of Brigadier General J. H. Reeves,
U.S.A., retired; Joe Cook, president of the Reserve Officer's Association
of Georgia; Colonel Frank S. Chalmers, Commander of the 123rd Infantry
Reserves; Quimby Melton, representing the National Commander of American
Legion; and Kenneth Murrell, Commander of Atlanta Post No. 1 to discuss
their opposition with J. H. Pearce, Sr., and Brenau's trustees.[19] The
conference basically dealt with the qualifications of Miss Rankin as a

[18]Athens Banner-Herald, December 17, 1934, p. 1; Athens Banner-Herald,
December 19, 1934, p. 1.

[19]Atlanta Constitution, December 8, 1934, p. 18; Atlanta Constitution,
December 17, 1934, p. 2.

professor to hold the proposed Chair of Peace.

Previously, the American Legion Post had made clear that their attack was not aimed at Brenau -- only at Miss Rankin. At this conference they even dropped all objection to the establishment of a "Chair of Peace" in order to focus attention on Jeannette Rankin. The American Legion wanted peace, but with military preparedness. Therefore, it objected to her pacifism and advocacy of total disarmament. Picturesquely, Captain A. L. Hinton described a disarmed American as a "dehorned bull in a herd of Texas steers."[20]

The American Legion Post No. 1 charged that Miss Rankin's connections with the American Civil Liberties Union, the National Council for the Prevention of War, The Women's Peace Union, Victor Berger Foundation, and the Peoples Council showed communistic association. The Legion charged that Seymour Waldman had headed the National Council for Prevention of War, and later became publisher of the Daily Worker, a Communist paper. Also they said that the National Council for the Prevention of War had received aid from the Garland Fund, which also partially supported Emma Goldman's anarchist-communist school. Furthermore, Miss Rankin's name, listed as vice-president of American Civil Liberties Union, was found on literature possessed by Angelo Herndon, a Negro recently convicted in Atlanta for attempting to incite insurrection. For these reasons the Legion urged her unfitness as a professor and lecturer.[21] The Executive Committee of Brenau's trustees agreed to take the Legion's protest under advisement.

---

[20] Atlanta Constitution, December 17, 1934, p. 2.

[21] Atlanta Constitution, December 19, 1934, p. 1.

Evidently the trustees were concerned about the allegations.
Jeannette Rankin asked Roger Baldwin, Director of American Civil Liberties
Union, to send material to H. J. Pearce about their activities, purposes
and associations of the Union. The trustees also requested additional
information from Frederick Libby about the National Council for the Prevention of War. In order to obtain Miss Rankin's own answers to the Legion
charges, Dr. Pearce sent her a stenographic report of the conference.[22]

To this report, Jeannette Rankin presented a rebuttal. As the American Legion claimed, she had been an honorary vice-president of the American
Civil Liberties Union, but since she was in New York irregularly, she did
not take an active part in the administration of its policies. Her endorsement of the American Civil Liberties Union was unqualified as long as it
was limited to activities to defending the right of free speech, free press,
and free assembly. "The director," she wrote, "was not a communist, and
that among other names on the letterhead was L. L. Hendren, Dean of the
University of Georgia."[23]

As to association with the Victor Berger Foundation, she had contributed five dollars, but had no other connection with it. She denied having
had any relationship with the Peoples Council, inactive for about seventeen
years.[24]

---

[22]H. J. Pearce to Jeannette Rankin, December 21, 1934, N. C. P. W.
Files, S. C. P. C.

[23]Jeannette Rankin to H. J. Pearce, December 21, 1934, Rankin File
Drawer, N. C. P. W. Files, S. C. P. C.; Columbia University, Oral History
Memoir of Roger Baldwin and American Civil Liberties Union, page 124 of
transcript -- named Jeannette Rankin as one of the early vice-chairmen.

[24]Jeannette Rankin to H. J. Pearce, December 21, 1934, Rankin File
Drawer, N. C. P. W., S. C. P. C.

Jeannette Rankin was proud of her position as Associate Secretary of the National Council for Prevention of War, and gave relentlessly of her time and energy to keep up with congressional measures and activities. She described the National Council for Prevention of War as comprising twenty-two participating organizations and ten cooperating ones, and including many distinguished public spirited individuals and educators. As far as she knew, none of these individuals or organizations were communist or participated in any communistic activities.[25]

Because Jeannette Rankin opposed military training both in high school and college and often chided her student audiences for their support of these agencies, the American Legion reported to H. J. Pearce that her speeches were unpatriotic and disrespectful. Miss Rankin denied telling students at a Griffin, Georgia, high school that "they should be ashamed to wear the uniform of the United States."[26] Similarly, she was charged with humiliating some old Confederate veterans who had gathered to participate in a parade by asking; "Why did they expect to be honored today?"[27]

These last charges by the Legion seemed to be deliberate attempts to prejudice the college trustees against Miss Rankin, and were actually foreign to any method of approach that she might have used. Blunt, unkindly remarks would have been quite contrary to her philosophy of interpersonal relations. She often spoke of the antiquity and futility of the educational methods of the war department, but never shamed anyone for symbolism they wished to reverence. Miss Rankin had a great respect for

[25]Ibid.

[26]Ibid.

[27]Ibid.

the individual, and for human life. To have lowered herself to this nature of attack, would have been self-degrading as well as indulging in the methodology of the opponent.

H. J. Pearce presented Jeannette Rankin's statements to the Executive Committee of the Brenau College trustees, and they decided that no action on the part of the committee was called for, even though some members were disturbed about the recent activities of the American Civil Liberties Union in defending free speech.[28] After thirty-five years, Haywood Pearce, Jr., remembered, "Only the fact that the National Commander of the Legion was a friend of mine, I and my two brothers had been in World War I." "These things got us off the hook."[29]

By the middle of January, 1935, the trustees had launched a campaign to raise $150,000 for a Department of Peace. Fifty thousand dollars were especially set aside to provide for the salary of the proposed professor. James H. Simmons, Secretary of the Brenau faculty, in a letter to a friend, wrote: "If the money is raised it is generally understood that the President will recommend Miss Rankin for the first occupant of the new chair."[30] The Brenau Bulletin of February, 1935, carried an announcement of the developing plans. Believing that world peace would come through education, and particularly of the younger generation, Brenau proposed to translate this conviction into action by instituting the first

---

[28]H. J. Pearce to Jeannette Rankin, December 28, 1934, Rankin File Drawer, N. C. P. W., S. C. P. C.

[29]Lucile Adams, Brenau Librarian and Dr. Pearce's sister, to Kenneth Clark, Brenau President, February 25, 1969 which included an excerpt from Letter Haywood J. Pearce, Jr., had written to her; Haywood J. Pearce to the author, April 29, 1969, both of these letters in personal file of the author.

[30]James H. Simmons to J. L. Kesler, January 18, 1935, Rankin File Drawer, N. C. P. W., S. C. P. C.

"Chair of Peace." The Professor was to formulate and organize from the
fields of History, Political Science, Economics, International Law,
Public Finance, and Sociology an integrated body of knowledge. He also
was to analyze and interpret contemporary institutions, events and idealo-
gies. The only obstacle seemed to have been financial, thus, the Bulletin
solicited the aid of its readers in securing funds and enlisting the
imagination of a philanthropist.[31] Despite these efforts, the dream for
a "Chair of Peace" died from a lack of funds.

Jeannette Rankin was never quite satisfied with the outcome of the
Brenau College controversy. She said, "I got such awful blasts from it
that I felt he [Pearce] owed me more than letting me speak a few times."[32]
She possibly felt "let-down" when the college invited the Legionnaires to
present "a plan for peace" and, then, eventually published their rebuttal
as a supplement to the February issue of the Brenau Bulletin. Equally,
she believed that the college pushed the publicity because it was good
advertising for the image of the school, and might also attract some
financial support to relieve the squeeze of the depression. If this was
the case, and it may well have been, it was equally true that any publicity
that would aid Brenau would also enhance Jeannette Rankin's position as an
adamant proponent for peace.

Sometime between 1928 and 1934, Jeannette Rankin and the Georgia Peace
Society fell from the good graces of the Macon newspapers, edited by W. T.
Anderson. In 1928, he had highly praised the initiative of the Georgia
Peace Society in calling the Georgia Conference on the Cause and Cure of

[31]Brenau Bulletin, XXVII (February, 1935), pp. 23-24.

[32]Jeannette Rankin, personal interview, January 30, 1969, p. 9
of transcript.

War, but in the Brenau Controversy in 1934, he captioned an editorial,
"Enough of Jeannette." Editor Anderson wrote that Rankin had spent the
greater part of her time for the past few years trying to undermine the
manhood and patriotism of this country. World War I would have been
shortened many months, he believed, had not Miss Rankin and others given
the German government the idea we would not fight. He believed that the
world situation was again very similar. Supporting Miss Rankin in preaching the virtue of renouncing war in any circumstance, according to the
Macon publisher, were the pacifists, defeatists, and communists. Finally,
he concluded his attack by writing, "All this pacifism just invites war,
and the more encouragement given to the people of the Rankin type, the
more certain is disaster."[33]

These attacks subsided until Jeannette Rankin returned to the Macon
area in the fall of 1935 to work for peace sentiment. She called a district meeting of the Georgia Peace Society to meet in Sandersville on
October 9-10, 1935. To the group assembled in the Washington County
Courthouse, Mrs. J. B. Dillard of Davisboro, chairman of the conference,
outlined the purpose of the meeting as to encourage the public to hold
the government to its pledge in the Kellogg-Briand Pact and to arouse
support for a consolidation of the army and navy into one defense department.[34] The first address at the conference was by former United States
Senator and Governor Thomas Hardwick. Earlier he had expressed hope that
the sessions would be well attended as Miss Rankin was a "sincere and
devoted advocate of peace." He set the tone for the conference by pointing

_____

[33] Macon Evening News, December 10, 1934, p. 4.

[34] Macon Telegraph, September 26, 1935, p. 12; Macon Telegraph,
October 10, 1935, p. 7.

out the similarity between the present conditions existing in the United States and those existing before World War I.[35]

The morning and afternoon sessions of the "District Conference," as it was called, were actually propaganda workshops for the Georgia Peace Society. They discussed such topics as "What Organized Groups Can Do to Prevent War," "Legislation Before Congress," and "Methods of Work -- Literature, Public Meetings, the Press, the Church, and Cooperation with National Organizations." The evening meeting aimed at educating and stimulating public opinion with addresses on "Youth and the Next War" by Virginia Smith, president of the International Relations Club of Georgia State College for Women, "The European Crisis" by Roberta Hodgson, and "What is National Defense" by Jeannette Rankin. Miss Rankin's speech was the usual exposition on the munition makers, the high cost of armaments, support for a referendum vote, and that coastal defense was all America needed.[36]

Thursday afternoon the Conference moved to the Washington County Fair where the Peace Society had a booth to distribute literature and to register those disapproving war and desiring peace.[37] At the fairgrounds, Jeannette Rankin spoke on "What the Voters Can do for Peace," the Reverend Mr. Joe Branch of Davisboro discussed, "War Propaganda," and Agnes Highsmith,

---

[35] Sandersville Progress, October 3, 1935, p. 1; Athens Daily Times, October 31, 1935, p. 1.

[36] Hand Bill on District Convention, October 9-10, 1935, Georgia Peace Society Folder, S. C. P. C.; Sandersville Progress, October 17, 1935, p. 1.

[37] In the Georgia Peace Society Folder at S. C. P. C., there were several Blue Horse Composition Books with signed names of people from all over Georgia who disapproved of war.

secretary of the Y. M. C. A. at Athens, talked on "Youth's Chance for the Future."[38]

At most meetings of the District Conference of the Georgia Peace Society attendance was small -- about twenty-five of which four or five were from Athens.[39] Sandersville was in Carl Vinson's district. If attendance at this meeting was an indication of public support for peace, Jeannette Rankin's work in prior years had not produced tangible results, although two things happened which may have affected attendance. First, interested persons could have been frightened away by the adverse publicity and the strong accusations against Miss Rankin by the American Legion in the Brenau College controversy in December of 1934 and the editorial by Macon Evening News, "Enough of Jeannette." The second was an anonymous letter sent to the chairman, Mrs. Dillard, in an envelope of the American Legion of Atlanta. It attacked the Georgia Peace Conference for having communist affiliations, and acting as a "camouflage and deceptive cloak for all these underground secret activity for non-Georgians."[40] Jeannette believed that many of the Sandersville residents had also received such information and were afraid to attend the meetings.

While the District Conference of the Georgia Peace Society met in Sandersville on October 9-10, 1935, Bill Janes, in his "Veteran's Corner" of the Macon Evening News, characterized Jeannette Rankin by writing, "Up Pops the Devil." He said that she was holding peace meetings, but that attendance would decrease when people find out what Jeannette stands

---

[38] Macon Telegraph, October 10, 1935, p. 7.

[39] Roberta Hodgson to Frederick Libby, November 20, 1935, Georgia Peace Society Folder, S. C. P. C.

[40] Roberta Hodgson to Frederick Libby, October 30, 1935, Rankin File Drawer, N. C. P. W. Files, S. C. P. C.

for and she will have to move on. Rankin returned to her boarding house
in Sandersville on the evening of the tenth just in time to take the Macon
Evening News off the porch. In it, she read,

> Jeannette Rankin was branded in the courts
> of Atlanta as being a rank communist and
> was accused of belonging to several such
> organizations. She was fired from the
> faculty of one of the South's finest
> schools, Brenau, for forming a so-called
> Chair of Peace, and advocating communistic
> ideas in our schools.[41]

Turning to her boarding house lady, she said, "Look what they said in the
paper." The lady replied, "Isn't it true?"[42]

The attack by the Atlanta Post of the American Legion, and now these
charges by Bill Janes in the "Veterans Corner," were just too much. Hoping
that it would stop the campaign against her, Jeannette Rankin, annoyed,
decided to attempt a libel suit.[43] She obtained the services of an Athens
lawyer, Walter G. Cornett. She wrote to Roger Baldwin of the American
Civil Liberties Union, Frederick Libby of the National Council for the
Prevention of War, and Fiorello H. La Guardia, Mayor of New York for
advice and encouragement. In the letter to Mayor La Guardia, she indicated that the American Legion was determined to destroy her work in Georgia
and that their continuous charges of communist influence were getting un-
bearable. Actually she wrote to ask him to make a deposition that she

---

[41] Macon Evening News, October 10, 1935, p. 4.

[42] J. R. Interview, January 30, 1969, p. 2.

[43] A second suit to be filed in Atlanta Division of U.S. Court was
planned against the American Legion for an alledged mimeograph slander
sheet distributed by them during the Sandersville District Conference.
This suit was never filed.

was not a communist.[44] The successful prosecution of the Schwimmer libel suit spurred Jeannette Rankin on until informed that the case was won on her being called "Bolshevist Agent" and "German Spy" and not on her being called "communist."[45] The American Civil Liberties Union, which support-ed many of the radicals when their freedom of speech was attacked, reluctant-ly advised against her suing a newspaper. Members of the newspaper world stuck together and were loath to give publicity to such suits. The Execu-tive Board of the National Council for the Prevention of War, for whom Miss Rankin worked, voted to support her libel suit by appropriating $500 provided competent counsel would advise the prosecution of the case.[46]

Walter Cornett outlined the four possible libel charges against Miss Rankin: (1) Branded in the courts of Atlanta as being a rank communist; (2) Fired from Brenau College, (3) That the Macon Telegraph and Evening News had carried editorials branding her as preaching un-American doctrines and (4) That a complete history of "the Jeannette Rankin Communist Case" may be obtained from A. L. Hinton or Atlanta Post No. 1 of the American Legion. He felt the false publication of either the first, third or fourth charges were libelous under Georgia law.[47]

To Harry F. Ward, Chairman of the Board of American Civil Liberties

---

[44]Jeannette Rankin to Fiorello H. La Guardia, n.d., Rankin File Drawer, N. C. P. W., S. C. P. C.

[45]Frederick Libby to Jeannette Rankin, November 22, 1935, Rankin File Drawer, N. C. P. W., S. C. P. C. Rosika Schwimmer, Hungarian feminist, came to the United States and eventually applied for citizenship. Because she would not swear to defend the nation with arms, citizenship was denied. Case upheld by the Supreme Court.

[46]Frederick Libby to Jeannette Rankin, November 22, 1935, Rankin File Drawer, N. C. P. W., S. C. P. C.

[47]Walter G. Cornett to Harry F. Ward, American Civil Liberties Union, November 4, 1934, Rankin File Drawer, N. C. P. W., S. C. P. C.

Union, Cornett quoted the Georgia law as follows:

> Any false and malicious defamation of another
> in any newspaper, magazine or periodical,
> tending to injure the reputation of any in-
> dividual and expose him to public hatred,
> contempt or ridicule, shall constitute a
> newspaper libel, the publication of such
> libelous matter being essential to recovery.[48]

He believed that the charges by Bill Janes were sufficiently strong enough
to bring obloquy and reproach upon Miss Rankin throughout the state and
expose her to public hate, contempt and ridicule. Thus, through the law
offices of Carlisle and Bootle in Macon, Walter Cornett filed a $50,000
libel suit on April 14, 1936 against both William Janes and the Macon
Evening News.

While the collection of monetary damages was the legal objective in
the suit, another objective was to vindicate the name and reputation of
Miss Rankin and to save from complete destruction the effectiveness of
her peace work in Georgia. Walter Cornett, deeply devoted to Rankin's
work, believed, "She will stand or fall in this State by the results of
the case, and if she is driven out of Georgia she will be followed elsewhere by the same forces."[49] He hoped to "sail her ship" between the
virtues and vices of Georgia prejudice and have a jury say that she has
reached a port of complete vindication.[50]

Jeannette Rankin believed the course case would bring the facts before
the people. "When a newspaper makes misrepresentations and fails to correct
them," she said, "the only alternative is to bring suit and have the fact

---

[48]Ibid.

[49]Walter G. Cornett to Harry F. Ward, November 4, 1935, Rankin File
Drawer, N. C. P. W., S. C. P. C.

[50]Ibid.

established in a court of law."[51] A National Council Press Release indicated that the Macon Evening News and Bill Janes must be made to know
and admit that Jeannette Rankin was not a communist. They looked on the
suit as a measure of stopping the false and insidious attempts to discredit advocates of peace and peace organizations by calling them
"communists," and by causing confustion among men and women who sincerely
want peace.[52]

H. J. Pearce, president of Brenau, wrote the editor of the Macon
Evening News to enter his protest of the "incorrect" and "unjust" statement. President Pearce stated in his letter that Jeannette Rankin had
not been fired from the faculty of Brenau, that none of her statements
were un-American and that the charge by the Atlanta Post of the American
Legion of her being communistic was never proved to any satisfaction.
Instead of being dismissed, he reported, she was encouraged to continue
the contract, and that he hoped that she would be able to return to Brenau
at a future date. His final paragraph carried the punch of his letter
and his support for Miss Rankin:

> I am in thorough sympathy with those who are
> endeavoring to establish Americanism in this
> country, but I greatly deplore the rabid
> attacks which have been made upon as good
> Americans as any of us, among whom I include
> Miss Rankin.[53]

The disposition of the libel suit really hinged upon the charges that
Jeannette Rankin "had been branded in the courts of Atlanta as a 'communist'"

---

[51]Press Release, National Council for the Prevention of War, January
20, 1936, Rankin File Drawer, N. C. P. W., S. C. P. C.

[52]Ibid.

[53]H. J. Pearce to The Editor, Macon Evening News, October 18, 1935,
Rankin File Drawer, N. C. P. W., S. C. P. C.

and "had been fired from the faculty of Brenau College." The published
statement that she was a communist resulted from the conviction in Fulton
County of Angelo Herndon already referred to. The Supreme Court of Georgia
in his case ruled; "The jury was amply authorized to infer that violence
was intended and that the defendant did attempt to induce others to combine in such resistance to the lawful authority of the State."[54]

In addition to communist literature found in Herndon's possession,
there was material from the American Civil Liberties Union. The letter-
heads indicated that Jeannette Rankin was a vice-president of the organization. Columnist Janes imagined that since Herndon had so much communist
association and had been convicted of insurrection, Jeannette Rankin,
whose name appeared on the letterhead of the ACLU, likewise must be a
communist and became so convinced as to say: "She had been branded in
the courts of Atlanta as a communist." Certainly, this attempt at conviction by association was damaging to the public image of Jeannette
Rankin, who already was "suspect" because of her "differentness."

Since the Janes charge of a court decision could not be proven and
because H. J. Pearce, Sr.'s letter declared that Jeannette Rankin had
not been fired, William T. Anderson decided to settle his company's part
of the case out of court. Miss Rankin reluctantly agreed to settle for
$1,000, court costs and a printed retraction of the statements. In a front
page story the Macon Evening News stated its conviction that Jeannette
Rankin "had never been discharged from the faculty of Brenau College; that

---

[54] Jeannette Rankin Suit, District Court of the United States for
Middle District of Georgia, Macon Division, April 14, 1936, pp. 1-2,
Rankin FIle Drawer, N. C. P. W., S. C. P. C.

she is not a communist and that she has never been branded as Janes alleged."[55] Anderson also believed, in common justice and courtesy to Miss Rankin, that he should go further than the legal settlement in making amends for any offense given her. He wrote: "She is held in the highest esteem for the sincerity of her efforts." Asserting that, "She has an international reputation as a pacifist," he added, "that this newspaper disagreed with her only in the matter of disarmament."[56] He concluded by saying that the article by Janes was not representative of the attitude or opinion of The News and "it got into The News only through rush and oversight."[57]

Julian Harris, formerly the daring and audacious liberal editor of the Columbus (Georgia) Enquirer-Sun, but now the Executive Editor of the Chattanooga Times, chastised the Macon newspaper in an editorial, "The Need for Accuracy." He wrote that the article by Janes was unfortunate not only because it contained incorrect statements concerning Miss Rankin's beliefs, but because it was an example of injustice frequently caused when terms are confused and misused. The editorial concluded by saying:

> It is to be hoped that the Macon newspaper's experience will result in a more careful use of terms which are by no means interchangeable and which, used inaccurately, harm and embarrass those to whom they are applied.[58]

Most of the charges in Georgia against Jeannette Rankin centered on her reputation as a pacifist by voting against World War I, and her

---

[55] Macon Evening News, November 16, 1936, p. 1.

[56] Ibid.

[57] Ibid.

[58] Chattanooga Times, November 29, 1936, p. 6.

association with the National Council for Prevention of War. The basic resources for this propaganda was Elizabeth Dilling's, The Red Network, a book dedicated to the "professional patriots" who encouraged her to expose the "truth about the Communist-Socialist world conspiracy....."[59] In Part I, the book carried general articles on the Russian Revolution, Communism, Socialism, Christian Socialism and Pacifism. Descriptive data concerning more than 460 Communist, Radical, Anarchist, Socialist and I. W. W. controlled organizations was in Part II. "Who is Who in Radicalism," the title of Secion III, contained the names of 1,300 persons associated with the organizations discussed in the previous chapter. Jeannette Rankin was described as:

> Former Congresswoman from Montana; national
> committee of the A. C. L. U.; national council
> of the Berger National Foundation; Associate
> Secretary for the N. C. P. W.; Women's Peace
> Union, 1929; lobbyist against national defense
> legislation; and her People's Council affiliation
> was exposed in the Lusk Report.[60]

For some reason, Mrs. Dilling overlooked Miss Rankin's close association with Jane Addams, who received severe criticism in the book, and her work with the National Consumer's League and U.S. Section of the Women's International League for Peace and Freedom, both of which were listed as Socialist-Communist. The American Legion purchased copies of this book and distributed them across Georgia to arouse suspicion about Jeannette Rankin and to counter the peace sentiment.[61]

---

[59] Elizabeth Dilling, The Red Network (Kenilworth, Illinois: Published by the author, 1934), p. 5.

[60] Ibid., p. 315. David Starr Jordan, who lobbied for the People's Council, named Jeannette Rankin as one of his contacts during her term as Montana Representative, p. 213.

[61] Walter G. Cornett to Harry F. Ward, November 4, 1935, Rankin File Drawer, N. C. P. W., S. C. P. C.

CHAPTER X

THE ZENITH

Frightened by the failure of the Geneva Disarmament Conference, the breakdown of naval status quo, collapse of collective and moral security in the Far East, and the threatening aggression in Europe, many Americans wanted to make sure the nation could avoid entanglement in what looked like an impending war situation. The Nye Committee report and sensational writing added to this popular opinion. One possible solution was to isolate the nation through neutrality legislation.[1]

Because America's traditional view of neutral rights and free trade on the seas had failed to keep the nation out of World War I, Jeannette Rankin supported an impartial neutrality. It prohibited trade with all belligerents and recognized the folly of free trade in modern warfare. Realizing that mandatory neutrality would curtail executive leadership, President Roosevelt and Secretary of State Cordell Hull proposed counter legislation that would give the President discretionary powers in applying the embargo. Immediately, the administration ran into difficulty with peace groups and with a Congress unwilling to risk involvement in

---

[1]Antecendents for neutrality legislation ran back to President Jefferson's Embargo. Secretary of State William J. Bryan called attention to the problems of neutrality and freedom of the seas prior to American entry into World War I. With growing desire to stay out of foreign conflicts, Congress passed in 1934 an act authorizing the president to prohibit the shipment of arms to Bolivia and Paraguay.

243

any "shade" of collective security.[2]

In the Spring of 1935, Senators Gerald P. Nye of North Dakota and
Bennett Champ Clark of Missouri and Congressmen Maury Maverick of Texas
and Frank Kloeb of Ohio introduced neutrality legislation. Collectively,
these bills prohibited the sale of munitions to belligerents, the extension of loans or credit to nations or citizens engaged in armed conflict, and a ban on American citizens traveling in war zones or in enemy
vessels. Strong Congressional leadership outmaneuvered the Roosevelt
administration in obtaining support for these bills and in registering
public opinion.

Jeannette Rankin and the NCPW lobbied against the inclusion of discretionary powers for the president. This reflected a continuing distrust
of executive initiative in designing foreign policy, evolving from the
conviction that Wilson had led America into World War I. While the NCPW
supported mandatory neutrality legislation, other peace groups, such as
the League of Nations Association, advocated legislation that would permit
the President to cooperate with the League of Nations in applying sanctions
against aggressors.

Helping the NCPW to spearhead the campaign for mandatory neutrality
legislation, Jeannette Rankin delivered speeches, wrote articles for
publication, and lobbied the Congress. In a letter for mass distribution,
she requested its readers to write the President, House Speaker Joseph W.
Byrnes, and Rules Committee Chairman John O'Connor and urge passage of
the Kloeb bill. In addition, she also wrote personal letters to one
hundred and seventy-five Congressmen, begging them not to conclude the

---

[2]Robert A. Divine, The Illusion of Neutrality (Chicago: University
of Chicago Press, 1962), pp. 62-8.

session "until they had safeguarded our country from involvement in another European war."[3] William Lemke, Congressman from North Dakota, replied that he not only would support her legislative endeavor, but "would cooperate...in creating a neutral sentiment that cannot ripen into war hysteria."[4]

On August 21, the Senate passed neutrality legislation designed by Key Pittman's Foreign Relations Committee. The scene then turned dramatically to the House, where the bill was tied up with Hull's encouragement, in Sam McReynold's Foreign Affairs Committee. Joyful over this victory in the Senate, Jeannette Rankin and Warren Mullins, NCPW Labor Secretary, stood by the House Chamber doors and urged the Representatives to encourage McReynold's committee to adopt neutrality legislation. Not talking it over with Frederick Libby because he might stop her, Jeannette Rankin surrepticiously approached, in McReynold's office, Congressman Kloeb, who had introduced one of the House resolutions. She suggested to him that the committee make the bill effective for only six months which would cover the period Congress was in recess. Rankin remembered, "In an hour they came out and said 'We've passed it for six months'."[5] Roosevelt acquiesced. As the Senate had done, the House accepted by a voice vote the committee's report of mandatory neutrality to extend until February of 1936.[6]

---

[3]Minutes, Annual Meeting of NCPW, October 19-20, 1938, NCPW Files, S.C.P.C.

[4]Letter of William Lemke to J. R., August 9, 1935, 1936, J. R. Correspondence Files, NCPW Files, S.C.P.C.

[5]J. R. Interview, January 30, 1969, p. 3.

[6]Wayne S. Cole, "Senator Key Pittman and American Neutrality Policies, 1933-1940", Mississippi Valley Historical Review, XLVI, March, 1960, p. 654.

Even though this First Neutrality Act was a basic revision of American foreign policy, Jeannette Rankin and other would have preferred a
stronger, more permanent version. Although dissatisfied with the bill,
she believed it did show Europe that America would neither profiteer on
their wars, nor participate in their collective efforts to secure peace.[7]
The NCPW considered neutrality legislation

> a step...in the process of passing from our futile
> "freedom of seas" position to an ultimate collective
> system of justice and peace.... Efforts to keep
> out of a general war are no substitute for the
> prevention of war through the World Court and a re-
> vised League of Nations....[8]

Jeannette Rankin later observed,"It was all that could be passed over the
opposition of foreign interests and our own racketeers."[9] Nevertheless,
she looked forward with hope to the convening of the next Congress.

During this six-month period, Jeannette Rankin knew that she must
effectively register public opinion on strategic Congressmen. Thus, she
envisioned a speaking tour through Sam McReynold's district in Tennessee.
Libby, head of NCPW, reluctantly agreed. Even though an arms embargo
was a popular topic, Rankin wanted to inform the people in order to
crystallize opinion in McReynold's district and to open channels of
communication to him.

In the late fall, she started her canvass in Chattanooga. She spoke
to high schools, labor groups, luncheons, teas, club meetings, on radio,
and even to a revival in Dayton. Despite a heavy snow storm, she continued

---

[7]J. R. MSS, for Southern Farmer, n.d., NCPW Files, S. C. P. C.

[8]Peace Action, I (May, 1935), p. 1; Peace Action, II (February, 1936),
p. 1.

[9]J. R., Article for Associated Press, November 11, 1935, NCPW Files,
S. C. P. C.

to all ten counties in the district. Rankin praised Tennessee for having such influence in international affairs since Cordell Hull was Secretary of State, Sam McReynolds was Chairman of the House Foreign Affairs Committee and Joseph W. Brynes was Speaker of the House. She praised their Congressmen's leadership and suggested that they write them and express support for arms embargo.[10]

Jeannette Rankin's visit evidently succeeded because McReynolds encouraged, supported and helped pass a somewhat stronger neutrality bill in February of 1936.[11] Still not satisfied, Jeannette said: "The President has pushed through a limited Neutrality Bill. The legislation is disappointing considering the tremendous sentiment for it in the country." Therefore, she urged that great pressure be brought on the President to recognize public opinion.[12] The climax to neutrality legislation came in May of 1937 with the inclusion of a "cash and carry" provision to the second law, a section forbiding Americans to travel on belligerent ships, and the directive that American merchant vessels were not to be armed. When Roosevelt refused, in July of 1937, to invoke the Neutrality Act with the resumption of the undeclared war between Japan and China,

---

[10]She was guest of Abby Crawford Milton, whose husband, George Ford Milton, publised newspapers in Chattanooga, Knoxville, and Memphis; Warren Mullins, also from the NCPW, went down to Tennessee and later reaped the wrath of McReynolds over false statements and insinuations that he purportedly made to a Chattanooga audience. cf. U.S., Congress, House of Representatives, Committee on Foreign Affairs, Hearings on American Neutrality Policy, 75th Congress, First Session on H. J. Res. 147 and 242, pp. 62-64.

[11]J. R. Interview, January 30, 1969, pp. 3-5, January 27, 1969, p. 11.

[12]J. R. to Executive Board Meeting, March, 1936, NCPW Files, S. C. P. C.

adherence to the law steadily declined. The Lend-Lease act circumvented it and America's declaration of war, nullified it.

During the mid-thirties, most peace groups began evaluating their approach to preventing war and realized that they needed new directives. In 1932 the NCPW, under Frederick Libby's leadership, changed its program from "peace education" to "peace action." The Georgia Peace Society, organized and led by Jeannette Rankin, took the initiative as the first of the peace action groups. Rankin said, "This is a new kind of peace work. No one fears the results of the peace worker who made sentimental speeches at ladies' teas, but when pioneer work is done among responsible citizens, it is a different story."[13] She believed this program represented the first practical means for effective promotion of peace.

By 1935, there appeared three distinct antiwar divisions in the peace movement: a radical element including Socialists and Communists, conservative educational societies, and political-activist groups. Failing to muster the necessary two-thirds' majority in the Senate for entrance into the World Court in January of 1935, the peace groups realized the emphatic need for dynamic programs using a united effort of peace forces. Ray Newton, Secretary of the Peace Section of the American Friends Service Committee, conceived of an "Emergency Peace Campaign." He secured the active support of leading pacifists John Nevin Sayre, Executive Secretary of Fellowship of Reconciliation; Frederick Libby, Executive Secretary of NCPW; and Kirby Page, staff member of FOR and editor of World Tomorrow. The purpose of the structure was "to promote a cooperative national campaign to keep the United States from going to war and to achieve world

---

[13]"Working Politically for Peace in Georgia," January 5, 1932, Georgia Peace Society Folder, S. C. P. C.

peace by:

> strengthening pacific alternatives to armed con-
> flict; bringing about such political and economic
> changes as are essential to a just and peaceable
> world order; and recruiting and uniting in a
> dynamic movement all organizations and individuals
> who are determined not to approve of or partici-
> pate in war.[14]

Jeannette Rankin, along with other staff members of NCPW, served on
the legislative committee of the Emergency Peace Campaign because they
had been deeply involved in political action.[15] In the summer of 1936,
EPC workers trained 223 young volunteers on the campuses of Duke, Ginnell,
and Whittier to work for peace in settlment houses, youth conferences, and
politically strategic legislative districts. From June 18 to 21, Jeannette
Rankin presented four lectures on "Organizing Public Opinion" to the Duke
Institute of International Relations, as this section was called. Because he was a leading advocate of military preparedness in Congress, Carl
Vinson's district in Georgia became a prime target for their peace propaganda.[16]

Believing, as she had told the students, that one of the ways to
prevent war was to elect Congressmen and Senators favorable to peace
legislation, Jeannette Rankin spent the summer and fall of 1936 organizing peace sentiment in the Sixth Congressional district of Georgia. Carl
Vinson, Chairman of the House Naval Affairs Committee and author of the

---

[14]"Emergency Peace Campaign Is Planned," Peace Action, II (March,
1936), p. 5.

[15]Charles Chatfield, For Peace and Justice: Pacifism in America,
1914-1941 (Knoxville: The University of Tennesses Press, 1971), p. 268.

[16]Among the participants was Susan B. Anthony, a niece of the
original Susan B. Anthony, The Ghost in My Life (New York: Chosen Books,
1971), p. 88.

Vinson-Trammel Act of 1934, advocated a strong military defense supported by an enlarged navy. He was one of the chief "militarists" whom
Miss Rankin opposed on Capitol Hill. She wrote:

> I feel Congressman Vinson is not aware of the
> peace sentiment in his district, and we plan
> to make him realize that this peace senti-
> ment must be represented....If we are success-
> ful, Congressman Vinson is going to feel our
> strength next fall.[17]

The Georgia Peace Society, working in Vinson's district since 1930,
had laid the groundwork for a supposed effective campaign. It had an
organization in each of the sixteen counties in the Sixth Congressional
District, and members in almost every precinct.[18] In addition to the
work of the Peace Society, Jeannette Rankin hoped for support from the
Farmers' Union and organized labor, but labor proved inconsequential
because Macon was the only "labor city" in the whole district. Thus, she
directed her campaign to win the rural votes. Significant aid came from
the Emergency Peace Campaign which was in full swing around the country.[19]
As a gesture of return help, Jeannette Rankin secured several of those
students, trained at Duke University, to assist her in a ten-week campaign in Georgia against the re-election of Representative Vinson.[20]

---

[17]News Release for Jeannette Rankin's proposed work in Georgia in
1936, Rankin File Drawer, N. C. P. W. Files, S. C. P. C.

[18]Ibid.

[19]Frederick Libby to Harold Hatch, June 29, 1936, Rankin File
Drawer, N. C. P. W. Files, S. C. P. C.

[20]A partial listing of the students showed four boys and six girls:
Kenson Kennedy, William Miller, Charles Penrose, _____ Flowery,
Mary Cason, Jo Marie _____, Kathrine Ruff, _____ Straub,
Helen Sixon, and Lucile Bowers. The last girl was the daughter of an
Athens dentist and she worked periodically as Miss Rankin's secretary;
Jeannette Rankin Campaign Report, Rankin File Drawer, N.C.P.W. Files,
S.C.P.C.

Miss Rankin planned to work intensively in the fourteen rural counties
of Vinson's district--possibly conceding Bibb with the city of Macon
in it and Baldwin, Vinson's home county. She estimated the cost of the
campaign at $3,400, exclusive of her salary and expenses.[21]

With the aid of the students in the Emergency Peace Campaign,
Jeannette Rankin began to wage a vigorous campaign against Vinson. Her
methodology included thousands of personal contacts, extensive literature
distribution, several mass meetings, and parades.[22] The parades took the
form of a children's pageant. The girls from the Emergency Peace Campaign,
with the help of local women, prepared the costumes and organized the
parades. The colorfully dressed children carried banners which depicted
peace slogans: "Join the Navy and See the Next World," "The Perfect
Soldier -- Headless," (A boy dressed in uniform with no head), "We Want
War", (three clowns with voluminous pockets to hold their profits), "War
Will Make Us Lame, Blind, Orphans, Armless, and Humpbacked," (all portrayed by children), and "Say Peace with Votes." In addition to the emotional
appeal of the slogans, the immediate motive for the children's parade was
to interest the community in a mass "peace meeting" to be held later at
a designated place.[23]

A truck equipped with a sound system, amplified the peace propaganda
and provided music for the parades as well as serving as a platform for

[21]Ibid.

[22]Letters from Charles Penrose to the author, January 29, 1972, and
March 18, 1972, substantiated this participation and general facts about
the campaign as presented in these paragraphs. Letters in the Author's
files.

[23]Fund raising form letter of Jeannette Rankin, May 15, 1936, Rankin
File Drawer, NCPW Files, SCPC.

the speeches. Music used in the parades was from George Gershwin's Broadway Musical, "Strike up the Band," a satire on war. It served as a tool for propaganda and as a means to attract attention. Miss Rankin felt one secion was especially good when it said,

> We're in a bigger, better war for your patrio-
> tic pasttime. We don't know what we're fight-
> ing for, but we didn't know the last time.[24]

There were problems with the campaign from the very beginning. Jeannette Rankin had initially hoped to put up a candidate against Representative Vinson, but the two prospects, W. O. Cooper and a Dr. Louis (no first name available), declined because they lacked financial backing. At the last moment, when worst came to worst, she persuaded a young man in the district to run, but he was too late to certify. With a shortage of money and no candidates, the campaigners could only hope for a moral victory in a battle of words and ideas.[25]

Lack of transportation also hindered the personal contacts planned for the campaign. The original idea called for several teams to divide up the precincts in each county and visit every registered voter. But, the Emergency Peace Campaign girls had only one or two cars at the most, and the boys had only one truck.[26]

Opposition to Rankin's peace campaign grew steadily. It was difficult to get local people to work because they were often intimidated by the

---

[24] J. R. Interview, May 24, 1969, p. 5; David Ewen, A Journal to Greatness: The Life and Music of George Gershwin (New York: Henry Holt and Company, 1956), pp. 205-207; George Gershwin, Strike Up the Band (New York: New World Music, 1930), pp. 115-118.

[25] Jeannette Rankin to Frederick Libby, June 22, 1936, Rankin File Drawer, NCPW Files, SCPC.

[26] Ibid.

strong and ardent supporters of Carl Vinson. The parades were perplexing to organize because the "militarist" would go to the costumed children and say, "You don't want to do this. You mustn't do this. You take this off."[27] This resulted in two of the "peace parades" being stopped. Even Miss Rankin began to complain, "It is hard to know which way to turn."[28]

When the votes were tabulated in the September Democratic Primary, which was tantamount to election in Democratic Georgia, there was no victory celebration by the Georgia Peace Society workers. Representative Vinson had polled 30,603 votes -- almost 10,000 more votes than he had received in the 1934 Democratic Primary. He gained in every county in his sixteen-county district, except his home county of Baldwin. Since the peace workers did not campaign intensively in his home county, this might have indicated that the voters were not aroused enough to get out and vote. The factor of "scratching the name of the candidate," which had been highly recommended by peace dodgers, was of little consequence; Representative Vinson received a total vote equal to the combined vote of the candidates in the governor's race.[29]

The actual effect of the campaign against Congressman Vinson in the 1936 Congressional election was uncovered in comparing Vinson's unopposed voting strength in the Democratic Primaries of 1932 through 1940. Prior

---

[27] J. R. Interview, May 24, 1969, p. 5.

[28] Jeannette Rankin to Frederick Libby, July 22, 1936, Rankin File Drawer, NCPW Files, SCPC.

[29] Georgia Secretary of State, Official Register for 1933-37 (Atlanta: Department of Archives and History, 1937), p. 643; Peace Campaign Dodger of 1936 -- "Our Votes Decide - Scratch the Names of all candidates who think it necessary to be ready to cross the seas to fight the wars of other nations," Rankin File Drawer, NCPW Files, SCPC.

to 1932, Vinson had represented the Tenth District, but after Congressional
redistricting, he ran from the Sixth District. In 1932, he received a
total of 17,027 votes.[30] His total for 1934 was up approximately 3,000
votes to 20,481. Then with the opposition of the Georgia Peace Society
led by Jeannette Rankin, Congressman Vinson polled 30,603 votes in 1936
or 13,000 more than he received in 1932 and 10,000 more than in 1934.
Without the opposition of the peace workers in 1938, a notable decrease
occurred as he recieved 5,000 fewer votes. Only by 1940 was he able to
regain the total attained in 1936. Allowing for a biennial increase in
voting and for a heavier turn-out on presidential election years, the
facts still pointed to an unusually high total in 1936. Instead of hurt-
ing him the peace campaign actually brought out the voters to give him the
largest victory to that date. The peace workers had expended several
thousands of dollars, much energy and talent, but all of it seemed to have
had little effect on the action of public voting and the "Congressional
militarist" returned to the Capitol unchecked.[31]

The years 1935 and 1936 showed great activity in Jeannette Rankin's
Georgia Peace Society, but also they were the beginning years of decline
and dissension among its members. Membership in the Athens nucleus, which
did most of the planning and carried out most of the activity, reached

---

[30]Atlanta Constitution, September 16, 1932, p. 12. The writer discovered, to the amazement of the Georgia achivist, that no official tabulation was available for the candidates in the races for the U.S. House
of Representatives -- neither in the office of the Georgia Secretary of
State nor in the records of the Department of Archives and History.
For some reason, maybe the same, these totals were not printed in the
Official Register covering that year.

[31]Georgia, Secretary of State, Official Register for 1933-37, p. 643
and Official Register for 1939-43, pp. 395 & 536. See voting tabulation
table in Appendix.

sixty in number, but attendance at meetings usually ran twenty-five or less.[32] Accordingly, Roberta Hodgson, a Georgia Peace Society member and professor of International Relations at Georgia State Teachers College, wrote:

> Some members of the Society object to the dictatorial methods....Some feel that when the name of the society is printed and meetings held in the 'name of the Georgia Peace Society' that some of the officers should be notified....I feel we have lost support and sympathy by this procedure.[33]

Duncan Burnet, University of Georgia Librarian and a close personal friend of both Miss Rankin and Miss Hodgson, felt Miss Hodgson's statement should be tempered by the fact that she, too, was a domineering career woman. Miss Rankin, in his opinion, was:

> ....much disinclined to look at facts in the face. She was devoted to her cause and adamant in her opinion. She was persuasive, but not dictorial.[34]

In the summer of 1936, the Society was further weakened by the loss of an active member and probably its last president as John Tate, director of the Wesley Foundation, moved to a pastorate in Barnesville, Georgia. With the decisive failure in the campaign to arouse peace sentiment in Congressman Vinson's district, the membership of the Georgia Peace Society dwindled away. Only occasional letters from Miss Rankin kept the members informed of the Society's work.[35]

---

[32]Mr. & Mrs. Pope Hill, Athens, Georgia, personal interview, January 25, 1969, p. 4.

[33]Roberta Hodgson to Frederick Libby, October 30, 1935, Rankin File Drawer, NCPW Files, SCPC.

[34]Duncan Burnet, personal interview, March 31, 1969.

[35]John Tate, personal interview, February 3, 1969, p. 1.

Prior to her organizing the Georgia Peace Society, Jeannette Rankin had supported S. O. Levinson's "Outlawry of War," Lynn Frazier's constitutional amendment to make war illegal, and the Kellogg-Briand Pact. It was then only natural for her to also back the thesis of a war referendum. In March of 1934, she appeared before a sub-committee of the House Judiciary Committee to testify in behalf of a constitutional amendment submitted by James Frear of Wisconsin to give Congress the power to declare war only after a majority of the states had approved it, excluding invasion of insurrection. Jeannette Rankin wanted the question "of going to war" put before the people so that they would be forced to make a decision, thereby thinking through the issue. She believed that people do not form decisive opinions unless they have the opportunity or power to express them.[36]

When questioned about whether the people would react differently than Congress, Rankin indicated that they might not at the present, but that a war referendum amendment would build peace habits. In retrospect of her World War I vote, she observed:

> I voted against war because for 7 years I had been following peace habits and thinking peace. ...I had answered every argument for war in my own mind, and acquired peace habits. Now the reason the men voted for war was that they had war habits in their tradition, history, and hearts. They think in terms of war and habit is something you use in any emergency. War is an emergency and consequently the reverted to their war habits.[37]

-----

[36]U.S., Congress, House of Representatives, Committee on the Judiciary, Hearings on Amending the Constitution with Respect to Declarations of War, on H. J. Res. 217 and 218, 73rd Congress, Second Session Sub-Committee #1, pp. 10, 11.

[37]Ibid., p. 11.

Jeannette Rankin believed that the decision-making process involved in this legislation would be an initial step in forming "peace habits."

Congressman Louis Ludlow, from Indiana, subsequently introduced a bill in the House of Representatives in 1935 which provided that, except in case of an invasion, Congress could not declare war without first consulting the people. As the possibilities for war became more evident in the late 1930's, the Ludlow Amendment became a measure to impede presidential leadership in foreign affairs and to establish the war decision-making power in the hands of the people.[38]

Supported by the NCPW, Rankin used every available ounce of energy to speak out for the war referendum bill. She wrote articles, lobbied Congressmen, and made speeches.[39] Referring to AAA legislation, she queried, "They let the farmers vote on whether or not they want to kill little pigs. Why shouldn't the mothers and fathers vote on whether they want their sons killed?"[40]

The NCPW and other peace groups generally produced widespread

----

[38]U.S., Congress, House of Representatives, Congressional Record, 74th Congress, First Session, LXXIX, p. 430, p. 1625. As early as 1922, Representative Edward Voight of Wisconsin had introduced a constitutional amendment to submit a war declaration to a vote of the people, and similar legislation was introduced annually through 1938. See Ernest C. Bolt, "The War Referendum Approach to Peace in Twentieth Century America: A Study in Foreign Policy Formulation and Military Defense Attitudes," unpublished Ph.D. dissertation at the University of Georgia, 1966.

[39]Great Falls Tribune, April 6, 1937; Radio Address, 1937; J. R. Speech to the 1937 Annual Business Meeting of NCPW, "Legislative Next Steps in Keeping our Country out of War," October 7, 1937. Louis Ludlow also addressed the group concerning his war referendum.

[40]A Radio Address in J. R. Folder or Speeches and Addresses, undated but clearly 1937 from the content, p. 3, NCPW Files, SCPC.

support among the American people for the Ludlow referendum. Public
opinion polls showed a high percentage of those questioned favored a war
vote. Even 218 Congressmen, enough to force it out of committee and on
to the floor for a vote, signed a petition approving it. After pressure
from the Roosevelt administration to defeat it, an attempt in January of
1938 to bring the bill out of the committee where it had been pigeonholed
failed by only twenty-one votes--188 to 209. The popularity of this
measure reflected the impact of peace propaganda, the distrust of executive
leadership in foreign affairs, and the zenith of sentiment for isolation
from war.[41]

As steps to destroying the war system, Jeannette Rankin pushed disarmament, investigation of the munitions industry, a reduction of military
appropriations, the suggestion anti-profit legislation and a war referendum.
Realizing that the Kellogg-Briand Pact signalled for a change in national
attitude toward war, Rankin believed that Congress needed to define clearly the nation's military policy. To fulfill America's commitment to the
Pact, she envisioned Congress' establishing a military plan to defend the
nation's shores from invasion and to maintain only those agencies necessary
for defense. All activities designed for aggression or foreign warfare
should be eliminated. With a statement of purpose, she observed:

> It would make it possible for us to know whether
> we were appropriating money for settling disputes
> by fighting wars across the sea or whether we were
> appropriating money to protect our shores from
> invasion.[42]

---

[41]Executive Board Meeting of NCPW, January 19, 1938, in NCPW Files,
SCPC; Report to the NCPW Annual Meeting, October 19-20, 1938, p. 3,
NCPW Files,SCPC.

[42] Undated statement in J.R. Files, NCPW Files, SCPC.

Within her own system, Rankin saw no need for an army or navy. Yet, she said, "As long as some people are in the habit of relying on force for protection, it may remove a certain amount of fear to have a National Defense Department."[43]

Jeannette Rankin thus proposed reorganizing the army and navy into one department with defense as its only objective.[44] In the midst of Franklin Roosevelt's "New Deal" proposals for overhauling major government departments and the need for curbing unnecessary national expenditures, Representative Gerald Boileau of Wisconsin introduced such a bill to combine the armed services into a National Defense Department.[45] Jeannette believed that this proposal would eliminate waste and duplication, save a tremendous amount of money for the taxpayer, create a feeling of security, and remove the feat which exists at home and abroad that the United States expects to fight a foreign war.[46] She believed that, if the European nations now preparing for war could be convinced of America's sincerity, problems would be greatly simplified. Namely, that by formulating a military policy conforming to the philosophy of the Kellogg-Briand Pact, Europeans would know that the United States "would not pull their chestnuts out of the fire. If they want to go to war, it will be theirs to pay for and fight. We must make it clear that we are protecting our shore and

---

[43]J. R. to Mrs. Harvey Emerson, December 21, 1932, NCPW Files.

[44]Jeannette Rankin, "Should America Have a New Deal in National Defense?" Congressional Digest, XII (April, 1934).

[45]U.S., Congress, House of Representatives, 7-th Congress, First Session, August 14, 1935, Congressional Record, LIX, p. 13195; of Nicholas M. Butler, Address at Parrish Art Museum, September 6, 1936, in J. R. MSS; "Miss Rankin Back in House Fighting War," Washington Post, February 9, 1935.

[46]J. R. Address, "Is Peace Possible or Can We Remain Neutral?" p. 2, NCPW Files, SCPC; cf J. R.'s article in Congressional Digest.

nothing more."[47]

Extending the above philosophy, Jeannette Rankin appeared before the Senate Committee on Naval Affairs in January of 1934 to oppose expansion of the naval building program. Under the strain of the Great Depression, she thought it quite incongruous to be cutting compensation of veterans and reducing high school budgets while increasing appropriations for the armed services and national defense. Based on testimony from admirals, she opposed this construction because its purpose was not to protect national shores. These, she thought, be best defended by mines, aircraft, and artillery. Jeannette deducted that conveying troops and fighting other ships were the sole purposes of the navy. Since the President said soldiers would not be used outside the United States, that left only fighting other navies.

Rankin then pointed out that the navy had become "obsolete as a fighting machine" because of aircraft bombers, inability to communicate during attack, and unmaneuverability. She based much of her argument on Wayne Francis Palmer's article in the New Outlook, which characterized the navy as being composed of "deaf and dumb" ships.[48] With radio interference, they lost their ability to communicate; and, when sprayed with artificial fog or smoke screen, these same ships could not move safely. Thus, Rankin called the navy "deaf, dumb, and blind."[49] She quoted one Congressman as

---

[47]J. R. Speech, undated, but probably as early as fall of 1931, p. 4, NCPW Files, SCPC; J. R., "A United Department of Defense," December 17, 1936, p. 3, NCPW Files, SCPC.

[48]Wayne Francis Palmer, "Deaf and Dumb Ships," New Outlook, Vol. 162 (November, 1933), pp. 36-39.

[49]U.S., Congress, Senate, Committee on Naval Affairs, Hearings on Construction of Certain Naval Vessels at the Limits Prescribed by the Treaties Signed at Washington and London on S. 2493, 73rd Congress, Second Session, pp. 13-14.

having said, "Our Navy is of no more value than 'so many wooden wash-
tubs'."[50] She concluded that the construction of additional ships was
wasteful and that it served only to make profits for the shipbuilders in
peace time at the expense of the taxpayers.[51]

Senator Richard Russell of Georgia, a member of the Senate Committee
on Naval Affairs and whose home in Winder was only a few miles from where
Jeannette lived in Bogart, realized that she opposed the construction
program on other than economic grounds. He asked about it. She replied
that she would prefer no armaments of any kind. Her idea of defense was:

> the kind that we have between the United States
> and Canada, but if anyone is afraid and wants
> defense, then it is perfectly all right to let
> them have defenses until we can get them to the
> place where they are not afraid.[52]

Knowing that the public was not ready for complete disarmament, Jeannette
Rankin settled for an intermediate step of shore defense. Additionally,
she estimated it to be relatively inexpensive.

Why was she willing to accept this line of defense? From her observations of history, Jeannette Rankin concluded that it was impossible for
an enemy to invade America's shores. She was in New Zealand shortly after
the British in World War I tried to land the Anzacs in Gallipoli. The
Turks stopped them, and the invasion failed miserably. Rankin heard the
people in New Zealand say, "You see, you cannot land troops on any enemy
shore." She also noted that New Zealand had no navy for its protection.

---

[50]J. R. Address, undated but probably 1934 or 1935, p. 4, in Speech
Folder, NCPW Files, SCPC.

[51]Flagstaff, Arizona Coconino Sun, November 10, 1933.

[52]U.S., Congress, Hearing on Construction of Naval Vessels, p. 15.

Britain was the only country with a navy large enough to attempt an invasion of America, and it was too strategically involved in other places
to try it if she wanted. Neither Canada nor Mexico would permit their
countries to become a battlefield for an invasion of the United States.
"With thousands of miles of ocean on two sides," Rankin often said, "we
cannot be successfully attacked." For her time, she was probably correct.[53]

Jeannette Rankin's tenure with the NCPW during the 1930's encountered
not only increasing militarism, but a nation facing acute social and economic adjustments during a depression. Her early opposition toward "New
Deal" legislation was evident in her statement, "In the little emergency
that we have had in the last three years, members of Congress voted for
legislation that they knew was in violation of the Constitution.[54] The
key that unlocked Rankin's economic and social philosophy was her attitude
toward "our stupid money system" based on the fetish of silver or gold. She
believed:

> If we had a gross national product worth a certain
> amount, out of it should come [enough money to run
> the] government, schools, health...[and other ser-
> vices]. If needed [within this framework], the
> people could do something for us in the free
> enterprise system. There would be no taxes and
> the government could provide all these things
> if they didn't spend half of it on the military.[55]

Jeannette felt that America's money system, which called some "poor"
and others "rich," divided the children and created class and misery of all

---

[53]Jeannette Rankin, "Reducing Armaments by a New Military Policy,"
Peace Action, IV (July, 1937), p. 4; cf. Thomas R. Phillips, "The Bombing
Plane Has Made America Invasion-Proof," Army Ordnance, September-October,
1941.

[54]U.S., Congress, Senate, Hearings Before the Special Committee
Investigating the Munitions Industry on S. Res. 206, 74th Congress, First
Session, April 10, 1935, p. 7162.

[55]J. R. Interview, October 19, 1971, p. 3.

kind. This was specifically upsetting to her when applied in the free lunch program for low income families. This program created distinctions and unnatural and false barriers between students. Whether or not a boy goes to college should not be determined by the wealth of his family, she insisted, was another example. She admired the socialistic system which takes care of a child from the time he is born until he dies by providing "a place to live, plenty to eat and all the education he wants."[56]

Henry George's "single tax" idea received Jeannette's approval because it taxed the increase in property value resulting from surrounding community and industrial growth. She disliked very much the principle of interest because the lender received pay for something which he did not earn. Because all savings accounts are not withdrawn at the same time, Rankin felt that the Federal Reserve and other banking institutions created false economic security by lending more money than they had actual resources. She considered this an unnatural use of the people's money for their own private profit.[57] In 1935, she wrote H. C. Eklund of Great Fall, Montana, "Our present efforts must be directed toward facing the facts and preparing for a peaceful elimination of the profit system."[58] Jeannette advocated setting up prime funds that could be given to people to use for a short time as progress demanded. In fact, she preferred using a monetary base that did not increase in value, as shells, beads, and stones of older

[56] J. R. Interview, October 19, 1971, p. 3.

[57] Edward K. Meador, "The Failure of the Federal Reserve System," pamphlet in J. R.'s personal possession.

[58] J. R. to H. C. Eklund, April 19, 1935, NCPW Files, SCPC.

societies.[59]

Having very progressive ideas about economic security, Jeannette Rankin found compatibility with the themes advanced in 1935 by Senator Huey Long of Louisiana, Dr. Francis Townsend of California, and Father Charles E. Coughlin, radio priest in Royal Oaks, Michigan. Overlooking his demogogery and racial prejudice, she admired Huey Long's populist idiom, expansion of governmental services in the state, and his national "share the wealth" plan. Considering his proposal to provide every family with an annual income of $2,500 and a homestead worth $5,000 in his attempt to redistribute wealth, Rankin wrote, "When you bring out the point that interest is usury..., it gives me great pleasure."[60] Long's whole approach, as interpreted appreciatively by Rankin, was to raise democracy and to stimulate thinking on the part of the people.

Emerging from California to bring hope to the masses of retired people, Dr. Francis Townsend, an elderly physician, attracted several million followers. His Old Age Revolving Pension Plan offered $200 per month to persons over sixty years of age, provided they spent it within the month to stimulate economy. Drawn by its concern for an area of destitute citizens, Jeannette Rankin began to advocade the establishment of "Townsend Clubs" in her speeches for the NCPW. To Harry E. Terrell, regional secretary for the Midwest, she wrote, "To me [it] has more possibilities than any of the programs.... It would help our peace program

---

[59] J. R. Interview, October 19, 1971, pp. 4-5; Will H. Kindig, "Five Easy Lessons on Money," pamphlet in J. R. personal possession; William Lemke, You and Your Money (Philadelphia: Dorrance & Company, 1938).

[60] J. R. to Huey Long, May 31, 1933, NCPW Files, SCPC; J. R. Interview, October 19, 1971, p. 7; T. H. Williams, Huey Long (New York: Knopf, 1969).

if for no other reason than there would be no more money left for war."[61]

As the depression lingered into the mid-thirties, Father Charles E. Coughlin, using the radio to stir the restless people in northern cities, became a vigorous antagonist of Roosevelt. Since the "radio priest" reflected much of her own sentiment, Jeannette Rankin regarded his views with approbation. Coughlin, as was characteristic of Jeannette, chastized "International Bankers" and Wall Street with populist slogans and demanded nationalization of banks, utilities, and natural resources.[62] This collection of power to the left of "New Dealism", led by Long, Townsend, and Coughlin, forced Roosevelt to make a serious evaluation of these popular grievances. The result was the passage of the Social Security Act, the National Labor Relations Act, and the Wealth Tax in the summer of 1935.[63]

By 1937, many Americans believed that the world faced the possibility of another global conflict. In fact, World War I in Europe had never really ended. While visiting the League of Nations on her first trip to Europe in 1931, Jeannette Rankin raised the question in a discussion group, "Why don't you go to the base of [Germany's problem] and modify the Treaty of Versailles?"[64] Shock waves rolled over the assembly. Rankin could not

---

[61]J. R. to Harry Terrell, March 4, 1935, NCPW Files, SCPC; J. R. Interview, January 22, 1970, p. 10; Abraham Holtzman, The Townsend Movement, A Political Study (New York: Bookman Associates, 1963).

[62]J. R. Interview, October 19, 1971, p. 11; Charles E. Coughlin, "Unregulated Debts," Copy of radio address given January 30, 1938, in J. R. personnal possession.

[63]Charles J. Tull, "Father Coughlin, the New Deal and the Election of 1936," unpublished Ph.D. dissertation at the University of Notre Dame, 1961; James P. Sheaton, "The Coughlin Movement and the New Deal," Political Science Quarterly, LXXIII (September, 1958), p. 361; W. E. Leuchtenburg, Franklin D. Roosevelt and the New Deal, 1932-1940 (New York: Harper and Row, 1963).

[64]J. R. Interview, March 2, 1971, p. 7.

have been more ostracized if she had suggested that they all take off
their clothes! Those attending the lectures on the League were horrified
that anyone would consider changing the Treaty. Obviously, they had not
appreciated the American Senate's reaction either.

Rankin's assessment of Europe's dilemma was more widely accepted
six years later. Accompanied by a nephew, John Kinney, who was to enter
Heidelburg University, Jeannette Rankin toured Western Europe in the late
summer of 1937. Shortly after her experience in Geneva in 1931, conditions
in Germany developed which permitted the rise of Adolph Hitler to power.
Other totalitarian regimes also rose in Italy and Spain. Encouraged by
Japan's unchecked foray into Manchuria, Benito Mussolini led the Italians
in annexing Ethiopia to Somaliland in 1935 and 1936. With the world
fretting over this situation, Hitler, who had assumed dictatoral power in
Germany, marched troops into the Rhineland in March of 1936 and began to
revitalize the nation's war machinery in violation of the Versailles
Treaty.

While these struggles took place in Europe, Japan, after an incident
at Marco Polo Bridge, dispatched troops in July of 1937 to overrun all
of North China. Against this ominous canvass of international affairs,
Jeannette walked the streets of Germany. In 1937 she said, "The planes
were flying over and you would think that war was almost there."[65] Unable
to speak their language, she could not secure the feeling of the common
people. Knowing his Aunt Jeannette spoke her mind, John Kinney was continually "hushing her up" because he was afraid she would say the wrong
thing.

---

[65]J. R. Interview, March 2, 1971, p. 9.

While visiting other countries in Europe, Jeannette observed "a general preparation for protection, but outside Italy and Germany, no nation appears to be wasting its men on great aggressive armies." Businessmen traveling in Sweden were of the opinion that, "barring accidents, Europe would not go to war." They said:

> None of the countries they represented had anything to gain by war except possibly Germany. And the German people recognize from the results of the last war that even in victory there is nothing to be gained by bloodshed and destruction.[66]

In England and France, Jeannette noticed widespread training in the use of gas masks. Signs were evident in all hotels and apartment houses which gave the location of the nearest gas-proof shelter in case of an air raid. English veterans of World War I held a reunion in London, while Jeannette was there. A bus driver in London told her, "The majority of war veterans organized in every country that participated in the last war would refuse to fight if another war is declared.[67]

Other Europeans believed that the international situation was exceedingly grave, but hoped that war might be averted with the passing of time. In making her own evaluation, Jeannette Rankin believed there was more serious discussion of peaceable disposition of international difficulties than there was a generation ago. She wrote:

> Italy and Germany, the most feared countries, are experiencing a desperate need of economic friendliness with European countries and will not rush into war in the immediate future. ...And may

---

[66]Jeannette Rankin and Belle Fligelman Winestein, "Europe Doesn't Want War," MSS in personal possession of B. F. Winestein, Helena, Montana, p. 1.

[67]Jeannette Rankin and Belle Fligelman Winestein, "Europe Doesn't Want War," p. 4.

     decide to cure their own economic troubles by
     friendly overtures rather than try to force
     their unwilling constituents into a much
     feared war.[68]

Unfortunately, military leaders scrapped her conclusions.

Jeannette Rankin returned to the United States just in time for
Franklin Roosevelt's Chicago speech in October of 1937. Given the inter-
dependence of the modern world, he said that it was impossible for any
nation completely to isolate itself from the economic and political up-
heavals in the rest of the globe. Alarmed by Japan's attack on China
in July and the restlessness of Europe, the President asserted that the
peace-loving nations must make a concerted effort in opposition to violation
of treaties and that war makers must be quarantined by the international
community.[69]

To Congressmen, Rankin suggested that Roosevelt's speech was intended
to prepare the way for increased armament appropriations. She wrote, "It
would doubtless meet the favor of the munitions and shipbuilding companies
and others because of its effect on the current depression."[70] Also, she
observed that his speech revealed the tendency of an executive to lead
the country into a position where war may seem to be inevitable. This can
be accomplished, she said, "by assuming it is a holy war and by arousing
fear of invasion. ...That will make people willing to make the sacrifice

---

[68]Ibid., p. 6.

[69]Samuel I. Rosenman, The Public Papers and Addresses of Franklin D.
Roosevelt, 1937 (New York: The Macmillan Co., 1941, pp. 409-10.

[70]J. R. to Senator James P. Pope, October 27, 1937, NCPW Files

a war demands."[71]

Proded by the direction of Roosevelt's Chicago speech and the defeat of the Ludlow Referendum in January of 1938, Jeannette Rankin redoubled her efforts to keep America from going to war. Testifying before the House Committee on Naval Affairs, she reminded the members that, through their control on authorizations and appropriations, Congress had the power to determine basic lines of foreign policy. Before authorizing construction of naval vessels to bring the United States to "treaty strength," she wanted Congress to secure a clear statement of policy from the Roosevelt administration. Having been told that the proposed increases were for defenses, Rankin questioned, "Defense of what?" Previously, the Navy had wanted to defend national policies, commerce, and control of the seas; the State Department desired to maintain orderly processes in Asia; and the President urged defense of the sanctity of treaties and of democratic principles.[72]

If Congress was to accept these directives, Jeannette Rankin believed, it would be negating the will of the people, abandoning the spirit of the Kellogg-Briand Pact, and reversing its own thrice-passed neutrality legislation. Continuing her argument from previous years, she asked for the justification of increasing expenditures for obsolete battleships in light of ill housed, ill fed, and ill clothed Americans. Furthermore, she suggested that these expenditures would "handicap normal business by making loans and supplies more difficult for it to obtain, and thereby raise the

---

[71]Statement of J. R., undated (probably between October of 1937 and January of 1938, NCPW Files, SCPC.

[72]U.S., Congress, House of Representatives, Committee on Naval Affairs, Hearings to Establish the Composition of the United States Navy on H. R. 9218, 75th Congress, 4th Session, January 31, 1938, pp. 2123-2124.

cost and reduce the standard of living." Lastly, Jeannette pointed out
that an abnormal naval building program would intensify international
tensions and distrust and "increase the speed with which humanity is
drifting into the general destruction of another war."[73]

Concurrent with the rise of war anxieties, according to Jeannette,
came an increased military propaganda. Its goal was to educate America
to the point of joining with England in threatening war or even going to
war. Rankin felt events were closely following patterns of pre-World War
I in that:

> The analogy is drawn between the Ludlow amendment
> and the McLemore resolution. [To forbid issuing
> of passports to American citizens traveling on
> belligerent ships.] Norman Davis is taking the
> place of Colonel House. English propaganda is
> being spread everywhere.[74]

John M. Coffee, Congressman from Washington State expressed these sentiments
picturesquely by writing, "I would prevent our diplomatic service, navy and
army from being used as the tail to the kite of British imperialism."[75]
With a touch of anglophobia, Rankin asserted, "England holds control over
the situation, but England will never permit war unless she is confident
the United States will do the fighting and paying for her."[76] Earlier,
she had hinted in California that Anthony Eden's cabinet fell when Cordell
Hull, United States Secretary of State, denied existence of a secret agreement with England and that "Great Britain is trying to force the United
States into war on foreign soil to pull John Bull's chestnuts out of the

---

[73]Ibid., pp. 2124-2125; New York Times, February 10, 1938.

[74]J. R. to Mrs. Pope Hill, January 31, 1938, NCPW Files, SCPC.

[75]John M. Coffee to Frederick Libby, August 5, 1938, NCPW Files, SCPC.

[76]Butte Montana Standard, undated copy in J. R. MSS (from content,
probably summer of 1938).

fire."[77]

While England attempted to justify its imperialism to save its empire, Hitler threatened Europe with war in the fall of 1938. Hoping to appease Hitler, England and France forced Czechoslovakia to give up its Sudenland sector to Germany in the Munich Agreement in September. For one who was not willing to credit England with much, Jeannette Rankin's reaction was enthusiastic. She hoped that Chamberlain had averted war and opened possibilities for an enduring peace. "Appeasement" was not a dirty word to her. She said, "I believe in it. You do anything to keep from killing men to settle a dispute."[78]

Jeannette Rankin continued to lobby for the NCPW until May of 1938, when it gave her a six-month leave of absence. Salary cuts and delayed payments were nothing unusual while working for the Council. Her trips to Europe in 1931 and 1937 were means of getting back salary since Frederick Libby liked for his staff to travel aborad. During the depression years, Jeannette received a salary cut of one-fourth and then in 1932 one-half. Beginning in 1936, the Emergency Peace Campaign competed with Libby for operational funds. Jeannette Rankin began in 1937 to make part of her salary by accepting speaking engagements. Then, in 1938 and 1939, the NCPW employed her for only six months. In spite of the fact that Libby offered no proposal for payment, Jeannette wrote her brother, Wellington, that she wanted to go to Washington in January of 1939 to work for three

---

[77]Hollywood Citizen-News, March 1, 1938.

[78]J. R. Interview, March 2, 1971, pp. 10-11; Frederick Libby to J. R., October 1, 1938, NCPW Files, SCPC; J. R. to Frederick Libby, October 17, 1938, NCPW Files.

months.[79]

Returning to the NCPW office in January, Jeannette Rankin lobbied Congress extensively over the next several months. First, she appeared before the House Naval Affairs Committee to protest the possible future fortification of Guam. This plan was supported privately by naval experts. She considered its fortification a strategic and diplomatic blunder because of its location in a labyrinth of Japanese military power. To her, "Guam would more readily become a hostage in enemy hands than a salient in ours."[80] A month later she testified before the Senate Committee, maintaining that the defense of Guam had become a political question of foreign policy. By fortifying Guam she believed, "We entered a political contest with Japan. ...Guam will not deter Japan. Why make a threat, especially when it is ineffectual?"[81]

Forced by declining funds, the NCPW wanted Jeannette Rankin to work full time for one-half salary, but she would not accept. Some of her co-workers expressed the opinion that she did not need a salary since her brother had a successful law practice. As the economic situation tightened,

---

[79]Margaret Thompson, Office Secretary, to J. R., November 9, 1937, NCPW Files, SCPC; NCPW Financial Report, October 5, 1937; NCPW News Bulletin, XI (November, 1932), p. 3; Frederick Libby to J. R., September 22, 1932, NCPW Files; NCPW Executive Board Meeting, December, 1938, NCPW Files; J. R. Interview, February 20, 1969, p. 6; NCPW Annual Business Meeting, October 13-14, 1939; J. R. to Wellington Rankin, December 7, 1938, NCPW Files; In June of 1938, J. R. went to North Dakota to spend a week speaking in behalf of the re-election of Senator Gerald Nye.

[80]U.S., Congress, House of Representatives, Committee on Naval Affairs, Hearings To Authorize the Secretary of Navy To Proceed with Construction of Certain Public Works, on H. R. 2880, 76th Congress, First Session, February 7, 1939, pp. 385-394.

[81]U.S., Congress, Senate Committee on Naval Affairs, Hearings on the Construction of Certain Public Works on S. 830, 76th Congress, First Session, March 9, 1939, pp. 105-109.

so did personal anxieties within the Council. Jeannette felt the staff

had not recognized her length of lobbying experience, her Congressional

"know-how," and had not given her the opportunity to contribute effective-

ly to NCPW policy. There was always a basic disarmament in technique

used in lobbying Congressmen. Having thought in terms of working only

three months, Jeannette Rankin resigned April 1, 1939. The Executive

Board paid Jeannette a consultative fee through June and gave her a

leave of absence to January of 1940. Before she left Washington, Rankin

presented a statement to the House Committee on Foreign Affairs encourag-

ing the strengthening of the arms embargo as proposed in the neutrality

legislation.[82] With the possibility of building a peace group in western

Montana and a residence in the Bitteroot, Rankin returned home.[83]

---

[82]U.S., Congress, House of Representatives, Committee on Foreign Affairs, Hearings on American Neutrality Policy, 76th Congress, First Session, April 18, 1939, pp. 229-233.

[83]J. R. Interview, February 20, 1969, p. 6; NCPW Executive Board Meeting, April, 1939, NCPW Files, SCPC; J. R. to Wellington Rankin, December 7, 1938, in NCPW Files.

CHAPTER XI

A FOOTNOTE IN HISTORY

After Hitler broke his pledge at Munich by overrunning the remainder
of Czechoslovakia in the spring of 1939, it was no surprise to the world
when German troops invaded Poland on September 1. While England and
France prepared to make war on Germany, Jeannette Rankin took up the
gauntlet for peace. She returned to Montana to encourage the people to
question America's role in world affairs, to gather their sentiment about
war, and to determine the possibility of her announcing for Congress in
1940. During that fall, she toured fifty-two of the fifty-six high schools
in the Western District. She wrote to the school principals and told them
that she would be in their area on a certain day and would like to speak.
Since Rankin gave them no return address, it was difficult for them to
answer negatively.[1]

Knowing her position on war, many of the school leaders were afraid
that Jeannette Rankin would attack President Roosevelt personally. They
had anxious moments about her speaking. Rankin usually introduced her
presentation by describing the situation in Europe as very serious. She
proceeded then to talk about her favorite subjects, war and peace. As had
been her custom for years, Jeannente concluded by asking the students to
write to their Congressmen and to the President. Having served in the

---

[1]Frances Elge Interview, September 10, 1970, pp. 1-2; J. R. Interview,
January 27, 1969, p. 6; typical of letters sent: J. R. to Superintendent
Conrad Orr, Dillon, Mont., October 2, 1939 in J. R. MSS.

274

House of Representatives, she explained the value of letters. She explained to the students that many Congressmen use form letters to answer
letters from their constituents. To get a personal answer, she suggested
writing often but "no more than once a week." To avoid giving themselves
away as school students, jokingly she told her audience, "Don't tell them
your age; I never do." To extend her influence, Jeannette always asked
the students to talk these ideas over with their parents before writing.[2]

The school students were responsive and quick to grasp Jeannette
Rankin's thesis. They enjoyed her stories, displayed an intelligent awareness of European problems, and asked significant questions. At the high
school in Kalispell, the students arranged for Miss Rankin to speak over
their own radio station which broadcast to the entire county. Jeannette
felt that these experiences with the students were interesting and valuable
as a means of disseminating peace propaganda.[3]

On September 29, Jeannette took time off from her tour of high schools
to make a radio address sponsored by the Business and Professional Women's
Club of Helena. She began by expressing empathy with fellow Montanians
as they tried to interpret the daily, mounting crisis in Europe compounded
by secret treaties and political commitments. Of one thing Rankin was
sure, "We have a moral responsibility to help correct the unspeakable
conditions that exist in the world."[4] Yet, that responsibility did not
include a commitment to war. To her, war always created more conflicts
than it solved because:

---

[2] J. R. Interview, Jan. 27, 1969, p. 7.

[3] J. R. Interview with John Board, August 29, 1963, p. 35.

[4] J. R. Radio Speech for B&PW Club of Helena, Montana, September 29,
1939, p. 1, NCPW Files, SCPC.

> ...The method itself is wrong. It violates moral
> laws which have been accepted as correctly stated
> for the individual, and therefore cannot be broken
> by a group of individuals although the group is as
> large as a state of nation.[5]

Declaring war as stupid and futile, Rankin told her radio audience that

America's expression of democracy should be to permit other governments

"to work out their own problems without our interference."[6]

After outlining her favorite defense thesis, "American shores cannot

be successfully invaded," Jeannette Rankin returned to the theme of democ-

racy. She said:

> It we want to preserve democracy for future gene-
> rations, we must do our individual part by express-
> ing our opinions now. Our interest is not with the
> forms of governments, deplorable as some of them
> are, but with our moral responsibility to help, by
> example, ...to abolish the war system.[7]

As a pacifist, Jeannette Rankin believed, morality required America to say,

"We do not like your Hitler methods; therefore, we are not going to use

violence." With the usual rhetoric, she concluded her speech by urging

her listeners to express their opinion that killing young men represented

permanent injury to world civilization.[8]

Before ending her propaganda and opinion sampling tour, Jeannette

Rankin returned to the East for several speeches and to help the National

Council for Prevention of War retain the embargo on arms and munitions.

Responding to pressure by the Roosevelt Administration, the Senate in

October of 1939, had approved a bill to repeal existing embargo legislation.

---

[5]Ibid.

[6]Ibid., p. 2.

[7]Ibid., p. 4.

[8]Ibid., p. 5.

Rankin answered Frederick Libby's urgent plea for assistance by coming
to Washington and lobbying the House for a week preceeding its vote.
A "cash and carry" embargo on arms and munitions was finally sustained.[9]
Before getting down to seriously considering campaigning in Montana,
Jeannette testified against battleship construction before the House Naval
Affairs Committee in February of 1940.

Using an interesting psychological technique, Jeannette Rankin sympathized with the Naval Affairs Committee in its work. She expressed
awareness that other committees, such as Military Affairs, had tried to
usurp its prerogatives. Obvious, too, she observed, was the lack of
coordination of the State, Army, and Navy Departments in developing unified
objectives. The result was confusion as to a consistent national policy
on foreign affairs. With these hardships, she realized it was almost impossible to adjust a naval program to such an uncertain national policy.[11]

To allevaite these difficulties, Jeannette Rankin submitted a resolution to the committee. She proposed that:

> The United States maintain a naval policy of de-
> fense only; to refrain from maintaining or establish-
> ing agencies of warfare other than those necessary to
> defend our shores from actual invasion and to eliminate
> from naval forces all such agencies...as are designed...
> for aggressive or foreign war.[12]

---

[9]Frederick J. Libby to J. R., Telegram, October 19, 1939, in NCPW
Files, SCPC; 1939 Report to Annual Business Meeting, NCPW Files; Spring-
field, Montana, Morning Union, December 5, 1939; Holyoke, Massachusetts,
Transcript Telegram, December 5, 1939.

[10]New York Times, February 6, 1940.

[11]U.S., Congress, House of Representatives, Committee on Naval Affairs,
Hearings on Establishing the Composition of the U.S. Navy pursuant to H.R.
8026, 76th Congress, 3rd Session, February 5, 1940, pp. 2166-2168.

[12]Ibid., p. 2169.

Under this framework, Jeannette believed that the committee and Congress could effectively carry out the desires of the American people.

To act responsibly on these issues, Jeannette Rankin concluded that she must run for Congress if there was any possibility of her winning. She spent the spring of 1940 contacting county committee chairmen, asking their advice and securing their opinion of the peace sentiment in the district. Complicating Jeannette's decision was her lack of public exposure in Montana since the last election. Except for vacations, she had worked out of the state exclusively and had spent considerable time in Georgia. Also, Rankin would have to overcome a Democratic majority of twelve thousand in the Western District. The final determining factor seemed to be, "At the last moment I kept saying to myself, 'If I don't run, the women [those who don't want war] will have no one to vote'."[13]

Judging that there was sufficient peace sentiment to put her in office, Rankin, on June 5, 1940, entered the Republican primary as a candidate for the House of Representatives. Opposing her were Jacob Thorkelson, incumbent Congressman, W. R. Allen and Winfield E. Page. In a letter announcing her candidacy, Jeannette indicated that the next session of Congress would be one of the most critical in history. Monetary standards, unemployment, security for the aged and unemployed, and national defense were sure to be some of the major issues. As to defense and European problems, she took as her slogan, "Prepare to the limit for defense; keep our men out of Europe."[14]

---

[13] J. R. Interview with John Board, August 30, 1963, p. 36.

[14] J. R. to Frederick Libby, May 2 and June 4, 1940, NCPW Files, SCPC; J. R. to Western District, undated, in J. R. MSS.

In the Primary campaign, Jeannette Rankin clearly stated her position
on the issues, including war. She did not personally attack any of our
other candidates, but emphasized her own ability. One woman asked, "What's
the matter with Thorkelson?" Rankin replied, "He's a good Congressman,
but I think I can do more than he. I know the men in Congress. I have
been lobbying and I know the rules of Congress. I think I can do more
for you."[15] According to Winfield Page, an opposing Republican, Jeannette
conducted a "gum-chew" campaign with the active backing of all the Rankins.
Being an old-line family with many ties, Jeannette found receptive voters
as she spoke, met people, and shook hands over Western Montana. Thorkelson's
reputation as a pro-Fascist and anti-Semitic may have aided Rankin's candidacy.
Yet, her most important assets were her own ability to campaign vigorously,
to present pleasing platform appearances, and to meet the issues honestly.
In the balloting on July 18, Western Montanians chose Jeannette Rankin
over Congressman Thorkelson, her closest opponent, 7,299 to 6,214. In writing to Frederick Libby, Executive Director of NCPW, Jeannette Rankin felt
her nomination "proved that the people in this district don't want to send
men to Europe."[16]

Jerry J. O'Connell of Butte received the Democratic nomination to the
November general election. He had established himself as a liberal while
serving in the House of Representatives from 1936 to 1938. During his term,

---

[15]J. R. Interview, January 27, 1969, p. 7.

[16]Winfield Page Interview with John Board, April 8, 1966, Missoula,
Montana, p. 3; Richard T. Ruetter, "Showdown in Montana, 1938: Burton K.
Wheeler's Role in the Defeat of Jerry O'Connell," Pacific Northwest
Quarterly, LIV (January, 1963), p. 28; Ellis Waldron, An Atlas of
Montana Politics, p. 285; Great Falls Tribune, July 7, 1940, July 12,
1940, July 19, 1940; J. R. to Frederick Libby, July 22, 1940, NCPW Files,
SCPC.

O'Connell supported the Ludlow Referendum, military unification, anti-war profit legislation, and Roosevelt's approach to a flexible neutrality policy. He also engaged in what was considered radical political and economic activity for his time. Some even labeled him as "communist". The quiet opposition of Senator Burton K. Wheeler, had defeated him for re-election in 1938, and personal family problems added to his difficulties in his bid for Congress in 1940.[17]

The Anaconda Company, normally a powerful force in Montana politics, was not happy with either candidate. Jeannette Rankin had earlier alienated the company by taking labor's side in the Butte mine strike of 1917. Jerry O'Connell, in 1938, called attention to Anaconda's evasion of an excise tax on imported copper and initiated legislation to stop its importation.[18] With such background, the Anaconda Company chose to remain still--very still.[19]

A radio address, delivered in Helena on July 8, 1940, was typical of Jeannette Rankin's approach. Taking note of the increasing war in Europe, she advocated more military efficiency, greater emphasis on airplanes and armored equipment, and a highly modernized military defense for peacetime. Jeannette believed that Montanians were opposed to sending men to Europe but willing to spend any amont to protect American freedom and its shore from invasion. Therefore, she proposed "to prepare to the limit to defend

---

[17]John E. Kennedy, "Liberal's Defeat--A Case History," The Nation, CXLVII (November 26, 1938), pp. 504-565; Richard T. Rueeter, "Showdown in Montana," pp. 19-28.

[18]U.S., Congress, House of Representatives, 75th Congress, First Session, Congressional Record, LXXXI, Part Two, p. 1264.

[19]J. R. Interview, January 27, 1969, p. 5.

our rights and shores and let the world know we are unwilling to send
our men to Europe to fight in foreign wars."[20]

Turning to domestic problems, Jeannette spoke of unemployment as the
most tragic. She expressed empathy with the large number of youth between
eighteen and twenty-four who were seeking a job. She called attention to
countless children who needed love and security and were hungry for food
in the midst of plenty. With increasing longevity, the future of the
aging citizen has created a new problem for America. As a beginning,
Jeannette suggested, "No adjustment of our economic institutions will be
satisfactory unless based on the astonishing fact that an abundance can
be made available." While this was being accomplished, she proposed to
increase consumption to match production. Untapped American markets
should be saturated before sending military establishments to foreign soil
to hold or to increase foreign markets.[21]

As a recognized suffragist and a champion for social legislation,
Jeannette spoke with authority in her appeal to women. Because she valued
highly women's past contributions to civilization, she encouraged their
involvement in helping to solve America's present problems. What could
be more important than your "traditional responsibility from time immemorial
to care for the children, to nurse the sick, to feed the hungry, and to protect the old?" she said. Identifying with them, she then pledged her best
efforts to finding practical solutions.[22]

Having spoken on the subjects of war, economics, and women, Rankin
concluded with a bid for votes. So that there could be no misunderstanding,

---

[20]U.S., Congress, Senate, 76th Congress, Third Session, Congressional
Record, LXXXVI, Part 17, p. 4836.

[21]Ibid.

[22]Ibid.

she stated her position clearly:

> If you do not want your boys to go to Europe to
> fight, if you want them kept at home and supplied
> with the most modern military equipment that
> science and ingenuity can produce to defend the
> greatest, most liberty-loving country, then I
> ask you to vote for me and you can depend . . .
> that in my efforts I will not fail you.[23]

The radio provided Jeannette with an effective tool for reaching most of the prospective voters - even those in Montana's remote areas. Arthur Acher, an attorney and partner of Wellington Rankin, and George Shepherd, an attorney for the Missoula Mercantile Company, developed a radio script which was widely used. Its format called for a master of ceremonies who would introduce several prominent women. They then gave prepared speeches in behalf of Jeannette Rankin. One woman would discuss Jerry O'Connell's unwarranted attack on the members of Montana's Supreme Court and his vicious attitude toward fellow Democrats. All this was to show his disregard for democratic institutions and his destructive rather than constructive pursuits.[24]

Another person compared O'Connell's labor record with Jeannette's. Quoting from a statement of David R. Robinson, President of the Brotherhood of Locomotive Firemen and Engineers, she said, "The fact is O'Connell has not supported labor generally. He opposed the Railroad Retirement Bill of 1937."[25] On the other hand, she read from a letter written by William Green, President of the American Federation of Labor which said, "During all her service here in Washington, Jeannette Rankin proved her value to

---

[23] Ibid.; See Butte Daily Post, October 30, 1940, for detailed coverage of another speech.

[24] Jeannette Rankin Radio Script, 1940 Campaign, J. R. MSS.

[25] Ibid.

the American Federation of Labor not only by her votes but by her actions in committees and conferences."[26] In addition to the support of the AF of L, Rankin received the endorsements of the Brotherhood of Maintenance of Way Employees, American Train Dispatchers Association, and the Brotherhood of Railway and Steamship Clerks.[27]

Not willing to miss an opportunity to increase suspicion of the Democratic candidate, the script insinuated that Jerry O'Connell had connections with Communists. The script writers based this on the fact that for two years O'Connell had promoted a pension plan which presently appeared on the platform of the Communist Party. Not to be outdone, O'Connell's men put out the word that Jeannette Rankin had been branded a Communist in Georgia. They printed a pamphlet containing a letter from the Athens American Legion attacking her patriotism. It also incorporated a statement by Kenneth Murrell, Commander of the Atlanta Post No. One, in which Murrell charged Jeannette Rankin with Communist association.[28] Many of O'Connell's statements were false and others were taken totally out of context. Friends of the Rankins tipped them off early as to the rumors and printed material.[29] With a few well-placed phone calls by Wellington Rankin, the Democrats quietly withdrew their pamphlets from circulation.

The radio script concluded with personal testimony by whomen who had known Jeannette in the early suffrage campaigns, in her first election to Congress and through the years as she worked for improved social conditions.

---

[26]William Green to James D. Graham, Montana State Federation of Labor, August 5, 1940, J. R. MSS.

[27]Butte Daily Post, November 1, 1940.

[28]Campaign pamphlet in J. R. MSS.

[29]Mrs. L. R. Packard to Wellington Rankin, October 31, 1940, J.R. MSS.

The radio script concluded with personal testimony by women who had known Jeannette in the early suffrage campaigns, in her first election to Congress and through the years as she worked for improved social conditions. Frances Elge, Rankin's personal secretary and treasurer of the Jeannette Rankin for Congress Club, organized and directed the presentation of several of the radio programs. Elge also accompanied Rankin on some tours through the district and assisted in "door-to-door" canvassing in the precincts.[30] In a lumbercamp in Northwest Montana, Frances Elge, referring to Rankin's attitude on war, told the men, "She [meaning Jeannette] would rather see them 'half shot' over here than 'shot' over there." Jeannette was horrified, but the story brought life to what many considered a rather dull campaign compared with the flambouyant contests of other years.[31]

To establish Jeannette Rankin's character and courage as compared to O'Connell's, the Republican State Committee secured commendations from reputable national leaders. Ruth Hanna McCormick Simms, Former Member of Congress from Illinois, wrote, "Her ability, courage and leadership add great strength to the Republican Party." Senator Robert M. LaFollette, Jr. of Wisconsin indicated "America needs leaders in Congress like Jeannette Rankin." Characterizing her as one of the great humanitarians of this age, Representative Harold Knutson of Minnesota said:

> Miss Rankin has labored . . . for legislation that
> would help the . . . underprivileged, the friend-
> less and the toiler. For twenty-four years I have

---

[30]Arthur Acher Interview, September 4, 1970, p. 5.

[31]Frances Elge Interview, September 10, 1970, p. 3; Butte Daily Post, November 4, 1940.

watched her effective work with ever growing . . . respect.[32]

From the Democratic side, Bennett Champ Clark, Senator from Missouri, wrote, "I had the pleasure of knowing you and of observing your work in the very trying position of being the first woman member of . . . a war Congress. I admired your courage and ability."[33] Probably one of the most enthusiastic endorsements came from Fiorello La Guardia, Mayor of New York and a close personal friend from Rankin's first term. He wrote:

> Jeannette Rankin has the training, experience and understanding to intelligently serve the people of Montana. ...I know of no one who has kept in closer touch with economic, social and political conditions in this country. ...This woman has more courage and packs a harder punch than a regiment of regular line politicians.[34]

In an interesting unused letter, Norman Thomas, Socialist candidate for President, surmissed, since there was no opposing Socialist, that he could endorese Jeannette Rankin. He wrote that this was his first support for an:

> Old Party candidate, but. . . I am willing to forgive her connection with the Republican Party! I know that she. . . cannot be charged with sympathy for or connection with any kind of totalitarianism, fascist or communist. She believes in American

---

[32]Campaign pamphlet, "Jeannette Rankin for Congress, "Republican State Central Committe, J. R. MSS; These original letters, containing the above excerpts, plus others were in the J. R. MSS: for example: Clifford R. Hope, Roy O. Woodruff, Thomas A. Jenkins, Katherine D. Blake, Styles Bridges, Frank B. Keefe, Francis Case, Charles McNary, Hamilton Fish ("No one outside of Congress did more or cooperated more effectively with me to keep us out of war."), Bruce Barton, George H. Tinkham, Lynn Frazier, Robert Taft, Everett M. Dirkson, Lenna Lowe Yost, Charles Tobey, Robert J. Corbett, and William Tyler Page.

[33]Ibid.

[34]Ibid.

democracy and wants to make it better. I think her
stand on social legislation will be enlightened."[35]

These letters gave status to the campaign, but the most important
contribution was Jeannette Rankin herself. A delightful and charming
speaker, she was also a disarming and logical debater. When these skills
were coupled with O'Connell's own weaknesses, the untiring loyalty and
devotion of women, and the perceptive, well informed political leadership
of Wellington Rankin, Jeannette's campaign manager, victory seemed inevitable. On November 5, while Democratic candidate Franklin D. Roosevelt,
Burton K. Wheeler, and James O'Connor were rolling up large pluralities,
sixty-year-old Jeannette Rankin, white haired Republican, defeated youth-
ful Jerry O'Connell by a margin of 56,616 to 47,352.[36]

By the time Rankin concluded her political victory, the Germans, in
addition to Poland, had successfully executed their military campaigns in
Belgium, the Netherlands, France, Denmark, and Norway. With the devious
German-Russian rapproachement, this temporarily left England to face alone
a German-dominated Europe. Given these facts, American public opinion
divided basically into two groups. First, the Committee to Defend America,
formed in May of 1940, felt it was most important to help England win the

---

[35]Norman Thomas to Jeannette Rankin, August 16, 1940, J. R. MSS; J. R.
voted for him for President each time he ran -- J. R. Interview, February
23, 1971, p. 8.

[36]Frances Elge Interview, September 10, 1970, pp. 4-8; Winfield Page
Interview, April 8, 1966, p. 6; Waldron, An Atlas of Montana Politics,
p. 288; Great Falls Tribune, November 7, 1940; New York Times, November
7, 1940; Jerry J. O'Connell to J. R., Telegram, November 6, 1940; "Congressman Returns to the House," Christian Century, LVII (November 20, 1940),
p. 1437.

war overseas, and to supply everything short of intervention.[37]

Secondly, as a challenge to the rapidly growing Committee to Defend America by Aiding the Allies, non-interventionists, headed by Robert Wood, established the Committee to Defend America First (popularly called the America First Committee). Jeannette Rankin encountered these two positions as she returned to Washington to take her seat on January 3, 1941. Without the fanfare of 1917, she became a member of the Seventy-seventh Congress and immediately began to deal with the increasing pressures of a world at war.[38]

Franklin D. Roosevelt, very conscious of non-interventionist sentiment and aware of American bitterness toward default of World War I debts, acted slowly. He favored aiding England but did not wish to antagonize an isolationist public. His solution came through an Executive Order, therefore bypassing Congress, to swap fifty aged destroyers for naval bases in Newfoundland, Bermuda and the Caribbean. In June of 1940, he declared that America "must be the arsenal of democracy." Roosevelt, by December, was ready to initiate a program to implement this ideal. He sent "Lend-Lease"

---

[37]In the beginning, William Allen White and Clark Eichelberger headed this committee; Selig Adler, The Isolationist Impulse (New York: The Free Press, 1957), pp. 262-263; John W. Mosland, "Pressure Groups and American Foreign Policy," Public Opinion Quarterly, VI (Spring, 1942), p. 118.

[38]J. R. to Rhoda Richardson, December 27, 1940, J. R. MSS; J. R. to Mrs. Harold Kennedy, December 14, 1940, J. R. MSS; There was no evidence that J. R. became a member of the America First Committee, but she did accept speaking engagements to their rallies, cf. Margaret B. Kennelly, Secretary of AFC Speakers' Bureau, December 9, 1941, J. R. MSS; U.S., Congress, House of Representatives, Congressional Record, 77th Congress, First Session, January 3, 1941, LXXXI, Part One, pp. 6-7.

legislation into the new Congress.[39]

The Lend-Lease Act, as proposed by the Administration, authorized
the President to lend, lease, sell, or barter arms, munitions, or military
information to any country whose defense seemed vital to the United States.
In the House, the bill by design carried a significant number--1776. For
several reasons, Jeannette Rankin opposed "Lend-Lease" legislation. Primarily she felt that the program brought the nation "one step closer to
war." Even though the bill did not specify any nation, Rankin was aware
that England would receive the greatest benefits. As a suspicious Anglephobe,
she envisioned men following this material in a short time to fight England's
war.[40]

In contrast to this measure, the will of the people, according to
Jeannette Rankin, supported unlimited expenditures for national defense
extending over the Western Hemisphere. "The people are equally strong,"
she said, "in their opposition to sending men to Europe to settle boundary
and commercial disputes of the Old World."[41] To protect this interest of
the people, she offered the following amendment to the proposed legislation:

> Nothing in this act shall be construed to autho-
> rize or permit the President to order, transfer,
> exchange, lease, lend or employ any soldier,
> sailor, marine or aircraft pilot outside the
> territorial waters of the Western Hemisphere
> without specific authorization of the Congress
> of the United States.[42]

---

[39] Richard W. Steele, "Preparing the Public for War: Efforts to
Establish a National Propaganda Agency, 1940-41." American Historical
Review, LXXV (October, 1970), p. 1640.

[40] U.S., Congress, House of Representatives, 77th Congress, First
Session, Congressional Record, LXXXVII, Part One, p. 791.

[41] Ibid., p. 792.

[42] Ibid., p. 791.

Supporting Jeannette's insistance that military preparation be limited to defense needs only was her firm belief, that with modern equipment, "Our country is impregnable."[43]

In addition to the immediate military implications of Lend-Lease, Jeannette Rankin inquired about future war aims. Not trusting England, she desired to know if they planned an invasion of Europe. Looking even farther ahead, she asked, "What terms can we accept as conditions for peace?" She believed that the answers to these questions would affect the human liberties of every American citizen. As the people's representative, she then reminded her colleagues, "People never make war. It is always governments."[45] Not won by her arguments, the House defeated her amendment, 82 to 137, and went on to endorse the principle of "Lend-Lease."[46]

Believing that the administration was preparing for war, Jeannette drafted, but did not introduce, legislation to "black out war profits." As suggested previously to a hearing considering war profits, she proposed that the Secretary of Treasury issue emergency currency upon a declaration of war. Every person would receive an amount of new money equal to his current holdings. Trading in regular currency would cease for the duration of the war, and the emergency notes would become legal tender. When the crisis ended, the currency in use would become void and good only as a momento of the war. Rankin's intent was to destroy the profit motive but the martial fever of Congress spoiled any possibilities for

---

[43] Ibid., 792.

[44] Ibid., p. 792.

[45] Ibid.

[46] Rankin's attitude toward "Lend-Lease" was supported by Senator Burton K. Wheeler of Montana who called it "New Deal's Tripple A foreign policy to plow under every fourth American boy"--Selig Adler, The Isolationist Impulse, (New York: The Free Press, 1957), p. 282.

its introduction.[47]

With continued Nazi harrassment of shipping, the United States began to provide convoy escorts and patrols for lend-lease goods in violation of the act. Many Montanians wrote Jeannette and expressed an opinion against increased convoy protection for English shipping. Before President Roosevelt announced his first extension of patrol operations on April 24, 1941, several hundred letters had crossed her desk. Typically, one of them wrote, "By doing all in your power toward keeping the United States out of this tragic threatening war, we citizens here will back you up 100%. You can depend on us - can we depend on you?"[48] Most Montanians who expressed themselves felt that the use of convoy patrols was dangerous and would lead eventually to war.[49] Another constituent bolstered Rankin's anti-British position by writing:

> America is aiding her [Britain] to resist totalitarian
> aggression and also to maintain British imperialism.
> I believe we are doing it because American financiers
> are so deeply involved in British imperialism that
> they can not afford to allow Britain to be defeated.[50]

To stop the convoy patrols, Jeannette supported New Hampshire's Charles W. Toby's Anti-Convoy Legislation and urged parents to write the President, expressing their opposition.[51] Not only did Rankin oppose the convoy system,

---

[47]Tentative draft of a Bill for Emergency Currency, March 29, 1941, J. R. MSS; cf also undated clipping, "Miss Rankin Urges Drafting of Money." J. R. MSS.

[48]Mrs. O. G. Marksen to J. R., April 20, 1941, J. R. MSS.

[49]Workers Alliance Local G-501 to J. R., April 25, 1941, J. R. MSS.

[50]Copy of letter sent to President Franklin Roosevelt from Francis Coyle, Great Falls, Montana, May 3, 1941, J. R. MSS.

[51]Statement of J. R. to the Montana First District Voters, May 10, 1941, J. R. MSS.

oppose the convoy system, but she protested against the arming of American merchant ships.[52]

In the middle Nineteen Thirties, Jeannette Rankin had lobbied for a national military policy. So, in May of 1941, she took advantage of her congressional seat by introducing similar legislation. She called upon Congress to establish a policy not to send armed forces outside of the Western Hemisphere or the territorial and insular possessions of the United States.[53] Failing to get her measure adopted, Rankin later attached an amendment to the Military Appropriations Bill of 1942. She chided the Democrats by paraphrasing their 1940 platform. Her amendment provided:

> That no appropriation in this act ... shall be used to send our army or airforces to fight in foreign lands outside of the Americas and our insular possessions except in case of attack.[54]

To accomplish this defense function, Rankin suggested reorganizing the military establishment into one unified department with clearly defined purposes. With ninety-five percent of her mail favoring the protection of American shores and staying out of Europe, Jeannette had expressed the will of the public opinion as it was expressed to her.[55]

But according to other public opinion polls, the mood of the people was changing to a position favoring aid to those allied against Hitler.

---

[52]Great Falls Tribune, Oct. 16, 1941; U.S., Congress, House of Representatives, 77th Congress, 1st Session, Congressional Record, LXXXVII, Pt. 7, p. 7901.

[53]U.S., Congress, House of Representatives, LXXXVII, Part Four, p. 3687; New York Times, May 7, 1941.

[54]U.S., Congress, House of Representatives, 77th Congress, First Session, Congressional Record, LXXXVII, Part Five, p. 4830.

[55]Ibid.

Adroitly, President Roosevelt committed America only one step at a time.
In the spring and summer of 1941, United States troops occupied Green-
land and Iceland through an agreement to protect supply routes. Rankin
criticized these moves because Roosevelt did not consult Congress as
the people's representatives.[56] With Germany's invasion of Russia in
late June of 1941, American "involvement" in Europe became even more com-
plicated. Would the United States support a "Stalinistic" totalitarianism
or should they continue to remain neutral? "Aid to Russia doesn't have
the people's support," Jeannette Rankin answered. The Great Falls Tribune
continued to quote her as saying, "They're simply not enthused about saving the Red Menace."[57]

Hitler's attack on Russia took the pressure off England but it in-
tensified propaganda in some American quarters favoring more aid to contain the Nazi power. By a narrow margin of 203 to 202, the House of
Representatives passed the extension of draft service in August, 1941 and
committed soldiers to areas outside the Western Hemisphere. Jeannette,
voting against the measure, was disappointed at the twenty-one Republicans
who supported the Administration. In progressive steps she thought the
United States was moving toward war. With the signing of the Atlantic
Charter on August 14, 1941 by Winston Churchill, English Prime Minister,
and Franklin Roosevelt, President of the United States, Jeannette saw the
consumption of American involvement in another European conflict.[58]

---

[56]J. R. to Mrs. J. W. Jewell, July 7, 1941, J. R. MSS.

[57]Great Falls Tribune, July 12, 1941.

[58]U.S., Congress, House of Representatives, 77th Congress, 2nd
Session, Congressional Record, LXXXV, Pt. 10, p. A4439.

While attention focused on Europe, international relations in the Pacific had grown considerably worse. With the sinking of an American ship, the Panay, in December of 1937, America's diplomatic association with Japan became definitely strained. As a response to continued Nipponese aggression in Southeast Asia, President Roosevelt in July of 1939, gave six months notice that the 1911 commercial trade treaty with Japan would be terminated. Shipments of critical items such as aviation fuel, scrap metal, machinery and oil ceased during 1940. Forced to turn elsewhere for economic and diplomatic friendship, Japan joined the defensive Tripartite Pact with Germany and Italy. When Hitler attacked Russia in June of 1941, Japan was free to occupy Indochina. To counter this move, the United States froze Japanese assets in American territories. This succession of events, Jeannette Rankin interpreted as the result of economic pressures, mounting tension and the inability of Japanese-American diplomacy to work out a compromise.

In relation to diplomatic negotiations during the pre-war period with Japan, Rankin commented:

> I commend patience to them. If their talks serve
> to put off or avert a war, I hope they go on tire-
> lessly. Here is an occasion for the much-derided
> diplomatic tea sipping and cake pushing to vindi-
> cate itself.[59]

Chastising both governments for surreptitious dealing, she pleaded for mutual loyalty, real sincerity, and good faith.[60] As neither side was willing to compromise and war seemed near, Jeannette hurriedly introduced

---

[59]U.S., Congress, House of Representatives, 77th Congress, First Session, Congressional Record, LXXXVII, Part Fourteen, p. A4715.

[60]Ibid.

on November 18 a resolution to order a national advisory election to
ascertain the will of the people on war.[61] The December 7th attack on
Pearl Harbor, with its immediate impact, rendered her war referendum
unnecessary.

Jeannette and her sister, Edna, heard the terrible news on the
Washington evening radio. Remembering that Congress debated the World
War I declaration for several days in 1917 and without contacting Majority
Leader, Joe Martin, Rankin decided to fulfill a speaking engagement in
Detroit. While listening to her radio along the way, she learned that
President Roosevelt would address a Joint Session of Congress at noon on
Monday. She left the train at Pittsburg and made a return trip to Washing-
ton during the night. Wellington Rankin telephoned and tried to persuade
her, since the nation had been attacked, not to vote against going to war.
To dodge the telephone and visitors during Monday morning, Jeannette Rankin
drove around Washington alone in her automobile. She remembered, "Oh,
that was a terrible thing to ride--just waiting for my execution."[62] With
her face registering extreme mental anguish, according to one of her friends,
Rankin returned to her office shortly before noon. As Sigred Scannell, her
personal secretary, was trying to console Jeannette, the session bell rang.[63]

Jeannette Rankin crowded her way onto the House floor. Meanwhile
back in the office, her secretaries, Frances Elge, Rosa Nell Spriggs, and

---

[61]U.S., Congress, House of Representatives, 77th Congress, First
Session, Congressional Record, LXXXVII, Part Nine, p. 9250.

[62]J. R. Interview, January 27, 1969, p. 9.

[63]Sigred Scannell to Ted C. Harris, March 16, 1969, in author's
personal file.

Sigred Scannell, listened sadly but intently to Franklin Roosevelt's
short address asking for a declaration of war against Japan. John
McCormack, Representative from Massachusetts, introduced the war resolution immediately after the House resumed business. Trying to delay
the procedures, Rankin objected to the question of a second to the resolution. The House Speaker, Sam Rayburn, ruled her objection was not in
order. Short speeches continued until McCormack called for the vote.
Again, Jeannette Rankin asked to be heard. Ignoring her, the Speaker
prepared for the roll call. For the third time, Jeannette tried to
speak. This time she called for a point of order. Rayburn then informed
her that a roll call may not be interrupted. Her frantic efforts, as described by the radio announcer covering the session, fell on the deaf ears
of House members who hoped for a unanimous vote. Not persuaded by the
arguments, Jeannette Rankin cast the single "no" vote in Congress.[64]

Even in the House cloakroom, Rankin was swamped with visitors and
guards. When they started to question, she ducked into a telephone booth
and called for help. Escorted by police, she returned to her office to
prepare a statement for the Montana papers. By casting the lone negative
vote, she felt she owed her district an explanation. She described it
this way:

> I felt there were not enough facts before us. . .
> to justify such hasty action. ...When I cast the
> only vote against war, I remembered the promise
> I had made during my campaign. ...I was thinking

---

[64] U.S., Congress, House of Representatives, 77th Congress, First
Session, Congressional Record, LXXXVIII, Pt. 9, pp. 9520-9537; J. R.
Interview, January 27, 1969, p. 9; Rosa Nell Spriggs Interview, June 11,
1971, p. 17; Washington Evening Star, December 8, 1941.

of the pledges I had made to the mothers and
fathers of Montana.

While I believed . . . that the stories [of
destruction of Pearl Harbor] . . . were probably true, still I believed that such a momentous
vote, one which could mean peace or war for our
country, should be based on more authentic evidence . . . .

It may be right for us to enter the conflict
with Japan, if so, it is my belief that all
the facts . . . should be given to the Congress
and the American people. So in casting my vote
today, I voted my convictions and redeemed my
campaign pledges.[65]

Reaction to Jeannette Rankin's second vote against war was much
stronger than the first. Probably the two factors influencing this most
were the "unexpected" attack at Pearl Harbor and the fact that hers was
the "sole" dissenting vote. In the vote against World War I, she had
fifty-five colleagues with her. Representative Harold Knutson, Republican from Minnesota, was the only other member of the House who had voted
against war in 1917. Letters, telegrams, and calls poured in by the hundreds. Some were favorable; a few were obscene; others were negative;
while still others disagreed but admired her courage to vote her convictions. In 1917, the Atlanta Constitution called her vote the expression of a woman's heart but in 1941 labeled it the work of a devious mind.[66]
Dan Whetstone, Republican National Committeeman from Montana, telegrammed,
"Redeem Montana's honor and loyalty, and change your vote at the earliest
opportunity."[67] Friends in the Athens area felt she was "an idealist who

---

[65] Statement of J. R., December 8, 1941, in personal possession of
Rosa Nell Spriggs.

[66] Atlanta Constitution, December 10, 1941; Atlanta Constitution, April
7, 1917.

[67] Dan Whetstone to J. R., Telegram, December 9, 1941, J. R. MSS.

was 'hipped' on one idea," and that her lone vote represented an "idealistic adhorrence to war rather than political isolationism."[68]

Roger Baldwin, American Civil Liberties Union, regarded Jeannette's
vote as a matter of principle. He wrote:

> Integrity is a virtue in public life rare enough
> in a crisis to command admiration even among
> opponents. You could only do what you did--and
> your act is heartening to all who cherish fidel-
> ity to principle and ideals.[69]

Jeannette expressed agreement with this evaluation when in commenting
about the vote, she wrote, "What one does in a crisis depends upon his
philosophy of life."[70] The Evening Kansan-Republican suggested that her
vote "makes Miss Rankin a martyr to an eternal principle that throbs in
the hearts of women."[71] Her vote then was interpreted as a stand in behalf of women in America who possess that feminine instinct against bloodshed and war.[72] As an unforgetable reminder of man's better self, Lillian
Smith, editor of the North Georgia Review and author of Strange Fruit and
Killers of the Dream, penned, "That one little vote of yours stands out
like a bright star in a dark night."[73] William Allen White lauded her
courage in his editorial in the Emporia Gazette. The former head of the
Committee To Defend America wrote:

> Rudyard Kipling coined the phrase: "The female
> of the species is more deadly than the male."

---

[68] Athens Banner-Herald, December 8, 1941.

[69] Roger Baldwin to J. R., December 9, 1941.

[70] J. R. to Mrs. John Nevin Sayre, January 27, 1942, J. R.MSS.

[71] Evening Kansan-Republican, December 12, 1941.

[72] cf. Congratulations from the Anti-war Mothers of America Clubs.

[73] Lillian Smith to J. R., December 13, 1941, J. R. MSS.

> Well--look at Jeannette Rankin. Probably a
> hundred men in Congress would like to do what
> she did. None of them had the courage to do
> it. ... When in a hundred years from now,
> courage . . . is celebrated in this country,
> the name of Jeannette Rankin . . . will be
> written in monumental bronze--not for what
> she did, but for the way she did it.[74]

"To admire her courage" was typical of all those who favored her vote
and many of these who disagreed.[75]

Yet, not all her publicity and letters were benevolent. Raymond
Clapper, noted journalist, wrote that Jeannette Rankin had "achieved her
small footnote in history. It is duly noted and can be forgotten as a
trivial, meaningless incident."[76] Henry McLemore's syndicated column,
"The Lighter Side," ridiculed Jeannette by saying that her pacifistic
qualities would make for an ideal wife. She would never declare war on
her husband at home.[77] One letter addressed her thusly: "Dear Jenny--
and you look it. You are an old fossil. Hitler aid--never should you
have been an official of any kind--rather an undertaker's assistant for
women only."[78] An anonymous letter from California thanked her for revealing herself and said, "If you had been as foxy as Senator Wheeler
and stayed away that day, it would have been harder for the people . . .
to have understood." It continued by insinuating association with Nazi
Fifth Column organizers because "they had promised her a husband."[79]

---

[74]Emporia Gazette, December 10, 1941.

[75]cf. see numerous letters in J. R. MSS.

[76]Raymond Clapper, "Don't Pass on Rumors," Montana Standard, December
11, 1941, p. 4.

[77]St. Louis Post-Dispatch, December 12, 1941.

[78]A. R. McCullock, Jacksonville, Fla., to J. R., December 8, 1941,
J. R. MSS.

[79]Anonymous Letter to J. R., December 91, 1941, J. R. MSS.

One interesting post card contained the following subtle message, "There is an old saying that wise men (and women) change their minds; fools never."[80] A former resident of Montana, disgusted with her vote, wrote to "Jeannette Bitch Rankin," saying that he was asking two hundred friends in the first district to repudiate her "filthy vote."[81]

Many letter, editorials, and groups of citizens called upon Rankin to resign. One petition containing ninety-nine signatures from the Veterans' Facility at Fort Harrison, Montana, and another from the Stillwater Grange #107 requested her immediate resignation as a result of her obnoxious and unpatriotic conduct.[82] John Nollen from Pittsburg, Pennsylvania, suggested that Jeannette resign because, "You are a disgrace and traitor to America. . . .Benedict Arnold is a Saint compared to you."[83] With less ingenuity but more directness, F. C. Pratley wrote, "Why in hell don't you leave that job--you disgrace the office you hold--damn such as you. . . .It is the work of a Beech [sic] that you did. . . .I am pay ng [sic] taxes for the likes of your kind--damn you."[84]

Several writers expressed opposition to Jeannette Rankin's vote as representative of womanhood. "For the first time in my life," Marion Denman wrote, "I am truly ashamed to be called a 'woman' after your vote today."[85]

---

[80]Miss L. K. Miller to J. R., December 11, 1941.

[81]Anonymous Letter.

[82]Petition from United States Veterans' Facility, n.d., J. R. MSS; Stillwater Grange #107, Whitefish, Montana, n.d., J. R. MSS.

[83]John Nollen to J. R., December 12, 1941, J. R. MSS.

[84]F. C. Pratley to J. R., December 8, 1941, J. R. MSS.

[85]Marion Denman to J. R., December 8, 1941, J. R. MSS.

Louise T. Hay, who had also worked for suffrage in the early years, believed, "You are the only living argument against giving unmarried women
the vote."[86] Another suffrage leader suggested that Rankin skip politics
and take a maid's job.[87]

With mail still flooding her office, Jeannette Rankin faced two more
war resolutions on December 11. After receiving requests from President
Roosevelt for declarations of war against Germany and Italy, the House
began its work. In near record time, the German war resolution was prepared. As the roll call began, Jeannette Rankin descended from the
galleries where she had been waiting with congressional secretaries.
When the clerk called, "Rankin of Montana," the chamber was soundless.
Weakly, she responded, "Present." The clerk did not understand; and she
spoke again, barely audibly. Monday, there had been hisses. At her
"present" vote on the declaration of war against Germany and later Italy,
there was applause. Later, as Rankin lunched on an apple and milk in
the cloakroom, the House voted to send another American Expeditionary
Force to fight anywhere in the world.[88]

Disheartened but not defeated, Jeannette Rankin bravely fulfilled
the remaining year of her Congressional term. With insight and courage,
she involved herself in protecting the interest of the people. As a
member of the Public Lands Committee, she listened to the hearings in
February of 1942 to amend the Raker Act. The amendment would allow

---

[86]Louise T. Hay to J. R., Telegram, December 8, 1941, J. R. MSS.

[87]Catherine Callanan to J. R., Telegram, December 9, 1941, J. R. MSS.

[88]U.S., Congress, House of Representatives, 77th Congress, 1st Session, Congressional Record, LXXXVII, Pt. 9, pp. 9665-9667; Washington
Post, December 12, 1941; Great Falls Tribune, December 12, 1941.

federally funded utilities to sell or lease surplus electric power to
private corporations. Rankin opposed this amendment because she felt
it would aid "private war profiteers" at the expense of the public.[89]

Jeannette Rankin's progressive spirit caused her to keep a close
watch on fiscal governmental responsibility. She opposed amendments to
the Civil Service Retirement Act extending coverage to the President and
members of Congress. She explained, "I am not eligible in years of service for this pension. Nevertheless, I think it is unfair to give it to
Members of Congress until all other people are provided for."[90] Responding to public opinion, Rankin introduced a repeal measure, removing the
obnoxious provisions for the President and for Congress. Camas Hot
Springs Exchange commented:

> We've got to hand it to Jeannette. She made us
> awfully mad a few months back . . . and hurt her-
> self politically. ... Still you must give her
> just dues. ... Now she has come out and has
> presented a bill for repeal of the "Grab Act."
> She deserves a big hand.[91]

Thus, one newspaper finally expressed what many Montanians felt privately.
They realized that Jeannette Rankin had voted her conviction and fulfilled
her campaign promises. Rankin was not trying to redeem herself but honestly
opposed the pension plan as irresponsible in the light of economic uncertainties that the average person encountered.

In other ways, Montanians saw Jeannette struggling to maintain the
ideal of a government responsible to the people. She worked hard to reduce

---

[89]U.S., Congress, House of Representatives, Committee on the Public
Lands, Hearings on Amending the Raker Act on H. R. 5964, 77th Congress,
1st Session, January 15-27, pp. 130-131, 370-373.

[90]J. R. to M. Crawford Vawter, February 24, 1942, J. R. MSS.

[91]Camas Hot Springs Exchange, February 19, 1942.

"boondoggling and unnecessary waste in Congressional appropriations."[92]
On other occasions, she inquired into certain bills to make sure there
were equal possibilities for large and small firms, inexperienced in
war production, to obtain and carry out government contracts.[93] To protect the government from possible fraud in its expenditure of billions
of dollars for national defense, Rankin advocated suspending the statute
of limitations during the war. She felt that in the three-year period
afterward, the Attorney General would have time to investigate and gather
evidence for prosecution. This thesis of serving the best interests of
the people and their government permeated her final Congressional year.

As early as June of 1942, Jeannette Rankin decided not to run for
re-election. Wellington, then, announced for the Senate. Jeannette
believed, "It is much more important to gain strength in the Senate" to
work with a projected Republican administration in 1944. Hopefully, she
said, "If there is a Republican trend at this time, there will probably
be a landslide in 1944, when I can come back."[94] Unfortunately, Wellington
Rankin was narrowly defeated, and Jeannette never found the opportunity
to politically return to Washington.

Jeannette Rankin became restless with all the war procedures in Congressional legislation. Yet, the item that disturbed her most was the
"New Deal's international policy." At the end of the war, she envisioned
Roosevelt's destroying America's traditional national policy by accepting
"responsibility for the rest of the world."[95] To call attention to the

[92]J. R. to Gladys Knowles, March 16, 1942, J. R. MSS.

[93] U.S., Congress, House of Representatives, 77th Congress, 2nd Session,
Congressional Record, LXXXVIII, Pt. 4, p. 4506.

[94]J. R. to Gladys Knowles, June 24, 1942, J. R. MSS.

[95]Ibid.

administration's manipulations in foreign affairs, Rankin placed "Some
Questions about Pearl Harbor" in the Congressional Record on December
8, 1942. She took advantage of the anniversary of her "no" vote to raise
inquiry into the administration's conduct of foreign affairs, especially
as they related to what Roosevelt called "the unprovoked aggression" by
Japan. Hers was one of the first attempts at "revisionist" historiography
for World War II.

Jeannette Rankin developed the thesis that British imperialists wanted American intervention in the Pacific to protect their disintegrating
colonial empire. They way to provoke a nation into war was to impose an
impossible ultimatum on economic sanctions. When would the United States
have agreed to such tactics? Rankin suspected the Atlantic Conference
attended by Roosevelt and Churchill in August of 1941. She thought it
strange that the President had refused to enforce the Neutrality Act
prior to August because it might bring on war. But, after the Atlantic
Conference, Roosevelt began imposing economic sanctions of ever increasing severity. The ultimatum, Jeannette interpreted, was the administration's
insistence on the principle of "non-disturbance of the status quo in the
Pacific." Why not just the Philippines? Why the whole of the Pacific? Because Roosevelt wanted to protect British and Dutch imperial interests in
the Orient was Rankin's answer. Thus, with his ultimatum and economic
sanctions, the President had provoked Japan into an attack to get us into
the war on the side of England. Choosing not to run for re-election and
Wellington's having been defeated, Jeannette Rankin could well afford to
expose what she considered the administration's conspiracy plot.[96]

---

[96] U.S., Congress, House of Representatives, 77th Congress, 2nd
Session, Congressional Record, LXXXV, Pt. 10, p. A4439.

The Roosevelt Administration ignored her, but Earl Godwin, radio commentator on the Blue Network's Ford Hour, did not. On December 23, 1942, he soundly denounced Jeannette Rankin for suggesting that Roosevelt accepted Churchill's game to embroil the United States in war with Japan. He said: "Seems to me that it [Rankin's thesis on Pearl Harbor] is about as low down a state of American mind as you could get without excavating pretty deeply."[97] In response to a letter supporting Jeannette, he continued his harangue:

> I have never believed in Jeannette Rankin. . . .
> She is not clear-out American. . . . I have no
> use for any women who stands in the place where
> a man ought to be - the United States House of
> Representatives.[98]

On this dramatic note, Jeannette Rankin packed and left for Montana. She turned the closing of the Washington office over to her secretary, Rosa Nell Spriggs.

During the next year, Jeannette rested on her brother's ranch, enjoyed the refreshing atmosphere and contemplated her future. Two options that appealed to her were to write a book on peace organizations in the United States, and to take a trip to India to study its contribution to the peace of the world.[99] A third alternative was to "work on some program with the women in Montana that will make it possible to avoid war in the future."[100] Instead of any of the above, Jeannette Rankin decided to visit her second home in Georgia.

---

[97]Earl Godwin's Radio Text, December 23, 1943 [sic], J. R. MSS.

[98]Earl Godwin to Lottie O'Neill December 30, 1942, J. R. MSS.

[99]J. R. to Harry Harrison, June 11, 1943, J. R. MSS.

[100]J. R. to Mrs. Kenneth Hayes, June 12, 1943, J. R. MSS.

In the late fall of 1943, Jeannette Rankin returned to Georgia.
Two years previously, an accidental kerosene stove explosion had burned
her "White House" on the Monroe Road.[101] She attempted to replace it
with a "tamped earth" structure in April of 1942 but gave up because of
insufficient help.[102] On this trip in 1943, Jeannette decided to move
to her other farm on the Mars Hill Road, two miles west of Watkinsville,
Georgia.[103] The only building suitable for inhabitance was a seventy-
five-year-old "tenant house," which she has remodeled through the years
into a very modest and comfortable dwelling under the "oaks of Shadygrove."

Jeannette retained until June of 1944 the hope of being re-elected.
Although she believed the women were behind her, Rankin told Frederick
Libby:

> It would take twice as much money as I have to
> make an easy race and a hard one even more.
> Since there is no way to know about the war
> situation in the future, im [sic] not willing
> to risk all I have. . . . I'm very disappoint-
> ed. . . . I shall always feel that I could have
> won if I had had the money and could have reach-
> ed the people.[104]

And thus closed, when she was 64, Jeannette's last serious consideration for
political office. Several times since, she has made overtures about running,
so, as she said, "to have someone to vote for."[105]

---

[101]She used to enjoy telling people that she had a "White House in
Georgia" before President Roosevelt did.

[102]The completed section of the "tamped earth" house remains strong
as Gibralter thirty years later.

[103]Rankin acquired this forty acre farm for a friend in 1930, but she
could not afford it, so Rankin kept it. J. R. Interview, January 30, 1969,
p. 7; Mrs. Mary Caldwell to J. R., September, 1933 (Recorded October 25,
1933) in Oconee County Warranty Deeds, Book T, p. 275.

[104]J. R. to Frederick Libby, June 2, 1944, J. R. MSS.

[105]Speech of J. R. to Georgia Anti-War Group, May 4, 1972.

With active political campaigning in the past, Jeannette Rankin
settled down to several years of study and travel. In contrast to most
tourists, Rankin's travels were purposeful. In 1915, she went to New
Zealand to observe their advanced systems of social legislation, while
the 1919 trip to Zurich, Switzerland, was to participate in a women's
international conference on peace. Frederick Libby, National Council
for Prevention of War, suggested that she attend a five-week session of
the League of Nations in 1931. Much of the 1937 trip to Europe observed
the war buildup in Western Europe and the Scandanavian approaches to social
problems. In Sweden, Rankin was very much impressed with cooperative
stores, cooperative apartment houses for middle income families, and a
large apartment complex for unwed mothers and children. During the day,
a nursery on the sixth floor cared for the pre-schoolers, while the
mothers worked. "This home for unwed mothers," Rankin thought, "was the
most intelligent thing found anywhere."[106] The coming of the war and
Jeannette's election to a second term in Congress postponed any foreign
travel until the late 1940's.[107]

Jeannette Rankin'a post-war travels began in 1945 with a short trip
to attend a Pan-American meeting in Mexico. She accompanied Abby Crawford
Milton, a Chattanooga feminist, to this gathering of women interested in
suffrage. In July of the following year, Jeannette began a world tour
including extendee visits in Turkey, where a friend, Harriet Yarrow,
served as a missionary, and in India. After Rankin introduced in 1918

[106]J. R. Interview, October 19, 1971, p. 2; cf. Interview with Belle
Fligelman Winestein, September 9, 1970, pp. 2-3.

[107]J. R. Interview, on travels, April 3, 1970, pp. 1-8.

a resolution for Irish freedom, an Indian, Lala Lajpat Rai, kindled her
interest in Mahatma Gandhi and Indian nationalism. To go to India in
1946 fulfilled a dream of many years. While there, she attended the All
India Congress and met with its president, J. B. Kripalani. She also obtained an interview with Jawaharlal Nehru.[108] Jeannette returned in
January of 1947 and remained constantly at the side of her ninety-three-
year-old mother until her death later in the spring.[109]

Enthused over her first trip to India, Jeannette Rankin returned for
a six-month visit in 1949. She scheduled her trip to coincide with a
World Pacifist Conference called by Gandhi before his death. Jeannette
brought her Ford automobile to India and hired a driver, whom she soon
dismissed because he knew less than she did. The first session of the
conference met in the South at Santinitetan, Tagore's last home; and
the second session, two weeks later, was held in Sevagram, Gandhi's last
home. Recalling an experience in the first session, she said:

> Imagine my dismay when I found the bed was made
> of hard boards and nothing else! All I had was
> a cotton saree and wool blanket. Someone found
> me a thin quilt and mat. I wishes I had more
> cushion on my bones.[110]

In addition to attending the peace conference, she drove over hundreds
of miles of the Indian countryside to study village life and its

---

[108]American Export Lines to J. R., June 11, 1946; J. R. MSS; Jeannette
Rankin, "Why I Am Going to India," J. R. MSS.

[109]New York Herald Tribune, January 24, 1947.

[110]Mimeographed statement of J. R. from India, January, 1950, J. R. MSS.

educational system.[111]

In the fall of 1951, Jeannette returned to India for a year, spending considerable time at Almara in the mountains. She returned to the United States in the summer of 1953 after a visit with her sister, Edna McKinnon, in Indonesia and a four-month tour of Africa. Over the next ten years, Rankin extended her travel to include Western Europe, Russia, and the Middle East. Each time her objective was the same: to simply study the life of the common people.[112]

---

[111]Ibid.; Clipping from Roundabout, April 16, 1952, J. R. MSS; undated clipping describing the 1949 trip, J. R. MSS; J. R. to Wellington Rankin, November 23, 1949, J. R. MSS; "Jeannette Rankin To Study Gandhi's Philosophy," Christian Century, LXVI (December 28, 1949), p. 1546; J. R. Interview, April 3, 1970, pp. 9-11.

[112]Edna Rankin McKinnon Interview, November 17, 1971, p. 8; J. R. Interview, April 3, 1970, p. 12; In subsequent years, Jeannette Rankin visited South America and India in 1956, India in 1959-60, Ireland, Russia, Turkey, and India in 1962, Mexico in 1965, and India again in 1970-71. In all, she made seven visits to India.

CHAPTER XII

FROM OBLIVION TO RESURGENCE

From 1943 to the mid-1960's, Jeannette Rankin spent considerable
time ranching in Montana, caring for an aging mother, remodeling her
"tenant" cottage in Georgia, and traveling abroad to study other cul-
tures. In this period, Gandhian pacifism attracted her to India six
times. Rankin anticipated discovering in India "a substitute for war"
and hoped to make application in the United States.[1]

Against the background of the Russian-American cold war in 1947,
Rankin prophesied, "Definitely the United States is going straight to
war unless we change our course." Asked how soon she thought the next
war would come, Jeannette replied, "It will be as soon as we get another
crop of men ready."[2] The Korean Police Action, as it has been called,
came sooner than she probably thought. As a part of the United Nations'
forces, American troops entered South Korea on the last of June, 1950.
Violence had broken out as Jeannette crossed the Pacific from her second
trip to study pacifism. Upon returning to the United States, she had
hoped to talk "morning, noon and night about settling disputes with
violence." Instead, she found a nation at war with communism.[3] "To my

---

[1] Great Falls Tribune, September 29, 1949.

[2] The New York Herald Tribune, January 24, 1947.

[3] J. R. to Frederick Libby, December 13, 1950, NCPW Files, SCPC.

great disappointment," she wrote Frederick Libby, "the warriors have succeeded in getting a good war started. . . .It is hard to see the sad faces of the young boys who are having to face this war."[4]

After three years and 25,000 casualties, Jeannette Rankin credited Dwight David Eisenhower, President, with bringing a conclusion to the Korean conflict. During his eight years in the White House, she additionally praised his avoidance of an active war. The cause for his success, Rankin reasoned, was that "the military can't put anything over on him."[5] Encouraged by this administration, Rankin supported in 1960 Richard M. Nixon, the Vice President, as the man best suited to succeed to the Presidency. "Nixon has been the closest to Eisenhower," she said, "and therefore knows the most about avoiding war."[6]

Yet, by a narrow margin, John F. Kennedy, the Democratic nominee and former Senator from Massachusetts, defeated Nixon. Paradoxical as it may be, this Democrat propelled Jeannette Rankin back into national prominence. Prior to the 1960 election, Senator Kennedy had written Profiles in Courage but had included no women. After being reprimanded, he quickly prepared an article for McCall's Magazine. In "Three Women of Courage," Kennedy honored Jeannette Rankin by writing, "few members of Congress have ever stood more alone while being true to a higher honor and loyalty."[7]

This reminder of Rankin's courage and opposition to war paralleled

---

[4] Ibid.; Great Falls Tribune, June 3, 1951.

[5] Great Falls Tribune, October 5, 1959.

[6] Ibid.

[7] John F. Kennedy, "Three Women of Courage," McCall's Magazine, LXXXV (January, 1958), pp. 37 and 55.

the buildup of American advisors in South Vietnam. Almost twenty years after her vote against World War II, Jeannette reiterated, "My views on war have never changed. I have always been an advocate of peace. I am fearful that warfare in this nuclear age will be the downfall of mankind."[8]

As the war in Southeast Asia escalated, Jeannette Rankin could receive no pleasure from an honorary doctorate awarded by Montana State College at Billings in August of 1961.[9] Three years later, Dr. Rankin and her brother, Wellington, received the Distinguished Service Award from the Alumni Association of Montana State University at Missoula.[10] In the interval between these awards, Kennedy was assassinated and Lyndon Johnson of Texas became President and sharply increased in 1965 the level of American military participation in South Vietnam.

Enduring it no longer, Jeannette Rankin began speaking out. She advocated immediate withdrawal of American troops from Vietnam "even if the Reds take over." As if expecting a rebuttal, she continued, "You don't do the right thing because of the consequences. If you're wise, you do it regardless of the consequences."[11] Later Rankin strengthened this position by adding, "I'm for immediate, total and unilateral disarmament."[12]

Believing that killing men in Vietnam was worse than the old Hebrew sacrifices, Jeannette Rankin called for withdrawal of American troops. She said the United States "just got into the war uninvited" and that

---

[8]Great Falls Tribune, June 6, 1961.

[9]Photo copy of Honorary Doctor of Laws Degree in J. R. MSS.

[10]Great Falls Tribune, October 15, 1964.

[11]Newsweek, February 14, 1966, p. 12.

[12]J. R. Interview, February 12, 1970, p. 6.

". . .we should just leave." She continued, "I don't know how you can
make it known and be nice about" the United States' leaving Vietnam, but
"the time has past for us to be nice. The army isn't polite when it
selects a young man and says, 'Come on and fight'."[13] Affirming that
Vietnam was "a unilateral war [meaning that ηo one had declared war against
us] and that we should have a unilateral peace," she proposed to "send the
ships and bring the boys home."[14]

Although she had proposed an immediate withdrawal from Vietnam,
Jeannette Rankin did not wish in the slightest way to express an "isolationist" position. She did intend to state firmly that the United
States must leave other nations alone politically. On the other hand,
it did have some responsibility for feeding the impoverished of the world.
She felt that America must help but not attempt to harness the social and
economic revolutions of underdeveloped nations. Its goal must be to provide assistance without enslaving a nation.[15]

To a public meeting at the University of Montana, her alma mater,
Jeannette summarized her views on war. She told the audience that all war
was immoral. "Not only are we wrong in fighting in Vietnam," she said,
"but Ho Chi Minh and company are likewise wrong." Explaining her opposition to the Vietnam War, she replied, "To me, it isn't this war or that
war. It's the war system. We've never settled any disputes by fighting."[16]

---

[13] Atlanta Constitution, May 19, 1967.

[14] The Peoples Voice, August 11, 1967; Santa Barbara News Press,
August 21, 1967.

[15] J. R., Interview, February 12, 1970, p. 6.

[16] The Missoulian, August 28, 1966; Bozeman Daily Chronicle, August
29, 1966.

Jeannette adhered to the principle that war, as a method of settling a dispute, sometimes had no relationship to the original conflict. She contended that the issues often changed in the interval from the beginning to the end of the war.[17]

Undaunted by the rhetoric of "holy war," "war to end all war" and "war for democracy," Jeannette Rankin believed that "war waged by the purest motives does not change the essential attributes of war."[18] She always pointed out that violence could not contribute to the adjustment of human relationships. War was a moral question to Jeannette. If it was morally wrong for an individual to lie, steal, hate, and kill, it was also wrong for a group.[19] Her standard phrase, needing no explanation, was "war is a stupid, futile method of attempting to settle disputes, regardless of who uses it or why."[20]

From "Preparedness that makes for Permanent Peace" to "immediate, total and unilateral disarmament" seemed like a change, or at least a progressive development in Rankin's peace philosophy. She insisted that it represented no change in her basic views. In her estimation, she had opposed war from the very beginning of her social work and political careers. The change, according to her, was in method or technique, not in philosophy. To her, it reflected only an adjustment to prevailing circumstances and conditions. The proposal of coastal defense in the 1920's and 1930's was only a logical first step to disarmament. She illustrated by saying:

---

[17] Bismarck Tribune, May 19, 1967.

[18] Radio Talk by J. R., November 11, 1936.

[19] Jeannette Rankin, "Can We Afford War?" Church Woman, August-September, 1967, p. 17.

[20] Ibid.; Jeannette Rankin, "Beware of Holy Wars," World Outlook (November, 1938), pp. 12-13, 39.

"You have to go with the machinery that you can use. At one time you used a train, then a car, and now a plane."[21]

Jeannette Rankin's greatest ambition was to substitute the American psychology of war with a psychology of peace. The place to begin was in the education of the thought of children. Unfortunately, she felt that children have learned to think the language of war. "Shooting games and suggestive [war] toys should be destroyed," she said. The child whose play was designed to teach him the rudiments of peace would think in terms of peace should be as a man sit at the council of diplomats. She assented to the doctrine in the proverb, "As the twig is bent, so is the tree inclined." Mothers, through definite construction education, could make peace instead of war a basic process of civilization.[22]

Once, when some children visited Miss Rankin's house, they sang a song about lovely soldiers and how they would like to be soldiers. Not able to refuse an opportunity for propaganda, she had them resing the verses but substitute the word "slave" for soldier whenever it appeared. They sang it lustily, she remembered. Then, she told them that soldiers were only slaves--doing what other people told them to do. In this way, Jeannette Rankin educated the children to know that soldiers "shoot and do things like that because someone tells them."[23] She was firmly convinced that the military blindly follow the leader and expresses no democracy.[24]

Another time she observed a kindergarten instructor on television

---

[21] J. R. Interview, February 12, 1970, p. 5.

[22] J. R. Interview, February 5, 1970, p. 6.

[23] J. R. Interview, January 22, 1970, p. 7.

[24] Ibid., p. 8.

teaching children to march. The teacher said, "Raise your knees like a soldier."[25] Rankin believed that the children were learning the war method unconsciously in an otherwise nice and friendly environment. She felt that teachers and mothers should anlayze what they are doing before subjecting it to the supple minds of children. This kindergarten program, to her, was "the most awful war propaganda that you could think of."

In building a psychology for peace, Jeannette Rankin emphasized the importance of establishing "peace" habits. Habits, she felt, were a silent factor in all decisions. Thought habituated to peace could never be expressed in terms of war. Believing that war was a "savage mutilation of youth and of a nation's strength, and that violence and bloodshed were always wrong in principle and disastrous in practice," Miss Rankin had no other alternative than to vote against war. She believed that her vote was a result of "peace" habits, while those who voted for war expressed "war" habits. Because America was educated to the war method, the use of war in settling disputes became a habit.[27]

To illustrate the significance of peace habits, Rankin recounted an experience at Tuskegee Institute where she had gone to speak in the mid-1930's. After the Tuskegee choir sang, the president asked Rankin if she had a favorite selection. To his chagrin, Jeannette chose "Ain't Gonna Study War No More." Later in her address, while speaking about peace habits, she noticed that all the boys were dressed in uniforms. This prompted her to say, "If you want to get rid of war, you have to get

[25] J. R. Interview, January 15, 1970, p. 1.

[26] Ibid.

[27] J. R. Interview, February 29, 1969, p. 3.

rid of the war habits. And you can't change your habits in a military uniform."[28] The students broke into spontaneous applause. Finally, after they had made a great fuss, Rankin reiterated, "You can't make peace habits in a military uniform." She remembered that the school authorities expected a riot at any time, but that everything turned out all right.

A subtle summation of Jeannette Rankin's peace philosophy was an illustration which she used in her talks. It concerned a test for mental retardation which used a dipper and a barrel of water being filled by a water faucet. The candidates were told to dip the water out of the barrel. Someone asked, "How do you know when they are feeble-minded?" She replied, "Them that ain't feeble-minded turn off the spickot." Rankin believed that turning off "the spickot of war" was the only way to get peace. Thus, she concluded, "Today, I'm for immediate, total and unilateral disarmament."[29]

In early 1967, Jeannette Rankin took time off from talking about the Vietnam war to design and build a home for elderly women. She envisioned their being self-sustaining, sharing in a type of communal living and eventually paying back her construction cost over a period of years. When the structure had been paid for, she anticipated giving the women the home. The design of the house was almost as unique as the idea. It was a "round house" with ten bedrooms surrounding a central living room. Opposite the entrance, on the other side of the living room, was a fully equipped kitchen. Jeannette also proposed to build a lake for boating and swimming, and offered land for a vegetable garden. Coupled with insufficient enthusiasm on the part of women and Rankin's preoccupation with other causes, the house

---

[28]Ibid.

[29]J. R. Interview, February 5, 1970, p. 9.

has yet to house its first elderly woman.[30]

With the military buildup in Southeast Asia continuing, Jeannette Rankin determined that women must use their "power" to stop the war. She attributed her philosophy of "feminine power" to Banjamin Kidd, a British sociologist. In his book, The Science of Power, he made a distinction between "force" and "power." Force was the constituent quality of the material universe, while power was the constituent quality of life. Men used force. Women used power. From his sociological inquiry, Kidd discovered, "It is in the woman that we have the future center of Power in civilization." He continued by writing, "She is the creature to whom the race is more than the individual; the being to whom the future is greater than the present."[31]

Kidd believed that women contained that ascendant and winning quality of life which he called "the Emotion of the Ideal." It was the expression of that ultra-rational capacity through which the individual woman senses her relation to future growth and development.[32] With their historical and procreative experience, Jeannette Rankin assumed that women were highly qualified to adjust the problems of human relations. Waiting nine months for the child to be born taught women that one day wasn't more significant than the other. They were all important. Conditioned by this experience, women always anticipated the future. They looked forward to the child's going to school, graduating, marrying, and having children. In adjusting

[30]Athens Daily News, June 4, 1967, Magazine Section, pp. 3-5.

[31]Benjamin Kidd, The Science of Power (New York: Putnam's Sons, 1918), pp. 194, 203, 219.

[32]Ibid., p. 198.

human relations, Rankin trusted women to think in terms of the future progress of world civilization. Men thought too much in the categories of might and force.[33]

In a very general assessment of historical sociology, Jeannette Rankin pointed out that women contributed to the stabilization of society. Early in time, women had interested men in raising crops to maturity rather than fighting and living a nomadic life. Musing to herself that things have not changed much, Jeannette said, "Women still raise the boys and men take them off to war and kill them."[34] Influenced by the consequences of this thought, Rankin launched a new campaign in May of 1967 to encourage women to help stop the war in Vietnam.

In February, the House of Representatives had given Jeannette Rankin a publicity boost by recognizing her entry into Congress fifty years previous.[35] Having thus received national attention, she was ready to accept an invitation from Nan Pendergrast, a stalwart of Atlanta, Georgia's Peace movement, to address a group called "Atlantans for Peace." Although she had been retired from public speaking for over twenty years, Rankin was not one to turn down an invitation to speak for peace.[36] Little did Jeannette realize that this meeting would be the beginning of a fast ascension to national prominence.

On May 18, Jeannette Rankin spoke to the sixty-five Atlantans for

---

[33]J. R. Interview, April 20, 1971, p. 2; J. R. to Montana Constitutional Convention, p. 5.

[34]J. R. Interview, January 16, 1969, p. 4.

[35]Atlanta Journal, February 28, 1967, p. 11.

[36]Warren Hinckle and Marianne Hinckle, "A History of the Rise of the Unusual Movement for Women Power in the United States, 1961-1968," Ramparts, VI (February, 1968), p. 26.

Peace at the Universalist-Unitarian Church and urged the nation's women
to band together to halt the war in Vietnam. She said, "If we had
10,000 women willing to go to prison that would end it. You cannot have
wars without the women." Noting that United States casualties had reached 10,000, Jeannette declared, "We've had 10,000 women sit back and let
their sons be killed in Vietnam."[37] Asked what women could do, Miss Rankin
suggested that they "picket everything. Do your part."[38]

Responding immediately in "An Open Letter to Jeannette Rankin" was
Edith O. Newly of New Mexico, who had not seen Jeannette for twenty-six
years nor heard from her in ten. She commended Rankin for her vote against
war and pointed out, "We are still under the illusion that we 'won' World
War II. That no one won anything is evidenced by the rapidly deteriorat-
ing situation throughout the world." Edith Newly praised the Montana
Congressman for trying to save the young men from being "thrown away like
garbage" while other women did nothing more than react with frenzied hysteria. Newly concluded by thanking Jeannette Rankin "for being the courageous American, the magnificent woman you are. That you go on in spite of
the past is in itself stupendous bravery."[39]

Meanwhile in California, Betty Meredith, a nursery school teacher in
Ross, read a news account of Rankin's speech. She thought Jeannette's
suggestion that ten thousand committed women could end the war made sense.
When Meredith mentioned the idea to her friend, Vivian Hallina, wife of
the San Francisco attorney Vincent Hallinan, things began to happen. In
August Vivian Hallinan traveled to Watkinsville to consult with Jeannette

[37] Atlanta Constitution, May 19, 1967.

[38] Bismarck Tribune, May 19, 1967.

[39] The Oconee Enterprise, May 27, 1967.

Rankin about strategy for organizing American women into a force powerful enough to end the war in Vietnam.[40]

While Vivian Hallinan and others were organizing what came to be known as "The Jeannette Rankin Brigade," Rankin undertook a speaking trip to the west coast and a visit to the Center for the Study of Democratic Institutions. In the Democratic struggle against Communism, she counseled, "Communism is an economic idea. You can't shoot an idea, put it in prison or change it by violence. You have to substitute a better idea."[41] On other occasions, she added:

> The only way to control Communism is to have a better system at home. . . . We haven't taken care of our children. We haven't done the things necessary to make a happy nation.[42]

By late November of 1967, organization of the Jeannette Rankin Brigade was well under way. To gain the widest spectrum of participants and support, leaders stressed a peaceful protest within strict compliance to the law. They desired no acts of civil disobedience. As a measure of avoiding factional strife, the Brigade was a coaltion of individuals rather than activist groups. Although this was the approach, the march received heavy support from Women Strike for Peace, Women's International League for Peace and Freedom, and the Black Congress. Chairman Rankin and Executive Secretary, Vivian Hallinan issued "A Call to American Women who are outraged by the ruthless slaughter in Vietnam and the persistent neglect of human needs at home" to come to Washington on January 15.[43]

---

[40]_Ramparts_, p. 26.

[41]_Santa Barbara News_, August 31, 1967.

[42]_Atlanta Constitution_, January 5, 1968.

[43]Jeannette Rankin Brigade Pamphlet in the author's personal file.

On this opening day of Congress, women, dressed in mourning black,
arrived from all parts of the nation. Reports listed large out-of-town
delegations from New York, Chicago, Cleveland, and as far away as San
Francisco and Seattle. They came to Washington bearing petitions against
grievances in Vietnam and social evils at home. The petitions demanded:

> 1. Congress shall, as the first order of busi-
> ness, resolve to end the war in Vietnam and imme-
> diately withdraw all American troops, 2. Congress
> shall use its power to heal a sick society at
> home; 3. Congress shall use its power to make
> reparations for the ravanged land we leave behind
> in Vietnam; 4. Congress shall listen to what the
> American people are saying and refuse the insatia-
> ble demands of the military industrial complex.[44]

The Brigade, representative of Rankin's philosophy, took on a larger
conotation than just an anti-war protest. It was a humanitarian dissent.

After gathering at 11:30 a.m. on the west side of Union Station, the
women, led by Jeannette Rankin, marched silently down Louisiana Avenue
in the snow. A huge banner, "End the War in Vietnam and Social Crisis
at Home," preceded the women. In addition to Rankin and Hallinan, the
marchers included Mrs. Dagmar Wilson, founder of Women Strike for Peace;
Correta King, Negro civil rights leader; Bobbie Hodges, member of the Black
Congress and Panthers; Mrs. Wayne Morse, wife of the dovish Oregon Democrat,
and her daughter, Judy Morse Eaton; Mrs. J. W. Fullbright, wife of the
Senator from Arkansas; and Mrs. Ernest Gruening, wife of the Senator from
Alaska who with Morse cast the only votes against the Tonkin Gulf Resolution. Some of the younger women brought their children. Benjamin Finzel,
four months, rode on his mother's back, papoose style, wearing a sign that

---

[44]Washington Post, January 16, 1969.

read, "Hell no, I won't go."[45]

Hundreds of policemen guarded the area and lined the half-mile route to the Union Square across from the Capitol. By invoking an 1882 law forbidding demonstrations on Capitol grounds, police barred the marchers from the Capitol itself. Jeannette Rankin, scoffing at the high level of security, said, "There is no reason why old ladies shouldn't be allowed to go into the Capitol."[46]

From three to five thousand women assembled around the statue of Ulysses S. Grant to hear Judy Collins, a folk guitarist, sing "This Land Is Your Land, This Land Is My Land." Along with other songs, the women joined in to sing "We Shall Overcome," a civil rights theme that many peace groups had adopted. After Swedish actress, Viveca Lindfors, read the official petition, the group boarded buses for an afternoon of conferences at the Shoreham Hotel.[47]

While the women were demonstrating at Union Square, Jeannette was busy talking to Congressmen inside the Capitol. She led a delegation of fifteen persons to talk to Speaker John W. McCormick. In a short amiable interview, he promised to refer their petition to the appropriate House committee. He did emphasize, though, that he disagreed with their views. Senator Mike Mansfield, on the other side of the Capitol, received only the Montana members of the delegation: Rankin; her sister, Edna McKinnon; and a niece, Dorothy Brown.[48] Jeannette observed that Mansfield

[45]Ibid.

[46]New York Times, January 16, 1968; Washington Post, January 12, 1968.

[47]Ibid.

[48]The Washington Evening Star, January 16, 1968.

was not nearly so brave as McCormick.

The "Women's Congress," convening in the afternoon at the Shoreham Hotel, heard reports from the delegation that visited Speaker McCormick and Senate Majority Leader Mansfield. They applauded a firey speech by Jeannette Rankin, who carried on with energy and spirit that belied her age. They discussed the law banning demonstrations on Capitol grounds and listened to speeches from other feminist leaders. The most militant point of the Congress came when Chairwoman Rankin introduced the wives of three men who had recently been indicted on charges of conspiracy to avoid the draft.[49]

While most observers and participants probably thought the activities of the Brigade was a model of deportment, an example of the way law-abiding citizens should present a petition to Congress, and a compliment to the wisdom of women, others disagreed. They would have favored a much more militant approach. Many of the younger women believed the demonstration was "good, but it didn't go far enough." For them, militancy had been compromised to attract moderate women.[50]

Unable to restrain themselves, approximately two hundred of these young women formed a rump "radical caucus." At the caucus, a group of black nationalist bitterly charged that the whole march was irrelevant. Later, one observed, "The march was a farce. The only part that was worth anything was the last thing [radical caucus] because it made people think."[51]

---

[49]Mrs. William Sloane Coffin, Jr., Mrs. Marcus Raskin, and Mrs. Mitchell Goodman; Washington Evening Star, January 16, 1968.

[50]Washington Post, January 17, 1969.

[51]Washington Evening Star, January 16, 1968.

On the other hand, Jeannette Rankin felt "this tremendous number of women, expressing their deep emotion against war, can't do anything but help."[52] Although they did not have the anticipated ten thousand women marching in Washington, the Brigade leaders thought they had demonstrated clearly, yet pacifically, women's opinion on Vietnam, poverty, and race. With apprehension on the part of some individuals, they had also succeeded in bring together a coalition of several thousand moderate to radical, middle-class American women.

After flirting with the thought of running again for Congress from Montana in 1969, Jeannette Rankin decided to rest, to complete her projected home for elderly women near Watkinsville, and to devote her energies to promoting peace and a more democratic electoral process. With anti-war sentiment increasing and the publicity received by the Brigade, Jeannette Rankin became a popular figure wherever she traveled. In an interview in California prior to the presidential conventions in 1968, she strongly supported Senator Eugene McCarthy, Democrat from Minnesota. "He is the only candiate," she said, "who recognized the influence of the military on our political situations."[53] Vice President Hubert H. Humphrey, to her, was absolutely the worst candidate. She prophesied that he would get the Democratic nomination because "the military has selected him as its candidate."[54] She went on to say that she would favor Richard M. Nixon or "anyone" over Humphrey.

---

[52]Arthur Alpert, Producer, and Kirk Browning, Director, "Mirror, Mirror on the World," Public Broadcast Laboratory of the National Educational Television and Radio Center.

[53]San Marino Independent-Star News, August 18, 1968.

[54]Monterey Peninsula Herald, July 24, 1968.

When President Richard Nixon, after his election, failed to end the
Vietnam War, Jeannette Rankin began to participate eagerly in anti-war
demonstrations. She spoke to the University of Georgia's Vietnam
Moritorium on October 15, 1969. Flanked by a "hippie band" and peace
posters, Jeannette addressed the 1500 students, professors, and University personnel. She stated that war had always failed and always will
fail and added that the war in Vietnam was being kept alive by mercenary
interest groups with great pressure in Washington. As she retired from
the speaker's stand, students, sitting on the ground, rose and gave
Rankin a standing ovation. She was, by far, the most popular speaker
on the program.[55]

Not one to permit the accolades to just ring in her ears, Jeannette
made a study trip to Czechoslovakia in 1969 to learn more about the Czech
people. She then planned a trip to Russia in May of 1970, but a broken
hip, received in a fall in Watkinsville a week before she was to leave,
prevented her from going. Hospitalized but still active, Rankin prepared a tape recording for an address she was to make to the Rankin Rank
and File, an anti-war group led by Clara d'Mia in New York City.

Before Jeannette Rankin broke her hip in May, friends in Washington
had planned to give her a "Ninetieth Birthday" party. Obviously enjoying
all the planning and not wanting to let her friends down, Jeannette encouraged them to proceed. So, on June 11, 1970, Jeannette Rankin, broken
hip, and wheel chair flew to Washington to greet about two hundred guests
in a birthday celebration. At the dinner Senator Margaret Chase Smith

---

[55]University of Georgia Red and Black, October 16, 1969; Atlanta
Constitution, October 16, 1969. A month later, she spoke to a similar
gathering in Monterey, California. Monterey Peninsula Herald, November
15, 1969.

expressed her indebtedness for Jeannette Rankin's pioneering for women,
independence, courage and dedication to peace. She continued by describing Jeannette as "ninety years young, tall as a giant in statesmanship
that is unparalleled in American history."[56]

After numerous testimonials from guests and the singing of "Happy
Birthday, Jeannette," Rankin stood up and addressed her friends for
twenty minutes. Having lost none of her ginger, she amazed her well-
wishers with an excellent analysis of her work for peace and democracy.
Rankin included an enthusiastic explanation of her latest idea, preferential voting. Although age had wrinkled her brow, it had not affected
her ability to speak and think. With Rankin charisma, she held the guests
in the "palm of her hand" all the time she spoke. In typical fashion, she
concluded, "We'd be the safest country in the world if the world knew we
didn't have a gun. Men are not killed because they get mad at each other.
They're killed because one has a gun."[57]

Before the end of the year, 1970, indomitable Jeannette Rankin was on
her seventh trip to India, her favoriate spot for rest and relaxation.
When she returned to the States, Jeannette embarked on the busiest years
of her retirement. Even though sentiment against the Vietnam was increasing, Jeannette Rankin observed that there was inadequate democratic machinery to register this conviction in Washington. Using John Stuart Mills'

---

[56]David Fisher, Tape of the Jeannette Rankin Birthday Dinner, June
11, 1970, Parts I and II, p. 15 of transcript; the author also has a
personal tape of the birthday proceedings in his personal files. Other
guests at the dinner included Montana Senators Mike Mansfield and Lee
Metcalf; Representative Arnold Olsen (Montana); Representative Patsy
Mink (Hawaii); former Senators Ernest Gruening (Alaska); Gerald Nye
(North Dakota), Burton K. Wheeler (Montana), and Claude Pepper (Florida);
and Alice Paul, an old friend from the National Woman's Party.

[57]Fisher, Jeannette Birthday Dinner Tape, Parts III and IV, p. 16.

idea of a "government of the whole people by the whole people represented," Rankin proposed changes in the election of legislators and of the
President. In a previous study of some state legislative assemblies,
Jeannette discovered in many instances a "government of the whole people
by a majority of the people exclusively represented."[58] She interpreted
this to mean a government of privilege in favor of the numerical majority
to a complete disfranchisement of the minority.

Rankin illustrated her idea by examining the sixty members of the
Oregon House of Representatives in 1917. In the last election, Republicans
cast 54,000 votes, Democrats 30,000, Socialists 7,000, and Prohibitionists
5,000. She then evaluated, "If the ideas of the people had been actually
represented . . . each party would have sent representatives to the legislature."[59] But, under the prevailing majority system, the Republicans
secured fifty-nine seats and the Democrats one. In order to avoid this
distortion of the electorate, Jeannette proposed a system of proportional
representation. Aware that this was a new idea tried only in a few
countries of Europe and Japan by 1917, she said:

> It is being found logical and simple, and readily
> commends itself as an indispensable instrument
> of a truly representative government.[60]

With such a system as this, Rankin believed the legislative bodies would
reflect a more accurate public opinion toward governmental policies.[61]

---

[58]J. R., Carnegie Speech, March 2, 1917, p. 24.

[59]Ibid.

[60]Ibid., p. 26.

[61]J. R., "To Give Every Party Voice in Laws," Chicago Sunday Herald,
October 21, 1971.

When the 1930 census revealed that Georgia would lose two Congressional seats, Rankin approached Richard B. Russell, Speaker of the Georgia
House and later Governor, with a multiple-member district plan. Jeannette
drove over to his home in Winder and suggested that the legislature divide the state into two equally populated districts with five representatives each. By this time, she had dropped the proportional idea, but
retained a provision for broader representation. She proposed a balance between urban and rural voters. Within a multiple-member district,
she pointed out that it was possible for the people to elect representatives with widely divergent backgrounds. Supposedly, rural, urban, labor,
capital, and others might all have their interests represented in Washington.[62]

With the emergence in the late 1960's and early 1970's of "court-
directed" reapportionment to achieve a balance of representation, Jeannette
revived her multiple-member district idea. The fact that she was ninety-
one years old did not deter her from spending several weeks lobbying the
Georgia legislature as it considered reapportionment in September of 1971.
This time, she simply suggested that the state be divided into multiple-
member districts. This encouraged several possibilities: two districts
with six representatives in one and four in another; two districts with
five representatives each; three districts in which two would have three
representatives each and the third would have four. "The way it is now,"
Rankin pointed out, "the people have no choice in Congressional elections.
Usually the two persons running have the same ideas."[63]

[62]J. R. Interview, January 15, 1970, p. 4; The Atlanta Journal and
Constitution, September 26, 1971, A15.

[63]Ibid., pp. A1, A15.

Another difficulty with single member districts, according to Jeannette Rankin, was that a small group in each locality controlled the outcome of elections. She estimated that forty percent of the people in a district favored a candidate, forty percent were against him, and twenty percent were undecided. Winning this twenty percent to the disregard of the eighty then became a candidate's primary objective. Multiple-member Congressional districts would alleviate this problem by making possible a broader representation of differing ideas in Congress.[64]

Remembering that she was elected in a multiple-member district, Jeannette Rankin appreciated the fact that the people could vote for both a man and a woman. She partially attributed her victory to this factor as it gave women an opportunity to express their opinions and to vote for a person to represent them in Washington. Rankin insisted that, under the present single-member district, the voter has only one choice; whereas, under a multiple-member district, "he could vote for a man and a woman, a black and a white, or an expert on education and a qualified person on local economic issues."[65] With Rankin's multiple-member Congressional district idea, the individual citizen would have more freedom of choice and the possibility of a wider representation of his interests. Her ideal of "participatory democracy" would find greater fulfillment as the electorate developed responsibility. Apathy, frustration and cynicism, so prevalent in today's voting populace, would diminish, according to Miss Rankin, if the voice of the people could be heard in the machinery of government.[66]

---

[64] J. R. Interview, March 2, 1971, pp. 1-2; J. R., "A Statement on Multiple-Member Districts," in author's personal files.

[65] Mimeographed letter to the members of the Georgia Legislature, October, 1971, in author's personal files.

[66] J. R., "A Statement on Multiple-Member Districts," in author's personal files.

Unfortunately, Jeannette Rankin's multiple-member idea ran afoul of federal law which permitted only single-member districts. Nevertheless, she hoped Congress would eventually change the law or that Georgia would become a test case for the federal courts.

As a second measure designed to implement the will of the people and to register their voice in public affairs, Jeannette Rankin began to advocate in the late 1960's a direct preferential vote for President of the United States. The closeness of the national elections of 1960 and 1968 emphasized flaws in the electoral system. Opinion polls showed a growing sentiment for reform. For the first time in her life, Jeannette Rankin was on the popular side of an issue. Broadening the electoral process was nothing new for the American people as at least seven amendments had extended the operation of the franchise since the adoption of the Constitution. The Fourteenth and Fifteenth Amendments gave the franchise to the black man. The Seventeenth provided for direct election of Senators, while the Nineteenth gave women the right to vote. In the Twenty-third, the District of Columbia obtained the ballot, and the Twenty-fourth outlawed the restrictive poll tax. In 1971, the Twenty-sixth Amendment lowered the voting age to eighteen.

Since her early years as a worker for women's suffrage, Jeannette Rankin had been interested in democratic processes which firmly established sovereign power in the hands of the people. As an initial step, she had advocated "votes for women." Slowly, she realized how Montana's direct nominating primary had revitalized interest in politics in contrast to the old nominating conventions. Enthused by the Constitutional amendment to provide for the direct election of Senators, Jeannette had proposed in 1917:

> We know we would have a greater influence in
> presidential elections if we had a direct vote
> for president. . . . It would increase the
> possibility of each vote having the same value.
> True democracy demands that each man has a vote
> and one man one vote.[67]

During the 1920's and 1930's, Rankin's interest in a Constitutional amendment to outlaw war and a war referendum vote could be interpreted as
examples of her continued interest in a government largely operated by
the consent of the governed. In the early 1950's, Jeannette became explicitly interested in "working for a new method of selecting a president."[68]
The eventual outcome was "the direct preferential vote for president."

In order to offer a greater degree of control to an increasingly better
educated and informed electorate, Jeannette Rankin broadened her plan for
selecting the President and Vice President of the United States. Designed
to challenge the voters' ideals, it expressed a politics of purpose and
affirmation rather than one of protest and rejection. Believing that
President Lyndon Johnson declined to run again in 1968 because he realized
the rejection by the American people of his Vietnam policies, she said,
"The 1968 political year demonstrated . . . we can throw a President
out, but we cannot elect one."[69]

The existing electoral machinery provided ample opportunity to express
negative feelings but no channels for promoting the peoples' positive ideas.

---

[67] Jeannette Rankin Carnegie Speech, March 2, 1917, p. 14, in J. R. MSS.

[68] J. R. to Thomas E. Kinney, Coeur d'Aline, Idaho, September 3, 1951,
J. R. MSS.

[69] J. R., "Case for a Direct Preferential Vote," mimeographed statement in the author's files and also is incorporated into testimony before
the House Judiciary Committee, February 26, 1969. The author heard Miss
Rankin present her statement to the committee.

From what Rankin had observed of the political scene, this lack of choice in presidential politics had alienated many young people, women, and members of minority groups. This frustration had thus driven large segments of the voting populace into the streets to demonstrate. Responding sensitively and creatively, Jeannette Rankin formulated a scheme whereby the people could vote for a candidate of their choice, rather than candidates pre-selected by party, politics, or pressure groups. To her, unless there was a free choice of candidates, voting became an empty, and ritualistic act. A direct popular vote, setting forth the preference of the people, was the next logical step in election reform.[70]

This preferential method of voting, as proposed by Jeannette Rankin, was not new or untried. Its basic previous handicap had been in the difficulty in tabulating the vote count for a large election. With the advent of optical character recognition equipment and programmed computers, the complex technological problems related to a preferential vote became easier to solve. With an assist from modern science, Jeannette pushed forward her idea for a direct vote of the people for the President.

Representative Emanuel Celler, Democrat from New York and a member of Congress when Jeannette was there, invited her to testify before the House Committee on the Judiciary on February 26, 1969.[71] Waiting until a nearly full committee was present and the hearing room packed, Jeannette Rankin finally arrived with the splendor of a visiting dignitary. Chairman Celler, greeting her cordially when the present speaker finished, invited her to witness. Standing, Jeannette began to speak. Interrupting

---

[70] J. R., "Case for a Direct Preferential Vote."

[71] Emanuel Celler to J. R., January 24, 1969, J. R. MSS.

with a flourish of small talk about their ages and length of service,
Chairman Celler urged her to sit. With typical Rankin wit, she replied,
"May I stand? I fight better standing."[72]

To introduce the committee to her background, Rankin told them, "I
have been working for 50 years--I won't say how much more--for improvement
in the electorate."[73] Her goal had been to give the voters a significant
opportunity to express themselves. She said, "I can trust the people and
I believe we have an educated, intelligent electorate."[74] In support of
her plan, she stated that every voter had one vote with which to declare
his choice. Only in a preferential election, she believed, could all
citizens have equal voting power and an equal chance to affect the final
decision. Also, the people would be assured that their vote counted directly for the candidate who came closest to satisfying their ideals.[75] One
distinguishing feature of this plan was its directness in the sense that
there was no intermediate step, such as the electoral college, between
the voter and his intention.

There were several ways names could be placed on the preferential
ballot. The explicit details Jeannette deferred to a Congressional
committee aided by the advice of experts. Yet, she did make some initial
suggestions. A bond, certifying that a candidate would obtain a definite
percentage of votes, might be required. A petition containing a certain
percentage of eligible voters would be another alternative. Selection by

---

[72]U.S., Congress, House of Representatives, Committee on the Judiciary,
Hearings on the Electoral College Reform on H. J. Res. 179 and 181. 91st
Congress, 1st Session, February 26, 1969, p. 374.

[73]Ibid., p. 374.

[74]Ibid., p. 375.

[75]Ibid., p. 374.

national political conventions provided a third possibility. Actually,
Jeannette had not thought through the qualifications and procedures for
getting a name on the ballot. Her mission, she believed, was simply to
present the idea.[76]

Jeannette Rankin described the balloting procedure for the direct
preferential by explaining that each voter would place the numeral "1"
by the name of his first choice. He then would indicate his preference
among the remaining candidates by writing the number "2" beside his second
choice, "3" adjacent to his third choice, and so on until the list was
completed. To begin tabulation of the ballots, the "first preference"
votes were totalled for each candidate. If a candidate received a majority of all votes cast, he won the election. However, if no one acquired
a majority of the first-place votes, the "second preference" votes were
added to the corresponding totals of the first. Then the cumulative totals
of the first and second preference votes were examined to see if a nominee
had attained a majority. If so, he was declared the winner. Provided no
candidate succeeded, the "third preference" votes were added to the cumulative totals of the first and second votes. Again the same method was used
to determine the person most preferred by the people. Yet, if still no
one emerged victorious, the procedure was continued with succeeding votes
until a majority candidate appeared or until the number of preferences
had been exhausted. In case the latter happened, a simple plurality of

----

[76]J. R., "Case for a Direct Preferential Vote for President," in
author's personal files.

the cumulative totals would determine the winner.[77]

In Jeannette Rankin's mind, the preferential vote was more than a means of casting a vote for President. It became an important avenue of expressing public opinion, providing an accurate and indepth assessment of the people's views. With more and more power being assumed by the President, especially in the area of international affairs, Rankin sensed a need for the people to express directly their opinion to the Executive.[78]

Jeannette Rankin also recommended the direct preferential method for electing the Vice President. It would greatly enhance the prestige and quality of his office to be chosen by the wishes of the people. Rankin indicated there would be little possibility of conflict between President and Vice President because she believed the voters' preference for President would influence a compatible choice for Vice President. Again, Rankin insisted that this would not destroy the party system. The parties could still hold conventions, write platforms, and nominate candidates; but the people's choice would not be limited solely to party nominations.[79]

In addition to expressing in action the ideal of the American democratic process, Rankin felt sure the direct preferential vote was practical.

---

[77]Handwritten note and flow chart in Rankin Folder on Election Reform, J. R. MSS; Miss Rankin was never too precise in explaining the mechanical details of how the plan worked because she felt this was the prerogative of a Congressional committee. She hoped the principle would be adopted by Constitutional amendment while leaving the implementation to Congress.

[78]U.S., Congress, Senate, Committee on the Judiciary, Hearings on Electing the President, 91st Congress, 1st Session, March 10, 1969, p. 171.

[79]J. R., "Case for a Direct Preferential Vote of President," author's personal files.

Without purchasing additional equipment, the computers and optical character recognition machines, already in use by various governmental agencies,
could be utilized to record and tabulate the ballots. As a further savings to the citizens, Rankin endorsed the preferential method's feasibility
from the standpoint of time and money. It would eliminate both the primary and a possible runoff afterwards.[80]

With the direct preferential voting method, a uniquely democratic
process, Jeannette Rankin hoped to channel the new political awareness
among American citizens. Asked if it was safe for the masses of people
to make such a decision, she replied, "The government asks the masses to
pay taxes . . . and even to fight and die for their country. Why should
they [the government] hesitate to ask the masses for an opinion?"[81] Rankin
expressed a complete faith in the people. Sometimes the electorate will
err, she acknowledged, but they will profit by their mistakes and will
learn to judge the candidates more accurately. This supreme trust of the
populace became the foundation for Jeannette Rankin's theory of the democratic process and a key to understanding her whole approach to life.

---

[80]Ibid.

[81]J. R., "Case for a Direct Preferential Vote."

CHAPTER XIII

THE DOWAGER OF WOMEN'S LIBERATION

In the resurgence of the feminist movement in the 1960's, Jeannette Rankin emerged as the link tying pioneering suffragists Susan B. Anthony, Lucy Stone, and Elizabeth C. Stanton to modern feminists Betty Freidan, Kate Millett, and Gloria Steinem. From her initial efforts in 1910, Rankin has exemplified feminism in America in both word and deed. Most of her ideas crystallized during the period of the 1910's and 1920's. For her "banner bearing" and peaceful agitation, Jeannette Rankin well earned the title of "the world's outstanding living feminist." The National Organization of Women betstowed this honor when they named her the first member of its Susan B. Anthony Hall of Fame in February of 1972.[1]

Having become accustomed to freedom in the West, Jeannette, by the time she was thirty, was ready to devote a lifetime of service to feminism. In comparison to the modern feminist movement, the national environment for Jeannette was more hostile and the odds even greater. These factors did not hinder nor phase "the woman from Montana." In retrospect, she observed, "I was fortunate to be raised in Montana in the pioneer days. There the men respected us. They readily gave their wives the vote."[2] The truth was that time and memory had mellowed and faded the picture of

---

[1] Nashville Tennessean, February 13, 1972.

[2] The Athens Daily News, January 28, 1972, p. 1.

337

Montana's hard fought campaign, won by a few thousand votes in 1914.
Yet, there was something distinctive about the Western states. They were
the early leaders in suffrage.

Why was woman's struggle for political equality in the West not nearly so long or strenuous as in the East and South? Jeannette Rankin attributed the reason not to the psychology of Western men, but to the character
of the Western country. This force made its impact upon both men and women
as they battled together the primal energies of nature. In contact with
these forces, they came to a common understanding of the fundamental principles of life. Side by side, the men and women first struggled with nature
to acquire their land, then with man-made laws which tried to control the
results of their struggle. Since they had shared common tasks in conquering the wilds of the West, the men soon recognized that the women should
thus participate in the formulating of laws. According to Jeannette Rankin,
this psychology prompted Montana men and women to establish political
equality based on a mutual understanding of the development of economic
forces.[3] Montana men found their women willing to share the burdens; so
they, in turn, were willing to share the privileges.

To illustrate this feeling, Jeannette recounted a story told by one
of Montana's feminine physicians. During the suffrage campaign, a young
man had come to her office. He recalled how early in the morning a woman
had left her cabin in the country to seek the nearest doctor. She rode
up the canyon, through the gulch, over the mountain, and down the other
side. After fording the river and crossing the plain, she arrived late
in the night in the mining camp. She had traveled sixty miles alone on

---

[3] Jeannette Rankin, "Why the West Leads the East in the Recognition
of Women," Chicago Sunday Herald, December 24, 1916.

horseback. That night, her son was born. The young man told the woman
doctor, "I am her son. I heard you were working for the vote, and so I
thought that I would tell you that I am for you." Jeannette felt that
men raised by such mothers could not help but believe in equality.[4]

By the time she ran for Congress, Rankin recognized a difference in
the thinking of the old and young men in Montana. In reference to her
campaign for the House of Representatives, the older men would say, "I
like her nerve," with an emphasis on the "like." They thought it was a
sporting thing to do. Not having had the appreciative experience of the
older men, the young men would taunt, "I like her nerve."[5] By stressing
the word "nerve," they showed that they were envious of her conviction
and dynamism.

Encouraged by articles of Jane Addams and others, Jeannette Rankin
began in 1910 to exhibit characteristics now regarded as typical of early
twentieth-century feminists. She was restless, eager to participate in
the intellectual vitality of the nation, desirous of encouraging the development of community life, and anxious to become an effective factor in
the development of the country through the vote. By the time the drought
ended for suffrage in 1910, Jeannette was ready to hold up the parade
banner, to speak from the soap box on the corner, and to develop the
organizational chart. For the next five years, she gave unselfishly of
her time and talents to the "woman movement," receiving only expenses
plus a minimal salary during much of the period.[6]

---

[4]J. R., Carnegie Speech, p. 5.

[5]J. R. Interview, September 27, 1971, p. 14.

[6]Jeannette Rankin, "What the Woman Movement Means," Chicago Sunday
Herald, December 17, 1916; William O'Neill, Everyone Was Brave (Chicago:
Quadrangle Books, 1969), pp. 146-168.

Jeannette Rankin brought both charm and personality to the suffrage movement. One woman said that Miss Rankin had no need of the vote, for men would grant her anything that she asked. To this, another woman replied:

> I tried to make her understand that it was this
> very gift of Miss Rankin's that was now being
> urged for the general benefit of womankind;
> that she was trying to give that powerful
> weapon, the ballot, to women who might be as
> worthy but neither had the charm nor personal-
> ity to influence mankind.[7]

The need for women to participate in the making of laws affecting themselves and their children stirred Jeannette Rankin to action. To illustrate this need, she told the following story at a open air meeting, held at the Como in St. Paul, Minnesota.:

> A husband and wife moved out to Colorado for the
> husband's health. He grew weaker and weaker.
> Finally, the support of both devolved on the
> wife. They had absolutely nothing excepting
> what she earned. One day after he had become
> so weak that he was confined to his bed, he
> asked for writing materials. She asked him
> what he was writing and was mused when he told
> her he was making a will. She could not under-
> stand what he had to will. After his death, she
> discovered that he had mailed a will to his rela-
> tives in the East bequeathing their unborn child
> to them.[8]

To correct such inequities, Jeannette Rankin worked hard to gain the vote for women as an expression of both social justice and equality.

Believing that suffrage was the greatest facet of feminism and held the key to future attainment for women, Jeannette Rankin encouraged them to participate in local and national affairs. She anticipated that their

---

[7]Mrs. George Marcus Kenyon, personal impressions of Jeannette Rankin, undated MSS in J. R. MSS.

[8]Ibid.

vote could influence legislation and would improve the quality of candidates seeking political office. It was to accomplish these goals that Rankin left social work per se and began campaigning for enfranchisement. Surveying the years, she evaluated, "Suffrage was the greatest organization of women that we have ever had. It was a great inspiration."[9] Jeannette observed that women in the states which had conducted suffrage campaigns have the best political sense today. Women in the South were slowed in political development because the Constitutional Amendment gave them the vote without their earning it.[10]

To Rankin's disappointment, women have not risen to the challenge of the vote. The zenith of the feminist movement came as women attained the national franchise through the Nineteenth Amendment. The years since, according to Rankin, have been beset with decline and mediocrity. Jeannette believed that World War I divided the women and that they have never regained the momentum nor the strength of pre-war years. Because of the restrictions on personal freedom, the divisive nature of war itself and the resulting social and economic transformations, she suspected that women, as well as men, lost their freedom at this time.[11] As to women's accomplishments since gaining the ballot, Rankin evaluated, "The reason women haven't done anything in the last fifty years is because they have lost their freedom."[12] When men lost their self-determination, so did women. She commented:

[9]J. R. Interview, September 27, 1971, p. 8.

[10]Ibid.

[11]J. R. Interview, March 23, 1971, p. 9; J. R. Interview, September 27, 1971, p. 5.

[12]J. R. Interview, March 23, 1971, p. 10.

> When I went to school, every boy was thinking
> of going into something independent. Now they
> are thinking of getting a job with a big com-
> pany. That's where they get the most pay and
> it's a sure thing. Men haven't the same
> freedom they used to have because they have
> to hold that job.[13]

Aware that few men now work alone and experience real freedom, Rankin advocated a return of the pioneer spirit that the farmer and professional
men once knew.[14]

With this emphasis Jeannette Rankin became more than a feminist.
She proposed, "Freedom has to be for all the people. You can't select
the blacks or the whites; the men or the women."[15] As long as one part
of humanity has lost its liberty, so has all the rest. With their husbands as slaves to the company, women could not speak out or get involved in political or social issues because he might lose his job. Thus,
Rankin deducted that men and women both had lost their individual integ-
rity.

Even though both were enslaved, Rankin believed woman's plight was
more serious. She never espoused the idea that women should have something just because men did. Women should attain equality as a result of
having something to contribute to society. If a woman volunteered her
services during the early suffrage campaign simply because she wanted
to vote, Jeannette was careful as to what work she was assigned. But, if
she believed in suffrage and that the government should be run by the consent of the governed: "We could send her any place because she would never

---

[13]Ibid.

[14]J. R. Interview, April 20, 1971, p. 8.

[15]J. R. Interview, March 23, 1971, p. 10.

make a mistake in dealing with people."[16]

Rankin characterized the unique relation of men and women by describing the human hands. She recognized that they were not the same and that their contributions were varied under diverse circumstances. She asserted, "They are both necessary. You can't say one is more important than the other."[17] Jeannette's basic goal was for male and female humans to learn to accept each other as persons.

Jeannette was sensitive to anything that divided people. In her speeches, she always began "men and women" rather than "ladies and gentlemen." She believed the latter phrase expressed an unequal connotation, that there were classes of people. For her, there was no distinction between people when one talked about human activity. When people called Jeannette "The Lady from Montana", she would remark quietly to her friends that she "resented it. . . . It should have been "The Woman from Montana." Once, when a policeman addressed her as a lady, she replied, "I'm no lady. I'm a woman!" Equally distasteful to her was the designation "Mrs.," which only served to say, "You're married, too bad, sex."[18] Women should be accepted as human entities, Rankin believed, and not as chattel belonging to their husbands.

During her first term in Congress, a female, Montana constituent went to China and married an American engineer while working there. Later, because her passport carried her maiden name, the authorities reclaimed it

---

[16]J. R. Speech to University of Georgia Chapter of Phi Alpha Theta, April 1, 1969, p. 4 of typescript.

[17]Ibid., p. 10; J. R. to Montana Constitutional Convention, March, 1972, p. 5.

[18]J. R. Interview, October 8, 1971, pp. 1-2.

when she went to have it extended. They contended that she was no longer
the person to whom it had been assigned. With a tinge of sarcasm,
Jeannette wondered curiously if the husband was still the same as before
marriage. "That marriage should change a woman's state is inconsistent
and absurd," she fumed. "It is a relic of the old common law idea that
held woman to be man's property."[19]

On another day during Rankin's first term, a group of secretaries
came running to her, exclaiming, "There is a man in the women's dressing
room." To Jeannette's surprise, she discovered Mary Walker, the Civil
War doctor who always wore a broadcloth coat and trousers. In the natural
conversation to follow, Jeannette asked her how long she had been wearing
men's clothes. Indignantly, Dr. Walker retorted, "I've never worn men's
clothes. I've always worn my own." Rankin recognized this as a truth
emphasizing that there should be no division of what belongs to men and
what belongs to women. All of it belonged to persons.[20]

Aware of woman's contribution to national development through profession and industry, Rankin anticipated their gradual recognition as
individuals. She looked forward to the time when laws would be made not
for men or women as such, but for human beings. Expressing more than
feminism, Rankin said, "The problems of today are human problems. What
affects men affects women."[21] Even more than that, she hoped for a basic
change in American attitudes in the concept of manhood and womanhood. Passing laws and vocalizing equality do not make equality accepted. Jeannette

[19] New York American, March 17, 1918.

[20] J. R. Interview, October 8, 1971, p. 4.

[21] J. R. Interview, April 20, 1971, p. 1.

often repeated, "Tradition and habit are stronger than laws."[22]

According to Jeannette Rankin, one of woman's most important contributions to civilization was children. Her dominant impulse was to create, and her fundamental responsibility was to take care of the young. This responsibility began in the cradle and continued to adulthood. With today's interest in "day care centers," Rankin said, "I don't think being separated from the children hurt them. I think it's what the mother does when she is with the child." She suspected that an hour of love and devotion at night was better than staying home and screaming at the child all day. Basically, whether a mother stayed home with her child or not was an individual decision, Rankin assessed.[23]

The "housewife syndrome" of modern women, as described by Betty Friedan in The Feminine Mystique, found sympathy in Jeannette Rankin only to the extent that she felt "women must be free to do what they want to do." If a woman wanted to have a career, nothing should hinder her. On the other hand, she suggested, it was just as much a challenge to have a family and to work within the household. Unfortunately, Jeannette sensed that men had robbed women's work of much of its purpose with the invention of mechanical tools. Washing at the stream and scrubbing on a rock has been reduced to the silly, artificial operation of the washing machine. Rankin summed up her philosophy, "It isn't a question of what work she does. It's what she contributed to society as a whole."[24]

----

[22]Ibid.

[23]J. R. Interview, April 20, 1971, p. 5.

[24]J. R. Interview, April 20, 1971, p. 2; Betty Friedan, The Feminine Mystique (New York: Dell Publishing Co., 1963), pp. 16, 281-282.

For this contribution to be significant, Jeannette Rankin added that women, as well as men, must be free to develop their lives along individually chosen paths. This seemed to be the philosophy Rankin has followed through life. In suffrage, politics, and peace crusades, her primary motive was service and not money. During her working years, Jeannette received only a modest income. The few luxuries she had were the gifts of a benevolent and loving brother. For later years, he established an annuity and provided a generous gift in his will. By choice, she still preferred to live very frugally in her home near Watkinsville, Georgia. In addition to being personally gratifying, the twinkle in her eye revealed a kind of "I-told-you-I-could-do-it" victory over the age of modern technolgoy.

Her grey, asbestos-shingled, frame house lacked central heating and running water. For about twenty years, she used a hand water pump; and only recently (1967) has she installed one cold water "faucet" over the bathtub. In a refurbished closet off her bedroom, Rankin placed an "airplane type" commode. An old "stripped" electric toaster provided heat for this miniature half-bath. The sitting room downstairs had a "tamped earth" floor on which she placed plastic, tar paper, and then carpet. Each room expressed a simple modesty, decorated with eclectic objects d'art representing her many travels. Her walls hanged heavy with pictures from India and fabrics from other parts of the world. Rugs from various countries covered the floors. Because of her love for India, these items dominated the furnishings. Jeannette also had an unusual ability to turn simplicity into usefulness. Burning New York Times, draped over an iron rod frame in the fireplace, provided extra heat for the living room upstairs.[25]

In regard to her life-style, Jeannette Rankin expressed agreement with modern feminists, "If I haven't had anything else, I've had freedom. I have never done a job long unless I've wanted to." She continued, "When I've been unemployed, I was never idle, but I couldn't see the purpose in most of the jobs I might have gotten (sic)."[26]

Although quite thrilled with the new feminine emphasis on freedom, Jeannette Rankin disliked their preoccupation with economics. "I wish they wouldn't waste their energy talking about money. Money shouldn't be a factor in our lives," she insisted. Referring to her own simple style of living, Rankin hoped to indicate the superfluousness of money. By not buying the conveniences of a modernized home, she saved money to give to the peace movement. To her, this was a more purposeful means for expression.[27] As a solution to eliminate many of the problems related to money, Jeannette Rankin proposed an equal income for everyone regardless of occupation. As a particular aid to widows, this income would permit them to raise their children without becoming dependent on society. Also unmarried women would then be able to live quite independently.[28]

To feminists gathered on the Georgia capital steps, Jeannette Rankin said, "The modern male looks too much at woman as a sex object. In the

---

[25]Many evenings the author interviewed Miss Rankin while warming to the burning papers in the fireplace and will attest to its efficiency.

[26]J. R. Interview, April 20, 1971, p. 2.

[27]New York Times, January 24, 1972, L, p. 24.

[28]J. R. Interview, April 20, 1971, p. 5.

animals sex is a matter of procreation.[29] In Jeannette's estimation, the
reason there has been so much stress on sex is that there is nothing else
to think about. Sex, to Rankin, was a creative work, stimulating to the
thinking and pleasureable. "Most of it is for enjoyment," she surmised,
but impishly added, "How would I know?"[30] Rankin believed in a relationship between fear and procreation. "When there is fear that the race is
going to be eliminated, procreation takes over," suggested Miss Rankin.
She pointed to the increased number of "war babies" to substantiate her
claim.[31]

Coinciding with the greater demand for sexual freedom by female
liberationists, Jeannette Rankin observed that men, too, are not monogamous.
From her personal observations and from her travels, polygamy could work
quite well. She thought that men preferred different types of wives at
various stages in the development of their life. Rankin explained that
a man may choose one woman for his sexual and social life, another as an
intellectual stimulus, and still another as the mother for his children.
Women ought to adjust to these facts, she believed and stop making a
tragedy out of it.[32]

With the election year of 1972 imminent, Jeannette Rankin began encouraging women to assert their power at every political level. Armed with
this purpose, early in 1972 she addressed women's political caucuses in
Atlanta, Nashville, and Little Rock. The goal of these bipartisan efforts

[29]Atlanta Journal, Mar. 8, 1970.

[30]J. R. Interview, Apr. 20, 1971, p. 7.

[31]Ibid., p. 8.

[32]Ibid., pp. 3-4.

was to gain equal delegate strength in the political process at the upcoming Democratic and Republican nominating conventions. Speaking at the Southern Women's Conference on Education for Delegate Selection in Nashville, Rankin deplored the circus atmosphere of the political conventions. "You can have all the balloons, the political games and the good times," she said, "but when all this is done there's still work to do. Why not get on with it?" Jeannette took her democracy very seriously and called the current machinery a "Model-T Ford."[33]

She also enunciated a strong feeling for equal participation by women in politics. Rankin evaluated, "It is unbelievable that we turn 50 per cent of our tax money over to men who corrupt our government and perpetuate the myth that political parties are responsible."[34] Jeannette, never a political hack, believed that there was very little difference in the major political parties. Jeannette complained of their approach to most issues, because their dissimilarity was almost insignificant. "This is one of the things they [the men] have put over on us so that they can divide and rule," she asserted.[35]

Chastising the men for permitting few women to participate in politics, Jeannette said, "You can't throw out half the people of the country and say that their minds and feelings are inferior."[36] This myth of inferiority, according to Rankin, was the greatest obstacle to women obtaining equal voice. Her solution for getting more women involved was "grass roots

---

[33]Nashville Tennessean, February 13, 1972; The Knoxville News-Sentinal, February 13, 1972; New Orleans States-Item, February 16, 1972.

[34]The Knoxville New-Sentinal, February 13, 1972.

[35]Ibid.

[36]Ibid.

organizing." She wanted to make every woman count, and one does not do this by coming to meetings and talking. Rankin advised, "There will be no revolution unless we go out into the precincts."[37] With a knowledge-able smile, she continued, "And when the men make fun of you, that's when you know you're getting along well."[38]

Previous to the experience of these political caucuses, Jeannette believed that women had progressed only "microscopically" since suffrage. Relative to the earlier efforts of the new feminist movement, she said, "The Woman's Liberation Movement is awfully good these days, but it is an awful bore. I've been talking about these same things for 50 years."[39] Excited about the possibilities of women learning political strategy, Rankin estimated, "This conference, and other like it, is the best thing that's happened in 50 years."[40] And, when she saw a month later the number of women participating in Montana's Constitutional Convention, she respond-ed, "This . . . has proved that the women . . . are going places and that you have to consider them in every activity."[41]

From the Nashville conference, Jeannette Rankin flew to New York. There the National Organization for Women (NOW) acclaimed her the "world's outstanding living feminist" and named her the first member of its "Susan B. Anthony Hall of Fame." According to Wilma S. Neida, President, the Hall of Fame was created to honor living women whose achievements can serve as

---

[37]Elizabeth Frappollo, "Jeannette Rankin," Life, LXXII (March 3, 1972), p. 65.

[38]Ibid.

[39]University of Georgia Red and Black, Dec. 1, 1971.

[40]New Orleans States-Item, February 16, 1972.

[41]J. R. Speech to Montana Constitutional Convention, March, 1972, p. 5 of transcript in author's files.

an inspiration and model for all feminists. In a life spanning more than nine decades, coupled with an enthusiasm for peace and equality, Jeannette Rankin had personified the goals of feminism.[42]

[42]The Atlanta Journal-Constitution, February 15, 1972; The Christian Science Monitor, February 25, 1972.

CHAPTER XIV

EPILOGUE

From a girl on a Montana ranch in the 1880's to the dowager of the
Women's Liberation Movement in the 1970's, Jeannette Rankin lived coura-
geously and independently. She worked hard, thought deeply and acted
according to her convictions. Many people knew her only for casting the
single negative vote against World War II. In most cases, they were not
aware that she had worked for woman suffrage, was the first woman elected to the United States' Congress, lobbied against war and then served
a second term in the House of Representatives.

Jeannette's vivacity roughly encompassed three areas of interest:
women, politics and peace. To delineate specific times when she was
more interested in one than another may be accomplished, but not convenient-
ly. Her ideological framework for the three areas were interestingly inter-
wined.

Rankin entered the suffrage movement because she felt women needed
to have more voice in the making of laws governing themselves. Then she
campaigned for Congress to represent the woman's point of view. Jeannette's
ideas on war and peace first emerged during college days. They assumed distinctive proportions in the early suffrage campaigns. She then envisioned
all of these activities as a deepening expression of democracy.

Endowed with a creative spirit, Jeannette Rankin found her early environment challenging, but her education boring. It just did not provide

352

the stimulation that she needed. On the other hand, the ranch and family became a training ground for learning the techniques of leadership and organization. Many times this primitive society challenged her well-spring of ingenuity. The West also provided an encounter in which women were respected for their talents and abilities and not just for their sex.

In addition to this small taste of pioneer spirit, John Rankin furnished his family with a style of living much above the average in Montana. They were among the elite of Missoula, having both a town house and a ranch. Within a laissez faire society, the Rankins exhibited all the trappings of affluence. This enabled Jeannette to secure a college education, to have access to magazines and books, to be able to travel and to come in contact with interesting and cultured people.

In the period, 1900 to World War I, Jeannette Rankin worked for typically "Progressive" programs. She trained for a career in social work, but applied it only sparingly. Recognizing that women needed the vote to change laws and institutions affecting them, Rankin spent six years speaking and organizing for enfranchisement.

Campaigning with the slogan, "Let the People Know," Jeannette Rankin reflected progressive ideas on government and democracy. She supported state primary elections, the initiative, referendum, recall, direct election of Senators, one man one vote principle, and the direct election of the President. Not only was she contemporary in her thinking, but in some instances ahead of her time.

This faith in the people to operate their government was a firm tenent of her philosophy. She felt that the people would vote correctly if they knew the facts and had an opportunity to express them with a secret ballot. It was for this reason that Rankin believed in organizing and working on the grass-roots level. She called her Georgia Peace Society an example of grass-roots organization, but its membership was not representative of Georgia's. The members were basically related to the University of Georgia and to the Athens community. Yet, her proposed "direct preferential vote for President" would give every candidate an opportunity to seriously campaign if he had the political backing. Also, it permitted every citizen to express his preference in the electoral system.

Jeannette Rankin's first term in Congress, 1917-1919, reflected substantial activity. She was concerned with women's status in the war economy; with labor; with maternity and infancy legislation; with woman suffrage; with citizenship for women independent of their alien husbands; and with a vote against war. For a junior Congressman, she expressed considerable initiative; yet, she was able to remain popular and delightfully feminine.

A survey of her friends during this period underscored the complexity and diversity within the Progressive Movement. They included persons of such dissimilarity as Jane Addams, a pacifist, to Theodore Roosevelt, a militarist; and from Robert LaFollette, liberal governor and Senator from Wisconsin, the Huey Long, demagogue from Louisiana. Representative of many Progressives in the 1920's, Jeannette continued her career in related fields of social legislation and peace.

Disillusioned that they had not made "the world safe for democracy" through a "war to end all wars," Americans rejected Woodrow Wilson's collective security and moral imperialism. They dropped the League of Nations idea and entered into a "non-interventionist" foreign policy. In this period of the 1920's and 30's, many historians saw a growing isolationism. Others, like Alexander DeConde, pointed out that isolation was nothing more than isolation from the war.[1]

Jeannette Rankin characterized the latter position. She was an isolationist only to the extent that she wanted to stop war. Believing that war was futile and immoral, Rankin formulated her isolationism in an antimilitaristic thesis. She supported disarmament conferences, the Kellogg-Briand Pact, an investigation of the munitions industry, reduction in military spending, unification of the military services into one department and a war referendum vote. Except for a period with the National Consumers' League, Jeannette worked professionally during the 1920's and 30's as an opponent of the war system.

While being an isolationist against war, Rankin was an internationalist in all other respects. She attended the Third International Conference for Women in Zurich in 1918 and addressed the Fourth Conference which met in Washington in 1924. In relation to the League of Nations, she opposed Article X in its Covenant, but valued the League as a channel of communication between nations. She, also, endorsed the idea of a World Court and believed that America should develop an amiable cultural and economic relationship with all nations.

Some Americans have gained renown through war. Others have suggested that the civilization we now enjoy would have been unattainable except through the advances of military technology. Undoubtedly, Americans have been a violent people. Yet, there has been a continuing,and at times surging, interest in peace. Certainly, Americans have not loved war.

Rather than emphasizing these violent tendencies, Jeannette Rankin preferred to talk about America's traditions for peace. Because many Anglo-Saxons were distrustful and weary of the European war system, she

---

[1]Alexander De Conde, Isolation and Security, p. 31.

believed that the founding fathers of the nation tried to eliminate the influence of militarism in the Constitution. They established civilian control over the armed services, two year limits for military appropriations and devised the concept of a Supreme Court to settle disputes without resorting to violence.

To further this philosophy, she supported S. O. Levinson's "outlawry of war" and "codification of international law." Later she endorsed the Kellogg-Briand Pact which contained the germ of this idea. During the 1930's, Rankin was representative of the peace movement as she supported the munitions investigation and neutrality legislation.

In the war crisis of the 1940's, Jeannette Rankin did not falter. She felt she could more effectively serve the cause of peace by being in the Congress. So, she campaigned and was elected. In the inner recesses of her heart, she believed that Roosevelt was leading the nation to war. When she vocalized it, Rankin became one of the first to express a revisionist approach to World War II. When the time came to vote on the Japanese declaration, she held tenaceously to her ideals and voted the lone negative ballot. Philosophically, she believed, the weak went down to defeat or compromised to save himself in this moment of national emergency.

History has accorded to Jeannette Rankin the distinction of voting against two world wars, which either evokes admiration or hatred. Yet, her significance extends far beyond these two widely separated events. The reasons she voted against war may be as much a contribution to social civilization as the actual vote was to political civilization. Jeannette placed high significance on this vote. It was woman's first vote and she had voted against war.

Jeannette Rankin believed that "the people" do not want to settle their disputes by war. The military, who gain dominance in the government, produce an enemy and frighten the people into supporting their program. To propagate for belief that people do not make war, she had thousands of buttons printed that read, "Governments make War."

In her vote against the war declaration, Rankin expressed the ideal and fulfilled her commitment to self. She was willing to do this regardless of the political cost. These votes against World War I and World War II were typical of her idealism and dedication to the cause of peace. In contrast to this, Rankin could be very practical at times. She used very pragmatic methods in campaigning and in lobbying. This was not to say that she was inconsistent, but only that she could be very idealist at times and again be very practicable. Realizing that she could not abolish the military system in one full sweep, Jeannette Rankin was willing to acquire her gains one step at a time. Again, this was a very practical approach to her ideal goal.

Basically, though, Jeannette Rankin was more interested in ideas, issues and concepts than in practicalities. She felt it was her mission to formulate the idea and then pass it along. Rankin was not always patient to work out the "nitty-gritty" of her proposals.

Jeannette Rankin encountered many battles, but scored few victories. Yet, success is not measured in the number of victories one wins, but in the efficacy of the cause for which one struggles. Perhaps this remarkable woman's career was best summed up when the War Resister's League at its 35th Annual Dinner on April 8, 1958 honored Rankin for her devotion and loyalty to peace. Tracy Mygatt, presently an eighty-seven year old pacifist who had watched the memorable vote in 1917 from the House gallary, presented her with a plaque which contained this inscription:

> **When others were swept away in the tides of passion, she stood her ground and gave an example of moral courage which has continued to inspire all those who love peace.** [2]

---

[2] Tracy Mygatt to the author, February 15, 1969, in the author's personal files; War Resister's League plaque is in the personal possession of Jeannette Rankin, Watkinsville, Georgia.

APPENDIX

COMPARISON OF CARL VINSON'S VOTING STRENGTH FOR THE
YEARS 1932-1940 IN THE DEMOCRATIC PRIMARY, SIXTH
CONGRESSIONAL DISTRICT, STATE OF GEORGIA[a]

COUNTIES	1932	1934	1936	1938	1940
BALDWIN	930	1,452	1,311	1,768	1,911
BIBB	4,026	5,172	7,018	6,382	8,219
BLECKLEY	1,055	698	1,269	767	1,339
CRAWFORD	92	485	759	520	705
GLASCOCK	465	415	666	555	834
HANCOCK	535	690	793	818	843
JASPER	758	902	1,533	1,142	1,115
JEFFERSON	1,391	1,389	2,211	1,653	1,743
JOHNSON	1,239	1,240	2,659	1,891	2,798
JONES	415	581	750	697	981
LAURENS	1,821	2,077	4,208	3,070	5,160
MONROE	541	1,328	1,891	1,584	1,542
PUTNAM	688	924	989	797	1,182
TWIGGS	531	587	1,055	803	930
WASHINGTON	1,536	1,514	2,112	1,931	1,872
WILKINSON	1,001	1,027	1,379	1,366	1,605
TOTALS	17,027	20,481	30,603	25,744	32,778

[a]Compiled from the Official Registers of 1933-37 (p. 643) and 1939-43
(pp. 395 and 536), and Atlanta Constitution, September 16, 1932, p. 12.

BIBLIOGRAPHY

BIBLIOGRAPHY

I. PRIMARY SOURCES

ORAL INTERVIEWS:

Acher, Arthur. Helena, Montana, personal taped interview with the
author on September 4, 1970.

Brown, Dorothy. Missoula, Montana, personal taped interview with the
author on September 5, 1970.

Burnet, Duncan, Athens, Georgia, personal interview with the author,
March 31, 1969. Mr. Burnet's wife was the first president of
the Georgia Peace Society.

Butler, Blanche, Watkinsville, Georgia, personal interview with the
author, February 13, 1969. Mrs. Butler was a member of the Girls'
Club and, presently, prepares lunch daily for Miss Rankin.

Columbia University. Oral History Project. Memoirs of Roger Baldwin
and the American Civil Liberties Union.

_____, Oral History Project. Memoirs of Frances
Witherspoon and Tracy Mygatt.

Coulter, E. Merton, Athens, Georgia, personal interview with the author,
February 6, 1969. Dr. Coulter was a charter member of the Georgia
Peace Society and president in 1934.

Elge, Frances. Billings, Montana, personal taped interview with the
author on September 10, 1970.

Elge, Frances and Gladys Knowles. Billings, Montana, personal taped
interview by John Board, November 27, 1964.

Fligelman, Freida. Helena, Montana, personal taped interview with the
author on September 3, 1970.

Ferguson, Mary Elrod. Missoula, Montana, personal taped interview with
the author on September 5, 1970.

Forbes, Stanton. Athens, Georgia, personal interview with the author,
March 7, 1969. Mr. Forbes was a nephew of Lucy Stanton in whose
studio the Georgia Peace Society originated.

361

Galt, Louise Rankin. Helena, Montana, personal taped interview by the author, September 4, 1970. This was Wellington Rankin's wife who has since remarried.

Gordon, Dave. Athens, Georgia, personal interview with the author, June 2, 1969. Mr. Gordon was a member of the Peace Society.

Hill, Joyce and Pope. Athens, Georgia, personal interview with the author, January 25, 1969. The Hill's were very close personal friends of Jeannette Rankin.

Huber, Mary Elizabeth Sedman. Douglaston, New York, personal interview with the author on September 12, 1971.

Knowles, Ted. Helena, Montana, personal taped interview with the author on September 2, 1970.

McGregor, Harriett. Douglaston, New York, personal taped interview with John Board, August 18, 1966.

McGregor, Harriett Rankin Sedman. Douglaston, New York, personal taped interview with John Board, August 18, 1966.

McKinnon, Edna Rankin. Carmel, California, personal taped interview with the author on November 16, 1971.

McLaish, Mrs. A.E. Fort Benton, Montana, personal taped interview by John Board, October 10, 1964.

Nunnally, Joe Watson. Bogart, Georgia, personal interview, July 5, 1969. Mr. Nunnally was the closest neighbor to Miss Rankin.

Nye, Gerald. Washington, D.C., personal taped interview with the author on June 10, 1971.

Rankin, Jeannette. Watkinsville, Georgia, personal taped interview with the author on the following dates: January 16, 26, 27, 30,1969; February 14, 20, 1969; May 24, 1969; June 25, 1969; September 5, 1969; January 15, 22, 1970; February 5, 12, 1970; March 31, 1970; April 3, 14, 21, 27, 1970; March 2, 9, 16, 23, 1971; April 6, 20, 27, 1971; May 4, 1971; September 25, 27, 1971; October 8, 19, 1971.

This series of interviews over three years totals about ninety hours of interviewing. The tapes have been transcribed and are in the personal possession of the author.

_____ and Josephine Wilkins. Athens, Georgia, personal taped dinner conversation with Vernon Edenfield and John Gay, April 28, 1972.

_____. Speech to Anti-War Rally on the campus of the University of Georgia, May 14, 1972.

_____. Birthday Party Tape, United States House of Representatives' Office Building, June 11, 1970.

_____. Dick Cavett Show Interview, February 23, 1971.

_____. David Frost Show Interview, January 25, 1972.

_____. Interview on the Merv Griffin Show, February 18, 1971.

_____. Missoula, Montana, personal taped interview by John Board, August 29 and 30, 1963.

_____. Speech to the Montana State Constitutional Convention, Helena, Montana, March 14, 1972.

_____. Speech to Phi Alpha Theta, University of Georgia, April 1, 1969. Taped by Katrina Cheek and used with her permission.

_____. Speech to Jeannette Rankin Rank and File, a New York City Peace Group, May 6, 1970. This address was taped by the author from her bed at Athens General Hospital.

_____. Personal interview with the Social Welfare Organization Classes at School of Social Work, University of Washington and School of Social Work, San Diego State College, December 4, 1968.

_____. "Sound of Youth," Talk Show produced in Atlanta, Georgia, April 4, 1971.

_____. "Today Show," National Broadcasting Corporation, March 20, 1972.

_____. Speech to War Resister's League Annual Convention, September 3, 1971 in Athens, Georgia. This address was taped by the author.

_____. Speech to the Wesley Foundation, University of Georgia, February 11, 1969. Taped by Katrina Cheek and used with her permission.

Rankin, Wellington D. Helena, Montana, personal taped interview by John Board, March 23, 1964.

Rittenour, Jimmie. Plains, Montana, personal taped interview with the author on September 5, 1970.

Ron Hovde, Virginia Sedman. Washington, D.C., personal taped interview with the author on June 11, 1971.

Spriggs, Rosa Nell. Chevy Chase, Maryland, personal taped interview with the author on June 11, 1971.

_____. Chevy Chase, Maryland, personal taped interview with John Board, on August 10, 1966.

Steven, Bailey. Library of the National Woman's Party in Washington, D.C., personal taped interview with the author on June 11, 1970.

Tate, John. Oxford, Georgia, personal interview with the author, February 3, 1969. John Tate was one of the presidents of the Georgia Peace Society.

Vernon, Mabel. Washington, D.C., personal taped interview by the author, April 7, 1972.

Wheeler, Burton K. Washington, D.C., personal taped interview with the author on June 10, 1971.

Whetstone, Dan. Cutbank, Montana, personal taped interview by John Board, October 18, 1964.

Wilson, Robert C. Athens, Georgia, personal interview with the author, April 22, 1969. Dr. Wilson, a professor in the Pharmacy School, was an associate of Henry C. White.

Wilkins, Josephine. Athens, Georgia, personal taped interview with the author on May 24, 1972.

Winestein, Belle Fligelman. Helena, Montana, personal taped interview with the author on September 2, 1970.

Winestein, Belle. Helena, Montana, personal taped interview with John Board, April 10, 1964.

Winestein, Belle and Norman. Helena, Montana, personal taped interview with the author on September 9, 1970.

PERSONAL CORRESPONDENCE:

Adams, Lucile to William Clark, Gainesville, Georgia, February 25, 1969, which contained an excerpt from letter of Haywood Pearce to Lucile Adams. Xerox copy in personal files of the author.

Anthony, Susan. Deerfield, Florida, Letter to the author, November 8, 1971. A niece of the original Susan B. Anthony and a student participant in the Duke Institute of 1936.

Mygatt, Tracy D. Letter to the author, February 15, 1969.

Pearce, Haywood. Letter to the author, April 29, 1969.

Penrose, Charles. Potsdam, New York, Letters to the author, January 29, 1972 and March 18, 1972. Penrose was a student in Jeannette Rankin's campaign against Vinson in 1936.

Russell, Richard B. Letters to the author, February 18, March 5, and April 10, 1969.

Scannell, Sigrid. Bismarck, North Dakota, Letters to the author, March 3, March 16 and April 27, 1969. Mrs. Scannell was a secretary to Miss Rankin during her second Congressional term.

Terrell, Harry E. Des Moines, Iowa, Letters to the author, October 29, 1971 and February 4, 1972. Terrell was in Des Moines branch of the NCPW.

Vinson, Carl. Milledgeville, Georgia, Letters to the author, March 26 and May 1, 1969.

Winestine, Belle Fligelman. Helena, Montana, Letters to the author, February 10 and 23, 1969. Mrs. Winestine was Miss Rankin's press secretary during the campaign of 1916 and a secretary during Miss Rankin's first term as Congresswoman.

MANUSCRIPT COLLECTIONS:

Carrie Chapman Catt Papers, Manuscript Division, Library of Congress.

Carrier Chapman Catt Papers, Manuscript Division, New York Public Library.

Georgia Peace Society, Swarthmore College Peace Collection. Folder
contained membership letters by Jeannette Rankin and publications
of the Society and the Georgia Committee on the Disarmament Conference from 1931 to 1937.

Harriett B. Laidlaw Papers, Schlesinger Woman's Library, Radcliffe
College. It also included a microfilm copy of the Harriett B.
Laidlaw Scrapbooks, 1912-1917, which was located in the New York
Historical Society, Albany, New York.

Catherine McCulloch Papers, Schlesinger Woman's Library, Radcliffe
College, Cambridge, Massachusetts.

National Consumers' League Papers, Manuscript Division, Library of
Congress.

National Council for Prevention of War, Swarthmore College Peace Collection.
Swarthmore College Peace Collection is the official depository of
National Council materials. There were two alphabetically arranged
file drawers of Rankin folders. Other Rankin information appeared
in the annual meetings and reports from 1930 to 1939.

National Woman's Party Papers, Manuscript Division, Library of Congress.
Contains records and reports of the early years.

New York Woman Suffrage Party Manuscripts, Manuscript Division, New York
Public Library.

O.H.P. Belmont Suffrage Scrapbooks, Library, National Women's Party,
Washington, D.C.

Jeannette Rankin Collection, Library, Montana Historical Society.

Jeannette Rankin Manuscripts, prepared and filed by the Manuscript
Division of the University of Montana, Missoula, Montana, but
presently in the possession of Jeannette Rankin.

Thomas J. Walsh Papers, Manuscript Division, Library of Congress. These
papers contained information relative to the campaign of 1918 as
Walsh was Miss Rankin's opponent in the general election.

U. S. Section, Women's International League for Peace and Freedom,
Swarthmore College Peace Collection. These materials contained
Rankin articles relative to her participation in the organization
and relative to her employment as Field Secretary.

Women's Peace Union, Swarthmore College Peace Collection. These papers
contained records, minutes, correspondence, press releases and

clippings. Rankin material appeared chiefly in 1929.

Woman's Rights Collection, Schlesinger Woman's Library, Radcliffe College, includes papers of Carrie Chapman Catt, Anna Howard Shaw, Maud Wood Park, C. L. Babcock, Alma Lutz, and other documents relating to the National American Woman Suffrage Association.

E. P. Wheeler Papers, Manuscript Division, New York Public Library.

Henry White Papers, Manuscript Division, Library of Congress.

GOVERNMENT DOCUMENTS:

Biographical Directory of the American Congress, 1774-1961. Washington
      Government Printing Office, 1961.

Georgia. Clarke County Deed Book, XLI.

_____. Oconee County Warranty Deeds, Book T.

_____. Journal of the House of Representatives, 1929. Atlanta: Stein
      Printing Company.

_____. Secretary of State. Official Register, 1929.

_____. Secretary of State. Official Register, 1933-37.

_____. Secretary of State. Official Register, 1939-41.

Montana. Reports of Cases Argued and Determined in the Supreme Court
      of the State of Montana. July 1, 1966-December 31, 1966. Official
      Reports, CXLVIII.

New York Legislature. Report of the Joint Legislative Committee
      Investigating Seditious Activities, filed April 24, 1920. Part I,
      Volumes 1 and 2.

United States Bureau of the Census. The Statistics of the Population
      of the United States (Washington: Government Printing Office, 1872),
      I, p. 46.

U.S., Congress, House of Representatives, 65th Congress, 1st Session,
      Congressional Record, LV, Parts 1, 3, 5, and 6.

_____, House of Representatives, 65th Congress, 2nd Session,
      Congressional Record, LVI, Parts 1, 8 and 9.

_____, House of Representatives, 65th Congress, 2nd Session,
      The Judiciary Committee, Minority Report on H. J. 3, Woman Suffrage
      by Federal Amendment.

_____, Senate, 67th Congress, 4th Session, Congressional Record,
      LXIV, Part 4.

_____, Senate, 71st Congress, 1st Session, Congressional Record,
      LXXI, Part 2.

_____, House of Representatives, 74th Congress, 1st Session,
      Congressional Record, LXXIX, Parts 1, 2, and 12.

_____, House of Representatives, 75th Congress, 1st Session,
      Congressional Record, LXXXI, Part 2.

_____, Senate, 76th Congress, 3rd Session, Congressional Record, LXXXVI, Part 17.

_____, House of Representatives, 77th Congress, 1st Session, Congressional Record, LXXXVII, Parts 1, 4, 5, 7, 9 and 14.

_____, House of Representatives, 77th Congress, 2nd Session, Congressional Record, LXXXVIII, Parts 4 and 10.

REPORTS:

Congress of the International Committee of Women for Permanent Peace. Report of the International Congress, Zurich, 1919. Zurich, n.d.

Congressional Union for Woman Suffrage. Report for 1914. Washington, D.C., 1914.

Lake Mohonk Conference on International Arbitration. Report of the 14th Annual Meeting. New York, 1908.

_____. Report of the 16th Annual Meeting. New York, 1910.

_____. Report of the 17th Annual Meeting. New York, 1911.

National American Suffrage Association. 43rd Annual Report. New York, 1911.

_____. Handbook and Proceedings of 45th Convention. New York, 1913.

_____. Handbook and Proceedings of 46th Convention. New York, 1914.

_____. Handbook and Proceedings of 47th Convention. New York, 1915.

_____. Handbook and Proceedings of 48th Convention. New York, 1916.

_____. Handbook and Proceedings of 49th Convention. New York, 1917.

National Education Association. Proceedings and Addresses, 1919. Washington, 1929.

Women's International League for Peace and Freedom. Report of the Fourth Congress. Washington, 1924.

JOURNALS:

The Suffragist. 1914-1920.

The Woman's Journal. 1909-1919.

The Woman Citizen. 1919-1920.

CONGRESSIONAL HEARINGS:

U.S. Congress. House. Committee on the Judiciary. Amend the Constitution with Respect to Declaration of War. Hearings on H. J. 217 and 218, 73rd Congress, 2nd Session. March, 1934.

_____. House. Committee on Foreign Affairs. American Neutrality Policy. Hearings on H. J. 147 and 242, 75th Congress, 1st Session.

_____. House. Committee on Foreign Affairs. American Neutrality Policy. Hearings. 76th Congress, 1st Session. April, 1939.

_____. House. Committee on Foreign Affairs. Arming American Merchant Vessels. Hearings on H. J. Res. 237, 77th Congress, 1st Session. October, 1941.

_____. House. Committee on the Civil Service. Civil Service Retirement for Certain Elective Officials. Hearings. 77th Congress, 2nd Session. February, 1942.

_____. Senate. Committee on Naval Affairs. Construction of Certain Naval Vessels. Hearings on S. 2493, 73rd Congress, 2nd Session.

_____. House. Committee on Naval Affairs. Authorize the Secretary of Navy to Proceed with Construction. Hearings on H. R. 2880, 76th Congress, 1st Session. February, 1939.

_____. Senate. Committee on Naval Affairs. Construction of Certain Public Works. Hearings on S. 830, 76th Congress, 1st Session. March, 1937.

_____. Senate. Committee on the Judiciary. Election of the President. Hearings. 91st Congress, 1st Session. March, 1969.

_____. House. Committee on the Judiciary. Electoral College Reform. Hearings. 91st Congress, 1st Session. February, 1969.

_____. House. Committee on Naval Affairs. Establish the Composition of the United States Navy. Hearings on H. R. 9218, 75th Congress, 4th Session. January 31, 1938.

_____. House. Committee on Naval Affairs. Establishing the Composition of the Navy. Hearings pursuant to H. R. 8026. 76th

Congress, 3rd Session. February 5, 1940.

_____. Senate. Special Munitions Investigating Committee.
The Munitions Industry. Hearings on S. Res. 206, 74th Congress,
1st Session. April 10, 1935.

_____. House. Committee on Labor. Hygiene of Maternity and
Infancy. Hearings on H. R. 12634, 65th Congress, 3rd Session.
January, 1919.

_____. House. Committee on Interstate and Foreign Commerce.
Public Protection of Maternity and Infancy. Hearings pursuant to
H. R. 10925, 66th Congress, 3rd Session. 1920.

_____. Senate. Committee on Appropriations. Navy Department
Appropriation for 1936. Hearings on H. R. 7672, 74th Congress,
1st Session. 1935.

_____. House. Committee on Foreign Affairs. Prohibit the
Exportation of Arms or Munitions. Hearings on H. J. Res. 93,
73rd Congress, 1st Session. March 30, 1933.

_____. Senate. Committee on Education and Labor. Protection
of Maternity. Hearings on S. 1039, 67 Congress, 1st Session.
April 25, 1921.

_____. House. Committee on Public Lands. Amending the Raker
Act. Hearings on H. R. 5964, 77th Congress, 2nd Session. January
of 1942.

_____. House. Committee on Military Affairs. Taking the
Profit Out of War. Hearings on H. R. 3 and H. R. 5293, 74th
Congress, 1st Session.

_____. House. Committee on Rules. Creating a Committee on
Woman Suffrage. Hearings on H. Res. 12. May 18, 1917.

_____. House. Committee on Woman Suffrage. Extending the
Right of Suffrage to Women. Hearings on H. J. Res. 200, 65th
Congress, 2nd Session. January, 1918.

_____. Senate. Committee on Woman Suffrage. Woman Suffrage.
Hearings on S. J. Res. 2, 65th Congress, 1st Session. 1917.

TELEVISION AND FILM DOCUMENTS:

Alpert, Arthur, Producer and Kirk Browning, Director. "Mirror, Mirror
on the World." Public Broadcast Laboratory of the National
Educational Television and Radio Center. This is a study of media
coverage of the Jeannette Rankin Brigade.

Fisher, David. "Jeannette Rankin: First Lady of Peace." A TV film
produced for WGTV, Athens, Georgia.

MUSIC:

Gershwin, George. Strike Up the Band. New York: New World Music
   Corporation, 1930.

SCRAPBOOKS, PLAQUES AND OTHER MEMORABILIA:

Hill, Joyce. Jeannette Rankin Scrapbook. Manuscript # 236, University
   of Georgia Libraries, Manuscript Division.

Sunshine Club Record Book in the personal possession of the author.

Susan B. Anthony Hall of Fame Award. First Annual Award given by the
   National Organization of Women. February 12, 1972.

War Resister's League. First Annual Recognition Award to Jeannette
   Rankin. April 8, 1958.

TRAFCO. American Profiles: Congressman Jeannette Rankin. May 30 and
   31, 1967; December 19, 1967. A recording distributed to radio
   stations for use in a syndicated program presentation.

ARTICLES:

Rankin, Jeannette. "American Women are Prepared to Share in War."
   Chicago Sunday Herald. May 27, 1917.

_____. "At the Front with the Women." General Federation
   Magazine, XVIII (August, 1918).

_____. "Beware of Holy Wars." World Outlook, n. vol. no.
   (November, 1938).

_____. "Can We Afford War?" The Church Woman, XXXIII
   (August - September, 1967).

_____. "Congressman Rankin Offers Solution of Wage Problem
   for Her Sex in the War." Chicago Sunday Herald. July 8, 1917.

_____. "Genuine Recognition of Woman's Wrath in Our National
   Crisis." Atlanta Constitution. July 29, 1917.

_____. "How Children's Bureau Proves Value of Woman in
   Politics." Chicago Sunday Herald. February 11, 1917.

_____. "How the War will Affect Women Workers." Chicago Sunday
   Herald. June 10, 1917.

_____. "How to Outlaw War." The Pilgrim, II (July, 1925).

_____. "I Would Vote No Again." Christian Science Monitor
   Weekly Magazine. April 1, 1936.

_____. "Jeannette Rankin Says." Chicago Sunday Herald. June 17, 1917.

_____. "Protect Women Workers in War is Demand of Congress-Woman." Chicago Sunday Herald. June 24, 1917.

_____. "Reducing Armaments by a New Military Policy." Peace Action, IV (July, 1937).

_____. "Save 10,000 Babies by Registration." Chicago Sunday Herald. February 18, 1917.

_____. "Should America Have a New Deal in National Defense?" Congressional Digest, XII (April, 1934).

_____. "To Give Every Part Voice in Laws." Chicago Sunday Herald. October 21, 1917.

_____. "Toil-Worn Child Workers on the Farm." Chicago Sunday Herald. May 13, 1917.

_____. "Twenty Years After." The Christian Herald, (April, 1937).

_____. "Two Votes Against War." Liberation III, (March, 1958).

_____. "U.S. Aid for Families of Soldiers." Chicago Sunday Herald. August 5, 1917.

_____. "U.S. Women's Problem to Keep Wage Standard During War." Chicago Sunday Herald. June 3, 1917.

_____. "What the Woman's Movement Means." Chicago Sunday Herald. December 17, 1916.

_____. "What We Women Should Do." Ladies Home Journal, XXXIV (August, 1917).

_____. "Why the Country Folk Did It." The Woman Voter, II (December, 1911).

_____. "Why the West Leads the East in the Recognition of Women." Chicago Sunday Herald. December, 1916.

_____. "Women Who Have Sure-Enough Men's Jobs." Chicago Sunday Herald. December 3, 1916.

Rathermick, A.E. "Early Days at Fort Missoula." Historical Reprints: Sources of Northwest History, Number 23.

"The Chair of Peace." Brenau Bulletin, XXVII (February, 1935).

II. SECONDARY SOURCES

BOOKS:

Addams, Jane. Newer Ideals of Peace. New York: The Macmillan
    Company, 1907.

_____. Peace and Bread in Time of War. New York: The
    Macmillan Company, 1922.

_____. The Second Twenty Years at Hull House. New York: The
    Macmillan Company, 1930.

Adler, Martiner Jerome. How to Think About War and Peace. New York:
    Simon and Schuster, 1944.

Adler, Selig. The Isolationist Impulse. New York: The Free Press, 1957.

Allen, Devere. The Fight for Peace. New York: The Macmillan Company,
    1930.

Altbach, Philip G. The American Peace Movement, 1900-1961: A Critical
    Analysis. Chicago: Hull Memorial Fund of the Jane Addams Peace
    Association, 1963.

Angell, Norman. Peace and the Plain Man. New York: Harper and Brothers,
    1935.

Angell, Norman and Ramsay McDonald. Patriotism, Ltd.: An Exposure
    of the War Machine. London: Union of Democratic Control, 1933.

_____. The Secret International: Armament Firms at Work. London:
    Union of Democratic Control, 1932.

Anthony, Susan B. The Ghost in My Life. New York: Chasen Books, 1971.

Atwater, Elton. Organized Efforts in the United States Toward Peace.
    Washington: The Digest Press, 1936.

Austin, Henry Wilfred. Moral Rearmament: The Battle for Peace.
    Toranto: W. Heinermann, 1938.

Bailey, Thomas A. A Diplomatic History of the American People.
    New York: Appleton-Century-Crofts, 1964.

Baker, Ray Stannard. Woodrow Wilson: Life and Letters. New York:
    Harper and Brothers, 1938.

Barber, Frederick Arthur. Halt, Cry the Dead: A Pictorial Primer on
    War and Some Ways of Working for Peace. New York: Associated
    Press, 1935.

Bartlett, Ruhl J. The League to Enforce Peace. Chapel Hill: The

University of North Carolina Press, 1944.

Beales, Arthur Charles. _The History of Peace_. New York: Dial Press, 1931.

Beard, Charles. _The Devil Theory of War_. New York: The Vanguard Press, 1936.

Bird, Caroline. _Born Female_. New York: David McKay and Company, Inc., 1968.

Blatch, Harriott S. Challenging Years: _The Memoirs of Harriott S. Blatch_. New York: G. P. Putnam's Sons, 1940.

Boccaccio, Giovanni. _Concerning Famous Women_. New Brunswick: Rutgers University Press, 1963.

Boeckel, Florence Brewer. _Between War and Peace: A Handbook for Peace Workers_. New York: The Macmillan Company, 1928.

_____. _The Turn Toward Peace_. New York: Friendship Press, 1930.

Bourne, Randolph Silliman. _Towards an Enduring Peace_. New York: American Association for International Conciliation, 1916.

Brailsford, Henry Noel. _Property or Peace_. London: V. Gollancz,1934.

Browder, Earl Russell. _Fighting for Peace_. New York: International Publishers, 1939.

Burlingame, Merrill G. and Ross Toole. _A History of Montana_. New York: Lewis Historical Publishing Company, 1957.

Butler, Nicholas M. _The Path to Peace_. New York: C. Scribner's Sons, 1930.

_____. _Why War? Essays and Addresses on War and Peace_. New York: C. Scribner's Sons, 1940.

Chatfield, Charles. _For Peace and Justice: Pacifism in America 1914-41_. Knoxville: University of Tennessee Press, June, 1971.

Conlin, Joseph R. _Bread and Roses Too: Studies of the Wobblies_. Westport: Greenwood Publishing Corporation, 1969.

Cordier, Andrew Wellington and Kenneth L. Maxwell. _Paths to World Order_. New York: Columbia University Press, 1967.

Curti, Merle Eugene. _Peace or War: The American Struggle, 1636-1936_. Boston: J. S. Cranner, 1959.

_____. _The American Peace Crusade_. Durham, North Carolina: Duke University Press, 1929.

Davids, Jules. America and the World of Our Time: U.S. Diplomacy in the Twentieth Century. New York: Random House, 1965.

Davis, Allen Freeman. Spearheads for Reform. New York: Oxford University Press, 1967.

Davis, Allen F. and Mary Lynn McCree. Eighty Years at Hull House. Chicago: Quadrangle Books, 1969.

Davis, Jerome. Contemporary Social Movements. New York: Appleton-Century, 1930.

DeConde, Alexander. A History of American Foreign Policy. New York: Scribner, 1963.

_____. Isolation and Security: Ideas and Interests in Twentieth Century American Foreign Policy. Durham: Duke University Press, 1957.

Degen, Marie Louise. The History of the Woman's Peace Party. Baltimore: Johns Hopkins University Press, 1939.

Detzer, Dorothy. Appointment on the Hill. New York: Henry Holt and Company, 1948.

Dilling, Elizabeth. The Red Network. Kenilworth: Published by the author, 1934.

Divine, Robert. Second Chance: The Triumph of Internationalism in America During World War II. New York: Atheneum, 1967.

_____. The Illusion of Neutrality. Chicago: University of Chicago Press, 1962.

Dubofsky, Melvyn. We Shall Be All: A History of the Industrial Workers of the World. Chicago: Quadrangle Books, 1969.

Dulles, Foster Rhea. America's Rise to World Power, 1898-1954. New York: Harper and Row, 1954.

Dulles, John Foster. War, Peace and Change. New York: Harper and Brothers, 1939.

Duniway, Abigal. Path Breaking: An Autobiographical History of Equal Suffrage Movement in Pacific Coast States. Portland: James Kerns and Abbott Company, 1914.

Dunn, Frederick Sherwood. War and the Minds of Men. New York: Published for the Council on Foreign Relations by Harper, 1950.

Ellis, L. Ethan. Republican Foreign Policy, 1921-1933. New Brunswick: Rutgers University Press, 1969.

Englebrecht, H.C. and F.C. Hanigher. Merchants of Death: A Study of the International Armament Industry. New York: Dodd, Mead and

Company, 1934.

Ewen, David. A Journey to Greatness, The Life and Music of George Gershwin. New York: Henry Holt and Company, 1956.

Faber, Doris. Petticoat Politics, How American Women Won the Right to Vote. New York: Lothrop, Lee and Shephard, Company, 1967.

Fay, Sidney B. The Origins of World War I. New York: Macmillan Company, 1931.

Ferrell, Robert H. American Diplomacy in the Great Depression: Hoover-Stimson Foreign Policy, 1929-1933. New Haven: Yale University Press, 1957.

_____. Peace in Their Time: The Origins of the Kellogg-Briand Pact. New Haven: Yale University Press, 1952.

Finn, James. Protest: Pacifism and Politics. New York: Random House, 1968.

Flexner, Eleanor. Century of Struggle. Cambridge: The Balknap Press of Harvard University, 1959.

Friedan, Betty. The Feminine Mystique. New York: Dell Publishing Company, 1963.

Fulford, Roger. Votes for Women: The Story of a Struggle. London: Faber and Faber, 1957.

Goldmark, Josephine. Impatient Crusader: Florence Kelley. Urbana: University of Illinois Press, 1953.

Goldsmith, Robert. A League to Enforce Peace. New York: The Macmillan Company, 1917.

Grattan, C. Harley. Why We Fought. New York: Vanguard Press, Reprint, 1969.

Gruberg, Martin. Women in American Politics, An Assessment and Source-book. Oshkosk: Academic Press, 1968.

Gulick, Sidney Lewis. The Fight for Peace. New York: Fleming H. Revall, 1915.

Harper, Ida. The History of Woman Suffrage. New York: National American Woman Suffrage Association, 1922.

Harrison, Harry P. as told to Karl Detzer. Culture Under Canvas: The Story of Tent Chautauqua. New York: Hastings House, Publishers, 1958.

Haymann, Hans. Plan for Permanent Peace. New York: Harper and Brothers, 1941.

Hemleben, Sylvester John. Plans for World Peace Through Six Centuries. Chicago: The University of Chicago, 1943.

Henderson, Arthur. Labour's Way to Peace. London: Methuen and Company, 1935.

Hirsch, Arthur H. The Love Elite: The Story of Woman's Emancipation of Her Drive for Sexual Fulfillment. New York: Julian Press, 1963.

Holtzman, Abraham. The Townsend Movement, A Political Study. New York: Bookman Association, 1963.

Hoover, Herbert C. The Problems of Lasting Peace. Garden City: Doubleday, Doran and Company, 1942.

Howard, Joseph Kinsey. Montana: High, Wide, and Handsome. New Haven: Yale University Press, 1943.

Irwin, Inez H. The Story of the Woman's Party. New York: Harcourt, Brace and Company, 1921.

Johnson, Julia Emily. Peace and Rearmament. New York: H. W. Wilson and Company, 1938.

Josephy, Alvin M., Jr. The Nez Perce Indians and the Opening of the Northwest. New Haven: Yale University Press, 1965.

Kidd, Benjamin. Social Evolution. New York: Macmillan and Company, 1894.

_____. The Science of Power. New York: G. P. Putnam's Sons, 1918.

Kraditor, Aileen S. The Ideas of the Woman Suffrage Movement, 1890-1920. New York: Doubleday and Company, 1971.

Kuhlman, Charles. Pacifism as the Unifying Thesis of All Social Reform. Boston: The Burham Press, 1922.

LaGuardia, Fiorello H. The Making of an Insurgent: An Autobiography. New York: Lippincott Company, 1948.

Lawson, Don. Ten Fighters for Peace: An Anthology. New York: Lothrop, Lee and Shepard, Company, 1971.

Leesen, Michael A. History of Montana, 1739-1885. Chicago: Warner, Beers and Company, 1885.

Lemke, William. You and Your Money. Philadelphia: Dorrance and Company, 1938.

Leonard, Eugenie. The Dear-bought Heritage. Philadelphia: University of Pennsylvania Press, 1965.

Leuchtenburg, W. E. Franklin S. Roosevelt and the New Deal, 1932-1940.
New York: Harper and Row, 1963.

Libby, Frederick J. To End War: The Story of the National Council for
Prevention of War. Nydck: Fellowship Press, 1969.

Lifton, Robert. The Woman in America. Boston: Houghton Mifflin, 1965.

Link, Arthur. Wilson: Campaigns for Progressivism and Peace, 1915-
1917. Princeton: Princeton University Press, 1965.

_____. Wilson the Diplomatist: A Look at His Major Policies.
Baltimore: Johns Hopkins Press, 1957.

Meiburger, Anne V. Efforts of Raymond Robins Toward Recognition of
Soviet Russia and the Outtawry of War 1917-1933. Washington:
Catholic University of America Press, 1958.

Miller, Joaquin. An Illustrated History of the State of Montana.
Chicago: The Lewis Publishing Company, 1894.

Millis, Walter. The Road to War. Boston: Houghton Mifflin Company,
1935.

Montana Historical Records Survey. Bozeman: The Historical Records
Survey, 1942.

Moritzen, Julius. The Peace Movement in America. New York: Putnam's
Sons, 1912.

O'Neill, William. Everyone Was Brave, The Rise and Fall of Feminism
in America. Chicago: Quadrangle Books, 1969.

_____. The Woman Movement: Feminism in the United States
and England. New York: Barnes and Noble, 1969.

Osgood, Robert E. Ideals and Self-Interest in America's Foreign Relations:
The Great Transformation of the Twentieth Century. Chicago: University of Chicago Press, 1953.

Page, Kirby. An American Peace Policy. New York: George H. Doran, 1925.

Patten, Simon N. The New Basis of Civilization. New York: Macmillan
Company, 1907.

Paxton, Annabel. Women in Congress. Richmond: The Dietz Press, Inc.,
1945.

Peck, Mary Gray. Carrie Chapman Catt: A Biography. New York: H. W.
Wilson Company, 1944.

Perkins, Dexter. America's Quest for Peace. Bloomington: University
Press, 1962.

Peterson, H. C. and Gilbert Fite. Opponents of War. Madison: University of Wisconsin Press, 1957.

Pethick-Lawrence, Emmeline. My Part in a Changing World. London: Victor Gollancz, 1938.

Rappard, William E. The Quest for Peace Since the World War. Cambridge: Harvard University Press, 1940.

Raymer, Robert G. Montana: The Land and Its People. New York: The Lewis Publishing Company, 1930.

Riegel, Robert Edgar. American Feminists. Lawrence: University of Kansas Press, 1963.

_____. American Women: A Story of Social Change. Rutherford: Fairleigh Dickinson University Press, 1970.

Ross, Ishbel. Sons of Adam, Daughters of Eve. New York: Harper and Row Publishers, 1969.

Rosenman, Samuel I. The Public Papers and Addresses of Franklin D. Roosevelt. New York: The Macmillan Company, 1941.

Sanders, Helen F. A History of Montana. New York: The Lewis Publishing Company, 1913.

Schuman, Frederick L. and George Soule. America Looks Abroad. New York: Foreign Policy Association, Inc., 1938.

Sinclair, Andrew. The Emancipation of the American Women. New York: Harper and Row, 1965.

Smith, Page. Daughters of the Promised Land, Women in American History. Boston: Little, Brown, 1970.

Solomons, Selina. How We Won the Vote in California. San Francisco: The New Woman Publishing Company, 1912.

Stoner, John E. S. O. Lavinson and the Pact of Paris. Chicago: University of Chicago Press, 1941.

Taylor, Elizabeth. The Woman Suffrage Movement in Tennessee. New York: Bookman Associates, 1957.

Terrell, Mary Church. A Colored Woman in a White World. Washington: Ransdell, Inc., 1940.

Vinson, John Chalmers. William E. Borah and the Outlawry of War. Athens: University of Georgia Press, 1957.

Wald, Lillian D. The House on Henry Street. New York: H. Holt and Company, 1938.

_____. Windows on Henry Street. Boston: Little, Brown and Company, 1941.

Waldron, Ellis L. An Atlas of Montana Politics Since 1864. Missoula: Montana State University Press, 1958.

Webb, Terrell D. Washington Wife: Journal of Ellen Maury Slayden, 1897-1919. New York: Harper and Row, 1962.

Wheeler, Burton K. and Paul F. Healy. Yankee from the West. Garden City: Doubleday and Company, 1962.

Williams, T. H. Huey Long. New York: Knopf, 1969.

Wiltz, John E. In Search of Peace: The Senate Munitians Inquiry, 1934-1936. Baton Rouge: Saint Louis Press, 1963.

Wittner, Lawrence S. Rebels Against War: The American Peace Movement, 1941-1960. New York: Columbia University Press, 1969.

ARTICLES:

"A Report to Make the Bones Fat." The Woman Citizen, III (March 29, 1919).

Anthony, Katharine. "A Basket of Summer Fruit." Woman's Home Companion, LIII (August, 1926).

_____. "Living on the Front Porch." Woman's Home Companion, LIII (September, 1926).

_____. "Our Gypsy Journey to Georgia." Woman's Home Companion, LIII (July, 1926).

Atwater, Elton. "Organizing American Public Opinion for Peace." Public Opinion Quarterly, I (April, 1937).

Barness, John and William Dickinson. "Minutemen of Montana." Montana, X (Spring, 1960).

Bates, J. Leonard. "Genius for Controversy." Montana, XIX (Autumn, 1969).

Bliven, Bruce. "Pacifism: Its Rise and Fall." New Republic, LXXXIX (November 18, 1936).

Board, John. "The Lady from Montana." Montana, XVII (July, 1967).

Broeckel, Florence. "A Woman's Vote on the War." Suffragist, V (April, 1917).

Bronner, E. B. "An Early Example of Political Action by Women." Bulletin of Friend's Historical Association, XIIIL (1954).

"Bureau of Engraving and Printing Meeting An Enormous Demand." The Plate Printer, XVI (July 7, 1918).

"The Capital Welcomes Jeannette Rankin." Suffragist, V (April 7, 1917).

Castles, Jean I. "The West: Crucible of the Negro." Montana, XIX (January, 1969).

"The Chair of Peace." Brenau Bulletin, XXVII (February, 1935).

Childs, Howard L. "Public Opinion and Peace." Annals of American Academy, XIICC (July, 1937).

Clapper, Raymond. "Don't Pass on Rumors." Montana Standard, December 11, 1941.

Cole, Wayne S. "Senator Key Pitman and American Neutrality Policies, 1933-1940." Mississippi Valley Historical Review, XLVI (March, 1960).

"Congressman Returns to House." Christian Century, LVII (November 20, 1940).

Daniel, Frank. "Pioneer Lady Solon A. Georgian." Atlanta Journal and Constitution, November 24, 1953.

Devine, E. T. "The New View of Charity." Atlantic Monthly, CII (December, 1908).

Duffield, Marcus. "Our Quarreling Pacifists." Harpers, CLXVI (May, 1933).

Dusenberry, Verne. "Chief Joseph's Flight Through Montana: 1877." Montana, II (October, 1952).

"Emergency Peace Campaign Is Planned." Peace Action, II (March, 1936).

Evans, Christine. "Woman Against War." Scribner's Commentator, XI (November, 1941).

Favre, Gregory. "Revel with a Cause." Atlanta Constitution and Journal Magazine, June 21, 1959.

Fay, Sidney. "New Light on the Origins of the World War." American Historical Review, XXV (July, 1920).

"Federal Mothers' Aid." Survey, XLI (February 1, 1919).

Filer, Bertha. "Our First Woman Congressman." McCalls, XVI (April, 1917).

"First Congresswoman Seeks to Return." Christian Century, LVII (September 4, 1940).

"First Woman Elected to Congress." Outlook, CXIV (November 22, 1916).

Fisher, Katherine R. "Our First Congresswoman." Suffragist, IV (November 18, 1916).

Fligelman, Belle. "First Woman Elected to Congress." Sunset, XXXVII (November, 1916).

Frapallo, Elizabeth. "Jeannette Rankin." Life, LXXII (March 3, 1972).

Hinckle, Warren and Marianne Hinckle. "A History of the Rise of the Unusual Movement for Woman Power in the United States, 1961-1968." Ramparts, VII (February, 1968).

Holt, Hamilton. "The Way to Disarm: A Practical Proposal." Independent, LXXIX (September 18, 1914).

Hunter, Allan A. "Pacifists and the United Front." Christian Century, LIII (January 8, 1936).

Justus, Lucy. "First Woman in Congress Still a Pacifist." Atlanta Journal and Constitution Magazine, May 7, 1967.

_____. "She Campaigns for Change." Atlanta Journal and

Constitution Magazine, February 13, 1972.

Kelley, Florence. "My Philadelphia." Survey, LVII (October 1, 1926).

Kennedy, John E. "Liberal's Defeat: A Cast History." The Nation, CXLVII (November 26, 1938).

Kennedy, John F. "Three Women of Courage." McCalls, LXXXV (January, 1958).

Kilgore, Margaret A. "Women Have Come a Long Way on Political Trail of Jeannette Rankin." Boston Sunday Globe, November 29, 1964.

Kimball, Mary Alice. "Women at the Peace Conference." The Public, XXI (November 30, 1918).

Kirkley, John. "An Afternoon with Jeannette Rankin." Georgia Advocate, VII (Fall, 1970).

Lennon, Bert. "The Lady From Montana." Chicago Sunday Herald, December 10, 1916.

Levinson, S. O. "The Legal Status of War." New Republic, XIV (March 9, 1918).

Levine, Louis. "First Woman Member of Congress Well Versed in Politics." New York Times, November 19, 1916.

_____. "Politics in Montana." Nation CVII (November 2, 1918).

MacFarland, Peter Clark. "Jeannette of Montana." Colliers, LIX (April 21, 1917).

Mallou, Winifred. "An Impression of Jeannette Rankin." Suffragist, V (March 31, 1917).

Masden, Bingham D. and Betty Masden. "The Diamond R Rolls Out." Montana, XXL (Spring, 1971).

Masland, John W. "Pressure Groups and American Foreign Policy." Public Opinion Quarterly, VI (Spring, 1942).

_____. "The Peace Groups Join Battle." Public Opinion Quarterly, IV (December, 1940).

"Member From Montana." Literary Digest, LIII (November 25, 1916).

Merz, Charles. "The Issue In Butte." New Republic

Michaelson, Judy. "Once More, A Date in Washington." New York Post, Magazine Section, December 23, 1967.

Mills, Harriett M. "A Suffrage Revival in New York." Woman's Journal,

XLIII (March 16, 1912).

"Miss Rankin Addresses 3,000." The Woman's Journal, XLVIII (March 10, 1917).

"Montana Member Predicts Victory." The Woman's Journal, XLV (March 7, 1914).

"Montana Passes Suffrage Bill." The Woman's Journal, XLIV (Feb. 1, 1913).

"Montana Safe if Vote not Tampered with." The Woman's Journal, XLVI (November 14, 1914).

Moque, Alice. "Miss Rankin has Busy Days." The Woman's Journal, XLVII (April 14, 1917).

"National Consumers' League." Survey, XL (December, 1920).

O'Neill, Mary. "How Montana Was Won." Suffragist, II (November 14, 1914).

Ouiatt, Alton B. "Fort Benton: River Capital." A History of Montana by Merrill G. Burlingame and K Ross Toole, New York: Lewis Historical Publishing Company, 1957.

"Our Busy Congresswoman." Literary Digest, LV (August 11, 1917).

Palmer, Wayne Francis. "Deaf and Dumb Ships." New Outlook, CLXII (November, 1933).

Parker, Adella M. "The Woman Voter of the West." The Westerner, XVI (August, 1912).

Pethick-Lawrence, F. W. "Motherhood and War." Harper's Weekly, LIX (December 5, 1914).

Phillips, Thomas R. "The Bombing Place Has Made America Invasion Proof." Army Ordance,

"Political Power in the Hands of a Woman." Survey, XXXVIII (July 21, 1917).

Ruether, Richard T. "Showdown in Montana, 1938: Burton K. Wheeler's Role in Defeat of Jerry O'Connell." Pacific Northwest Quarterly, LIV (January, 1963).

Salutes, Theodore. "The Montana Society of Equity." Pacific Historical Review, XIV (December, 1945).

Schaffer, Ronald. "The Montana Woman Suffrage Campaign, 1911-1914." The Pacific Northwest Quarterly, LIV (January, 1964).

_____. "The New York City Woman Suffrage Party, 1909-1919." New York History, XLIII (July, 1962).

Sheaton, James P. "The Coughlin Movement and the New Deal." Political

Science Quarterly, LXXIII (September, 1958).

Shipton, Clifford. "The Shaping of Revolutionary New England."
Political Science Quarterly, L (December, 1935).

Shriner, Sara. "Of War and Peace." Capitol Hill Spectator, February 1,
1968.

_____. "Of War and Peace." Capitol Hill Spectator, February
15, 1968.

Smith, Ethel. "What a Congresswoman has done for Working Women." The
Woman Citizen, I (July 2, 1917).

"Social Progress Moves on the Feet of Women." The Union Printer, LXXI
(May 5, 1945).

Steele, Richard W. "Preparing the Public for War: Efforts to Establish
A National Propaganda Agency, 1940-41." American Historical Review,
LXXV (October, 1970).

"The Lady From Montana." Independent, LXXXVIII (November 20, 1916).

"The International Congress of Woman." Nation, CVIII (March, 1919).

"The Suffragist Germ in Washington." The Woman's Journal, XLI (March 5,
1910).

Thompson, Dorothy. "Who Wants Peace?" Survey Graphic, XXVI (Feb., 1937).

Trueblood, Elton. "The Renunciation of Hatred." Christian Century, LIII
(April 15, 1936).

Vindex, Charles. "Radical Rule in Montana." Montana, XVIII (January,
1968).

Wilhelm, Donald. "Lady From Missoula." The Independent, XC (Apr. 2, 1917).

"Woman's Movement for Constructive Peace." Suffragist, III (Jan. 16, 1915).

"Women to Put Masses Power Back of Peace." Christian Science Monitor,
April 15, 1932.

"Worthy Tribute to Miss 'Congressman' Rankin." Commercial West, July
27, 1918.

NEWSPAPERS:

<u>Anaconda Standard</u>. 1916

<u>Athens Banner-Herald</u>. 1927, 1928, 1930, 1931, 1934, 1935, 1941.

<u>Athens Daily News</u>. 1967, 1972.

<u>Athens Daily Times</u>. 1934, 1935.

<u>Atlanta Constitution</u>. 1911, 1917, 1928, 1929, 1932, 1934, 1941, 1967, 1968, 1969.

<u>Atlanta Journal</u>. 1917, 1934, 1963, 1967, 1970, 1971, 1972.

<u>Baltimore Son</u>. 1913, 1934.

<u>Bismarck Tribune</u>. 1967.

<u>Boston Advertiser</u>. 1925.

<u>Boston, Massachusetts Post</u>. 1916.

<u>Boston Traveler and Evening Herald</u>. 1914.

<u>Bozeman Dailey Chronicle</u>. 1966.

<u>Brenau Bulletin</u>. 1935.

<u>Brooklyn Eagle</u>. 1917.

<u>Buffalo News</u>. 1917.

<u>Butte Daily Bulletin</u>. 1918.

<u>Butte Daily Post</u>. 1940.

<u>The Call</u>. 1912.

<u>Camas Hot Springs Exchange</u>. 1942.

<u>Chattanooga Times</u>. 1936.

<u>Chicago Evening News</u>. 1919.

<u>Chicago Sunday Herald</u>. 1917.

<u>The Christian Science Monitor</u>. 1972.

<u>Cleveland News</u>. 1925.

<u>Cleveland Plain Dealer</u>. 1925.

Concord Evening Monitor. 1915.

Daily Missoulian. 1904, 1905, 1914, 1916, 1951.

Denver, Colorado Post, 1925.

Emporia Gazette. 1941.

Evening Kansan - Republican. 1941.

Fargo Forum and Daily Republican. 1913.

Flagstaff, Arizona Coconeno Sun. 1933.

Florida Times - Union. 1913.

Gainesville Eagle. 1934.

Gainesville News. 1934.

Great Falls Tribune. 1925, 1934, 1937, 1940, 1941, 1949, 1951, 1959,
    1961, 1964.

Hartwell Sun. 1931.

Helena Independent. 1911, 1914, 1916, 1917, 1918

Hollywood Citizen - News. 1938.

Jackson, Michigan Citizen Patriot. 1934.

Journal of Labor. 1934.

The Knoxville News Sentinal. 1972.

Macon Evening News. 1930, 1934, 1936.

Macon Telegraph. 1928, 1931, 1935.

The Missoulian. 1966.

Montana Progressive. 1913, 1914, 1916.

Montana Record - Herald. 1916.

Monterey Peninsula Herald. 1968, 1969.

Springfield, Montana Morning Union. 1939.

Nashville, Tennessean. 1914, 1930, 1972.

NCPW News Bulletin. 1932.

New Orleans States - Item. 1972.

The New Republic. 1934.

The New York American. 1917, 1918.

New York Call. 1912.

New York Evening Journal. 1917.

New York Evening Post. 1914.

New York Herald. 1931.

New York Tribune. 1917, 1947.

New York Suffrage Newsletter. 1912.

New York Sun. 1917, 1918.

New York Times. 1916, 1917, 1918, 1919, 1932, 1938, 1940, 1968, 1971, 1972.

Nonpareil (Council Bluffs, Iowa). 1934.

The Oconee Enterprise. 1967.

Omaha, Nebraska News. 1917.

The Peoples Voice. 1967.

The Portsmouth Times. 1916.

Saqinaw, Michigan Daily News. 1913.

St. Louis Post - Dispatch. 1941.

Sandersville Progress. 1935.

San Marino Independent Star News. 1968.

Santa Barbara News Press, 1967.

Washington Daily News. 1937.

Washington Evening Star. 1913, 1917, 1935, 1937, 1941, 1968, 1969.

Washington Post. 1941, 1968.

UNPUBLISHED MANUSCRIPTS:

Board, John C. "The Lady From Montana: Jeannette Rankin." Unpublished
  M.A. Thesis, University of Wyoming, 1964.

Bolt, Ernest Collier. "The War Referendum Approach to Peace in Twentieth
  Century America: A Study in Foreign Policy Formulation and Military
  Defense Attitudes." Unpublished Ph.D. Dissertation, University of
  Georgia, 1966.

Bowers, Robert E. "The American Peace Movement: 1933 - 1941." Unpublished Ph.D. Dissertation, University of Wisconsin, 1947.

Burbank, Lyman Besse. "Internationalism in American Thought, 1919 - 1929."
  Unpublished Ph.D. Dissertation, New York University, 1950.

Coleman, Ronald George. "A Historical Survey of the Rhetorical Proofs
  Used by Women Speakers of the Suffrage Organizations, 1869 - 1919."
  Unpublished Ph.D. Dissertation, Case Western Reserve University, 1968.

Kuusisto, Allen A. "The Influence of the National Council for Prevention
  of War on United States' Foreign Policy, 1935 - 1939." Unpublished
  Ph.D. Dissertation, Harvard University, 1950.

Schaffer, Ronald. "Jeannette Rankin: Progressive-Isolationist." Unpublished Ph.D. Dissertation, Princeton University, 1959.

Stone, Fern E. "History of the National Council for Prevention of War."
  Unpublished manuscript in the Files of the National Council For
  Prevention of War, Swarthmore College Peace Collection.

Tull, Charles J. "Father Coughlin, The New Deal and the Election of 1936."
  Unpublished Ph.D. Dissertation, University of Notre Dame, 1961.

DISSERTATIONS
IN
AMERICAN BIOGRAPHY

An Arno Press Collection

Breault, Judith. **The Odyssey of a Humanitarian, Emily Howland, 1827-1929.** 1982

Christen, Robert J. **King Sears.** 1982

Donoghue, John. **Alexander Jackson Davis, Romantic Architect, 1803-1892.** 1982

Endelman, Gary Edward. **Solidarity Forever.** 1982

Formwalt, Lee William. **Benjamin Henry Latrobe and the Development of Internal Improvements in the New Republic 1796-1820.** 1982

Frederick, Olivia Mae. **Henry P. Fletcher and United States-Latin American Policy, 1910-1930.** 1982

Goodell, John. **The Triumph of Moralism in New England Piety.** 1982

Grundfest, Jerry. **George Clymer.** 1982

Guerrero, Linda Dudik. **John Adams' Vice Presidency.** 1982

Harris, Ted. **Jeannette Rankin.** 1982

Hartig, Thomas H. **Robert Lansing.** 1982

Howson, Embrey Bernard. **Jacob Sechler Coxey.** 1982

Ifkovic, John William. **Jonathan Trumbull, Junior, 1740-1809.** 1982

Irving, John D. **Mary Shaw.** 1982

Jones, Robert A. **Cass Gilbert.** 1982

Keller, Rosemary Skinner. **Abigail Adams and the American Revolution.** 1982

Kershner, James William. **Sylvanus Thayer.** 1982

King Joerger, Pauline N. **A Political Biography of David Lawrence Gregg.** 1982

Kirsch, George B. **Jeremy Belknap.** 1982

Lipstadt, Deborah E. **The Zionist Career of Louis Lipsky, 1900-1921.** 1982

Marabell, George Peter. **Frederick Libby and the American Peace Movement, 1921-1941.** 1982

Martin, Roger A. **John J. Zubly.** 1982.

McKee, James R. **Kit Carson.** 1982

McLean, David. **Timothy Pickering and the Age of the American Revolution.** 1982

Mitchner, Clarice James. **Senator John Sherman Cooper.** 1982

Moser, Maynard. **Jacob Gould Schurman.** 1982.

Murray, Craig C. **Benjamin Vaughan (1751-1835).** 1982

Peterson, Larry Richard. **Ignatius Donnelly.** 1982

Platt, John D.R. **Jeremiah Wadsworth.** 1982

Ratzlaff, Robert K. **John Rutledge, Jr.** 1982

Ruderman, Terry Jane. **Stanley M. Isaacs.** 1982

Sahli, Nancy Ann. **Elizabeth Blackwell, M.D. (1821-1910).** 1982

Schmidt, Philip R. **Hezekiah Niles and American Economic Nationalism.** 1982

Shelton, William Allen. **The Young Jefferson Davis.** 1982

Thompson, Julius Eric. **Hiram R. Revels, 1827-1901.** 1982

Trendel, Robert A., Jr. **William Jay.** 1982

Tripp, Wendell Edward, Jr. **Robert Troup.** 1982

Walker, Jeffrey B. **The Devil Undone.** 1982